STUDIES IN
CHINESE SOCIETY

Contributors

Emily M. Ahern   Jack M. Potter
Myron L. Cohen   G. William Skinner
Donald R. DeGlopper   Marjorie Topley
Stephan Feuchtwang   Arthur P. Wolf
Winston Hsieh   Margery Wolf
Burton Pasternak

STUDIES IN
CHINESE SOCIETY

Edited by ARTHUR P. WOLF

Stanford University Press, Stanford, California   1978

Books published in the series
STUDIES IN CHINESE SOCIETY

Maurice Freedman, ed., *Family and Kinship in Chinese Society* (1970)
John Wilson Lewis, ed., *The City in Communist China* (1971)
W. E. Willmott, ed., *Economic Organization in Chinese Society* (1972)
Mark Elvin and G. William Skinner, eds., *The Chinese City Between Two Worlds* (1974)
Arthur P. Wolf, ed., *Religion and Ritual in Chinese Society* (1974)
Margery Wolf and Roxane Witke, eds., *Women in Chinese Society* (1975)
G. William Skinner, ed., *The City in Late Imperial China* (1977)

Stanford University Press
Stanford, California
© 1978 by the Board of Trustees of the Leland Stanford Junior University
Printed in the United States of America
Cloth ISBN 0-8047-1006-6   Paper ISBN 0-8047-1007-4   LC 78-62272

Contents

Introduction

ARTHUR P. WOLF

The papers presented here derive from conferences sponsored by the Social Science Research Council and the American Council of Learned Societies between 1966 and 1973, and were first published in the seven-volume series Studies in Chinese Society (Stanford University Press, 1970–77). The present selection is intended to serve the needs of students in courses taught by anthropologists, sociologists, and social historians. It reflects not only my judgment but that of a dozen colleagues currently teaching courses on China in the United States and Great Britain.

The first paper, by G. William Skinner, is included despite its difficulty because it presents a unique and important perspective on Chinese society. Chinese society was traditionally treated as either a largely undifferentiated whole or a loose conglomeration of independent villages. Skinner showed that it was instead made up of a hierarchy of cellular structures shaped by the exigencies of topography, distance, and population density. At the bottom of the hierarchy is the standard marketing community, consisting of a small town and 15–20 satellite villages; at the top, the great metropolis; and between these extremes, six or seven intermediate classes of cities ranging from relatively small and simple to relatively large and complex.

In a seminal series of articles published in 1964–65, Skinner discussed the implications of his model for the study of Chinese culture, arguing that the standard marketing community was the culture-bearing unit in the traditional society, largely because the great majority of all peasants married within their standard marketing area.[1] In the paper reproduced here he extends his analysis to include the relationship between the

[1] See G. William Skinner, "Marketing and Social Structure in Rural China, Part I," *Journal of Asian Studies*, 24, no. 1 (1964): 3–43.

hierarchy of central places formed by economic transactions and that established by the imperial bureaucracy for the purposes of field administration. His most remarkable conclusion is that "Ch'ing field administration was marvelously adapted to the realities of regional structure within the empire." Instead of a government crippled by corruption, incompetence, and blind conservatism—the picture painted by many historians—we find, in Skinner's revisionist view, a government whose officials possessed a highly intelligent appreciation of the essential features of their society and the ability to organize their administration accordingly.

Winston Hsieh's paper exemplifies the insights that can be gained by the careful application of Skinner's analysis of the marketing hierarchy. Taking as his topic two of the many peasant insurrections that jolted the Canton delta in 1911, Hsieh demonstrates that "the stage on which the drama of peasant insurrection unfolded . . . was not an undifferentiated platform on which the peasant actors moved at random, but rather a hierarchical structure of nested local economic systems in which urban centers occupied strategic positions." Who revolted, where, when, and with what result all become clearer when the events and the actors are placed in the communities created by the marketing centers. The student who has trouble with Skinner's abstractions may prefer to begin his reading with Hsieh's case studies.

Though the next two papers, Stephan Feuchtwang's and mine, are concerned primarily with religion, they carry on many of the themes introduced by Skinner and Hsieh. In traditional China government and religion were so closely related that the imperial bureaucracy, temple organization, peasant insurrection, and popular conceptions of the supernatural all belonged to the same sphere. The point is made in both papers, but from different perspectives. In Feuchtwang's paper we view religion and ritual from the point of view of the imperial bureaucracy. We see a distinction drawn between an official religion and a popular religion and discover that both were employed as agents of social control. In my paper the perspective is reversed. Taking the point of view of the peasant, we find that the gods were thought to have essentially the same characteristics as posted officials. Many of the deities despised as heterodox by the mandarins of the imperial bureaucracy were in fact inspired by their example.

More generally, my paper argues that the supernatural world of the Chinese peasantry was a faithful replication of their view of the Chinese social landscape. The gods were officials; the ghosts were bandits and beggars; the ancestors were parents, grandparents, and great-grandparents. Thus the paper is as concerned with the family as it is with religion and may be profitably read together with the contributions by Myron Cohen, Burton Pasternak, and Margery Wolf. Though they begin with radically different views on the subject, all three papers focus on related aspects of kinship and family organization.

Many discussions of Chinese society treat property rights, the domestic economy, and family dynamics separately as aspects of law, economics, and kinship, respectively. Myron Cohen, by contrast, examines the ways in which the family estate, the family economy, and the makeup of the family are interdependent. The result is not only a clear demonstration of the need to relate family relations to their material base, but also a new appreciation of the family's ability to adapt to changing economic circumstances. What had appeared to be an inflexible institution doomed to founder on the shoals of modernization now looks as though it may survive considerable change without losing its essential identity.

A large part of the striking variation in the size and complexity of Chinese families is illusory. Elementary families grow in size and complexity as sons marry and are then reduced to elementary forms again as fathers die and households divide. Whether a family is large or small, complex or simple, depends in large part on where it is in this cyclical process. But the variation one sees in family conformations at a point in time is not entirely an illusion. Some families grow into large, complex units with thirty or forty members before they are finally divided; others never achieve a form more complex than that of the stem family.

In most analyses of Chinese family life this variation in family size and complexity is attributed to wealth. Since the wealthy marry early, live long, and are better able to control their sons, their families are larger and more complex than those of poor farmers who marry late if at all, die young, and see their sons migrate in search of employment. But why then, one must ask, is there so much variation in family size among the poor? Why are complex family forms common in some communities and rare in others? One kind of answer is offered in Pasternak's comparison of two villages in southern Taiwan. Like Cohen, Pasternak argues that the Chinese family is a flexible institution, readily responding to changed economic circumstances. He attributes the striking difference between the family forms characteristic of the two villages to differences in labor demand arising from the fact that one village draws its water from a large-scale irrigation system whereas the other depends on rainfall. The paper illustrates the value of comparative studies as well as the power of ecological explanations.

Margery Wolf's paper approaches the family from a very different perspective. Where Cohen and Pasternak explain the shape of the family as a response to material conditions, Wolf seeks an explanation within the family. For property rights, market conditions, and water control she substitutes the experience of family life and its effect on adult relationships. The difference between the two approaches is most apparent in the authors' treatment of the fraternal relationship. Cohen's and Pasternak's analyses imply that people decided whether or not to divide a joint household on rational grounds and largely with reference to such variables as labor demand and economic diversification. Wolf concedes the relevance of such considerations but insists that emotional and psychological factors are also important. Thus adult brothers may not remain together even when it is clearly to their economic advantage to do so because their relationship as children has made it impossible for the younger to accept the older's authority.

Wolf's paper also serves as an introduction to the papers by Marjorie Topley and Emily Ahern. "Chinese society," she writes, "has given a father both the power and the authority to manage his adult sons. A mother's authority is not so clearly stated, and so she must establish her power in a more subtle fashion." Here in brief is the outline of a theme that Wolf later developed into a full-fledged analysis of female strategies in traditional China.[2] Her essential point is that because women were deprived of all authority, they sought power by co-opting the loyalty of their male children. Unable to control their fates as daughters, as wives, or as women, they made the most of the opportunity they were offered as mothers.

Chinese women generally had little choice but to marry and make the best of the consequences, yet a marriage resistance movement flourished in parts of rural Kwangtung in the late nineteenth and early twentieth centuries. Under what conditions did this movement emerge? Why did it succeed in a few communities in the Canton delta but not elsewhere? How did it manage to persist for a century? And why did it eventually decline? These are only a few of the questions raised by Marjorie Topley's fascinating analysis. Until we know why and how some women refused marriage, or, having married, refused to live with their husbands, we cannot claim an adequate understanding of women's place in the traditional order.

In traditional China, as in many other societies, women were regarded

[2] See Margery Wolf, *Women and the Family in Rural Taiwan* (Stanford, Calif.: Stanford University Press, 1972), pp. 32–41.

as ritually unclean and dangerously powerful, and were excluded from many activities lest their presence cause harm to others. Emily Ahern's paper describes these beliefs in detail and then asks why people felt that way. Why were women regarded as dirty? And why was their impurity seen as dangerous? The paper considers three possible answers, one having to do with the emotional significance of birth and death, one with the threat women posed to their husbands' families, and one with transgression of the boundaries that separate people and groups from one another. The reader who follows Ahern's subtle argument through its full course will not feel cheated when, in the end, she refuses to commit herself to any single answer.

The last two papers in the volume stand as counterweights to the distant views of Chinese society presented in the opening papers. From Skinner's abstract overview of Chinese society as a whole, we move to Donald DeGlopper's fine-grained analysis of business relations in Lukang. And from Feuchtwang's analysis of official religion and its relation to popular religion, we proceed to Jack Potter's colorful account of shamanism in a Cantonese-speaking village in Hong Kong.

DeGlopper describes the old port of Lukang as lying "like a beached whale three kilometers inland from the west coast of Taiwan." Once the second-largest city on the island and the economic center of its region, Lukang has "slipped down the central-place hierarchy" and is now a placid country town. DeGlopper implies that the particulars of Lukang's history may account for some of the business practices he describes; but most of these practices are more or less typical of small towns elsewhere in Taiwan. One interesting difference is that in Lukang "there are no large, complex businesses run jointly by several brothers and their sons." One wonders why.

Potter's rich description of a group seance and the life of a practicing shaman relate to several of the themes developed earlier in the book. The subject of Cantonese shamanism raises questions concerning official versus popular religion and the distribution of beliefs across regional systems. The shamans are all women; we wonder how this relates to the fact that women are regarded as powerful but unclean. We learn that female shamans obtain their powers through their children, and we are reminded of Margery Wolf's analysis of the maternal relationship. And when Potter tells us that "in Ping Shan numerous ghosts of brothers come back to haunt their living brothers and their families," we recall the questions raised by Cohen and Pasternak about the causes of family division.

The eleven papers in this volume are only one possible selection from the eighty-odd papers published in the Studies in Chinese Society series. We hope interested students will be moved to look into the seven volumes of that series and read some of the many fine papers that could not be included here.

Cities and the Hierarchy of Local Systems

This paper considers the place of cities in imperial China's spatial structure.[1] Two hierarchies of central places and of associated territorial systems are distinguished, one created and regulated by the imperial bureaucracy for purposes of field administration, the other given shape in
the first instance by economic transactions. The first reflected the bureaucratic structure of "official" China—a world of yamens and ranked
officials arrayed in a formal hierarchy of graded administrative posts.
The second reflected the "natural" structure of Chinese society—a world
of marketing and trading systems, informal politics, and nested subcultures dominated by officials-out-of-office, nonofficial gentry, and important merchants.

In this paper I attempt to model these two structures and their interaction. It should be noted at the outset that administrative capitals were
but a subset of economic central places, for all capitals performed significant economic functions for their hinterlands. In the eighteen provinces of China proper in the 1890's, there were some 39,000 economic
central places, only 1,546 of which served as capitals in the imperial
field administration.[2]

Despite the role of capitals as both administrative and economic central places, the distinction drawn between the two hierarchies is by no
means simply a heuristic device. The boundaries of administrative units
seldom coincided with those of marketing or trading systems. Thus, a
given capital city fitted into two empirically distinct spatial structures.
It is this feature that enables us to view low-level capitals as the locus
of articulation between the official structure of field administration and
the nonofficial structure of societal management.

My approach here gives some analytical precedence to commercial as against other central functions. In taking this stance I mean neither to imply that commercial functions outweighed all others nor to suggest that all or even most cities and towns originated as primarily economic centers.[3] But there are three senses in which economic central functions may be seen as basic. First, market towns and commercial cities were central nodes in the flow of goods and services, money and credit, and persons pursuing their livelihood and other economic interests. This meant that trading centers at all levels were logical sites for such public institutions as communal temples, schools, and benevolent institutions as well as for headquarters of the nonofficial structures exercising political, administrative, and even military control. In this sense, commercial centers attracted other types of central functions; thus there was a distinct tendency for religious "parishes," the catchment areas of schools, and the jurisdictions of parapolitical structures to coincide at local levels with the economic hinterlands of trade centers and to reflect their nodal structure.[4] Second, since the extraction of economic surplus is everywhere a critical enabling mechanism of politics, it was efficient for political institutions to focus on commercial centers in their efforts to control and regulate the means of exchange and (indirectly) production, and to tap the wealth of any given local system. Thus the headquarters of secret-society lodges and of other parapolitical institutions were normally located in market towns and cities in part because control of markets and of other key economic institutions figured prominently among the prizes of political competition.[5] Thus, too, a regular feature of the periodic adjustments and reorganizations of the imperial field administration was the incorporation as capitals of newly prominent trading centers.[6] Third, trade appears to have been far more potent than administrative transactions—or, for that matter, any other form of interurban linkages—in shaping *systems* of cities within China. This followed in part from the low intensity of bureaucratic field administration but more importantly from the fact that commerce, ever sensitive to cost distance, was more sharply constrained by physiographic givens than administration was. Thus, geographic constraints and trading patterns tended to reinforce one another in shaping urban systems.

For reasons implicit in these remarks, I begin with an analysis of China's cities and towns as commercial centers and take up field administration only after placing economic central places in the context of physiographic regions.

Modeling the Economic Hierarchy

The general economic importance of a settlement in late imperial China, as in most traditional agrarian societies, was in large part a function of three factors: (1) its role in providing retail goods and services for a surrounding tributary area or hinterland; (2) its position in the structure of distribution channels connecting economic centers; and (3) its place in the transport network.* In what follows I start with a theoretical discussion of the first factor, presenting an idealized model that I subsequently modify to incorporate elements of the other two factors.

Central-place theory in the strict sense is concerned solely with retailing.[7] The basic notion is that higher-level centers purvey more specialized goods and consequently have more extensive maximal hinterlands than lower-level centers do. The two key concepts here are the *demand threshold* of the supplier and the *range* of a good. Demand threshold may be defined as the area containing sufficient consumer demand to enable the supplier to earn normal profits. It reflects economies of scale in the provision of certain services and agglomeration advantages accruing from locating centralized retailers near to one another. The chief determinant of threshold is purchasing power per unit of area, itself a function of population density and the extent to which household economies are dependent on the market. Range may be defined as the circumscribed area beyond which buyers would not be willing to travel to purchase the good in question. The main determinants of the range of central goods are economic distance (i.e., geographic distance converted into transport costs) and production costs. If transport costs and demand density do not vary by direction from the central place, then the areas of both demand threshold and range will be roughly circular, with the radius of the circle varying for different goods and services.

Using the concepts of threshold and range and hewing to a number of stringent assumptions,† central-place theory predicts hierarchical patterns of trading centers on the landscape. Common goods in heavy demand are available in all centers at whatever level, whereas more specialized goods are available only at higher-order centers in accordance with the extent of their range. Thus, the set of goods supplied by a more complex center includes all goods supplied by simpler centers plus an increment of different higher-order goods. The result is a system in

---

* In a traditional agrarian society, industrial production tends to be relatively atomized and dispersed, and the location of handicraft industry closely reflects the three factors specified. Thus industrial location has not been incorporated in the models developed here.

† Most notably, full knowledge of market conditions on the part of both suppliers and consumers, full rationality on the part of suppliers in seeking to maximize profits and on the part of consumers in seeking to minimize costs, perfect competition, and a sufficient number of suppliers to meet all "threshold" demand.

which marketing centrality is discretely stratified, yielding functionally distinct levels of centers. A consequent feature of every regular central-place system is that the number of centers steadily decreases and the average size of hinterlands steadily increases as one moves up the hierarchy.

On the assumption of uniform demand density, centers at any given level will be spaced according to an isometric grid, as if at the apexes of space-filling equilateral triangles; since the size of threshold areas is affected by distance from competing suppliers in neighboring centers, hinterlands tend to be hexagonal rather than circular in shape. Thus, a honeycomb of hexagonal hinterlands develops, each in contact with six others at the same level. Finally, centers at one level are interdependent with their neighbors at adjacent levels in the sense that increased development of one higher-order town will result in the lesser development of the low-order centers in its immediate hinterland. The tributary nature of the system means that larger centers draw trade from nearby smaller centers and thus restrict their commercial growth.

One of the more common central-place patterns is diagramed in Figure 1, where four levels of centers are shown. Although this kind of model is derived from a theoretical analysis of the behavior of retailers and consumers, the geography of wholesale trade is at least as important as that of retailing in accounting for the location of cities and the structure of urban systems.* I shall argue briefly that, in a preindustrial economy lacking mechanized transport and communication, regular central-place hierarchies of the kind modeled in Figure 1 are optimal not only for retail marketing but also for the collection and export of local products, for the import and distribution of exogenous products, and for the wholesaling, transport, and credit functions essential for these activities.

Let us assume that the major transport routes on the hypothetical landscape of Figure 1 are those connecting A centers (each route passing through one B center and two C centers), that the next most important routes are those connecting B centers (each passing through one C center and two D centers), and so on. Efficiency alone dictates that the importance of particular centers as transport nodes should decline as the number and variety of suppliers and the size of the market decline. Given this pattern of nodes and links, and assuming uniform transport costs (i.e., that the friction of distance does not vary), the collection

---

* The convention within location theory is to define "central place" narrowly as a retail center. In this paper, however, the term has reference to all kinds of central functions, including but not limited to retailing.

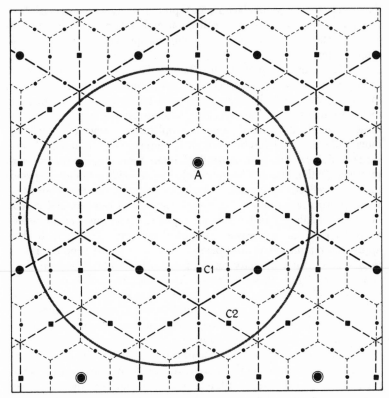

FIG. 1. A REGULAR CENTRAL-PLACE HIERARCHY, BOUNDLESS AND BOUNDED. The limits of D-level hinterlands are not shown.

◉ A centers   ● B centers   ■ C centers   • D centers

points for rural goods would normally be the nodes of the lowest-level (i.e., D-level) systems. How far up the hierarchy goods move is a function not only of such factors as their range (in the case of consumer goods) and of the location of processing and manufacturing industry (in the case of commercial crops and other raw materials), but also of the level of the nodes of systems that are themselves at the same level. For instance, the nodes of some D-level systems are C and B centers, and in these cases collection and bulking of goods of relatively high demand might cease at the center of first collection; there goods would be processed and distributed to lower-level centers throughout the C-level or B-level system whose node was the original collection point. In accordance with these variable factors, local products might pass through few or many nodes (here seen as collection and bulking centers), but in any case the movement of goods would recapitulate the hierarchy of retail centers.

Similar reasoning applies to distribution. The products of enterprises in or near an A center, or exogenous goods imported by firms located in an A center (which, of course, might be expected to participate more heavily than lower-level centers in long-distance trade), would be most efficiently distributed to retail suppliers in remote D centers by moving down the hierarchy through B centers and C centers. We are concerned here with the demand of retail firms and productive enterprises (rather than of households), but, as with retailing, demand threshold reflects economies of scale and agglomeration advantages. Range in this case refers to the area within which retailers find it economically feasible to seek wholesale supplies, credit, and transport services. Hierarchical patterns are predicted by a logic analogous to that applied to retailing in central-place theory. Small-scale simple services in general demand by petty retailers would be available, say, in all C centers and higher, whereas large-scale or specialized higher-order services would be available, in accordance with the extent of their range, only in B or A centers. Thus, the number and variety of wholesaling, credit, and transport facilities would be greatest in A centers, declining steadily as one descends the hierarchy.

Three points should be made about this ideal model of spatial distribution before introducing the more realistic assumptions needed to apply it to the Chinese case. First, it is clear that centers at the same level in the hierarchy are differently favored in terms of location in relation to higher-level centers. Suppliers in the ring of D centers immediately surrounding an A center are better off in terms of transport, credit facilities, wholesale prices, and goods selection than suppliers in the D centers immediately surrounding a B center; D centers lying on the roads connecting C centers are still less favorably situated. Even in a regular central-place hierarchy, then, the selling prices of retail goods and the purchase prices for local products at a D center may be expected to vary systematically according to that center's position in the overall structure. Second, the regular model ensures spatial competition because a center at any level is oriented to two (in the particular system modeled in Figure 1) or more higher-level centers. Thus, in Figure 1, retailers in every D center may choose between wholesalers in two higher-level centers; this means that wholesalers in a given higher-level center are competing with wholesalers in another higher-level center to supply each intervening D center. Third, the two-way trade and transport linking higher-level towns with their dependent lower-level centers strongly reinforce the systemic integrity of central-place subsystems. This is another facet of the interdependence described above in terms of the diversion of trade from lower-order centers to their higher-order neighbors.

The model developed so far assumes an idealized landscape characterized by (1) a flat and featureless topography, (2) an even distribution of demand or purchasing power, (3) equal transport facility in all directions, and (4) an indefinite extension of the same invariant pattern in all directions. In order to proceed to an analysis of the Chinese landscape, we must deal systematically with departures from these unrealistic assumptions.

The Structure of Regional Systems

In conceptualizing regional systems in agrarian China, I have drawn on four different approaches. The first equates regions with the maximal hinterlands of high-level central places.[8] As applied to nineteenth-century China, this approach would distinguish as first-order regions the trade areas of the highest-order goods and services supplied by such major metropolises as Sian, Wuhan, and Canton. Alternatively, a region might be defined as the maximal extent of the network of wholesale credit transactions centered on a given metropolis. One difficulty with this "metropolitan-dominance" approach is that the outer limits of the metropolitan region may give way to rural areas that consume none of the diagnostic higher-order goods or services. And in fact, China in the nineteenth century provided several instances of rural borderland areas that were not linked with any nodal region we could define using the above approach.

A closely related approach focuses on functionally integrated urban systems.[9] If we connected all the central places on a landscape by lines whose thicknesses were proportional to the magnitude of the trade between any given points, then the cores of economic regions would appear as a concentration of heavy lines connecting clusters of higher-level cities. The network of lines would thin toward the peripheries, and small market towns on regional frontiers would be assigned to one region or another on the basis of the direction of the greater trade flow.

The third approach is concerned with the differential distribution of economic resources. The concentration of critical resources may be indexed by such data as per capita income, demand density (purchasing power per unit of area), and (in an agrarian society) the value of agricultural production per unit of land or even the proportion of land that is arable or cultivated. In following this approach, I take population density as the major indicator of resource concentration on the grounds that it is a major component of demand density and correlates strongly with agricultural productivity both as cause (labor inputs) and as effect (the carrying capacity of the land).[10] As applied to China, this involves plotting county-level population densities, from which contours are derived showing density gradients. Extensive pockets of high population density are taken as the cores of economic regions, and regional boundaries are assumed to pass through the areas of lowest density between cores.

The fourth approach of concern here begins with physiographic features. The particular tradition on which I draw dates back to the eighteenth century, when Philippe Buache visualized the earth's land surface as consisting of river basins separated by mountain chains that provided convenient boundaries.[11] Taking the river basin as the essential regional determinant is particularly appropriate in the case of agrarian China, where crop inventories and productive techniques were specifically adapted to a plains-and-valley ecology and where water transport was of the greatest importance. In most Chinese physiographic regions, the river system provided the skeleton of the transport network that underlay the region's functional integration.[12] Although the definition of river-basin units involves a number of operational problems (see p. 212 above for their resolution in the Chinese case), watersheds are readily identified and taking them as regional boundaries leaves no areas unaccounted for.

When these four approaches are followed in regionalizing nineteenth-century China, the results are in large part mutually reinforcing and/or complementary. Nine major "islands" of relatively dense population were identified, each surrounded by concentric gradients of declining densities. Each high-density "core" was wholly contained within one of the nine physiographic macroregions shown in the map on page 9,* and with minor exceptions the watersheds that constituted regional boundaries passed through areas that were sparsely populated, at least in relation to the populations of the cores.

With the exception of Yun-Kwei and Manchuria, the maximal commercial hinterland of each region's major metropolis was wholly contained in, but did not exhaust, that physiographic region. (As of 1893,

---

* For background information on the maps on pp. 9 and 10, see the appendix, pp. 74–78. Although the maps show a single undifferentiated core within each macroregion, the distribution of population densities within most of these cores would permit further delimitation of concentric density zones.

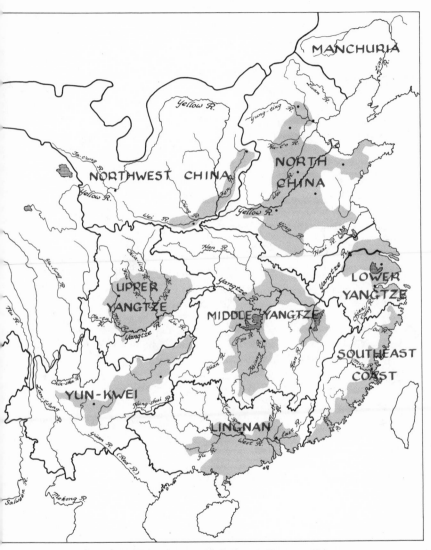

PHYSIOGRAPHIC MACROREGIONS OF AGRARIAN CHINA IN RELATION TO
MAJOR RIVERS, WITH REGIONAL CORES INDICATED BY SHADING

PHYSIOGRAPHIC MACROREGIONS IN RELATION TO PROVINCES,
AND SHOWING METROPOLITAN CITIES, 1843

the metropolises and their regions were Peking in North China, Sian in Northwest China, Chungking in the Upper Yangtze, Wuhan in the Middle Yangtze, Shanghai in the Lower Yangtze, Foochow in the Southeast Coast, and Canton in Lingnan.) In each case, the major commercial cities of the region had stronger economic links with one another than any had with cities outside the region,[13] and the densest interurban trade was almost wholly contained within the regional core. Moreover, the densely populated and urbanized core areas were closely associated with riverine lowlands.

Since it is virtually axiomatic that in a traditional agrarian society population density is a close function of agricultural productivity per unit of area, I will not document the assertions that a higher proportion of land was arable in the cores of regions than in the peripheries, that arable land in the former was generally more fertile than it was in the latter, and that the proportion of irrigated acreage in the cores was generally greater than that in the peripheries. The level of capital investment in drainage, reclamation, irrigation, and flood control was far higher per unit of arable land (and in some cases per capita) in cores than in peripheries, and in fact the very extent of a core was in many instances shaped by decisions to invest or not to invest in such waterworks. For reasons spelled out in the appendix (pp. 74–78), investment in transport—roads and bridges, canals and locks—was also comparatively heavy in core areas. Finally, because of the relatively low cost of transport in cores and their denser transport net, the local economies of core areas were consistently more commercialized than those of peripheral areas, both in the sense that more commercial crops and handicrafts were produced for the market and in the sense that households were more dependent on the market for consumer goods.

We are now in a position to modify the idealized model of central-place systems discussed in the previous section to accord with the structure of China's major regional systems. We may begin by abandoning the assumption that the same invariant pattern extends indefinitely in all directions. Suppose a landscape is bounded by high mountains along the circumference of the shaded circle in Figure 1. The system of central places within the circle now includes one A center, three B centers, fifteen C centers, and 62 D centers. All four of the B-level hinterlands (three whose nodes are B centers and one whose node is A) are contained in A's hinterland and dependent on the A center. All 19 of the C-level hinterlands (15 whose nodes are C centers, three whose nodes are B centers, and one whose node is A) are contained in one or more B-level hinterlands and dependent on one or more of the higher-level centers. And all 81 of the D-level hinterlands (62 whose nodes are D centers, 15 whose nodes are C centers, etc.) are contained in one or more C-level hinterlands and dependent on one or more of the higher-level centers. Thus the whole constitutes a single system of centers whose hinterlands form nested subsystems at four levels.

Adding boundedness to the model has two other consequences that deserve mention. First, spatial competition is generally reduced, and for many centers near the newly introduced system-limits it is elimi-nated entirely. Note that the three B centers are now oriented to only one A center, that several of the C centers near the periphery are now oriented to a single B center, and that many D centers around the rim are oriented to only one C center. Second, an additional element of differentiation among centers at the same level is introduced through truncation of the transport network around the rim of the system. For instance, in the unbounded model the locations of centers C_1 and C_2 were equally favorable in terms of transport to the nearest B and A centers, but in the bounded model C_2 is doubly disadvantaged: it is no longer on a road connecting B centers, and it is more distant than C_1 from the sole A center. Thus, boundedness alone creates a core-periphery structure within the central-place system.

If we now equate the bounded model just delimited with the upper reaches of the central-place system of one of the seven major macro-regions in agrarian China, we are constrained to modify the three other major assumptions of classical central-place theory. The notion of a uni-formly flat and featureless topography must be replaced by one of sys-tematic variation ranging from a productive level plain in the vicinity of the central metropolis (the A center) to relatively nonproductive and impenetrable terrain at the regional periphery. (In most of China, the rim of regional peripheries was marked by rugged mountains; by swampy saline marshes, as along much of the littoral of North China; or by des-ert, as along most of the Inner Asian peripheries of North and Northwest China.) The assumption of uniform demand density must be replaced by one of variable distribution whereby population density and the de-gree of market dependency both diminish toward the periphery. And finally, the notion of uniform transport facility must be replaced by one of systematic variation in transport costs from low values in the gener-ally low-lying and well-watered core areas to high values in the rela-tively rugged periphery.

Given these modifications of the central-place model, we can postu-late, first, that the average distance between centers at each level will be smaller in the core than in peripheral areas. Thus, moving from the core toward the periphery, the average area of trading systems increases. (One can imagine Figure 1 printed on a rubber sheet and then stretched so that distortion increases with distance from center A.) The rationale for this expectation is less simple than might appear at first glance, for transport efficiency has an effect on the spacing of centers (and hence on the size of hinterlands) that countervails the effect of demand density. Regional cores tend to couple high demand density with efficient transport; the former favors a close spacing of centers (small trading systems), whereas the latter favors a dispersed spacing of centers (large trading systems). The reverse is true in regional peripheries, where low demand density has the effect of increasing the distance between centers and inefficient transport has the effect of decreasing it. In practice, however, the effects of transport efficiency were strong enough to counteract those of demand density in only a few areas, such as the core of the Lower Yangtze region, characterized by a dense network of navigable waterways.

Second, we can postulate that within each class of central places the size of the market (that is, the volume of business transacted per unit of time) will be relatively large for centers near metropolis A and will decline steadily as we approach the periphery. At any level of the central-place hierarchy, then, peripheral cities will be likely to have fewer firms in the same business than core cities, and thus less competition.

Third, within each class of central places, peripheral cities will tend to have fewer *types* of firms purveying high-order goods and services than will their counterparts in regional cores. We have seen that a center's level (A, B, C, or D in Figure 1) is determined by the availability in it of specialized goods not obtainable at a lower level. But certain of the goods that are diagnostic of C centers in the core may be available in the periphery not in C centers but only in B centers. This upward displacement may occur at any and all levels of a central-place system, and it has the important consequence that subsystems occurring at the same level but differently situated with respect to the structure of the region may be characterized by somewhat different schedules of diagnostic incremental goods.[14]

Let me now characterize economic central places and their hinterlands in China with respect to the expectations derived from central-place and regional-systems models. On my analysis the economic hierarchy in the late nineteenth century consisted of eight levels.* In ac-

---

* An account of the procedures followed and criteria used in classifying central places by level in the economic hierarchy is given as an appendix to this paper in G. William Skinner, ed., *The City in Late Imperial China* (Stanford, Calif.: Stanford University Press, 1977), pp. 347–51.

cordance with the expectations of central-place theory, the number of
centers decreased sharply with each step up the hierarchy. In ascending
order, I have classified the economic centers of agrarian China in 1893
as follows: standard market towns (27,000–28,000), intermediate market towns (ca. 8,000), central market towns (ca. 2,300), local cities
(669), greater cities (200), regional cities (63), regional metropolises
(20), and central metropolises (6).*

The standard market town, which typically serviced a hinterland of
fifteen to 30 villages, met the week-to-week marketing needs of peasant
households. (I have discussed elsewhere the essential characteristics of
this basic town-plus-hinterland as an economic system: transport, trade,
industry, and credit were all structured within it spatially according to
the principle of centrality and temporally by the periodicity of its market days.[15]) Standard marketing systems were nested within intermediate systems, and so on in the manner suggested by central-place models,
but always subject to the constraints of topography and the distorting
effects of the transport grid. According to my analysis, this structure ultimately culminated in 26 metropolitan trading systems, which in turn
formed eight great economic systems, each essentially coterminous with
one of the physiographic macroregions shown in the maps on pages 9
and 10. The spatial characteristics of the full hierarchy will be illustrated below by reference to the Upper Yangtze region.

Macroregional cores were, of course, more urbanized than their surrounding peripheries, but the models now before us make it possible to
specify two distinct ways in which this was true. Table 1 shows that at
each ascending level of the economic hierarchy a higher proportion of
central places were situated in cores as against peripheries, the difference being greatest at the two highest levels. The table also shows that
for each level in the hierarchy city size was significantly larger in regional cores than in peripheries. It would be wrong, however, to interpret these population differentials as a simple consequence of the pri-
mordial physiographic aspects of regional structure. On the contrary, it
was Chinese patterns of occupance that transformed physiographic regions into city-centered functional systems whose very "natural" features
were to a considerable degree man-made. Urbanization itself contributed to core-periphery differentiation, and large cities have had the
effect of intensifying the core-like character of their environs. The ecological consequences of Chinese urbanization may be illustrated with
respect to deforestation and the disposal of human waste.

* The shift in terminology from market "town" to "city" between the third and
fourth orders is not meant to imply a critical distinction; it appears to me that the
orders constituted an integrated and evenly graded hierarchy.

TABLE 1. LOCATION OF CENTRAL PLACES IN REGIONAL CORES OR
PERIPHERIES BY LEVEL IN THE ECONOMIC HIERARCHY,
SHOWING MEAN POPULATIONS, 1893

Level in the economic hierarchy	Cores		Peripheries	Total	Mean population of cities/towns in class	
	No.	Pct.			Cores	Peripheries
Central metropolis	6	100 %		6	667,000	
Regional metropolis	18	90.0	2	20	217,000	80,000
Regional city	38	60.3	25	63	73,500	39,400
Greater city	108	54.0	92	200	25,500	17,200
Local city	360	53.8	309	669	7,800	5,800
CMT[a]	1,163	50.2	1,156	2,319	2,330	1,800
IMT[a]	3,905	48.7	4,106	8,011	690	450
SMT[a]	13,242	47.8	14,470	27,712	210	100
Total	18,840	48.3%	20,160	39,000		

[a] CMT, IMT, and SMT stand for central, intermediate, and standard market towns, respectively.

From time immemorial Chinese architecture has relied on timber as
the basic structural material. Wooden pillars and beams provided the
framework not only of houses and shops but also of urban public buildings: palaces and yamens, academies and examination sheds, gate houses
and drum towers, guildhalls and covered markets. Thus, an enormous
amount of timber was required for the construction of a Chinese city,
more than was needed for urban construction in most other civilizations,
which placed a greater emphasis on stone and brick. These cities of
wood with their narrow streets were subject to continual fires that were
difficult to contain. Between the burning of cities in wars or rebellions
and the burning of them in accidental conflagrations, much timber was
reduced to ashes. Additional inroads on China's forest cover were made
to supply charcoal for urban industry (including the firing of roof tiles),
fuel for urban residences, and paper and black ink (made of soot from
burnt pine) for administrative records, scholarly essays, and merchant
account books.[16] Since the forest cover of regional cores was depleted
fairly early, by late imperial times forest products for urban consumption came largely from mountainous areas in the peripheries. These developments had two important consequences: there was a direct transfer
of fertility through the conversion of peripheral timber to peri-urban
ash, and there was an indirect fertility "migration" as a result of erosion
caused by deforestation in peripheral highlands. The river systems that
formed the skeletal structure of most Chinese macroregions removed a
great deal of soil by erosion from the peripheral highlands and deposited it as silt in the lowlands of the core. Part of this silt was further

redistributed in the alluvial plains by the canal systems, irrigation works, and dikes that were also concentrated in lowland cores.[17] The mud that collected in canals, ditches, and other lowland waterways was, of course, periodically removed, if only to avoid obstruction; if the sludge was not applied directly to adjacent fields, it was dried for transport and sale to enrich the soil of nearby farms.[18] In the process, ash and silt whose ultimate origin was in the regional periphery enhanced the fertility of peri-urban agricultural areas in lowland cores.

The zones of high soil fertility that surrounded all of the larger cities in China's regional cores owed even more to the characteristically Chinese practice of husbanding night soil for use as fertilizer. Buchanan refers to the relevant process as the "continuous transfer of fertility from often distant hinterlands to supply urban populations with food."[19]

The organic and nutrient content of this food, in the form of human excreta, is eventually returned to the soils of the peri-urban area and these soils show a high humus, nitrogen, and base content which makes possible very high and stable yields. This use of night soil diminishes sharply with increasing distance from the cities, [which are consequently] surrounded by concentric zones of diminishing fertility; as a corollary . . . it is evident that the remoter food-supplying regions must be undergoing a continuous depletion of fertility as a result of this outflow of nutrients (including the phosphorus loss due to export of animal products).

Thus, urbanization in lowland areas helped bring about the higher fertility and dense rural populations characteristic of regional cores. And the very process of urbanization in regional cores proceeded at the expense of urbanization potential in the surrounding peripheries. In this sense, urban development in the core areas caused urban underdevelopment in the peripheries.

The Economic Hierarchy in the Upper Yangtze Region

I want now to focus on a single macroregion, the Upper Yangtze, in order to analyze the structure of its regional urban system. This section aims to present the contextual significance of cities at each level and to suggest the ways in which level in the hierarchy of economic central places necessarily implies position in a regional urban system.[20]

Map 1 presents an overview of the upper levels of the regional economy of the Upper Yangtze. The regional core, defined in terms of population density, included the major navigable stretches of the region's river system and, as one might expect, coincided rather closely with the Red Basin. As of 1893, the population density of the core was approximately 294 persons per sq. km., and that of the periphery about 47. Note

MAP 1. THE UPPER YANGTZE REGION, 1893, showing the extent of the regional core, rivers, central places down to the level of local cities, and the approximate extent of regional-city trading systems. The dotted line bisecting the region separates the economic sphere of Chengtu from that of Chungking.

that most of the region's high-ranking economic centers were situated in the core: both metropolises, five of the six regional cities, and sixteen of the 21 greater cities.

In the 1890's, the relative economic centrality of the region's two metropolises, Chengtu and Chungking, was in transition. In the early nineteenth century, Chengtu had been unequivocally the central metropolis and Chungking merely a regional metropolis; by the 1920's, however, the roles of the two cities would be decisively reversed.[*] Even in the 1890's, however, Chungking had become the chief center of both intra- and extraregional trade, and in this sense the region as a whole may be taken as the maximal hinterland of Chungking. The dotted line on Map 1 separates the economic sphere of Chengtu from that of Chungking and defines the limits of the region's two metropolitan trading systems.

Map 1 also shows the approximate boundaries of the Upper Yangtze's eight regional trading systems. Three points are worthy of notice here. First, around the periphery of the region, the limits of trading systems almost without exception followed the mountain ridges separating basins of tributary river systems. Second, whereas in peripheral areas local and greater cities were oriented to single higher-level centers, in the more central areas a number of cities were oriented to two or more regional-city trading systems; no fewer than four greater cities and 21 local cities are shown at the boundaries of trading systems, reflecting their economic dependence on two or more of the eight nodes of regional-city trading systems. Third, with the exception of Kuang-yüan's trading system, which lay entirely in the regional periphery, each of the regional-city trading systems included core as well as peripheral areas. The general structure, then, was one in which regional-city trading systems tended to be discrete around the periphery and interdigitated within the core.

It is apparent that economic centers were sited on navigable waterways whenever possible, a preference that was general throughout China. An inspection of Map 1 reveals that of the 29 greater and higher-

[*] The chief explanations for this reversal of roles are all ultimately related (1) to the steady growth of extraregional trade via the downriver Yangtze route (both absolutely and as a proportion of the Upper Yangtze's total extraregional trade) and (2) to the fact that transport modernization within the region was limited almost entirely to waterways prior to the 1950's. Long before 1896, when the first steamship successfully breached the gorges between I-ch'ang-fu and Wan-hsien, Chungking had benefited from the increased economic activity in the Lower and Middle Yangtze regions that had followed the opening of Shanghai and Hankow as treaty ports and the introduction of mechanized transport in those regions. As of 1893, Chengtu was still the more populous of the two cities, although Chungking probably surpassed it in the number of shopkeeper households.

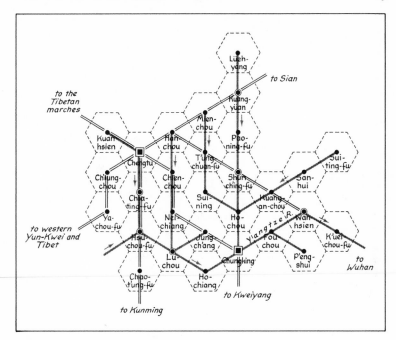

Fig. 2. Greater-City Trading Systems in Relation to Rivers and Major Roads (Schematized), Upper Yangtze Region, 1893. Arrows show direction of flow of rivers.

level cities in the Upper Yangtze region, only one (Chao-t'ung-fu) was not sited on a river. (The Ch'ing-i River, on which Ya-chou-fu was situated, was unnavigable for certain downstream stretches.) This means that 27 cities of this class were served for at least part of the year by at least small craft.[21]

The essential structure of the region's transport network is schematized in Figure 2. It shows not only those portions of the Yangtze River and its tributaries that linked higher-level cities, but also the most important of the official roads (*kung-lu*), all of which radiated from Chengtu, the provincial capital of Szechwan.[22] In many respects, the highway that ran from Ya-chou-fu through Chengtu to Kuang-yüan (continuing on to Sian and eventually to Peking) was the functional equivalent in Chengtu's metropolitan trading system of the Yangtze River in Chungking's metropolitan trading system. It is apparent that the structure of the river system virtually determined the siting of the region's higher-level economic centers and that major roads had the

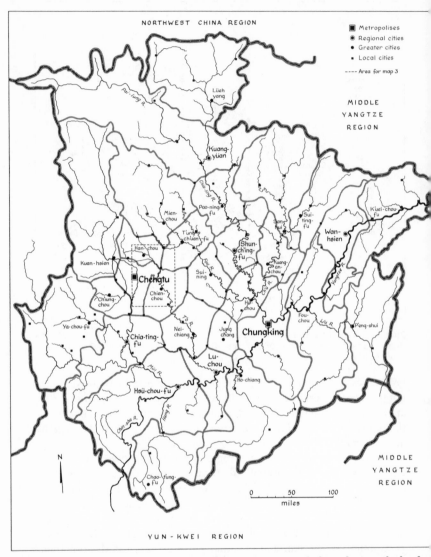

MAP 2. THE UPPER YANGTZE REGION, 1893, showing rivers, central places down to the level of local cities, and the approximate extent of greater-city trading systems.

effect of compensating for deficiencies of the river system in linking those cities.*

Map 2 shows greater-city trading systems, the next level below the regional-city trading systems shown in Map 1. In general, the pattern noted in Map 1 is recapitulated for the hinterlands of greater cities. System boundaries in the periphery were relatively impermeable, following mountain ridges that limited intercourse between cities in the various drainage basins, whereas those in the core passed through numerous local cities that were members of two or more greater-city trading systems.

Two of the most important ways in which transport systematically distorts the regularity of the central-place hierarchy were apparent in the Upper Yangtze, as in most other regions of late imperial China. First, major transport routes of all types foster linearity by attracting (as it were) central places that would otherwise be sited on a triangular lattice. This effect is evident in the siting of two local cities (rather than one) between higher-level cities along major rivers. On Map 2, note the placement of local cities between Wan-hsien and Fou-chou on the Yangtze, between Pao-ning-fu and Shun-ch'ing-fu on the Chia-ling River, between T'ung-ch'uan-fu and Sui-ning on the Fou River, between Chien-chou and Nei-chiang on the T'o River, and between Chia-ting-fu and Hsü-chou-fu on the Min River. A second distorting effect, wholly expectable in a regional system whose basic transport network is a river system, is the tendency for cities to be situated within their hinterlands off-center in the downstream direction. Examples apparent on Map 2 are the greater-city trading systems of Lüeh-yang, Kuang-yüan, Mien-chou and Kuan-hsien in the northwest, of Ho-chiang and P'eng-shui in the southeast, and of Sui-ting-fu and San-hui in the northeast.

It is dramatically evident in Map 2 that the areas of greater-city trading systems at or near the periphery were larger than those in the regional core. This pattern illustrates the expected effect of sparse population and low commercialization in fostering large trading systems. Another feature of the Upper Yangtze system that has general significance is the contrast between relative irregularity in the spatial patterning of regional cities (and higher-level centers) vis-à-vis greater cities,

---

* In general the importance of navigable waterways in structuring regional urban systems was comparable in four other macroregions—the Middle Yangtze, the Lower Yangtze, the Southeast Coast, and Lingnan—to what we have seen for the Upper Yangtze. The importance of roads and overland transport was relatively greater in North China, absolutely greater in Northwest China, and overwhelmingly greater in Yun-Kwei.

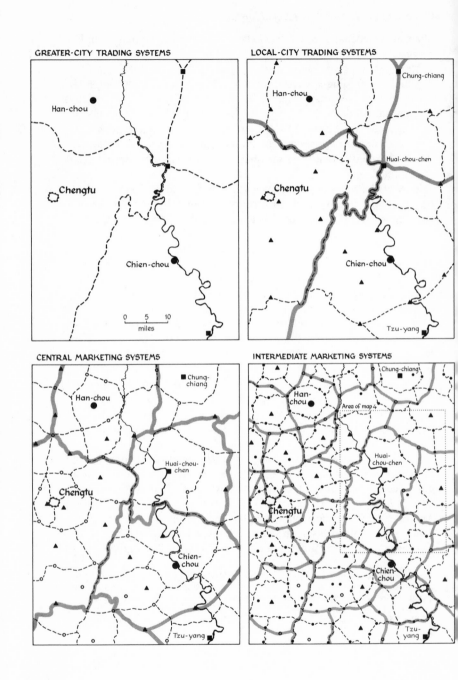

GREATER-CITY TRADING SYSTEMS

Han-chou
Chengtu
Chien-chou

0   5   10
miles

LOCAL-CITY TRADING SYSTEMS

Han-chou
Chung-chiang
Huai-chou-chen
Chengtu
Chien-chou
Tzu-yang

CENTRAL MARKETING SYSTEMS

Han-chou
Chung-chiang
Huai-chou-chen
Chengtu
Chien-chou
Tzu-yang

INTERMEDIATE MARKETING SYSTEMS

Han-chou
Chung-chiang
Area of map 4
Huai-chou-chen
Chengtu
Chien-chou
Tzu-yang

Map 3 (*opposite*). A SMALL PORTION OF THE UPPER YANGTZE REGION, 1893, showing the approximate extent of greater-city and local-city trading systems and of central and intermediate marketing systems. The wide shaded boundaries show the next higher system level in each case: the limits of greater-city trading systems upper right, of local-city trading systems lower left, and of central marketing systems lower right. Greater cities are shown as large solid circles, local cities as solid squares, central market towns as solid triangles, and intermediate market towns as open circles.

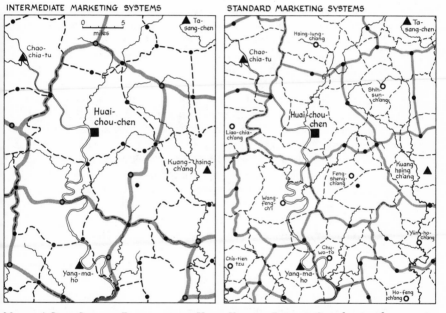

INTERMEDIATE MARKETING SYSTEMS · STANDARD MARKETING SYSTEMS

Map 4. A STILL SMALLER PORTION OF THE UPPER YANGTZE REGION, 1893, showing the approximate extent of intermediate and standard marketing systems. The wide shaded boundaries show the next higher system level in each case: the limits of central marketing systems on the left and of intermediate marketing systems on the right. Local cities are shown as solid squares, central market towns as solid triangles, intermediate market towns as small open circles, and standard market towns as dots.

as against fairly regular patterning at lower steps of the economic hierarchy. Note in Figure 2 that the pattern established by the siting of Kuang-yüan, Shun-ch'ing-fu, Wan-hsien, Chungking, and Lu-chou vis-à-vis their dependent greater cities was broken in the western portion of the region, a function in part of "irregularities" in the structure of the river system, whereby the major river confluences at the sites of Lu-chou and Hsü-chou-fu are exceptionally close together, and in part of the "clumping" of resources in the Chengtu Plain, along the Yangtze between Hsü-chou-fu and Lu-chou, and northwest of Lu-chou along the T'o River. Such "coarse-grained" variations took their toll of regularity in the siting of regional and higher-level cities in most macroregions.

In general, within the same subsystem of centers I find that discrete stratification prevailed and that upward shift of functions to centers of the next higher level occurred in peripherally situated trading systems. Of the enterprises listed in the appendix (p. 351) as being diagnostic of local cities in the regional core of the Upper Yangtze, pawnshops are among those most often mentioned in gazetteers and other contemporary sources during the 1875–1912 period. Despite reservations about negative evidence, it is worth reporting that of all cities in the region for which the presence of pawnshops is documented during this period, those situated in the periphery were limited to greater and higher-level cities whereas those in the regional core included scores of local cities.

The arrangement of greater-city trading systems, as shown on Map 2, bears scant resemblance to an array of fitted hexagons. Nonetheless, it is apparent from Figure 2 that at the greater-city level the region's central places were generally distributed on a triangular grid. A count of the sixteen greater-city trading systems that did not abut on the regional boundary yields an average of 5.3 neighbors, with 6.0 representing perfect geometric regularity.

Map 3, which continues the progression down the hierarchy of nested economic systems, is necessarily limited to a small portion of the region, namely the area in the vicinity of Chengtu enclosed by the dotted rectangle on Map 2. The upper-left panel of Map 3, like Map 2, shows greater-city trading systems, thereby conveying a feel for the sharp increase in scale. Each of the other three panels of Map 3 takes us a step lower in the economic hierarchy. The upper-right panel shows local-city trading systems and central places down to the central market town; the lower-left panel shows central marketing systems and central places down to the intermediate market town; and the lower-right panel shows intermediate marketing systems and central places down to the standard market town. In each case, system boundaries at the next higher level are indicated by wide shaded lines, thereby dramatizing the manner in which economic centers and hinterlands at each level were related spatially to those at adjacent levels in the hierarchy. In conjunction, they illustrate a general feature of the hierarchy of local economic systems, namely that whereas higher-level systems completely enveloped only one system at the next lower level (the one with the same node), they enveloped several systems at the level below that. We also see at each level the interstitial placement of orders that is characteristic of a regular central-place hierarchy: note in particular that the great majority of intermediate market towns fell at the borders of central marketing systems, i.e., were oriented economically to two or more central market towns, and that the great majority of standard market towns were similarly situated with respect to intermediate marketing systems.

The effect of topography may be seen in the coincidence of systemic boundaries at each level along the crest of the Lung-ch'üan Mountains, which range is penetrated by the T'o River just northwest of Huai-chou-chen. This feature illustrates the general principle, already noted with respect to higher-level systems in the regional periphery, that topographic barriers impede the usual overlapping of systems at adjacent levels of the hierarchy. The tendency for higher-level centers (in this case central market towns on up) to favor through transport routes is apparent along the course of the T'o River.

Map 4 completes the progression down the hierarchy of local economic systems. It is limited to a still smaller portion of the landscape, namely that enclosed by the dotted rectangle shown in the lower-right panel of Map 3. To ensure visual continuity, the left panel of Map 4 repeats at the larger scale what is shown within the dotted rectangle of Map 3. The right panel of Map 4 makes clear that nodes of standard marketing systems were not limited to standard market towns, but also included intermediate market towns, central market towns, and local cities. It shows that standard market towns were normally situated interstitially between higher-level towns and that standard marketing systems were invariably split between intermediate marketing systems. It was these spatial features, all predicted by central-place theory, which, through replication at successively higher levels, integrated local economic systems into the complex interlocking network of higher-order trading systems.

There is no space here to present a schematization of the landscapes shown in Maps 3 and 4. However, the chief point that might thereby be conveyed visually can be suggested quantitatively by neighbor counts at the various levels. It was noted above that inspection of sixteen greater-city trading systems in the central area of the Upper Yangtze region indicated an average of 5.3 neighbors per system. The corresponding figures for lower-level systems wholly or partly included in Map 3 are 5.7 for the nine local-city trading systems, 5.8 for the 31 central marketing systems, 5.9 for the 75 intermediate marketing systems, and 6.0 for the 230 standard marketing systems. Such progressions were characteristic of core areas throughout agrarian China. We may conclude that within regional economic systems the arrangement of central places conformed most closely to the regular central-place model at lower levels of the hierarchy and in core areas as against regional peripheries.

A Comparison of Regional Urban Systems

Because of the unique physiographic configurations of China's macroregions and the semi-independent nature of their various economic histories, no two urban systems were alike. The Middle Yangtze and the Southeast Coast are sharply subregionalized by physiographic features, whereas North China and the Lower Yangtze are not. Great variation obtained in the relative size and shape of the core and in the centrality of its location within the region, which factors strongly conditioned the characteristics of the various urban systems. Nonetheless, systematic comparison across all regions reveals regularities of some interest.

Table 2 sets out for each of the eight macroregional systems the num-

TABLE 2. NUMBER OF CENTRAL PLACES BY REGION
AND BY LEVEL IN THE ECONOMIC HIERARCHY, 1893
(*Down to Central Market Towns*)

Region	\multicolumn{6}{c}{Level in the economic hierarchy}	Total
	Central metropolis	Regional metropolis	Regional city	Greater city	Local city	Central market town	
Northwest China	1	2	7	18	55	178	261
Yun-Kwei	—	2	3	13	36	112	166
Lingnan	1	2	7	24	71	223	328
Middle Yangtze	1	3	10	25	115	403	557
Upper Yangtze	1	1	6	21	87	292	408
Southeast Coast	—	1	4	11	42	147	205
North China	1	6	18	64	189	697	975
Lower Yangtze	1	3	8	24	74	267	377
Total	6	20	63	200	669	2,319	3,277

ber of central places at each level of the economic hierarchy down to and including central market towns. (Note that the urban system of the Upper Yangtze was about average in terms of number of central places.) The implications of these regional data are brought out in Table 3, which displays the average areas and populations of trading systems at five levels of the hierarchy. In relating Table 3 to the figures of Table 2, it should be remembered that high-level cities have multiple concentric hinterlands. A regional city is the node not only of a regional-city trading system but also of a greater-city trading system, of a local-city trading system, and of a central marketing system. Thus, the numbers of trading systems in Table 3 are cumulations of the numbers of centers shown in Table 2. Regional cities, for instance, were nodes of only 63 of the 89 regional-city trading systems, the others being accounted for by the twenty regional metropolises and the six central metropolises. As expected, the size of hinterlands, whether measured by area or population, decreased decisively in each region from one order to the next lower order in the hierarchy.

Rather more interesting are the comparative size regularities to which attention has been called by ordering the regions according to their average population densities. The pattern that holds in general for trading systems at all levels appears most clearly in the case of central marketing systems: whereas the average area of hinterlands at a given level is related linearly to population density (with area declining steadily as density increases), the average hinterland population shows a curvilinear relationship, increasing along with density up to a point and thereafter decreasing with still higher densities. The overall dynamics of these interrelationships can be captured by comparing four groupings of regions without reference to within-group differences. Demand density (purchasing power per unit of area) was highest in the Lower Yangtze, relatively high in the Southeast Coast and in North China, middling in the Upper and Middle Yangtze regions and Lingnan, and low in Yun-Kwei and Northwest China. It is apparent that as demand density decreases (moving up the table), hinterland area increases by way of compensation. It does not keep pace, however, because a declining population density is related not only to the decrease in demand density but also to an increase in the distance from the center in question to the limits of its hinterland. If the area of hinterlands were to be enlarged in proportion to the decline in demand density, then purchasing power in the more remote areas would be lost to *any* center by reason of excessive transport costs. Thus, in that portion of the regional continuum with relatively sparse populations, one sees a trade-

TABLE 3. CITY-CENTERED ECONOMIC SYSTEMS, BY REGION, 1893

Region[a]	Area (sq. km.)	Pop. (000)	Density (persons per sq. km.)	Metropolitan trading systems			Regional-city trading systems		
				No.	Ave. area (000)	Ave. pop. (000)	No.	Ave. area (000)	Ave. pop. (000)
Northwest China	746,470	24,000	32	3	248.8	8,000	10	74.6	2,400
Yun-Kwei	470,570	16,000	34	2	235.3	8,000	5	94.1	3,200
Lingnan	424,900	33,000	78	3	141.6	11,000	10	42.5	3,300
Middle Yangtze	699,700	75,000	107	4	174.9	18,750	14	50.0	5,357
Upper Yangtze	423,950	53,000	125	2	212.0	26,500	8	53.0	6,625
Southeast Coast	190,710	26,000	136	1	190.7	26,000	5	38.1	5,200
North China	771,300	122,000	158	7	110.2	17,429	25	30.9	4,880
Lower Yangtze	192,740	45,000	233	4	48.2	11,250	12	16.1	3,750
Total	3,920,340	394,000	101	26	150.8	15,154	89	44.0	4,427

[a] Regions are ordered according to population density, low to high from top to bottom.

Region	Greater-city trading systems			Local-city trading systems			Central marketing systems		
	No.	Ave. area	Ave. pop. (000)	No.	Ave. area	Ave. pop. (000)	No.	Ave. area	Ave. pop. (000)
Northwest China	28	26,660	857	83	8,994	289	261	2,860	92
Yun-Kwei	18	26,140	889	54	8,714	296	166	2,834	96
Lingnan	34	12,500	970	105	4,047	314	328	1,295	101
Middle Yangtze	39	17,940	1,923	154	4,543	487	557	1,256	135
Upper Yangtze	29	14,620	1,828	116	3,654	457	408	1,039	130
Southeast Coast	16	11,920	1,625	58	3,288	448	205	930	127
North China	89	8,670	1,370	278	2,774	439	975	791	125
Lower Yangtze	36	5,350	1,250	110	1,752	409	377	511	119
Total	289	13,570	1,363	958	4,092	411	3,277	1,196	120

off whereby the average area increases (with declining demand density) at so gradual a rate that the average hinterland population declines. In Northwest China and Yun-Kwei, goods appropriate to centers at a given level had ranges that were, in a manner of speaking, unduly restricted for the ecological environment, whereas firms appropriate to such centers had thresholds that were unduly extended; the result of this "squeeze" was that hinterlands were at once overlarge in area and not large enough in population.

In that portion of the regional continuum with relatively dense populations, purchasing power becomes critical in understanding the relationships revealed in Table 3. The Lower Yangtze as a whole was far more commercialized than the Southeast Coast, which in turn was more commercialized than the Middle Yangtze. The implication is that 1.2 million people in the Lower Yangtze (the average population of a greater-city trading system) generated at least as much demand as 1.6 million in the Southeast Coast and 1.9 million in the Middle Yangtze. And there is no reason to doubt it; one would, in fact, expect the *total* purchasing power of a greater-city trading system, say, to be smaller in the Middle than in the Lower Yangtze (rather than the same) owing to the effect of higher transport costs in limiting hinterland size. In short, the curvilinear relationship of population density with average hinterland population is but a manifestation of a more basic linear relationship with the total purchasing power of the various regions.

Note the following irony. The Upper Yangtze was chosen as the region for detailed analysis in part because of its typicality: an internal physiography that fell midway between the extremes, an urban system of average size, and an overall population density that put it closer than any other region to the empirewide average. Yet its city-centered trading systems were among the most populous in all of China.

The Official Administrative Hierarchy

Most of China's central places that ranked as local cities or higher in the economic hierarchy also served as administrative capitals. For instance, in the Upper Yangtze as of 1893, all eight of the regional cities and metropolises were capitals, as were twenty of the 21 greater cities, 68 of the 87 local cities, and 43 of the 292 central market towns. I now turn to a description of field administration in order to explore the ways in which the administrative central functions of cities and their place in the administrative hierarchy interacted with their economic central functions and place in regional economic systems.

The Ch'ing field administration[23] may be conveniently described as

having four levels below the imperial capital.* At the highest level, the
eight governor-generalships and eighteen provinces were interdigitated
to constitute in effect nineteen governments in as many capital cities.
Only three of the eight capitals with a governor-general's yamen (Canton, Wu-ch'ang-fu, and Kunming) also housed a governor's yamen. Three
provinces (Shansi, Honan, and Shantung) belonged to no governor-
generalship, and two governor-generalships consisted of a single province each (Chihli and Szechwan). Nanking, capital of the Liang-chiang
governor-generalship, was situated in Kiangsu, whose provincial government was at Soochow; nonetheless, the Nanking government included several high officials (e.g., a lieutenant governor and a provincial
director of education) otherwise found exclusively in provincial capi-
tals.²⁴ In any case, the present analysis ignores the administrative distinctions among the nineteen cities that served as capitals of provinces
and/or governor-generalships.

The eighteen provinces were subdivided into 77 circuits (tao), some
of which were classified as military circuits. In some respects, circuit
yamens resembled specialized offices of the provincial government more
than administrative offices at a separate level of the territorial hierarchy.
For instance, circuit intendants were primarily responsible for diplomatic relations with foreigners even within the circuit that contained
the provincial capital. The official educational hierarchy concerned with
supervising and accrediting scholars and administering imperial examinations bypassed circuits altogether. Nor were official temples and altars
prescribed for the circuit level, as they were for the other three levels
of field administration. Nonetheless, the circuit intendant maintained a
yamen in a city within the territorial area of his circuit, and prefects
and other officials at the next lower level were directly accountable to
him for a wide range of civil and military affairs. And despite anomalies,
circuit yamens were traditionally located in cities that were capitals by
virtue of having yamens for other levels of the administrative hierarchy.

---

* This analysis is limited to agrarian China minus Manchuria and Taiwan, specifically to the eight macroregions shown in the maps on pp. 9–10. As of 1893, the
combined territory of these regions contained 1,576 county-level units, inclusive of
areas directly administered from prefectural-level capitals. At that time the empire
as a whole contained approximately 80 additional county-level units, not treated
here; most of the excluded units were in Sinkiang, Manchuria, and Taiwan, but
several were located in the arid and/or mountainous periphery of China proper, most
notably northern Chihli, western Szechwan, and northwestern Yunnan (see the
map on p. 10). The 1,576 county-level units under consideration contained only
1,549 capitals because yamens of adjacent county-level units were occasionally located in the same city.

The next lower level included three types of administrative units: prefectures (*fu*), by far the most numerous; autonomous *chou*, also called independent departments (*chih-li chou*); and autonomous *t'ing*, also called independent subprefectures (*chih-li t'ing*). The relative importance of these prefectural-level units is suggested by the bureaucratic rank of the superior incumbent official, normally 4b for a prefecture, 5a for an autonomous *chou*, and 5a or 6a for an autonomous *t'ing*.* This rank order was reflected in the relative population of prefectural-level capitals. On the average, the capitals of prefectures were more populous than those of autonomous *chou*, which in turn were more populous than those of autonomous *t'ing*.[25] The classic contemporary description of Ch'ing administration tells us that autonomous *t'ing* "represent a lower form of local government," having been "made independent of the prefectural government because of their importance or territorial magnitude." Moreover, autonomous *chou* and *t'ing* "represent intermediate stages in the transformation of ordinary [*chou* and *t'ing*] into prefectures. For this reason they are observed to be most numerous on the borders of the Empire."[26] We shall have reason below to modify and elaborate this interpretation, but for the moment it may serve to signal the status of autonomous *chou* and *t'ing* as at once lower ranking than prefectures and somehow special.

Three different types of units were also found at the fourth and lowest level of bureaucratic administration, namely, counties (*hsien*), by far the most numerous; ordinary *chou*, also known as dependent departments (*san-chou* or *shu-chou*); and ordinary *t'ing*, also known as dependent subprefectures (*san-t'ing* or *shu-t'ing*).† All three types of county-level units could be subordinate to prefectures, whereas with one exception ordinary *chou* and *t'ing* were never subordinate to autonomous *chou* or *t'ing*.[27] By contrast with the prefectural level, where autonomous *chou* and *t'ing* were outranked by prefectures, at the county

* There were nine bureaucratic ranks, each divided into an upper (a) and lower (b) subrank. Rank 1a was highest, 9b lowest.

† Arguably a still lower level of administration existed in embryonic form. Certain county-level units contained subdistricts (*ssu*) whose "capitals" were towns where a special category of deputy magistrate (*hsün-chien*) served. Since such towns typically ranked among the most important within their counties, there would be good reason for keeping them distinct in analysis. On the other hand, subdistricts were never considered a regular administrative unit at the subcounty level—on the contrary, *hsün-chien* were considered an integral part of the county-level government—and their number was repeatedly reduced during late imperial times. At any event, in the present analysis I have reluctantly merged this small class of subadministrative towns with nonadministrative centers—a decision that greatly simplifies presentation without materially altering the results.

level ordinary *chou* and *t'ing* officially outranked counties. The chief bureaucrat of an ordinary *chou* was normally of rank 5b and that of an ordinary *t'ing* of rank 6a (occasionally 5a), whereas the rank of a county magistrate was normally only 7b. City size, however, suggests a different ordering. True enough, *chou* capitals tended to be larger than either *hsien* or *t'ing* capitals, but *t'ing* capitals were smaller on the average than *hsien* capitals, not larger—as might be expected from the official ranking.[28] This discrepancy will be explained when the regional distribution of types of capital cities is considered below.

The hierarchical ordering that ran from province to prefecture to county was seen as the standard administrative arrangement. Prefectures and counties, as we have seen, greatly outnumbered other administrative units at their respective levels. Moreover, provincial capitals were invariably capitals of prefectures (never of autonomous *chou* or *t'ing*), and prefectural capitals were invariably capitals of counties (never of ordinary *chou* or *t'ing*). The standard hierarchy of province-prefecture-county was structured in the manner familiar to us from most modern administrative arrangements. The territory of a province was exhausted by prefectural-level units, and the capital of one of these, termed hereafter the metropolitan prefecture, also served as the provincial capital. Similarly, the territory of a prefecture was exhausted by county-level units, and the capital of one of these, termed hereafter the metropolitan county, also served as the prefectural capital. Thus, every provincial capital had minimally three yamens, one each for the provincial governor, the prefect, and the county magistrate, and every prefectural capital had minimally two yamens, one each for the prefect and the county magistrate.

The arrangement was quite different in the case of an autonomous *chou*, whose territory was not exhausted by its subordinate counties. Rather, what would otherwise be considered the metropolitan county-level unit had no government of its own. Known as the *pen-chou* (the "root" *chou*, or *chou* proper), it was administered directly by the government of the autonomous *chou*, whose capital thus lacked a county-level yamen. The entire category of *pen-chou* tends to be lost in administrative records and to be overlooked in analyses of Ch'ing administration since *pen-chou* do not appear as administrative units in official compendia such as the *Hui-tien* or the *Chin-shen ch'üan-shu*. Autonomous *t'ing* were more anomalous still in that, with two exceptions, they lacked subordinate county-level units altogether. Thus, the county-level "*pen-t'ing*" (the term was not used) exhausted the territory of the prefectural-

TABLE 4. SPAN OF CONTROL BY TYPE OF ADMINISTRATIVE CENTER, 1893
(*Prefectural and Higher-level Capitals Only*)

Span of control[a]	Capitals of									
	Metropolitan prefectures		Ordinary prefectures[b]		Autonomous chou		Autonomous t'ing		Total	
	No.	Pct.	No.	Pct.	No.	Pct.	No.	Pct.	No.	Pct.
1			4	13%		0%	28	88%	32	100%
2			4	27	9	60	2	13	15	100
3			8	25	24	75		0	32	100
4			21	53	19	48			40	100
5		0%	22	71	9	29			31	100
6	2	6	22	71	7	23			31	100
7–8	3	6	48	94		0			51	100
9–10	4	16	21	84					25	100
11–13	4	29	10	71					14	100
14+	7	78	2	22					9	100
Total	20	7%	162	58%	68	24%	30	11%	280	100%

[a] I.e., the number of county-level yamens supervised by a given prefectural-level yamen.
[b] Includes the two sectoral capitals in the imperial prefecture that served as circuit capitals.

level autonomous *t'ing*, and there was of course only a single administrative yamen in the capital city.[*]

This last distinction draws our attention to span of control, a formal feature of field administration that sharply differentiated the three types of prefectural-level units. The analysis pursued here refers solely to control of county-level yamens by their superior prefectural-level yamens. Span is said to be narrow when the superordinate office has only a few subordinate offices to supervise, and broad when the subordinate offices are many. In Ch'ing China, the number of county-level units per prefectural-level unit ranged from one to eighteen, not counting the exceptional imperial prefecture, which had 24; the mean fell between five and six. Table 4 shows the span of control of all prefectural-level units

[*] In fact some "rectification of names" would have been in order in the field administrative system of late Ch'ing. Two autonomous *t'ing* (Pai-se in Kwangsi and Hsü-yung in Szechwan) and six prefectures (Hsing-i, Shih-ch'ien, Ssu-chou, Ssu-nan, and Ta-ting, all in Kweichow, and Ssu-en in Kwangsi) were structurally identical to autonomous *chou*, and I have been unable to ascertain any reason why they were not so designated. The anomalous *t'ing* each contained one county in addition to the directly ruled area, and in the anomalous prefectures what would have been the metropolitan county was a directly ruled area analogous to a *pen-chou*. The six prefectures thus constitute an exception to the general rule given in the text that every prefectural capital contained at least one county yamen. Where appropriate in subsequent statistical analyses, these anomalous cases are classed with the capitals of autonomous *chou*.

TABLE 5. SPAN OF CONTROL BY TYPE OF CAPITAL, 1893
(*County-level Capitals Subordinate to Prefectures Only*)

County-level capital	Span of control[a]							
	−6		7–8		9+		Total	
	No.	Pct.	No.	Pct.	No.	Pct.	No.	Pct.
Hsien	225	25%	242	27%	421	47%	888	100%
Chou[b]	37	27	48	35	51	38	136	100
T'ing	26	43	10	17	24	40	60	100
Total	288	27%	300	28%	496	46%	1,084	100%

[a] Span of control refers here to the number of units in the prefecture to which the county-level unit in question belonged.
[b] Excludes sectoral capitals in the imperial prefecture.

by type of prefectural-level capital. We have already noted that the span of control of autonomous *t'ing* was normally only one, and it is clear from the table that autonomous *chou* had relatively narrow spans; they ranged from two to six with a mean of 3.7. Ordinary prefectures had spans clustered in the range from four to ten, with a mean of 6.6, whereas metropolitan prefectures (i.e., those whose capitals were provincial or higher capitals) had still broader spans, ranging from six to 24, with a mean of 11.9.

At the county level, too, units were distinguished by span of control. It follows from what has already been said that counties in autonomous *chou* would be more closely supervised (in the sense of belonging to superordinate units with relatively narrow spans of control) than counties in prefectures. However, there is no a priori reason for expecting differences among the three types of units within prefectures. Nonetheless, as shown in Table 5, ordinary *t'ing* were disproportionately found in prefectures with narrow spans (six or less), ordinary *chou* in prefectures with intermediate spans (seven to eight), and *hsien* in prefectures with broad spans (nine or more).

The key to span variations at both levels of the administrative hierarchy lies in the distinctive locational patterns of different types of capitals within regional urban systems, a subject I take up in the following section. But first a summary of the various types of capital cities is in order. Details are presented in Table 6, where the numerical preponderance of prefectural and county capitals at their respective levels is immediately apparent. Table 6 also points up the peculiar distribution of circuit yamens. If circuits had fitted "properly" into the field-administrative system, then all higher-level capitals would also have been circuit capitals and all circuit capitals would also have been prefectural-level capitals. However, exceptions to both expectations are apparent

TABLE 6. CAPITALS BY ADMINISTRATIVE LEVEL AND RANK, 1893

Capitals of	Also circuit capitals		Not also circuit capitals	Total
	No.	Pct.		
Provinces and/or governor-generalships	16	84%	3	19
Sectors of the imperial prefecture[a]	2	50	2	4
Prefectures[b]	41	26	119	160
Autonomous *chou*	6	9	62	68
Autonomous *t'ing*[c]	2	7	28	30
Chou in prefectures	2	2	134	136
T'ing in prefectures[d]	3	5	57	60
Nonmetropolitan *hsien* in prefectures	5	1	883	888
Hsien in autonomous *chou*	0	0	184	184
Total	77	5%	1,472	1,549

[a] Of the four sectors into which Shun-t'ien *fu*, the imperial prefecture, was divided, three formed one circuit whose capital was at Ch'ang-p'ing-chou, which also served as capital of the North sector. The East sector, together with Yung-p'ing *fu*, formed a separate circuit whose capital was at T'ung-chou, which also served as capital of the East sector. Thus, the capitals of the South and West sectors, Pa-chou and Wan-p'ing (the latter one of Peking's two metropolitan counties) did not serve as circuit capitals, and Peking (which does not appear elsewhere in this table) was not itself a circuit capital.

[b] The Wuhan conurbation, which in this analysis is counted as a single economic center, appears in this row as two prefectural capitals, Wu-ch'ang-fu and Han-yang-fu, both also circuit capitals. This was not strictly true in the latter case, for the circuit yamen was located in Hankow, an otherwise nonadministrative center in the metropolian county of Han-yang *fu*.

[c] Kuei-sui, which in this analysis is counted as a single economic center, appears in this row as two *t'ing* capitals. Sui-yüan also served as a circuit capital, whereas Kuei-hua-ch'eng did not.

[d] Chiang-pei-t'ing, situated directly across the Chia-ling River from Chungking, is in this analysis considered together with that prefectural capital as a single economic center. However, it appears in this row as a separate capital.

from the table. Peking and three provincial capitals (Soochow, Hangchow, and Canton) did not serve as circuit capitals, whereas ten countylevel capitals did. These administrative irregularities, together with the functional anomalies of circuits mentioned previously, can best be understood when related to China's spatial structure, to which we now return.

The Regional Basis of Field Administration

In late imperial China, field administration was designed not only to promote social order and foster the well-being of the populace, but also—and more importantly—to ensure the regular flow of revenue, to defend the various parts of the realm against internal and external enemies, and to prevent the concentration or consolidation of local power that might pose a threat to imperial control. It is my thesis that all of these administrative concerns varied in rough correspondence with the structure of physiographic regions, and that in consequence so did administrative arrangements and the character of capital cities.

rested?
Since?

In a word, I argue that revenue and defense were inversely related in regional space such that in the central areas of regional cores local government was preoccupied with taxation to the virtual exclusion of military affairs, whereas along regional frontiers local government was preoccupied with defense and security to the virtual exclusion of fiscal affairs. As for the potential threat of local power, I would suggest that in core areas the chief danger lay in concerted action by the leading elements of society, whereas in peripheral areas it lay in the mobilization of heterodox elements. Finally, I believe it can be shown that the political structure, and above all the leadership of local social systems, varied according to place in the overall regional structure in such a way that the burden of societal management to be shouldered by local government was relatively lighter in cores than in peripheral areas. If, as these propositions suggest, the mix of administrative priorities and tasks varied systematically through the spatial structure of regions, then the central functions of administrative capitals would have been differentiated accordingly.

Let us begin with the distribution of the various types of capitals as between regional cores and peripheries. Table 7 summarizes the relevant data for the eight macroregions combined. We see in the upper portion, which focuses solely on administrative centers within prefectures, that the capitals of metropolitan prefectures (i.e., provincial and higher-level capitals) were far more often located in regional cores than were nonmetropolitan prefectural capitals. Moreover, county-level units

TABLE 7. CAPITALS OF DIFFERENT LEVELS AND TYPES BY
LOCATION IN REGIONAL CORES OR PERIPHERIES

| | Cores | | | |
Capitals of	No.	Pct.	Peripheries	Total
Metropolitan prefectures	17	85%	3	20
Ordinary prefectures	80	53	70	150
Other counties in prefectures	468	53	420	888
Chou in prefectures[a]	63	45	76	139
T'ing in prefectures	13	22	47	60
Autonomous *chou*[b]	31	41	45	76
Hsien in autonomous *chou*	72	39	112	184
Autonomous *t'ing*[c]	6	19	26	32
Total	750	48%	799	1,549

[a] Includes T'ung-chou, Ch'ang-p'ing-chou, and Pa-chou, sectoral capitals in the imperial prefecture.
[b] Includes capitals of the two autonomous *t'ing* and six prefectures that were structurally analogous to autonomous *chou*.
[c] Includes capitals of the four prefectures with only a single subordinate *hsien*.

within prefectures were sharply differentiated in this respect by administrative type. Ordinary *chou* were more likely to be peripherally situated than nonmetropolitan counties, and ordinary *t'ing* were still more strongly concentrated in regional peripheries. This reflects two systematic biases: (1) only the more peripherally situated prefectures were likely to contain any *chou* or *t'ing* at all; and (2) within such prefectures, the *chou* and/or *t'ing* were situated more peripherally than were counties. In the lower part of the table we see that capitals of autonomous *chou* and their component counties were somewhat more peripheral in their distribution than were ordinary *chou*, and that autonomous *t'ing* were concentrated no less heavily in the peripheries than were ordinary *t'ing*. As one might suspect, the rough dichotomization of regions into cores and peripheries obscures another regularity that in fact obtained: within regional peripheries, *t'ing* tended to be more peripherally located than *chou*.

The next question concerns the extent to which the differences in span of control that were found above to be associated with level and type of administrative capital were themselves simply a reflection of place in the core-periphery structure of regions. We see in Table 8 that for higher-level capitals of each type the span of control was relatively broad in the regional cores and relatively narrow in regional peripheries. Once again, there obtained a fairly regular progression that is partially obscured in Table 8 by the simple dichotomization of the core-periphery variable: the broadest spans tended to occur in the centers of regional cores, and the narrowest ones toward the rim of the regional peripheries. This resulted not only from a concentration of autonomous *t'ing* (typically with a span of one) in the far periphery and of autonomous *chou* (with spans of two to six) in the intermediate range, but also from systematic variation in the number of county-level units within both prefectures and autonomous *chou* according to their specific location within the region's core-periphery structure. Note, however, that span of control is not simply a function of the prefectural-level unit's position in the core-periphery structure; that is, type of capital has an independent effect, a point that can be readily grasped by focusing on units with the same span. Of those with a span of six, for instance, the proportion situated in the cores declined from 71 percent of the autonomous *chou* to 39 percent of the prefectures to none of the provincial and higher-level capitals.

As for the different types of units at the county level, we have already established that peripherally located prefectures were more likely to

TABLE 8. SPAN OF CONTROL BY LOCATION IN REGIONAL CORES OR PERIPHERIES, 1893
(*Prefectural and Higher-level Capitals Only*[a])

Provincial and higher-level capitals

Span of control	Cores		Periph-eries	Total
	No.	Pct.		
6		0%	2	2
7–10	6	86	1	7
11+	11	100	1	11
Total	17	85%	3	20

Prefectural capitals

Span of control	Cores		Periph-eries	Total
	No.	Pct.		
–3	4	24%	13	17
4–5	14	34	27	41
6	9	39	14	23
7	11	44	14	25
8+	32	59	22	54
Total	70	44%	90	160

Capitals of autonomous *chou* and autonomous *t'ing*

Span of control	Cores		Periph-eries	Total
	No.	Pct.		
1–2	6	15%	33	39
3	7	29	17	24
4	7	37	12	19
5	5	56	4	9
6	5	71	2	7
Total	30	31%	68	98

[a] Span of control in this table refers to the number of county-level units subordinate to the prefectural-level yamen in the capital in question. Sectoral capitals in the imperial prefecture are not included. Han-yang-fu is counted separately from Wu-ch'ang-fu, and Kuei-hua-ch'eng is counted separately from Sui-yüan. Status as circuit capitals is not taken into account in the classification of capitals. The core/periphery classification relates here to the prefectural-level capital per se, not to the prefecture as a whole; cf. Table 10.

Table 9. Span of Control by Location in Regional Cores or Peripheries, 1893
(County-level Capitals Subordinate to Prefectures Only[a])

	Hsien in prefectures[b]				Ordinary chou[c]					Ordinary t'ing			
Span of control	Cores No.	Pct.	Peripheries	Total	Span of control	Cores No.	Pct.	Peripheries	Total	Span of control	Cores No.	Pct.	Peripheries	Total
–6	64	27%	168	232	2–3		0%	3	3	–5		0%	16	16
7	46	36	82	128	4–7	14	25	42	56	6–8	4	25	16	20
8–10	144	46	168	312	8–10	16	36	28	44	9	8	30	16	24
11–13	69	57	53	122	11+	18	50	18	36					
14+	93	78	26	119										
Total	416	46%	497	913	Total	48	35%	91	139	Total	12	20%	48	60

[a] Span of control in this table refers to the number of units in the prefectural-level unit to which the county-level unit in question belonged. Chiang-pei-t'ing is counted separately from Chungking. Status as circuit capitals is not taken into account in the classification of capitals. Reconciliation: from Table 8: 20 + 160 + 98 = 278; from this table, 913 + 139 + 60 = 1112. In addition, there were 186 hsien in autonomous chou, not shown here. The total number of county-level units covered by this analysis is 278 + 1112 + 186 = 1576.

[b] Includes 25 "extra" hsien whose capital was shared.

[c] Includes Tung-chou, Ch'ang-p'ing-chou, and Pa-chou, which also served as sectoral capitals within the imperial prefecture.

include ordinary *chou* and *t'ing* among their subordinate units and that *t'ing* in particular were concentrated in the most peripheral prefectures. As shown in Table 9, this finding is also closely associated with differences in span of control. One could conclude either that prefectures had been made smaller in areas where proportionately many of the county-level units were *chou* and *t'ing* (which areas were empirically concentrated in regional peripheries) or that prefectures had been made smaller in regional peripheries (where *chou* and *t'ing* happened to be concentrated); but either way, *t'ing* yamens were likely to be more closely supervised than *chou* yamens, which in turn were likely to be more closely supervised than *hsien* yamens.

We are now in a position to demonstrate that the span of control of prefectural-level units varied systematically not only with position in the regional core-periphery structure but also with the level of their capitals in the economic central-place hierarchy. Since the spans of prefectural-level units at any given level tended to be narrower in the periphery than in the core, it is parsimonious to present the data by grouping peripheral capitals at one level of the economic hierarchy with core capitals at the next lower level of the economic hierarchy, as in Table 10. This arrangement in effect shows the span of control of all capitals at the prefectural level or higher arranged by position in their respective economic systems. The message of the table is unmistakable. Cities whose economic centrality was exceptionally high tended to be capitals of extra-large prefectures with extraordinarily broad spans of control (upper-right corner of the table). Span declined steadily and regularly with the capital's economic centrality until, in the lower-left corner of the table, cities of exceptionally low economic centrality are seen to have been capitals of very small prefectural-level units with extraordinarily narrow spans of control.

A part of the explanation for this relationship undoubtedly relates to the effective distance between the prefectural-level yamen and the yamens of its subordinate counties. In the prefectures at the upper-right of Table 10, counties on the average were relatively small in area (though large in population), and transport costs were relatively low. County-level units in the diagonally opposite corner, however, were on the average much larger in area (though small in population), and transport costs were relatively high. Thus, in terms of the friction of distance to be overcome in reaching subordinate capitals from the prefectural-level capital, the most distant county capital in a fourteen-county prefecture (upper right) might well be closer than the closest subordinate capital in a two-county autonomous *chou* (lower left).

TABLE 10. SPAN OF CONTROL BY POSITION IN REGIONAL ECONOMIC SYSTEMS, 1893
(I.e. by a Classification Combining Level in the Economic Hierarchy with Location in Regional Cores and Peripheries, Prefectural and Higher-level Capitals Only)

Level in the economic hierarchy	Regional cores (C) or peripheries (P)[a]	Span of control[b] 1-2 No.	1-2 Pct.	3-4 No.	3-4 Pct.	5-7 No.	5-7 Pct.	8-9 No.	8-9 Pct.	10-13 No.	10-13 Pct.	14+ No.	14+ Pct.	Total No.	Total Pct.
Central metropolis	C		0%		0%		0%		0%	1	20%	4	80%	5	100%
Regional metropolis	C		0%	2	12	3	18	3	18	5	29	4	24	17	100
Regional metropolis / Regional city	P / C	1	4	2	7	10	36	7	25	7	25	1	4	28	100
Regional city / Greater city	P / C	2	3	9	13	33	49	13	19	10	15	0		67	100
Greater city / Local city	P / C	12	15	24	30	33	41	5	6	6	8			80	100
Local city / Central market town	P / C	12	22	27	49	12	22	3	5	1	2			55	100
Central market town	P	20	71	8	29	0		0		0				28	100
Total		47	17%	72	26%	91	33%	31	11%	30	11%	9	3%	280	100%

Pct. of county-level units in core	Prefectural-level capital in core or periphery?	Classification of prefectural-level unit
51-100	C	C
	P	C
30-50	C	C
	P	P
-29	C	P
	P	P

[a] In analyses of span of control within prefectural-level units, the core-periphery distribution of all capitals within the prefecture is taken into account in assigning the prefecture to either the core or periphery.

[b] I.e., the number of county-level units subordinate to the prefectural-level yamen in the capital in question.

Although this factor is helpful in understanding the feasibility of the arrangements indicated by Table 10, it does not speak to their underlying rationale. My argument, to be developed below, is that the critical factors were fiscal strategy and defense policy. A broad span of control and the standard administrative arrangement of counties in prefectures appear to have been optimal for revenue collection in the hinterlands of cities with high economic centrality, whereas a narrow span of control and the peculiar administrative arrangement of *chou* and *t'ing* appear to have been optimal for defense and security, which were particularly salient in regional peripheries.

Post designations. Support for this line of interpretation may be drawn from an important feature of Ch'ing field administration not yet introduced. The superior bureaucratic post in every county- and prefectural-level yamen was officially characterized according to the presence or absence of four stereotyped attributes.* These post designations, as I shall refer to them, consisted of the various combinations of four binary variables, each indicated by the presence or absence of a Chinese character. Altogether there were sixteen possible designations, one consisting of all four characters, four consisting of combinations of three characters, six consisting of combinations of two characters, four consisting of a single character, and one without any characters. The four elements of these post designations may be briefly described as follows. *Fan* ("troublesome, abundant") was conventionally taken to signify a great deal of official business at the yamen in question. *Ch'ung* ("thoroughfare, frequented") was held to indicate a center of communications; more closely than any of the other three characters, it indicated a capital's commercial importance. *Nan* ("difficult, vexatious") purportedly referred to a post that had to cope with an unruly, crime-prone populace. *P'i* ("fatiguing, wearisome") referred to the difficulty of collecting taxes.[29]

The sixteen possible post designations were assigned with quite different frequencies. Capitals boasting a four-character post were fairly rare, numbering only 59 altogether; they were strongly concentrated (59 percent) in regional cores. By contrast, capitals with a no-character designation were the most numerous (424 altogether) and were poorly represented in regional cores (only 30 percent). For the rest, the four characters occurred in post designations as follows: *nan* (hereafter N), "insecure locale," 697; *fan* (hereafter F), "busy yamen," 637; *ch'ung* (hereafter C), "trade center," 526; and *p'i* (hereafter P), "unremunera-

---

* The posts of circuit intendants were similarly designated, but post designations at the circuit level are excluded from the present analysis.

tive post," 258. A frequency analysis of the two- and three-character designations reveals patterning that may be diagrammed as follows:

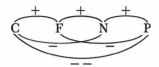

When arranged in this sequence, the affinity of any character for another is a function of proximity. Each has a positive affinity only for its immediate neighbor(s), and C and P constitute the least compatible pair.

The internal logic of this symbolic system is fairly straightforward. That C and P should be incompatible makes eminent sense if—as my previous analysis suggests is reasonable—we assume that an important transport node–cum–trade center was likely to be the center of an extensive high-level trading system. A yamen situated in such an economic central place would hardly be expected to experience revenue problems or to be considered an unremunerative post. As shown in Table 11, CP was by far the least common of the six character pairs, and the two three-character designations containing both C and P were rare indeed by comparison with the other two combinations. The lesser incompatibilities of C with N and of F with P become more readily understandable if the connotation of F is expanded slightly to include the idea of a politically sensitive or important post. If a city was important as a trade center and hence as a source of revenue (C), *and* located in an area with problems of security or social control (N), then its yamen was almost by definition a politically sensitive post, so that one would ex-

TABLE 11. FREQUENCIES OF TWO- AND THREE-CHARACTER POST DESIGNATIONS AND THEIR DISTRIBUTION AMONG CAPITALS IN REGIONAL CORES AND PERIPHERIES

Character designations			Actual	Expected	Ratio	Cores		Peripheries	Total
						No.	Pct.		
CFN	FNP		280	196	143▲	173	62%▲	107	280
CFP	CNP		22	106	21	8	36	14	22
	Total		302	302		181	60%	121	302
CF	FN	NP	357	275	130▲	181	51%▲	176	357
CN	FP		85	144	59	33	39	52	85
CP			12	35	34	3	25	9	12
	Total		454	454		217	48%	237	454

pect C plus N to occur only rarely without F. Hence the underoccur-
rence of CN and the overoccurrence of CFN. As for the combination of
F with P, since the latter character implies a post that was unimpor-
tant as a source of revenue, what else (within the limits of the scheme)
could be the cause of a post's heavy work load and political sensitivity
if not activities related to defense and/or local security? Thus F plus P
should occur only rarely without N.

Simply taking the three-character designations at their face value,
one would expect CFN, rather than FNP, to have been assigned to capitals whose political importance rested heavily on high revenue potential and the problems of controlling transient traders and a large merchant population. In fact, on my analysis, nearly half of the CFN posts
were in greater cities or higher-level economic central places as against
less than a third of the FNP posts. Taking the two-character posts at
face value, one would expect CF and FN to have been assigned to capitals that were less important overall than CFN or FNP capitals but more
important overall than NP capitals, and one would further expect that
a comparison of CF and FN cities would show the former to have had
greater economic centrality. In general, these expectations are borne out
by tabulations of cities with the post designations in question. CFN and
FNP designations were overrepresented among cities that ranked high
in both the economic and the administrative hierarchies, CF was overrepresented among cities whose economic level was higher than their
administrative rank, FN was overrepresented among cities whose administrative rank was higher than their economic level, and NP was overrepresented among cities that ranked low in both hierarchies.[30]

Table 11 also makes the interesting point that the uncommon, internally inconsistent post designations were seldom assigned to cities in
regional cores. I attribute the concentration of anomalous post designations in peripheral areas (1) to the irregularities that, as we have already
noted, were frequently encountered around the periphery of regional
central-place systems, and (2) to the greater diversity of administrative
problems posed by peripheral as against core cities.

The system of post designations was rather less straightforward (and
more informative) than the above description suggests because it was
also designed to serve as a general importance rating. The importance
of posts was held to be indicated by the number of characters in their
designation. The official importance rating (four categories ranging
from very to least important) was printed in the *Chin-shen ch'üan-shu*
directly adjacent to the CFNP post designations, and among bureaucrats
assignments were known colloquially as "four-character posts," "three-

character posts," etc. Nothing in the Chinese or the Western literature suggests that the importance rating was anything other than a direct translation of the number of characters, but in fact I found that for 170 posts (11 percent of the total) the assigned importance rating was higher than indicated by the post designation. It was as though each such post designation included an unspecified or invisible character that served to raise its importance rating. I have dubbed this invisible character the "secret" strategic component on the grounds that everything about the geographical location of the posts so designated and their administrative characteristics suggests that it flagged capitals strategically situated for the defense of regional cores and their principal cities.

Before pursuing this lead for what it can tell us about the defense functions of late imperial cities, let us briefly consider its implications for the system of post designations. That the military component of local administration should be indicated by an invisible code is, after all, not particularly surprising in a sophisticated bureaucracy that was dominated by Confucian values (which exalted normative over coercive power) and that subordinated specialized military officials in both form and symbol to their civil counterparts. But if the coding were to have validity, it would obviously have been necessary to bring the designations of nonstrategic posts into perfect agreement with their importance rating. I suggest that the usual procedure in such cases was to add or subtract P as necessary to bring the designation into alignment with the rating. P was unquestionably the most protean of the four characters. In some contexts it was a foil for C, indicating the unremunerative nature of the post. In other contexts, it was a foil for F, indicating a low-pressure post of no particular political importance or sensitivity. Clearly it had neither connotation when used with all three other characters, for CFNP was the designation of the most important capitals in the realm, e.g., Peking, Soochow, Nanking, Canton, Sian, Chengtu, and Kunming. CFNP cities were themselves military prizes and often the centers of military command, to be sharply differentiated from cities whose significance stemmed from a strategic site on a single approach to the center of a macroregion. Thus, it appears that P also functioned as a foil for the secret strategic component of post designations. When necessary to up the importance rating of a "nonstrategic" city beyond the number of characters yielded by the appropriate assignment of C, F, and N, the character P was added, thereby salvaging the significance of the secret component.

Defense. We are now in a position to muster all relevant evidence concerning the distribution within regions of capitals with a significant

TABLE 12. THE "SECRET" STRATEGIC POST
DESIGNATION IN RELATION TO CHARACTER DESIGNATIONS, 1893
(*All Capitals Except Those Whose Designations Included
All or None of the Four Characters*)

		"Deficit" of designation characters?		
Character designations	No	Yes No.	Pct.	Total
FN	97	39	29%	136
F	46	6	12	52
N	112	13	10	125
F and/or N with C or P	547	38	7	585
F or N with C and P	21	1	5	22
P	22	1	4	23
CP	12	0	0	12
C	111	0	0	111
Total	968	98	9%	1,066[a]

[a] By definition, capitals (59 in all) with the FCNP designation cannot show a deficit of designation characters. Of the 424 capitals with a no-character designation, 17 percent show a "deficit." Reconciliation: 59 + 1066 + 424 = 1549, the total number of capitals.

defense function. We may begin by scrutinizing the character portion of post designations that included the "secret" strategic component. As shown in Table 12, the latter occurred most frequently with FN, the combination whose face value pointed to politically sensitive security problems, and least frequently, which is to say not at all or only very rarely, with CP, C, and P, components unrelated to, or even negating, the notion of strategic importance. These findings and the logic of the intermediate gradations provide circumstantial support for the interpretation offered here for a deficit of designation characters. A mapping of the cities in question offers still firmer support. With few exceptions, cities whose post designations included the "secret" component were sited at the approaches to strategic passes, in mountainous areas subject to attack by non-Han peoples, on roads breaching a regional frontier, on islands or rivers commanding the approach to seaports or major inland waterways, at strategic sites along major rivers, and on roads approaching high-level capitals.

On the assumption that strategically important cities would be distributed in accordance with the strategic significance of different types of frontiers, I classified all administrative cities into seven categories according to whether the county-level units of which they were the capital lay on or near external or internal frontiers. The external categories were three: (1) China's international borders to the south and south-

TABLE 13. THE "SECRET" STRATEGIC POST DESIGNATION IN RELATION TO THE
FRONTIER SITUATION OF CAPITAL CITIES, 1893

Location of capitals in relation to frontiers	"Deficit" of designation characters?			
		Yes		
	No	No.	Pct.	Total
External frontiers				
1. South and southwest	15	23	60.5%	38
2. Inner Asian	68	21	23.6	89
3. Maritime	182	24	11.7	206
Internal frontiers				
4. Regional only	94	12	11.3	106
5 + 6. Provincial[a]	672	72	9.7	744
Removed from any frontier	348	18	4.9	366
Total	1,379	170	11.0%	1,549

[a] Two categories are here combined, capitals situated near provincial boundaries but not regional frontiers and capitals situated near both, there being no difference between them in the proportion of "secret" post designations.

west; (2) the Inner Asian regional frontiers, that is, those regional boundaries of Yun-Kwei, the Upper Yangtze, Northwest China, and North China that abutted on Inner Asian territories rather than other regions of agrarian China; and (3) the coastal or maritime frontier. Internal frontiers were classified as (4) regional only (that is, lying on the boundaries of my physiographic regions but not on provincial boundaries); (5) both regional and provincial; and (6) provincial only. The seventh category included county-level units removed from frontiers of any kind. Table 13 shows the distribution according to this scheme of cities with the "secret" strategic post designation. The heavy use of the "secret" component for cities along the empire's more sensitive frontiers is telling, as is its negligible use for posts removed from any frontier.

Table 14 displays span of control in relation to the same categorization of frontiers. It is notable that apart from maritime frontiers (of which more below), the distribution of narrow control spans closely parallels that of the "secret" strategic component. These data strongly support the notion that a narrow span of control was held to be advantageous in the case of militarily vulnerable capitals.

Finally, let us contrast the different types of capitals. With respect to the telltale deficit of characters in post designations, the differences were stark. The "secret" strategic component was present in the post designations of 75 percent of ordinary *t'ing* capitals and 65 percent of autonomous *t'ing* capitals (the difference reflecting not the lesser strategic

TABLE 14. SPAN OF CONTROL IN RELATION TO THE
FRONTIER SITUATION OF CAPITAL CITIES, 1893

Location of capitals in relation to frontiers	Span of control							
	1–5		6–8		9+		Total	
	No.	Pct.	No.	Pct.	No.	Pct.	No.	Pct.
1. South and SW international frontiers	27	71%	11	29%		0%	38	100%
2. Inner Asian frontiers	44	49	27	30	19	21	90	100
4. Internal frontiers: Regional only	44	41	38	35	26	24	108	100
5. Internal frontiers: Reg. *and* prov.	167	36	176	38	116	25	459	100
6. Internal frontiers: Provincial only	89	31	88	30	114	39	291	100
3. Maritime frontiers	35	16	83	38	101	46	219	100
7. Removed from any frontier	60	16	134	36	177	48	371	100
Total	466	29%	557	35%	553	35%	1,576	100%

importance of the latter but rather their greater general importance, whence post designations with more characters on the average). The corresponding figures for capitals of prefectures and of *chou*, both autonomous and ordinary, clustered around 17 percent. As for ordinary *hsien*, whether in prefectures or autonomous *chou*, the incidence of the "secret" component was less than 4 percent; for provincial and higher-level capitals it was nil. We may also discern a distinct tendency toward spatial specialization in the defense function. At the borders of the empire—the international boundaries to the south and southwest, the Inner Asian frontier, and the seacoast—the main burden of defense was carried by the capitals of autonomous and ordinary *t'ing*. As for internal frontiers, the major burden was borne by ordinary *t'ing* capitals along regional frontiers that were distinct from provincial boundaries; by autonomous *chou* capitals along regional frontiers that coincided with provincial boundaries; and by both autonomous and ordinary *chou* capitals along provincial boundaries within regions. In the areas away from any frontier, the defense function devolved largely on ordinary *chou* capitals.[31] From the perspective of the major cities at the heart of regional cores, then, the first and second lines of defense were associated primarily with the capitals of ordinary and autonomous *chou*, respectively, whereas more distant defense perimeters were marked largely by *t'ing* capitals. It will be recalled that of these four types of capitals (all characterized by relatively narrow control spans), the narrowest spans were associated with autonomous *t'ing*, concentrated at the outermost periphery, and the broadest with ordinary *chou*, concentrated at the innermost defense perimeter. It is scarcely necessary to add that when the "secret" component was used for prefectural-level capitals other than those of autonomous *t'ing*, it was heavily concentrated among units with exceptionally narrow spans of control.

The thrust of my first argument should by now be apparent. A narrow span of control, entailing as it does close supervision and minimal competition for channels of communications, was highly desirable for centers vulnerable to military invasions, uprisings, or other violent disruptions. In military terms the odd arrangement of the autonomous *t'ing* was ideal, for the subprefect in charge of the strategically important town reported directly to a military circuit intendant or to provincial-level officials rather than indirectly through a prefectural-level yamen. The peculiar administrative arrangement of the *pen-chou* also made military sense in that the *chou* city itself (as opposed to the entire area of the autonomous *chou*) was normally the strategic prize; direct control of the *pen-chou* by the prefectural-level official had the effect of putting the man in charge of the *chou* city's defense under the direct command of high-level military officers. The fewer the counties supervised by the magistrate of an autonomous *chou*, the less distraction there would be in times of military emergency. Similarly, the narrower the span of a prefecture to which an ordinary *chou* or *t'ing* belonged, the less disruptive it would be in times of crisis to monopolize the communication channels from the prefect to higher-level authorities with orders and reports relating to the emergency.

It is notable that all autonomous *chou* and *t'ing* (but not all prefectures) fell into the category of administrative units whose ranking posts were filled through nomination by the governor or governor-general from among acting or probationary officials under his own control. Such appointments were restricted by statute to men with at least three years of prior experience.[32] As a result, the official in supreme command of a province could be certain that subordinates in the most strategic of local posts would be experienced officials who had earned his confidence. Moreover, unlike *hsien* posts, most of which were available for a first appointment, all ordinary *chou* and *t'ing* posts, whether controlled by the Board of Civil Office or by the governor, could be filled only by men with previous administrative experience.[33]

This analysis calls into question Brunnert and Hagelstrom's contention that autonomous *chou* and *t'ing* should be viewed as transitional forms eventuating in prefectural status. It is true that the capitals of ordinary *chou* were normally selected as the capitals of newly formed autonomous *chou*, but not more than twenty autonomous *chou* were ever converted to prefectures, and against these must be set an even greater number of contravening changes. The history of Ch'ing field administration provides no support whatsoever for a developmental sequence from ordinary *t'ing* to autonomous *t'ing* to prefecture. One response to the growing threat of British power off the Chekiang coast in the 1840's was to change the status from *hsien* to *t'ing* of Ting-hai, an administrative unit encompassing the archipelago that commanded the approach to Ningpo and Hangchow.

A certain congruence may be noted between the defense function of many frontier cities and the special character of other administrative functions in the more remote portions of regional peripheries. It was along China's regional frontiers that local society assumed its most heterodox and variegated guise: there one found tribes of non-Han aborigines and pockets of incompletely sinicized groups; autonomous kongsis pursuing illicit productive activities beyond the reach of the law and of tax collectors; heterodox sodalities ranging from religious sects to seditious secret societies; and bands of bandits, many imbued with romantic-rebel ideologies.[34] The populace at large included disproportionate numbers of smugglers, outcasts, political exiles, sorcerers, and other deviants. In dealing with such elements, normative strategies of administration were largely ineffective, and frontier administrators necessarily relied on repression, containment, and divide-and-rule strategies. Thus the military posture and coercive power needed for defense around the rim of regional peripheries were also appropriate to the other objectives of field administration in such areas—the maintenance of social order and the prevention of local concentrations of power that might pose a threat to imperial control.

Revenue collection. Let me now turn to fiscal strategy. We start with the proposition that revenue collection, both of land tax and of commercial levies, was most efficient (in the sense of greater tax take per unit of administrative effort) in regional cores, particularly in the environs of cities high in the economic hierarchy. Among the myriad reasons are the high levels of productivity and per capita income, the high density of taxable units (households, farms, business firms, periodic markets, etc.) per unit of area, the comparatively strong leadership of local social systems, and a local populace with relatively firm community roots and relatively high aspirations. In general, the efficiency of tax collection may be seen to decline as one moves outward from the center toward the periphery of the economic region and downward through the hierarchy of trading and marketing systems.[35] The continuum in question may be conceptualized as in the row labels of Table 10. Somewhere along this continuum, a break-even point was reached where the tax take was barely covered by the costs of collecting it, and below that point county-level units were dependent for part of their operational budget on subsidies from higher-level yamens.[36]

It is widely recognized that provincial governments, and above all the imperial government, looked to a limited number of populous, commercialized, and relatively rich areas for the great bulk of their revenue. My point here is that these areas may be specified with some precision in terms of (1) the relative urbanization of the eight great regional economies (with the Lower Yangtze at the head of the list and Yun-Kwei at the tail), and (2) position within each of these regional economic systems as specified in Table 10.

The strategy followed, or so I infer, was to extend the area under the jurisdiction of key tax yamens (i.e., those in high-level capitals that were at once regional cities and metropolises in the economic hierarchy) so as to include within their boundaries as much as feasible of the high-revenue areas, and to concentrate in this small number of supervisory posts the ablest and most trustworthy personnel in the imperial bureaucracy.[37] Thus, the optimal administrative arrangement for areas of highest revenue potential was very nearly the reverse of that for areas of greatest strategic importance. In the latter, it was desirable to make both county-level and prefectural-level units as small as possible, the former in terms of area and the latter in terms of component units. In areas of highest revenue potential, by contrast, it was desirable to make both county-level and prefectural-level units as large as possible, the former in terms of population and the latter in terms of component units.

I wish now to show that the gradation of capitals by revenue potential was precisely indicated by the system of post designations already described. I begin by establishing the significance of these designations for city population size. As demonstrated in Table 15, F tended to be assigned to the most populous cities (which makes sense if one assumes volume of official business to be a function of urban population),[38] and P to the least populous cities (which also makes intuitive sense on the assumption that relatively small capitals were disproportionately located in sparsely populated counties with poor transport where tax returns were likely to be low in proportion to bureaucratic effort). C and N were intermediate with respect to city population, but on the average C was assigned to more populous cities than was N. Table 15 also makes it clear that the *number* of characters in the post designation was positively associated with city population.

TABLE 15. POST DESIGNATIONS IN RELATION TO CITY SIZE OF THE
CAPITALS INVOLVED, 1893[a]

A. Cities whose yamen posts received 3- and 4-character designations

| | Population classes | | | | | | | |
| | Over 16,000 | | 4,000–16,000 | | Under 4,000 | | Total | |
	No.	Pct.	No.	Pct.	No.	Pct.	No.	Pct.
FCNP	37	63%	18	31%	4	7%	59	100%
FCN	61	37	92	56	12	7	165	100
FNP CNP FCP	21	15	67	49	48	35	136	100
Total	119	33%	177	49%	64	18%	360	100%

B. Cities whose yamen posts received 2-character designations[b]

| | Population classes | | | | | | | |
| | Over 8,000 | | 2,000–8,000 | | Under 2,000 | | Total | |
	No.	Pct.	No.	Pct.	No.	Pct.	No.	Pct.
FC FN FP	86	29%	197	67%	11	4%	294	100%
CF CN CP	53	23	150	66	26	11	229	100
NF NC NP	60	21	184	65	39	14	283	100
PF PC PN	11	11	57	57	32	32	100	100
Total number of characters	(210)		(588)		(108)		(906)	
Total number of capitals	105	23%	294	65%	54	12%	453	100%

C. Cities whose yamen posts received single-character designations

| | Population classes | | | | | | | | | |
| | Over 4,000 | | 2,000–4,000 | | 1,000–2,000 | | Under 1,000 | | Total | |
	No.	Pct.	No.	Pct.	No.	Pct.	No.	Pct.	No.	Pct.
F	23	45%	23	45%	6	10%		0%	52	100%
C	29	26	36	32	40	36	6	5	111	100
N	19	15	29	23	54	43	23	18	125	100
P	2	9	5	22	9	39	7	30	23	100
Total	73	24%	93	30%	109	35%	36	12%	311	100%

[a] For purposes of this table, the following multiple-nuclei conurbations are counted as single cities and classified according to the population of the whole. First we have Wuhan, Kuei-sui, and Chungking (together with its satellite Chiang-pei), even though each contains two capitals. Second are the two anomalous cases of Hui-chou-fu (Kwangtung) and Feng-yang-fu (Anhwei), each with a separate walled city in which the yamen of the metropolitan county was located. Third are three twin cities involving one capital and one nonadministrative center: Lao-ho-k'ou and Kuang-hua, a *hsien* capital (Hupeh); Fan-ch'eng and Hsiang-yang-fu (Hupeh); and Ch'ing-chiang-p'u and Ch'ing-ho, a *hsien* capital (Kiangsu). The 422 capitals with no-character designations, not shown, have a size distribution between that of N-designated cities and P-designated cities. Reconciliation: 360 + 453 + 311 + 422 = 1546, the number of cities involving capitals.

[b] Each city covered by Subtable B appears twice, i.e., in the rows for each of its designation characters. FC posts are, of course, the same as CF posts, and so forth; the order of each pair is reversed so as to point up the significance of the groupings in each row.

The pecking order established by the population significance of the four components establishes a rank-order of the sixteen designations. On the basis of their correlations with several other urban variables, three significant "breaks" were established in this series, yielding four groupings here designated High (FCNP and FCN), Medium (FCP, FNP, CNP, FC, and FN), Low (FP, CN, CP, NP, F, C, N, and P), and No-character.[39] When post designations, so grouped, are cross-tabulated with the level and type of capital city, as in Table 16, it is apparent that, apart from the two types of *t'ing*, the rank-order of post designations closely parallels the official ordering of capital types. (The "exceptionally" high frequency of Medium post designations for autonomous and ordinary *t'ing* results, as we might expect, entirely from an excess of the FN designations that signaled their strategic importance.)

If my overall argument is correct, rank-ordered post designations should have indexed not only the population and the ranking of capitals but also span of control. Table 17 demonstrates that they did just that for prefectural-level capitals. The remarkable fact is that rank-ordered post designations served to differentiate prefectural capitals and the capitals of autonomous *chou* into three grades each, so related that the bottom grade of prefectural capitals was still distinguished from the top grade of *chou* capitals. The net result was that, in conjunction with type of capital, post designations marked out eight graded types of prefectural-level capitals, the entire series being correlated with the span of control.

It remains to show that rank-ordered post designations in fact differentiated cities according not only to span of control but also to the position of capitals in regional economic systems. We have already observed (see Table 10) the pervasive tendency to match the size of prefectural-level units (i.e., the number of component county-level units) to the revenue potential of the economic system centered on the prefectural-level capital. Table 18 is designed to test the proposition that the post designations of prefectural-level capitals varied according to all the factors built into Table 10—that is, according to a complex calculus that took into account the city's level in the economic hierarchy, its location in the regional core-periphery structure, and the span of control of the administrative unit of which it was the capital. The grid of the upper diagram recapitulates the structure of Table 10, and the data in tabulations A and B relate to the five diagonal groupings of cells defined on that grid. Diagonal 1 includes prefectural-level capitals that ranked at the top of the hierarchy of economic central places, that were centrally located in their regional economies, and whose administrative jurisdiction encompassed an extraordinarily large number of counties with

TABLE 16. POST DESIGNATIONS IN RELATION TO LEVEL AND TYPE OF
ADMINISTRATIVE CENTER, ALL CAPITAL CITIES, 1893

Capitals of	Post designations[a]									Total	
	High		Medium		Low		No-character				
	No.	Pct.	No.	Pct.	No.	Pct.	No.	Pct.		No.	Pct.
Provinces, etc.	20	100%		0%		0%		0%		20	100%
Circuits[b]	38	63	17	28	2	3	3	5		60	100
Prefectures	51	46	40	36	19	17		0		110	100
Autonomous *chou*[c]	17	24	36	51	8	11	9	13		70	100
Ordinary *chou*	16	12	40	30	53	39	26	19		135	100
Hsien in prefectures	71	8	224	25	323	37	265	30		883	100
Hsien in autonomous *chou*	7	4	39	21	71	39	67	36		184	100
Autonomous *t'ing*[d]	2	7	10	33	4	13	14	47		30	100
Ordinary *t'ing*	3	5	11	19	3	5	40	70		57	100
Total	225	15%	417	27%	483	31%	424	27%		1,549	100%

[a] This classification of the sixteen possible post designations is based on a generalized pecking order, established empirically, of F, C, N. P. High includes FCP, FNP, CNP, FC, and FN. Medium includes FCN. Low includes the other eight character designations.
[b] Capitals of provinces and governor-generalships that are also circuit capitals are not included. The total includes 40 capitals of prefectures, six of autonomous *chou*, two of autonomous *t'ing*, two of sectors in the imperial prefecture, two of ordinary *chou*, five of *hsien*, and three of ordinary *t'ing*.
[c] Includes capitals of the two autonomous *t'ing* and six prefectures that were structurally analogous to autonomous *chou*.
[d] Includes the four prefectures with only a single component *hsien*.

TABLE 17. SPAN OF CONTROL BY TYPE OF ADMINISTRATIVE CENTER AND BY POST DESIGNATIONS, 1893
(*Prefectural and Higher-level Capitals Only*)

Capitals of	Post designations[b]	Span of control[a]														Total	
		1		2–3		4		5–8		9–10		11–13		14+			
		No.	Pct.	No.	Pct.	No.	Pct.	No.	Pct.	No.	Pct.	No.	Pct.	No.	Pct.	No.	Pct.
Provinces, etc.[c]	High				0%		0%	5	25%	4	20%	4	20%	7	35%	20	100%
Prefectures	High			2	2	5	6	51	62	15	18	7	9	2	2	82	100
	Medium			5	10	7	14	30	60	5	10	3	6		0	50	100
	Low			3	15	8	40	8	40	1	4		0			20	100
Autonomous *chou*[d]	High			9	43	6	29	6	29		0					21	100
	Medium			18	47	10	26	10	26							38	100
	Low		0%	10	59	4	24	3	18							17	100
Autonomous *t'ing*[e]	—	32	100		0				0							32	100
Total		32	11%	47	17%	40	14%	113	40%	25	9%	14	5%	9	3%	280	100%

[a] I.e., the number of county-level units supervised by a given prefectural-level yamen.
[b] The few No-character designations are grouped here with Low designations.
[c] Includes the two sectoral capitals in the imperial prefecture that served as circuit capitals.
[d] Includes capitals of the two autonomous *t'ing* and six prefectures that were structurally analogous to autonomous *chou*.
[e] Includes capitals of the four prefectures containing only a single *hsien*.

TABLE 18. POST DESIGNATIONS IN RELATION TO LEVEL IN THE ECONOMIC HIERARCHY, LOCATION IN REGIONAL CORES OR PERIPHERIES, AND SPAN OF CONTROL, PREFECTURAL-LEVEL CAPITALS ONLY, 1893

Definition of "diagonal classes" simultaneously indicating level in the economic hierarchy, location in regional cores or peripheries, and span of control

Level in the economic hierarchy	Regional cores (C) or peripheries (P)[a]	Span of control[b]											Total
		1	2	3	4	5	6	7	8	9–10	11–13	14+	
Central metropolis	C												5
Regional metropolis	C										1		17
Regional metropolis	P												28
Regional city	C												
Regional city	P									2			67
Greater city	C												
Greater city	P							3					80
Local city	C												
Local city	P				4								55
Central market town	C												
Central market town	P	5											28
Total		32	15	32	40	31	31	29	22	25	14	9	280

Table 18, *continued*

A. Post designations classed in terms of High, Medium, Low, and No-character

Diagonal class	High		Medium		Low and no-character		Total	
	No.	Pct.	No.	Pct.	No.	Pct.	No.	Pct.
1	32	100%		0%		0%	32	100%
2	27	64	15	36		13	42	100
3	45	51	32	36	11	13	88	100
4	20	24	41	48	24	28	85	100
5	1	3	11	33	21	64	33	100
Total	125	45%	99	35%	56	20%	280	100%

Post designation[c]

B. Post designations classed in terms of C and F components

Diagonal class	C and F[e]		C or F		Neither C nor F		Total	
	No.	Pct.	No.	Pct.	No.	Pct.	No.	Pct.
1	32	100%		0%		0%	32	100%
2	34	81	8	19		2	42	100
3	55	63	31	35	2	2	88	100
4	37	44	33	39	15	18	85	100
5	3	9	14	42	16	48	33	100
Total	161	58%	86	31%	33	12%	280	100%

Post designation[a]

[a] In analyses of span of control within prefectural-level units, the core-periphery distribution of all capitals within the prefecture is taken into account in assigning the prefecture to either the core or periphery. See Table 10 for operational definitions.

[b] I.e., the number of county-level units supervised by a given prefectural-level yamen.

[c] For the classification of post designations into High, Medium, and Low, see Table 16.

[d] C stands for *ch'ung*, F for *fan*.

[e] Includes three cases in which the post designation of the prefectural yamen shows one character and that of the county yamen the other.

above-average populations. In all these respects, successive diagonals 2, 3, and 4 grade cities from that extreme to its opposite, diagonal 5, which includes capitals that ranked exceptionally low in the economic hierarchy, were situated peripherally with respect to their regional economies, and whose jurisdiction encompassed at most three sparsely populated county-level units.

Tabulation A of Table 18 shows that post designations did indeed closely reflect the factors encompassed in the definition of the diagonals. Note in particular that every one of the 32 cities in diagonal 1 had a high post designation. (It is not unlikely that in the late nineteenth century the 31 prefectures and one autonomous *chou* involved supplied nearly half of all revenues received at Peking.) Tabulation B indicates the particular diagnostic value of the F and C components of the post designations. Finally, the data presented in Table 19 show that at *all* levels of the administrative hierarchy, and in regional peripheries as well as cores, the post designation of a capital closely reflected its place in the hierarchy of economic central places.

One beauty of the post designations was their value for posting officials of varying competence, experience, and trustworthiness in accordance with the posts' importance for sustaining the flow of imperial revenues. Positions in the field administration were filled either through direct appointment by the Board of Civil Office in Peking or through nomination by the governor (or governor-general), subject to the Board's approval. Whereas the Board's appointments could be made from the pool of expectant officials who had never before served in office, the governor's nominations were by statute limited to men who had served under him for a minimum of three years (five in certain categories). Posts classified as "most important" or "important" (that is, all three- and four-character posts plus others containing the "secret" strategic component) were controlled by the province,[40] thereby establishing a floor of experience and trustworthiness for the most critical assignments. For all incumbents, no matter how appointed, there were elaborate procedures for the periodic evaluation of performance. Post assignments, as well as promotion or demotion within the bureaucratic ranks, depended on the results. In the triennial "great reckoning" (*ta-chi*), which assessed the achievements of each local official, "by far the most important criterion was his ability to collect taxes. Thus a magistrate was not eligible for recommendation if he had been unable to collect the land tax according to the quota."[41] The data presented in Tables 18 and 19 imply that so long as bureaucratic "promotions" involved transfers to posts with higher designations (e.g., from No-character to

TABLE 19. The Relationship Between the Post Designation of Capitals and Their Level in the Economic Hierarchy, 1893

(*Showing Tabulations Separately for High-level as Against Low-level Capitals and for Regional Cores as Against Regional Peripheries*)

HIGH-LEVEL CAPITALS/REGIONAL CORES
Post designations

	High		Medium		Low and no-char.		Total	
	No.	Pct.	No.	Pct.	No.	Pct.	No.	Pct.
Regional cities & higher	43	81%	9	17%	1	2%	53	100%
Greater cities	24	50	19	40	5	10	48	100
Local cities	12	39	14	45	5	16	31	100
CMT's	0	0	0	0	3	100	3	100
Total	79	59%	42	31%	14	10%	135	100%

HIGH-LEVEL CAPITALS/REGIONAL PERIPHERIES
Post designations

	High		Medium		Low and no-char.		Total	
	No.	Pct.	No.	Pct.	No.	Pct.	No.	Pct.
Regional cities & higher	14	74%	3	16%	2	11%	19	100%
Greater cities	18	37	24	49	7	14	49	100
Local cities	13	30	21	48	10	23	44	100
CMT's	1	8	3	25	8	67	12	100
Total	46	37%	51	41%	27	22%	124	100%

LOW-LEVEL CAPITALS/REGIONAL CORES
Post designations

	High		Medium		Low		No-char.		Total	
	No.	Pct.	No.	Pct.	No.	Pct.	No.	Pct.	No.	Pct.
Greater cities & higher	16	30%	24	45%	9	17%	4	8%	53	100%
Local cities	48	18	101	39	79	30	34	13	262	100
CMT's	6	2	49	19	114	44	89	34	258	100
IMT's & SMT's	0	0	0	0	12	30	28	70	40	100
Total	70	11%	174	28%	214	35%	155	25%	613	100%

LOW-LEVEL CAPITALS/REGIONAL PERIPHERIES
Post designations

	High		Medium		Low		No-char.		Total	
	No.	Pct.	No.	Pct.	No.	Pct.	No.	Pct.	No.	Pct.
Greater cities & higher	9	22%	16	39%	4	10%	12	29%	41	100%
Local cities	15	6	73	32	91	39	52	23	231	100
CMT's	5	2	60	19	132	41	125	39	322	100
IMT's & SMT's	0	0	1	1	13	16	66	83	80	100
Total	29	4%	150	22%	240	36%	255	38%	674	100%

C, from FP to FC, or from CNP to FCN), they were likely to entail a step up the economic central-place hierarchy and/or a move to a city whose prefectural-level unit had a broader span of control—i.e., to a post of greater fiscal importance.

Special cases. It is, of course, an oversimplification to portray the administrative salience of security as everywhere inversely related to the administrative salience of revenue. We have already pointed to a possible departure from this generalization in the case of cities along China's maritime frontiers. The incidence of the "secret" component of post designations (Table 13) suggests that the proportion of cities with an important defense function was somewhat higher along the coast than near internal frontiers; the distribution of control spans (Table 14) suggests that the same was true of cities important for revenue. This anomaly resulted from the fact that the maritime "frontiers" of several regional cores lacked the peripheral zone that everywhere buffered cores along their internal regional frontiers. The critical question concerns the extent to which the two functions were conjoined in the same coastal cities. Many seaports in core areas were indeed the nodes of high-revenue trading systems, whence the high incidence of broad control spans along the maritime frontier as a whole. However, prior to the rise of ocean ports in the late nineteenth century, the typical pattern was for important seaports to be sited upriver from the immediate coastline, with their seaward approaches being guarded by fortresses or smaller defense-oriented capitals. Canton, Foochow, Ningpo, and Tientsin are classic cases.* Nonetheless, by its very nature, the maritime frontier did have an exceptionally high proportion of cities for which commerce and defense were both important. A prominent example was Amoy, a deepwater port located on an offshore island and hence highly vulnerable to attack. Not surprisingly, its administrative status was that of a *t'ing* capital and its post designation included the "secret" strategic component. At the same time, it was the most important commercial city in its highly commercialized subregion and ranked as a regional city in the economic hierarchy.

Significantly enough, Amoy was also a circuit capital, a fact that points us toward resolution of the anomalies surrounding circuits in the Ch'ing field administration. After its recapture from Koxinga, Amoy

---

* Chen-hai, a county capital with the "secret" strategic component in its post designation, guarded the entrance to the river on which Ningpo was sited 18 km. upstream. For a map of that area that also shows the location of three fortresses built in early Ming times for maritime defense, see Yoshinobu Shiba, "Ningpo and Its Hinterland," in G. William Skinner, ed., *The City in Late Imperial China* (Stanford, Calif.: Stanford University Press, 1977), p. 402.

was seen by the Ch'ing as essentially a military outpost, and in the 1680's it was incorporated into the administrative system as an ordinary *t'ing*. Meanwhile, the unwonted security brought to the Taiwan Strait by the Ch'ing after their annexation of Taiwan enabled Amoy, despite its vulnerability, to thrive as never before, taking full advantage of its excellent harbor. In 1727, by which time Ch'üan-chou-fu had lost the bulk of its maritime trade to Amoy, the circuit yamen was moved to the *t'ing* capital.[42] From a garrison town, Amoy had developed into a city from which the defense and trade of the entire subregion could be controlled and coordinated.

It was the special character of the circuit intendant's role that caused the court to favor as capitals cities, like Amoy, that were strategically situated for both defense and trade. We noted above that the intendant was responsible for dealing with foreigners who penetrated his circuit, and it may be added here that he normally also served as the superintendant of customs.[43] As a preliminary formulation, then, we might say that the circuit intendant's primary mission was the conduct of "local" foreign relations—trade, diplomacy, and war—and that his local administrative role concerned the coordination and control of activities within the circuit only insofar as they affected these larger concerns of the court. The departures from a regular administrative chain of command to which I earlier called attention make sense in these terms. Of the four high-level capitals that lacked circuit yamens, Peking, the imperial capital, and Canton, the open port to which the Ch'ing directed foreigners from overseas, both had specialized alternative institutions for handling foreign relations. Hangchow and Soochow, the other two capitals involved, provide examples of "forward" siting, whereby circuit yamens were situated within their territories off-center in the direction of foreign pressure. The circuit in which Hangchow fell was headquartered in Chia-hsing-fu to the northeast, whereas the eastern approach to Hangchow Bay was under the supervision of the circuit intendant at Ningpo. Soochow had been the capital of Su-Sung-T'ai circuit until 1730, when the yamen was transferred to Shanghai,[44] a growing but much smaller city that had, however, come to dominate the Lower Yangtze's coastal trade with both northern and southern ports and that had emerged as the focal link between these two branches of the coastal trade and the commercial network of the Lower and Middle Yangtze regions.

The other kind of administrative anomaly—circuit yamens located in cities that were not even prefectural-level capitals—may also be attributed to the court's overriding concern to locate intendants in whatever city within the circuit was most strategically situated for their mission. The pragmatic responsiveness to external developments that caused circuits to be established during the eighteenth century in Amoy and Shanghai, both county-level capitals, was no less evident during the subsequent era of Western encroachment. In 1861, the court transferred the yamen of Han-Huang-Te circuit (Hupeh) from Huang-chou-fu to Hankow, the commercially dominant nonadministrative component of the Wuhan conurbation.[45] Later in the century, in response to French aggressiveness and the growth of the Tonkin trade, the government established circuit yamens in Meng-tzu (an ordinary county capital in Yunnan), by then a regional city in the economic hierarchy, and in Lung-chou (an ordinary t'ing capital in Kwangsi), by then a greater city.[46]

As of 1893, the Chinese ecumene was ringed by 25 circuit capitals: eight along the northern Inner Asian frontier, four on the western frontier facing Tibet, three on the southern frontier facing Tonkin, and ten along the coast. Though many of these were, in fact, the largest and most important prefectural-level capitals within their circuits, others were lower-ranking or smaller capitals whose more peripheral position was strategic for the coordination of trade with, and defense against, the relevant "barbarians."

Still, circuits at the periphery of the imperial domain accounted for fewer than a third of all circuits, and the preoccupation of their intendants with foreign relations in the strict sense should perhaps be seen as a peculiarly intensified manifestation of the intendant's role. A more generic formulation of it might be phrased as responsibility to see that the external affairs of his circuit conformed to the strategic policies of the court. Here we have a rationale for the intendant's peculiar mixture of concerns—regional defense, long-distance trade, revenue from commerce, and control of outsiders—and for his peripheral role with respect to education, justice, the land tax, and other matters primarily affecting the local populace.

The variable guise of the circuit intendant—here primarily occupied with military affairs, there with customs, elsewhere with negotiations with non-Han border peoples—is only to be expected from our survey of inter- and intraregional differentiation. If one asks why the seat of T'ung-Shang circuit (Shensi) was situated at the southeastern border of its territory in an ordinary t'ing capital of no particular commercial importance, the answer lies in the great strategic value of the San-men Gorge, through which the Yellow River flows from the Northwest physiographic region into North China. It is notable that T'ung-Shang's neighboring circuits in adjacent provinces—in this area the river constituted the boundary separating Shansi province from Shensi and Honan (see the map on p. 10)—were also headquartered in small cities cited directly on the Yellow River, namely P'u-chou-fu (Shansi) at a strategic site above the gorge, and Shan-chou (Honan) at a comparable site below it. Other anomalies may be accounted for primarily in terms of the hierarchy of economic central places. Why was it not always the most important trade center among the prefectural-level capitals in a circuit that was made the capital? The answer in several cases is that the circuit's most important economic center was a nonadministrative city, in which case the capital of the county-level unit in question was made the circuit capital. Feng-yang-fu (Anhwei) and Ching-chou-fu (Hupeh), for instance, both merely local cities in their own right, were nonetheless circuit capitals, and their prefect posts carried four-character designations; each owed its administrative preeminence to the presence within the metropolitan county of a nonadministrative center ranking as a regional city in the economic hierarchy—Lin-huai-kuan and Sha-shih, respectively. Hsiang-yang-fu (Hupeh) and Li-chou (Hunan) are comparable cases, their status as circuit capitals and their FCN post designations reflecting in each case close proximity to nonadministrative greater cities—Fan-ch'eng and Ching-shih, respectively. Hsin-yang (an ordinary *chou* capital in Honan) and Wu-hu (an ordinary *hsien* capital in Anhwei), both circuit capitals of long standing, were regional cities in the economic hierarchy.

These examples suffice to account for the logic of anomalies in the administrative status of circuit capitals and to make the point that the flexibility and responsiveness peculiar to the circuit level of administration often served to bring a city's place in the administrative hierarchy into closer alignment with its level in the economic hierarchy. It should also be clear why so many circuit capitals were exceptions to the general rule that military and fiscal salience did not go together in the same urban posts.

Finally, a word about ordinary *chou* capitals, whose role in defense, as we have seen, was often to guard the immediate approaches to high-level capitals. Being situated on major roads in regional cores, many *chou* capitals were also commercial centers of some importance. A number of them, interestingly enough, carried the anomalous post designation of CN, signifying their modest importance for both trade and security. It should now be clear why the official ranking of county-level units within prefectures (declining from *chou* to *t'ing* to *hsien*) differed from their ordering by population size—from *chou* to *hsien* to *t'ing*. The official elevation of ordinary *chou* and *t'ing* above counties reflected their strategic importance, but the distinctive strategic role of each meant that *chou* capitals were likely to have greater economic centrality than county capitals whereas *t'ing* capitals normally had less.

Informal governance. In an earlier analysis of marketing in rural China, I argued that in most respects the organization of informal politics paralleled the structure of marketing systems found at the lower reaches of the economic hierarchy as described in this paper.[47] At a level that was one or two steps removed from villages, the arenas of politics and the units of informal administration were standard marketing systems, and politico-administrative action, like economic activity, was centered in the market town and reflected the periodicity of the marketing week.[48] In most parts of China, such informal power structures extended up the hierarchy at least to central marketing systems and often to local-city trading systems or higher.[49] It should be emphasized that the leadership bodies involved were not town councils, even though they usually met in the central place; leaders were drawn from throughout the relevant territorial system, and hinterland and town were "administered" as an undifferentiated unit. Naturally the more powerful leaders were involved at more than one level, and the considerable degree of such vertical overlap in the corps of leaders was accompanied by some horizontal overlap, as when a resident of an intermediate market town played a role in the power structures of both central marketing systems to which his native place was oriented.

In relating the arrangements for informal governance to the formal administrative hierarchy, two points are of particular significance. Since political arenas and marketing systems were spatially coterminous, and since the interrelations of parapolitical systems recapitulated the hierarchy of economic systems, the interests of local traders coincided with those of local gentry leaders more closely than might otherwise have been the case; in any event, gentry control of leading merchants was facilitated. In the usual case, the leading merchants of the market town or local city were brought into leadership councils by the gentry "establishment," and in intersystem conflicts economic and political issues were closely intertwined. Second, the element of spatial competition inherent in the overlapping hierarchical mode that we have shown to characterize the natural economic hierarchy rendered local-level politics particularly flexible and adaptive. The parapolitical system centered in a standard market town might align with higher-level systems centered on any of the neighboring higher-level market towns or, if power were roughly balanced, find itself in a position to play one off against another. By the same token, neighboring high-level political systems were in competition for the allegiance of intervening low-level systems.

The nature of the hierarchy also permitted a kind of territorial aggrandizement that was not possible in political systems contained within administrative boundaries. An exceptionally powerful political structure at the local-city level might dominate all of the systems centered in the surrounding ring of central market towns and even extend its sway to the intermediate systems on the far side of those central market towns, thereby truncating the political structures centered on neighboring local cities.

We have already established the point that the population of economic systems at the same level of the hierarchy (say, central marketing systems) varied according to position in the regional structure: populations were smaller in such poorly endowed and underdeveloped regions as Yun-Kwei and larger in richer, better developed regions such as the Lower Yangtze; smaller in peripheral areas and larger in regional cores; smaller in the case of systems whose nodes were central market towns and larger in the case of systems centered on local or higher-ranking cities. The same pattern held for the total economic demand within the system and for the total volume of business transactions. On first principles, we would expect comparable patterning in the strength of the informal political structures that inhered in these economic systems. In particular, of course, elites were disproportionately concentrated in more favorably situated, richly endowed, "urbanized" marketing systems, so that the nonofficial elite and, a fortiori, the bureaucratic elite would be far more numerous in a central marketing system whose node was a greater city in the regional core than in a central marketing system whose node was a central market town situated in the far periphery. Consequently, leadership councils would be more selective in systems of the former type, with comparatively heavy representation of officials-out-of-office and powerful merchants. Finally we would expect territorial aggrandizement (of the kind described above) by a strong parapolitical system within a regional core at the expense of more peripherally situated neighboring systems. Thus, we would have every reason to believe that the relative power of informal politico-administrative systems and the standing of their leaders varied systematically in accordance with the model developed above of regional economic systems.

The first point of contact between the hierarchy of local parapolitical systems and the hierarchy of bureaucratic administrative units was normally the county-level capital. That critical intersection was, in most cases, in a local city or central market town, but in this respect, too, there was sharp variation in accordance with place in the regional structure. Over 60 percent of the high-level economic centers (greater cities or above) that housed county-level yamens were situated in regional cores. The corresponding figures are 49 percent for local cities, 40 percent for central market towns, and 32 percent for intermediate market towns; the handful of standard market towns that served as capitals were all located in regional peripheries. Thus, the range of variation was great on two counts. The local leaders who dealt with the magistrate of a peripheral county were likely to have headed the unusually weak power structure of a relatively small central marketing system, encompassing, say, a population of 50,000; few among them would have been graduate degree-holders or former officials of any importance. By contrast, local leaders who confronted the magistrate of a metropolitan county in a core city were likely to have headed the exceptionally strong power structure of a relatively large local-city trading system, encompassing a population that most likely exceeded half a million; few among them would not have been graduate degree-holders or former officials of great power. In the one case the scope for informal governance below the intersection with the bureaucratic government was fairly restricted, in the other case extremely broad.

It would appear, then, that the strength and resources of informal parapolitical systems varied through regional space in an approximation of complementary distribution with the capacity of bureaucratic government to attend to those aspects of governance not focused on the court's overriding concern with revenue and defense. We may conceive of the matter in terms of a variable division of labor. The "services" at issue included resolving civil disputes and maintaining local order; apprehending and punishing criminals; dispensing famine and disaster relief and other welfare services; promoting education and supervising institutions related to imperial examinations; constructing and maintaining public works; and licensing and regulating certain semiprofessionals and businessmen. For simplicity's sake, let me lump these activities together as societal management and social control and point to the obvious fact that the extent to which formal government could shoulder responsibility for them was a function of administrative intensity.

It was possible, I argue, to make a go of giant prefectures at the heart of great economic systems—that is, bureaucrats could concentrate on revenue collection in such prefectures—only by allowing much of the responsibility for societal management to devolve on informal parapolitical structures. And it was in just such areas that local parapolitical structures were largest and strongest. In the rich core areas where counties were populous and span of control broad, nonofficial societal management was institutionalized under the leadership of urban elites, merchants as well as gentry, whose "governmental" activities so reduced the routine of county-level yamens that control by the prefectural yamen was not necessarily perfunctory despite the broad span of control;[50] it was even possible for overburdened prefects to rely on native officials-out-of-office to help keep tabs on county magistrates. In less favorably situated areas near the transition between core and periphery, where both county populations and spans of control were closer to the empirewide average, local parapolitical structures tended to be weaker, less effective, and controlled by less exalted leaders; and there county-level yamens were in a position to shoulder more of the responsibilities of governance, and prefectural-level yamens were able to spread their attention more evenly over the whole range of governmental functions.

If one asks how the government induced leaders throughout the nested hierarchy of local systems to serve as its informal agents, the answer appears to rest heavily on the state's control of the status symbols that defined and graded elites, namely the "academic" degrees associated with the imperial examination system. The manifest function of that system was to cultivate and identify talented men for recruitment to government service, but it also enabled the state to monopolize the most important status symbols in the society at large and to control their significance and distribution by setting quotas, fixing the academic content of the examinations, canceling or adding examinations, and (of particular importance in this context) denying certain groups access to the examination sheds.[51] It is hardly coincidental that the local systems most strongly caught up in the government-sponsored academic competition were found in those very areas where field administration was least intensive. Academically successful localities in Ch'ing China were heavily concentrated in the local-city trading systems of cities that were at once greater or higher-level cities in the economic hierarchy *and* prefectural or higher-level capitals in the administrative hierarchy.[52] These corresponded in large part to the metropolitan counties of the prefectural-level units whose capitals are shown in the first and second diagonals of Table 18.

It all fits together. Areas of high revenue potential had the resources to invest heavily in grooming young men for academic success, producing in the process degree-holding elites that were dependent on bureaucrats and particularly susceptible to their normative controls. And these were the elites whose leaders would man the extensive and elaborated parapolitical structures on which so much of local governance necessarily devolved by virtue of the highly extensive form of field admin-

TABLE 20. DISTRIBUTION OF CENTRAL PLACES BY LEVEL IN THE
ADMINISTRATIVE AND ECONOMIC HIERARCHIES, 1893

Level in the economic hierarchy	Level in the administrative hierarchy[a]						
	Imperial	Provincial	Circuit[b]	Prefectural and aut. *chou*[c]	Low-level[d]	Non-adm.	Total
Central metropolis	1	3	2				6
Regional metropolis		15	1	3	1		20
Regional city		1	26	20	8	8	63
Greater city			19	77	85	19	200
Local city			12	62	494	101	669
CMT				17	581	1,721	2,319
IMT					106	7,905	8,011
SMT					12	27,700	27,712
Total	1	19	60	179	1,287	37,454	39,000

[a] Wuhan and Kuei-sui are counted as single cities, and Chiang-pei-t'ing is counted as part of Chungking. See notes to Table 6.

[b] Excludes the sixteen provincial capitals that were also circuit capitals. The table appears to lack one circuit capital, since the yamens of two circuits are housed in Wuhan, which is counted here as a single city.

[c] Includes the two autonomous *t'ing* that were structurally analogous to autonomous *chou*.

[d] Includes capitals of prefectural-level units (25 autonomous *t'ing* and four prefectures) that contained but a single county-level unit.

istration favored in areas with a high revenue potential. Where obverse conditions produced local leaders who were less reliable agents of local yamens, more intensive administrative arrangements reduced the state's reliance on informal governance.

An obvious problem with the basic strategy of Ch'ing field administration was how to enlist the services of local gentry and merchants as informal agents of bureaucratic government without so strengthening them and the parapolitical structures they controlled that their power could pose a threat to bureaucratic control. As suggested above, institutional arrangements that tied the interests of local elites to those of the state were doubtless the chief means of coping with this problem. They did not preclude additional precautions, however. It appears likely to me, for instance, that where the potential danger from concentrated local power was greatest, administrative boundaries were deliberately drawn with an eye to their divisive consequences.

The kind of entrenched power that involved illicit connivance between officials-in-office and local elites was effectively contained in Ch'ing China by such bureaucratic devices as rules of avoidance and rapid turnover of incumbents. Thus, the greatest danger lay in collusion between powerful gentry and wealthy merchants in areas where both were concentrated. From evidence available to me, it appears that within the informal political systems discussed above, cooperation between gentry and merchants was less than exceptional,[53] and as one source of a community of interests I pointed to the fact that for gentry-man and trader alike the field of operations at each level was identical, namely the commercial hinterland of a given central place. Above the level of intersection between the "natural" economic hierarchy and the formal administrative hierarchy, however, the relevant arenas of the two leading social groups tended to diverge, as the interests of the gentry were pulled inexorably toward the hierarchy of official administrative units. If for no other reason than that the regular academic ladder recapitulated the structure of field administration, the concerns of the higher gentry were largely contained within and focused on the hierarchy of counties, prefectures, and provinces, whereas those of merchants related to the hierarchy of trading systems centered on greater cities, regional cities, and metropolises.

To what extent did the two hierarchies coincide? Part of the answer may be seen in Table 20, which shows the distribution of cities by level in the administrative and economic hierarchies. It is evident that there was considerable divergence between the maximal administrative and economic hinterlands of particular cities, especially those in the middle range. The leading gentry of a given prefecture, for instance, might find their political action focused at a city whose leading merchants were concerned either with a local-city trading system that was much less extensive than the prefecture or with a regional-city trading system that extended well beyond the prefectural boundaries. Cities classified in the upper-right cells of Table 20 all point to more or less extreme cases of misalignment whereby extensive trading systems climaxed in cities that were not even capitals of the smaller prefectural-level administrative units wholly contained within them. Chou-chia-k'ou, for instance, one of eight nonadministrative regional cities, was the base of great merchants whose area of operations extended far beyond the prefecture (Ch'en-chou) in which it was located, a prefecture whose capital was a city of relative insignificance. Focusing on the column of Table 20 showing low-level capitals, we may note that the one county-level capital that served as a regional metropolis (Wei-hsien in Shantung), the eight county-level capitals that served as regional cities (including Te-chou in Shantung, Wu-hsi in Kiangsu, and Wan-hsien in Szechwan), and most of the 85 county-level capitals that served as greater cities were all centers of commercial systems that extended beyond the prefectural-level administrative units to which the counties in question belonged. In these instances, not only were the commercial systems to which great merchants were oriented and the administrative systems to which leading gentry were oriented of different territorial magnitude; they were also differently structured in space, being centered on quite separate nodal cities.

It should be clear, moreover, that the data in Table 20, showing the alignment of *centers*, seriously understate the amount of misalignment between *systems*. By the very nature of the two structures of territorial systems—the uniform discreteness of the one, the indiscrete overlapping of the other—the alignment of systems was necessarily grossly imperfect. And, to focus on the point at hand, they could be made to diverge radically by deliberately drawing administrative boundaries to minimize convergence.

Limiting examples to the exalted level that can be illustrated by reference to the map on page 10, we may focus our attention on the cores of the Lower Yangtze and North China regions. Had the former been included in a single province—and the Lower Yangtze as a whole would have made a smaller-than-average province in terms of area —the hierarchy of administrative units would have coincided all too closely with the hierarchy of commercial systems within the region.

In an area that included the strongest concentrations of rich merchants *and* of powerful gentry in the entire realm, potential collusion between the two groups at all levels extending up to the central metropolitan trading system would have posed a very real threat to imperial power. By drawing provincial boundaries so that the core of the region was divided among three provinces *and* so that the metropolitan trading systems were split between administrative units (the entire portion of the regional core in Anhwei province, for instance, was oriented economically to Nanking in Kiangsu province), the region's powerful gentry were fractionated into competing elites, and the hierarchy of administrative systems within which each provincial gentry group was focused was sharply differentiated from the commercial territorial hierarchy that shaped the interests of Lower Yangtze merchants. It will be noted, moreover, that of the three provinces involved, Kiangsu and Anhwei each included a portion of the North China regional core, while Chekiang incorporated the northern portion of the Southeast Coast regional core. Thus, in interprovincial competition, the Lower Yangtze gentry within each province allied with gentry in the core of different regional economies.

In that part of the North China core farthest from the imperial capital, provincial boundaries strongly suggest high-level gerrymandering. One effect of extending a leg of Chihli deep into the southern portion of the regional core was to split the metropolitan and the regional-city trading systems of both Kaifeng and Tung-ch'ang-fu between two provinces and to tie the interests of the powerful gentry of Ta-ming *fu* (the prefecture forming the southern leg of Chihli) to the metropolitan province rather than to Honan or Shantung, the provinces on which the interests of Ta-ming merchants were focused.

I am inclined to interpret in similar terms a fairly rare and highly peculiar administrative arrangement at the local level. If the concentrated power of merchants and gentry within local parapolitical structures reached dangerous proportions anywhere, it would have been in the local-city trading systems centered on cities ranking high in both hierarchies—such Lower Yangtze cities as Soochow, Nanking, Hangchow, Yangchow, Ch'ang-chou-fu, Hu-chou-fu, and Shao-hsing-fu; and such metropolises elsewhere as Peking, Sian, Chengtu, Changsha, Hengyang-fu, Nanchang, Foochow, and Canton. The administrative peculiarity in question was common to all of these cities, and it resulted from the fact that each served as the capital of more than one county, three in one instance (Soochow), two in all others. In such cases, the county boundary ran through the city, and the yamen of each county was located in the appropriate sector.* This administrative sectoralization of the city's immediate hinterland meant that there was no county-level yamen to which the extraordinarily strong power structure of the local-city trading system as a whole could relate. As a result, their political focus would have been directed upward to the prefectural yamen. In all probability, this escalation served to weaken the informal political system in two ways. Lesser merchant and gentry leaders whose interests did not extend beyond the local-city trading system and whose standing was uncomfortably low for negotiations with the bureaucrats posted to such high-ranking prefectural yamens may well have declined to participate, focusing their political activities at the next lower level. As for the more exalted leaders of the system, escalation would have brought out the divergent interests of gentry and merchants, whose respective systems of reference at the higher level—the prefecture and the greater-city trading system—were spatially differentiated.

Conclusions

In this paper I have described how regional urban systems were shaped by physiography and how they in turn structured the economy of different physiographic regions. The economic centrality of cities was shown to vary from one region to another and systematically within each region in accordance with its core-periphery structure and transport grid. Although the details of this analysis provide what I believe to be a useful framework for investigating the economy and society of late imperial China, the close correspondence found between central-place systems and physiographic regions, on the one hand, and the relative autonomy of those regional economies, on the other, might well be expected in the case of an agrarian society of subcontinental magnitude lacking mechanized transport.

* Altogether 24 cities throughout China served as the capitals of more than one county. All but two of these cities were located in regional cores, and thirteen were found in the Lower Yangtze region. They included ten of the twenty provincial and higher-level capitals, ten prefectural capitals, and only four county capitals. In addition, *chou* and *t'ing* capitals provide examples—only two to my knowledge—of cities that were administratively divided. T'ai-ts'ang, the capital of an autonomous *chou* in Kiangsu, housed not only the *chou* yamen but also the yamen of Chen-yang, a subordinate county, and the boundary running through the city separated the county from T'ai-ts'ang *pen-chou*. Hsü-yung, the capital of an autonomous *t'ing* in Szechwan, consisted of two separately walled components on either side of a river, with the yamen for the *t'ing* on the west bank and that for its subordinate county, Yung-ming, on the east bank; the boundary between the county and the directly ruled area followed the course of the river.

My findings concerning the regional basis of field administration, however, are less than intuitively obvious. I am led to conclude that Ch'ing field administration was marvelously adapted to the realities of regional structure within the empire. On the one hand, the revenue potential of different localities was largely a function of their place in the hierarchy of nodal economic systems that culminated in eight regional economies, each with a core-periphery structure. On the other hand, defense requirements varied in conformity with the structure of physiographic regions; critical defense perimeters were closely associated with regional frontiers, and other strategic sites guarded the major approaches to the heartland of physiographic regions, whose rich resources and great cities constituted the ultimate military objectives. The basic strategy underlying the design of field administration was to adjust the size of county-level units in accordance with position in the macroregional structure—maximizing county populations in the high-revenue portions of the core and minimizing county areas in the insecure and vulnerable areas along the regional frontiers—and then to form prefectural-level units that contained many county-level units at the core (so as to incorporate in as few prefectures as possible the key economic areas on which the empire depended for the bulk of its revenue) but few at the periphery (so as to simplify the chain of command and achieve closer supervision of local officials in times of crisis). The capstone of the system was the meticulous classification of capitals that faithfully reflected the core-periphery structure of regions, the capital's level in the hierarchy of economic central places, span of control, and the relative salience of distinctive administrative tasks. This complex scheme, involving post designations as well as administrative level and rank, enabled the central government to deploy its bureaucratic cadre to maximum advantage. Finally, the specialized functions of circuits introduced some critical differentiation into the administrative chain of command and modified the basic design as necessary to serve broader geopolitical goals.

These findings effectively dispose of the notion that cities in imperial China were but microcosms of empire, more or less uniform creations of an omnipotent state. Rather, they give evidence of skilled husbanding and deployment of the limited bureaucratic power that a premodern court could effectively control. Bureaucratic government may have imposed elements of formal uniformity on Chinese cities, but in practice field administration expressed rather than suppressed functional differentiation within the urban system.

Our investigation of urban networks in relation to regional structure has underlined the remarkable degree to which cities were at once embedded in society and essential to its overall structure. The point can be phrased in terms of hinterlands. That cities shape their hinterlands is axiomatic. This analysis points to the probable virtues of turning the matter around and examining cities in terms of the number, size, and characteristics of their various hinterlands, and of the degree of coincidence and overlap among them. For in a manner of speaking, these determined variation in urban social structure. The relative strength of gentry and merchants in a given city and their propensity to cooperate in urban governance were functions not only of its position with respect to the two hierarchies of central places (as tabulated in Table 20) but of the degree of fit between the city's economic and administrative hinterlands. Similarly, the relative importance of the bureaucratic element in the governance of cities depended not on administrative level alone but rather on the entire interrelated structure of commercial hinterlands and administrative units. We have also found it useful to relate local parapolitical systems to the hinterlands of economic centers, and to examine their intersection with bureaucratic governance in terms of the superposition of two contrastive modes for stacking hinterlands.

The overall fit, throughout the core-periphery structure of a region, between administrative intensity and the political strength of local systems, together with the complex interaction between economic and political power within regional systems of cities, directs our attention to the mechanisms of dominance and dependency that expressed and reinforced the structure as a whole. The present analysis virtually requires us to ask in what ways the exceptional development of such regions as the Lower Yangtze was dependent on underdevelopment in interior regions, and to what extent development in the cores of regions *caused* underdevelopment in their peripheries. Those who pursue these questions are likely to find differentiation among cities and interurban relations close to the heart of the matter.

Appendix

Fairly early in my research on Chinese cities it became clear that in late imperial times they formed not a single integrated urban system but several regional systems, each only tenuously connected with its neighbors. In tracing out the overlapping hinterlands of the cities in each one of these regional systems, I came to the realization that the region they jointly defined coincided with minor exceptions to a physiographic unit. In short, it appears that each system of cities developed within a physiographic region. I eventually came to conceive of urban development—the formation of cities and the growth of their central functions—as a critical element in regional development—the processes whereby regional resources of all kinds, social and cultural as well as economic and political, were multiplied, deployed with greater effectiveness, and exploited with increased efficiency.

First-order regional units are depicted in the maps on pages 9 and 10. Without exception they are defined in terms of drainage basins. All regional boundaries follow watersheds (except in the few places where they cross rivers) and more often than not follow the crests of mountain ranges. There were two critical questions that had to be answered in setting regional boundaries. First, in the case of great river systems spanning two or more regions, precisely where along the trunk river's course was the critical cut to be made? And second, with which regions were self-contained interior drainage basins and small river systems along the coast to be aligned? The criteria for answering these questions had to do with transport efficiency and trade flows as well as with physiography per se.

Together the nine regions include virtually all of agrarian China, i.e., that part of the empire where sedentary agriculture as traditionally practiced by the Chinese was feasible. In the west, regional boundaries were defined to exclude the arid and otherwise inhospitable basins of six rivers upstream from the cutting points shown in the map on page 9. The Yun-Kwei region, a plateau in which virtually no rivers are navigable and all official and commercial transport moved by land, was defined to include the upper reaches of the Hung-shui (a tributary of the West River), of the Wu (a tributary of the Yangtze), and of the Chin-sha (as the Yangtze is known along its upper course) from approximately the point where each becomes unnavigable even for small junks.

For the rest, regional definitions presented few problems. Lingnan is the drainage basin that includes the West, North, and East rivers. The Southeast Coast includes the basins of the myriad rivers that flow from the Wu-i mountains to the sea. The Lower Yangtze, whose core is the fertile Kiangnan area that figures so prominently in the literature on imperial China, includes the basins of the Ch'ien-t'ang and other rivers that flow into Hangchow Bay. The Middle Yangtze region includes the great basins of four major tributaries—the Han, Kan, Hsiang, and Yüan rivers. The Upper Yangtze region has as its core the fertile Red Basin of Szechwan. Northwest China, consisting in large part of the upper basin of the Yellow River, has been extended, as is customary, to include the internal drainage systems in which the chief oases of the Kansu corridor are situated. North China includes the lower basin of the Yellow River plus the drainage areas of the Huai, the Wei, and the host of smaller rivers that cross the North China Plain.

Manchuria, the ninth region of agrarian China, is excluded entirely from my analysis, as it is also from the coverage of the book as a whole. The chief reason is that settlement of the region by Han Chinese got under way on a large scale only in the last decade of the Ch'ing period. Thus Manchuria was little developed by the 1890's, and its urban system was embryonic or at best emergent; the rapid changes that were to transform Manchuria into China's most highly urbanized region were all twentieth-century developments. Moreover, it was only in the first decade of this century that the regular Chinese system

THE MACROREGIONS OF AGRARIAN CHINA, EXCLUDING MANCHURIA:
AREAS, ESTIMATED POPULATIONS, AND POPULATION DENSITIES,
1843, 1893, and 1953[a]

Macroregion	Area (sq. km.)	1843		1893		1953	
		Population in millions	Density	Population in millions	Density	Population in millions	Density
North China	746,470	112	150	122	163	174	233
Northwest China	771,300	29	38	24	31	32	42
Upper Yangtze	423,950	47	111	53	125	68	160
Middle Yangtze	699,700	84	120	75	107	92	131
Lower Yangtze	192,740	67	348	45	233	61	316
Southeast Coast[b]	226,670	27	119	29	128	36	159
Lingnan[c]	424,900	29	68	33	78	47	111
Yun-Kwei	470,570	11	23	16	34	26	55
Total	3,956,300	406	103	397	100	536	135

[a] See note 4, p. 708, of my "Regional Urbanization in Nineteenth-Century China," in G. William Skinner, ed., *The City in Late Imperial China* (Stanford, Calif.: Stanford University Press, 1977), for the procedures followed in constructing the estimates in this table.

[b] Includes Taiwan. The corresponding figures for the Southeast Coast region excluding Taiwan are area, 190,710 sq. km.; 1843 population, 26 million; 1843 density, 136; 1893 population, 26 million; 1893 density, 136; 1953 population, 29 million; 1953 density, 152.

[c] Includes Hainan.

of civil field administration was extended to Manchuria, so that classification of cities according to administrative rank as of 1893 is not possible for Manchuria as it is for the other eight regions. My analysis, then, covers agrarian China minus Manchuria, a total territory that is roughly equivalent (see the map on p. 10) to the traditional "eighteen provinces" of Ch'ing China.

Though the eight regions treated here are equivalent in physiographic terms, they are by no means commensurate. The accompanying table shows for each the approximate area, the estimated population, and the population density as of 1843 and 1893 (1953 data are given for comparison). Regional differences in area and population were reflected in the number of cities at any given level in the urban hierarchy that were "supported" by the region's resources or, to turn it around, the number required to perform the region's central functions at a given level. For instance, from the map (p. 10), which plots all metropolitan cities as of 1843, it may be seen that the Southeast Coast had only one such city, whereas at the other extreme North China had seven.

In human geography, the term region refers to any partition of activity-space made according to one of two criteria: (1) the homogeneity of things to be considered, producing a set of *formal* or *uniform* regions; or (2) the interrelatedness of things to be considered, producing a set of *functional* or *nodal* regions. The regions just defined are of the second type, and if the map on page 9 appears novel to most readers it is because we are used to regionalizing China according to the homogeneity criterion, producing uniform regions about which generalizations can be made, whether the subject be soils, climate, agriculture, or ethnicity. In contrast to uniform regions, functional regions are internally differentiated and constitute systems in which activities of many kinds are functionally interrelated. In the regions of China under discussion here, cities are the nodes of the systems, the "command posts" that serve to articulate and integrate human activity in space and time.

We are now in a position to account in general terms for the fact that in each of the major physiographic regions there developed a reasonably discrete urban system, i.e., a cluster of cities within which interurban transactions were concentrated and whose rural-urban transactions were largely confined within the region. We start with the key fact that each region was characterized by the concentration in a central area of resources of all kinds—above all, in an agrarian society, arable land; but also, of course, population and capital investments—and by the thinning out of resources toward the periphery. As I have described in the text, ecological processes, natural as well as technological (e.g., the transfer of fertility through erosion, on the one hand, and the use of irrigation and of fertilizer, on the other), boosted agricultural productivity in the lowland cores. An indication of where regional resources were concentrated, Manchuria aside, is given in the map on page 9, where each region's area of highest population density is shaded.

It will be noted that, with the exception of Yun-Kwei, these regional "cores" are river-valley lowlands, which almost by definition had major transport advantages vis-à-vis peripheral areas. Because of the low unit cost of water as against land transport, navigable waterways dominated traffic flows in all regions except Yun-Kwei and the Northwest; and even where rivers were unnavigable their valleys typically afforded the most efficient overland routes. Thus the transport network of each region climaxed in the lowland cores, where most of the transport nodes were situated. River systems aside, the less rugged terrain of the core areas made it relatively inexpensive to build roads and canals.

For these reasons it is hardly surprising that the major cities of each region grew up in the core areas or on major transport routes leading into them, and that all cities within a physiographic region developed hierarchical transaction patterns culminating in one or more cities in the regional core.

Transactions between the centrally located cities of one region and those of another were minimized by the high cost of unmechanized transport and the great distances involved. It cost as much to transport grain 200 miles on the back of a pack animal as it did to produce it in the first place, and the corresponding figure for coal was less than 25 miles. Transport costs of this order of magnitude effectively eliminated low-priced bulky goods from interregional trade. Moreover, we have to take into account the increased expense of transport in the more rugged terrain that characterized most portions of the regional peripheries; even the most advantageous routes between adjacent regions often traversed mountain passes or hazardous gorges.* It should be emphasized that systematic differences in transport efficiency affected politico-administrative and social transactions no less than commerce: interregional intercourse was depressed in all spheres.

---

* The exceptions, navigable water routes linking macroregions, are of course crucial to an understanding of the extent and nature of interregional integration.

Peasant Insurrection and the Marketing Hierarchy in the Canton Delta, 1911-1912

WINSTON HSIEH

In the wake of the Wuchang Uprising of October 10, 1911, many thousands of peasant bands in the Canton delta region rose at their local market towns and marched toward the cities. In a few weeks some of these poorly equipped but enthusiastic "people's armies" (*min-chün*) had reached the regional capital of Canton, while others had taken over county capitals throughout the delta. It would be an exaggeration to say that the armies conquered Canton; they simply swarmed over it unresisted. For several weeks they dominated the Canton scene. Carried away by iconoclastic fervor, some of them stunned the public by attempting to destroy the Temple of the City God and by other acts of violence. From surrounding towns came the more alarming news that the rebels controlled many county governments, that some were forcing travelers to cut off their pigtails, and that others had gone so far as to attack the houses of the privileged gentry.

The spontaneity and destructive power of the people's armies astonished many contemporary Western observers, but in the context of local history they seem less extraordinary. Peasant disturbances and mass uprisings were a familiar element of local politics in the Canton delta. Gazetteers and other Chinese sources record numerous instances of collective violence during the century preceding 1911, including inter-village and interlineage feuds, mass attacks on tax collectors, luddite destruction of silk-reeling machines, fighting between local militia and government troops, and secret-society rebellions. Information is far richer and more specific on the people's armies of 1911 than on dissident forces in earlier years, thanks to the special attention given the Revolution of 1911 in Chinese historiography.[1] Thus, the case of the people's armies is a strategic one for illuminating collective violence and the wide distribution of paramilitary forces in the delta region. The study of people's armies in 1911 also provides historical perspective on the armed peasant forces that were to play such a prominent role during the Republican period in the revolts against Yüan Shih-k'ai and various warlord regimes, in the conflicts between communist-directed peasant associations and traditional militia organizations on the eve of the Northern Expedition, and in the anti-Japanese guerrilla activity along the Pearl river tributaries during World War II. Specifically, what we learn about the geographic origins, composition, main sources of support, and basic motivations of the dissident peasant forces of 1911 is often applicable to the dissident peasant forces of later decades as well.*

Since information on given local uprisings during 1911–12 is usually incomplete and superficial, I have fleshed it out with socioeconomic data from local gazetteers and geographic data from large-scale local maps both contemporary and of more recent vintage. Such supplementary data not only help correct for the errors inevitable in such sources as the reminiscences of participants, but also shed light on many otherwise isolated or seemingly insignificant events. Most important, however, tracing the movements of insurrectionary armies on the map of local marketing systems helps to reveal the channels through which these bands were drawn to the centers of conflict and the patterns of mobilization at various levels of the marketing hierarchy.

These historical and methodological considerations underlay my selection of the two case studies presented below: the Shih-ch'i uprising in Hsiang-shan (now Chung-shan) county and the Kuan-lan uprising in Hsin-an (now Pao-an) county. With the help of five consecutive editions of Hsiang-shan gazetteers, spanning 250 years of the county's history, I have been able to reconstruct the trend of urbanization in the city of Shih-ch'i, where a major uprising was staged in 1911. The second case involves a movement encompassing several towns near the border of the Hong Kong New Territories. Using a recently unearthed daily chronicle on the uprising in conjunction with large-scale local maps, I have been able to demonstrate the central role of market towns in local uprisings and to delineate the pattern of revolutionary mobilization.

The Shih-ch'i Uprising

On the eve of the uprising, the secret organization of the revolutionary party, the T'ung-meng Hui, had infiltrated much of the county of Hsiang-

---

* This chapter is part of an ongoing research project on the Canton delta region. For substantive comments and advice, my thanks go to the two editors of this volume and to those participating in the Canton Delta Seminar at the University of Hong Kong in 1973.

shan, which bordered on the Portuguese colony of Macau and was cut through by many waterways connecting delta cities with Hong Kong (see Map 1). More specifically, Hsiang-shan students and émigrés in Hong Kong, Macau, and Honolulu had used their family and personal connections to build a secret network in Lung-tu, an area west of and commercially dependent on the central market of Shih-ch'i, the county capital of Hsiang-shan. Naval officers assisted the revolutionaries by smuggling weapons into the walled city, and revolutionary fervor was so intense that the commander of the militia and the chief of the county magistrate's bodyguards had both joined the T'ung-meng Hui. An enterprising Shih-ch'i merchant, certain that a local uprising would follow the Wuchang Uprising within days, made up a batch of several hundred republican flags for sale.

The T'ung-meng Hui's clandestine activities were not limited to the Shih-ch'i area. Contacts were maintained with pirates in the town of Hsiao-lan to the northwest. Efforts were also made to infiltrate the New Army at Ch'ien-shan, a military stronghold overlooking the Macau border. Following the T'ung-meng Hui's decision to appeal to the local armed bands for revolutionary action, a headquarters was set up at Macau to coordinate and finance the various activities across the Hsiang-shan border. On November 2, the pirates made the first move, taking over Hsiao-lan; the next day, a band of militia sent by the magistrate to suppress the pirates joined them instead. Two days later, the major uprising took place at Shih-ch'i.[2]

Mobilization of the insurrectionary troops. The peasant bands from the Lung-tu area first gathered at their local centers and then marched to Shih-ch'i. When the bands met in front of the Temple of the Dragon Emperor at the Shih-ch'i market, they were organized into two brigades, one marching into the walled city by the West Gate, the other by the South Gate. Because the militia officers at the West Gate and the garrison forces at the county magistrate's yamen cooperated with them, they took over the city without difficulty. The *hsün-fang-ying* patrol forces attempted to resist at the South Gate, but they were easily routed and their commander was slain on the spot.[3] By this time the uprising had developed into a spectacle, with thousands of people watching along the riverside. The county magistrate, who had studied in Japan and was sympathetic to the ideas of revolution and change, made a public pledge to support the republican cause and to remain in his post for the transition period. Gentry and merchant leaders with lineage ties to the rebels offered to raise funds. For the office of the new government, the ancestral hall of the Kao lineage was preferred to the county yamen, symbol of the old regime.

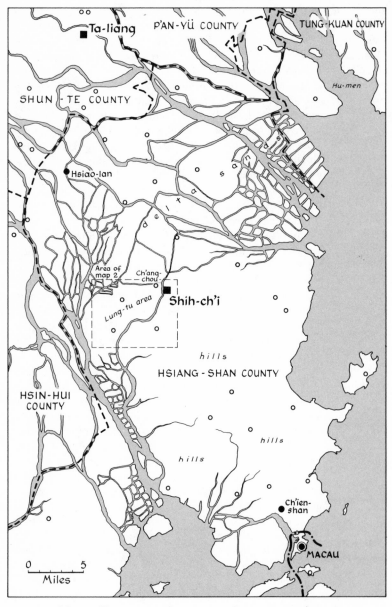

MAP 1. HSIANG-SHAN COUNTY AND SURROUNDING AREA

The fall of Shih-ch'i alarmed the provincial authorities in Canton, who dispatched a gunboat to suppress the uprising. But the people's armies had both banks of the river near the Shih-ch'i market under heavy guard, and when New Army forces under revolutionary command arrived from Ch'ien-shan the gunboat left. Most Chinese accounts of the uprising shift their focus at this point, leaving Shih-ch'i itself and going on to relate how the New Army troops were reorganized into the Hsiang-shan Army (*Hsiang-chün*), how the Army acted in Canton, and how it was incorporated into the expeditionary force sent to fight the Ch'ing army at Nanking. Our concern, however, is with what the process of mobilizing a people's army was actually like, and for this we must piece together data on the local uprising and analyze them in the light of background material provided by local gazetteers.

The reminiscences of Cheng Pi-an, a T'ung-meng Hui leader, provide crucial information: the names of the commanders of the ten major bands participating in the uprising, the names of the communities where the bands originated, and the surnames of the majority of the soldiers in each band (see Table 1). The correspondence of followers' and leaders' surnames suggests that the bands were organized along lineage lines; and indeed Cheng remarks that the band from An-t'ang consisted of the young men from the Lin lineage, the Hsi-chiao band of those from the Liu lineage, and so on. In each case the lineage cited by Cheng for which documentary sources are available is shown to be the principal lineage of the community in question.[4]

The impressive number of volunteers from each of these lineages suggests that each band was supported by the whole lineage. Cheng estimates the total number of volunteers involved in the uprising at between 2,000 and 3,000 men. Since it is unlikely that a smaller number could have halted the gunboat from Canton, Cheng's estimate seems reasonable. Thus the average lineage would have provided some 200 to 300 volunteers, which should cover almost all the young males in a local lineage who were capable of fighting. In earlier times such a massive turnout would have occurred only in a major lineage feud.

Cheng's account also suggests that the leaders whose names he gives, though belonging to the lineages involved, may have been titular rather than actual commanders of the bands, since many of them no longer resided in their native towns. Indeed, they were, in a sense, outside agitators. As Cheng recalls, some were activists from overseas Chinese communities who had hurried home to participate in the revolution. Some had been studying in Hong Kong. Probably all of them were T'ung-meng Hui members, for otherwise Cheng would not have been so likely to remember all their names.

TABLE 1. MAJOR BANDS PARTICIPATING IN THE
SHIH-CH'I UPRISING, 1911

Local community	Dominant lineage	Band commanders
An-t'ang	Lin	Lin Hsiu Lin Shao-yü Lin Yao-nan
Hsi-chiao	Liu	Liu Cho-t'ang Liu Wei-ch'ih Liu Jih-san
Nan-wen	Hsiao	Hsiao —— - ——
Lung-chü-huan	Liu	Liu Han-hua
Hsiang-chiao	P'eng	P'eng Hsiung-chia
Hao-t'u	Kao	Kao Sheng-hu
Shen-ming-t'ing	Yang	Yang Tsao-yün
K'an-hsia	Liang	Liang Shou
Kang-t'ou	Hu	Hu K'ung-ch'u
Ch'ang-chou	Huang	Huang Yao-han Huang P'u-ming

SOURCE: *Hsin hai ko ming hui i lu*, 2: 338–42.

Thus the mobilization can be reconstructed as follows. T'ung-meng Hui agitators were sent to local communities where they had family ties to win over the leaders who controlled the lineages' fighting bands, to spread revolutionary propaganda, and to prepare for the uprising. When the call finally came, they marched with the local bands, armed with guns acquired for use in the local feuds, to the Temple of the Dragon Emperor in Shih-ch'i. (Thus, two prominent T'ung-meng Hui members, Lin Chin-hun, the top leader of the uprising, and his cousin Lin Chün-fu, were both natives of An-t'ang; and the Lins from An-t'ang formed the largest band that fought at Shih-ch'i, numbering over 500.) The success of the uprising was undoubtedly furthered by money from Hong Kong and Macau and by the persuasive power of republican agitators, but there would have been no uprising without personal access to the existing "war machine" for lineage-based feuds.

It should be pointed out that this pattern of mobilization has its limitations. In the immediate neighborhood of the villages that produced revolutionary forces, many other communities played no part in the uprising (Map 2). While the revolutionaries' lack of access to the lineage-sponsored armies in these communities provides a major explanation, certain questions remain. Why, for instance, did such powerful communities as Hsi-chiao and Shen-ming-t'ing fail to sway their neighbors and,

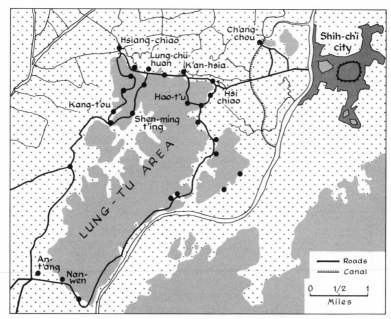

MAP 2. PLACES OF ORIGIN OF THE MAJOR BANDS PARTICIPATING IN THE SHIH-CH'I UPRISING, 1911. Areas over 20 feet in elevation are shaded. Settlements from which few or no participants originated are not labeled.

in particular, how does one account for the inactivity of the intervillage militia bureau, which had come into existence in the mid-nineteenth century specifically to coordinate local forces? The events of 1911 seem to indicate that control of such forces had shifted from the general militia office to individual villages. Could this shift, then, be taken as an index to the general decline of the traditional, intervillage dependence of the area under the modern impacts from the Shih-ch'i market? What looms large in the background of the revolutionary mobilization seems to be a situation close to what Skinner found in his rural marketing study: As individual villages were increasingly pulled to the modern urban trading system, "much of their communal significance devolves on component villages, and a gradual change in emphasis places the self-interest of each little community above intervillage cooperation."[5] To grasp the nature and scope of such changes, we must investigate the urbanization process in the Shih-ch'i marketing system during the decades preceding 1911.

Differential urbanization. As a comparison of Table 1 and Map 2 will show, nine of the ten lineage-sponsored bands involved in the Shih-ch'i rising came from an area traditionally known as Lung-yen-tu, or simply Lung-tu, and the tenth from an area between Lung-tu and Shih-ch'i called Ch'ang-chou. Although the Lung-tu and Ch'ang-chou areas were separated from the market by the Shih-ch'i "sea," a major branch of the Pearl river system in the delta region, all evidence suggests that both areas had belonged for centuries to a local marketing system dependent on Shih-ch'i.* For instance, the 1911 gazetteer map, which was the basis for Map 3, shows five major wharves along the Shih-ch'i sea: three of these were apparently for the long-distance steamer and junk lines connecting Shih-ch'i with Shun-te, Macau, and Hong Kong; but two were for local ferries to Ch'ang-chou and Lung-tu. The canal in Map 2 used by Lung-tu ferryboats to reach Shih-ch'i is discussed in the 1759 gazetteer, which indicates that such ties across the Shih-ch'i "sea" had developed long before the arrival of steamers.

On the other hand, there is no record of major bands coming to join the uprising from any place outside the Shih-ch'i marketing area. The pirates who had taken over Hsiao-lan a few days earlier showed no interest in joining the Shih-ch'i insurrection, nor was there any response from the area known as "Sixteen Delta Sands of the Eastern Sea" (*Tung-hai shih-liu-sha*), an area of alluvial land to the northeast of Shih-ch'i, where the local self-defense organization had probably the best fighting capacity in the county. Since it is hard to imagine the T'ung-meng Hui overlooking this potential source of support, we must look elsewhere for an explanation. One is provided by the local gazetteers of Hsiang-shan and Shun-te counties, which reveal that although the Sixteen Delta Sands area was officially under the jurisdiction of Hsiang-shan county, the local militia organizations had actually been under the control of gentry leaders in neighboring Shun-te county for decades, if not centuries. Hsiang-shan magistrates had repeatedly attempted to wrest

---

* In its narrowest sense "Shih-ch'i" designated the market district that centered on the Grand Temple of Shih-ch'i and extended from the waterfront of the Shih-ch'i sea to the West Gate of the walled city. This is the district loosely described in gazetteers and in Tables 2 and 3 as "Outside the West Gate." However, the Shih-ch'i market directly served a major sectoral marketing system within the city trading system, whose precise boundaries are difficult to determine but which clearly extended westward from the West Gate, across the river, and through Ch'ang-chou to the Lung-tu villages. I call this system the "Shih-ch'i marketing system."

The Shih-ch'i market also provided services, as a higher-level market, to the less developed sectoral marketing communities outside the walled city's other three gates, thus gaining such dominant status that its name was commonly extended to the city as a whole. In formal administrative terms, the city was sometimes referred to as Hsiang-shan because it was the county capital; but in local references and among Hsiang-shan emigrants I interviewed in Hong Kong and elsewhere the city is called Shih-ch'i.

TABLE 2. HOUSEHOLD DISTRIBUTION IN SHIH-CH'I

District	Kind of household		Total	District percentage of total urban population
	Regular	Irregular		
Walled city	803	239	1,042	8%
Outside the West Gate	4,341	683	5,024	36
Outside the South Gate	2,486	484	2,970	21
Outside the North Gate	1,778	690	2,468	18
Outside the East Gate	1,294	366	1,660	12
Hou-hsing Street (northwest to the city)	659	69	728	5
Total	11,361	2,531	13,892	100%

SOURCE: The 1910 census survey, cited in HSHCHP, 1924 ed., ch. 2, pp. 1b–2a.

NOTE: "Irregular" households are those HSHCHP designated *fu-hu,* which seems to mean either recent settlers or temporary residents whose officially recognized native places were elsewhere. The disproportionate number of such households in the northern district is probably to be accounted for by the location in that district of the *hsün-fang-ying* provincial patrol forces, for families of the soldiers could have been counted as *fu-hu.*

control of this richly productive area from Shun-te leaders, but to no avail.[6] Thus the local bands of the Sixteen Delta Sands were indifferent to the Shih-ch'i uprising because they were controlled by Shun-te gentry leaders.

Seemingly, then, the Shih-ch'i uprising was confined to a single marketing community, namely the Shih-ch'i sectoral marketing system, and there was no spontaneous response from other sectoral marketing communities even within the large trading system centered on Shih-ch'i. This case fits the general proposition that revolutionary energy, the explosive potential underlying the uprisings during the autumn of 1911, was concentrated in certain marketing communities rather than evenly permeating the peasantry of the Canton delta.

Why should the Shih-ch'i marketing community have been more readily mobilized for revolution than adjacent communities? To answer this question, it is necessary to investigate the development of Shih-ch'i during the decades preceding the revolution, during which the city grew to some 14,000 households, with a population of around 70,000. Table 2 shows an enormous degree of urban expansion by 1910: over 90 percent of the population lived outside the walled city.

Map 3 shows Shih-ch'i in 1911. The district lying outside the West Gate, in which the Shih-ch'i market was located, was the most heavily settled part of the city, with a total of over 5,000 households, almost five times more than within the walled city. Here also were the thickest concentration of streets and the city's more modern institutions, e.g. the post office, telegraph station, and Western hospital. The data in Table 3,

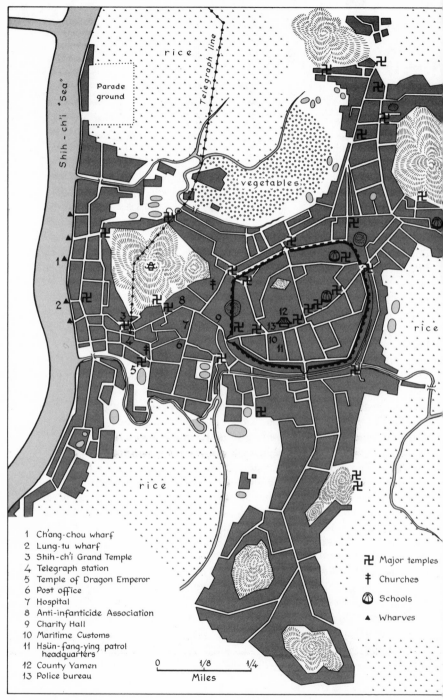

1 Ch'ang-chou wharf
2 Lung-tu wharf
3 Shih-ch'i Grand Temple
4 Telegraph station
5 Temple of Dragon Emperor
6 Post office
7 Hospital
8 Anti-infanticide Association
9 Charity Hall
10 Maritime Customs
11 Hsün-fang-ying patrol
   headquarters
12 County Yamen
13 Police bureau

卐 Major temples

✝ Churches

🅢 Schools

▲ Wharves

0   1/8   1/4
Miles

MAP 3. THE CITY OF SHIH-CH'I ON THE EVE OF THE REVOLUTION

TABLE 3. GROWTH OF DISTRICTS OUTSIDE THE WALLS OF SHIH-CH'I
(*Number of li*)

District	1673	1750	1827	1873	1911
Outside the West Gate	1	10	15	15	30
Outside the North Gate	2	5	13	15	8
Outside the East Gate	4	9	10	11	6
Outside the South Gate	12	14	14	21	21
Total	19	38	52	62	65

SOURCES: HSHCHP, 1673, 1750, 1827, 1873 and 1924, sponsored by Shen Liang-han, Pao Yü, Chu Huai, T'ien Ming-yao, and Li Shih-chin, respectively. Although the latest edition (by *Li*) was published in 1924, most of its data precede 1911.

NOTE: *Li* refers to a territorial unit whose basic function in the late Ch'ing period was probably the allocation of tax quotas.

taken from five successive editions of the county gazetteer, point up the rapid growth of the western district in the decades immediately preceding 1911. In fact, whereas all four suburbs expanded during the two centuries preceding 1873, growth after that year was limited to the western district.

The spectacular growth of the western district and the simultaneous attrition of the other districts were perhaps opposite aspects of the same development. It often happens that when the introduction of more efficient transportation favors trade at a particular location, commercial facilities in nearby centers relocate; thus the western district seems to have absorbed many of the marketing functions of the northern and eastern districts. With marketing activities now increasingly shifted to the western district, the center of gravity of the city also shifted there. This helps explain the rebels' easy takeover of the other districts of the city following the conquest of the Shih-ch'i market.

The impact of commercialization. A major factor in the rapid growth of the Shih-ch'i market was the introduction of steamboats. By virtue of its location, the western district monopolized steamshipping, and between 1873 and 1911 the city's major wharves increased from three to five. The map in the 1873 gazetteer shows a cluster of market streets surrounding the Grand Temple, with shops spreading along the roads connecting the temple with the wharves and with the West Gate; to the south of these streets there were still many vacant areas marked with the character *t'ang* (ponds). On the 1911 map, not only has the market expanded enormously, but all the areas previously marked *t'ang* are filled with streets and residential lanes. Nothing like the same growth occurred in the other districts.[*]

[*] The tremendous impact of steamboats on transportation and marketing in China was due not merely to their shipping capacity and speed, but also to their low cost

Even prior to the introduction of modern transportation, Hsiang-shan county exported agricultural products to the urban centers of Shun-te and other delta counties. The introduction of steamboats on the Shih-ch'i "sea" encouraged farmers near the city to grow rice primarily as a commercial crop. By 1911 the seasonal export of rice from Hsiang-shan reached such high levels—an annual value of over five million taels, or almost three-quarters of the county's total exports—that some 300,000 taels' worth of cheaper Siamese rice had to be imported annually for local consumption.[7] Shih-ch'i had thus developed into a leading transit port for rice on the delta, and Lung-tu merchants had become prominent in the rice trade, as they are in Hong Kong to this day. In addition to its high-quality rice, the Lung-tu area was noted for the production of raw silk and silk cocoons and of fruits and vegetables, and exports of these products also initially increased with the growth of steam transport. Commercialization was particularly marked in the Lung-tu area, not only because of its intimate ties to the Shih-ch'i market but also because of the favorable ecological setting of the village communities in question. Almost all of those involved in the Shih-ch'i uprising were situated on the outer rim of a hilly area—note the twenty-foot contour on Map 2—between the level fields where rice and mulberry were cultivated and the hills where fruits and vegetables were grown.

Precisely because Lung-tu villages had responded vigorously to the initial steady expansion of commercial opportunities, they were particularly vulnerable to subsequent fluctuations in the export markets. Indeed, Lung-tu was hard hit in the first decade of the twentieth century not only by instability in the fruit and vegetable trade but by a secular decline in silk exports. A major blow came in 1911 with the full use of the Canton-Kowloon railroad, which made it possible to ship Siamese rice to various delta cities directly from Hong Kong and greatly reduced demand for the higher-priced rice from Hsiang-shan county.

Resentment against the Ch'ing government. Considering the impressive and long-sustained urban growth of the Shih-ch'i marketing community, one may well question whether the economic setbacks immedi-

---

per ton-mile—a factor hardly noticed until J. Lossing Buck's study of China's rural economy supplied the relevant data. Although one may question whether Buck's 1929–33 data are applicable to the late Ch'ing period, steamboat shipping clearly cost far less than the two common forms of transportation on the Canton delta: flat-bottomed junks and human runners carrying loads balanced at both ends of a pole. Using Buck's data (*Land Utilization in China, Statistics* [Nanking, 1937], pp. 346–47, Tables 3 and 4), G. William Skinner calculates the following comparative costs in silver dollars per ton-mile for medium distance transportation in early twentieth-century China: pole-carrying runner, 1.39; junk, 0.21; railroad, 0.09; steamboat, 0.08.

ately preceding 1911 warranted so extreme a response as an uprising. But the absolute measurement of such setbacks is far less important than their perceived effect, exacerbated in this case by the dashing of expectations nurtured by a prolonged period of prosperity. T'ung-meng Hui agitators in the county made every effort to blame its economic troubles on the evil rule of the Manchu dynasty, and to transform the widespread dissatisfaction into revolutionary action. Meanwhile, the representative of that dynasty in Kwangtung, as if playing into the revolutionaries' hands, pushed through a series of reformist programs to strengthen political control, build up new armies, and increase revenues. To cite one especially unpopular instance, a province-wide police system, an unprecedented innovation, was established in 1910. In Hsiang-shan county this meant a corps of 515 men in eleven bureaus—seven in Shih-ch'i and four more in the local market towns, including one in Lung-tu and one in Ch'ang-chou.[8]

All these reforms, of course, cost money. Indeed, the form of governmental oppression most acutely felt by Hsiang-shan people during the late Ch'ing period was the seemingly endless tax increases.* Tax riots were frequent in the Canton delta, as elsewhere, in the years before 1911, and on occasion census surveyors, mistaken for tax collectors, were beaten up.[9] An episode in June 1910 attests the widespread resentment concerning taxes in the Shih-ch'i area.[10] When a bureau was established in the city to collect the newly imposed "levies on witches, priests, monks, and nuns," a group of priests and monks came together on June 7 to organize resistance; envoys were dispatched to surrounding towns and villages. On June 12, a mob—many from Lung-tu—formed in front of the bureau and began demolishing the building. About 9 P.M., when the *hsün-fang-ying* patrol forces moved in to back up the local police, the mob stoned the battalion commander, knocked his sedan chair to pieces, and beat up the chief of police. The new tax bureau was completely destroyed by 10 P.M., when the mob, now swollen to several thousands, moved on to assault the house of Ch'en Shan-yü, collector of the taxes for coastal defense and the excise tax on pottery. At midnight, when Ch'en's house was demolished, the mob turned to the salt-monopoly

* For a dramatic illustration of the Ch'ing government's aggressive and persistent efforts to tighten administrative control in Kwangtung during the years leading up to 1911, see my "Triads, Salt Smugglers, and Local Uprisings: Observations on the Social and Economic Background of the Waichow Revolution of 1911," in Jean Chesneaux, ed., *Popular Movements and Secret Societies in China, 1840–1950* (Stanford, Calif.: Stanford University Press, 1972), pp. 145–64. The drastic increase in salt taxes in the Waichow region in 1909–11, which cut deeply into the well-established and secret-society-based salt trade, looms unmistakably in the background of the Waichow uprising.

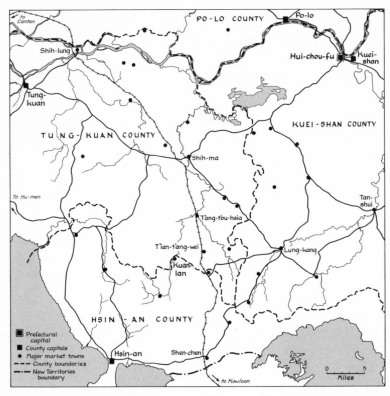

MAP 4. SETTING OF THE KUAN-LAN UPRISING

bureau, which was looted and burned. This riot dramatizes the widespread resentment against the Ch'ing government, a feeling that must have contributed to the T'ung-meng Hui's rapid success in raising people's armies throughout the Canton delta.

The Kuan-lan Uprising

The background of the second uprising we shall examine had much in common with that of the first. Bordering on the British colony of Hong Kong—in fact, with a large portion of its land recently carved off as part of the Kowloon New Territories—Hsin-an county had been as directly exposed to Western influences as Hsiang-shan. The impact of urbanization and commercialization was also felt strongly here, if only because of the demand for servicing metropolitan Hong Kong. And finally, the newly built Canton-Kowloon railroad had brought economic reverses to certain districts of both counties. In particular, the Kuan-lan market, where the forces of the uprising were first rallied, had recently felt the competition of a booming new market in nearby T'ien-t'ang-wei, the railroad station; and many other market towns involved in the Kuan-lan uprising, as we shall see, were also located on or near the railroad's southern section, which had been in use since 1906.

Possibly, then, our explanation of the Shih-ch'i uprising may be applicable to Kuan-lan: namely, that insurrectionary forces tended to appear in those marketing systems in which expectations raised during a sustained period of urbanization and commercialization were dashed by a sudden sharp reversal of economic fortunes. Although there is abundant documentation for a detailed study of urbanization in Hsin-an county in the decades preceding 1911, I would prefer to use my space here to explore some other facets of the Kuan-lan uprisings. In particular, thanks to the recent publication of a daily chronicle kept by the commander of the revolutionary troops and annotated by a fellow participant, both members of the T'ung-meng Hui, we have a rare opportunity to observe in detail the actual development of an uprising and the metamorphosis of a people's army. The next four paragraphs offer a résumé of this chronicle, and much of what follows is based on it.[11]

The initial uprising was staged in Kuan-lan on October 30; the major battle was won in a neighboring town, Lung-kang, on November 3. On their way back to Kuan-lan from this battle on November 4 the revolutionaries were ambushed by a band from the town of Tan-shui, which attempted to take custody of the captured government troops. A patrol officer from the *hsün-fang-ying* troops stationed in Hsin-an city defected to the rebels at Kuan-lan on November 5, bringing 80 soldiers with him.

On November 6 news arrived that the county authorities at Hsin-an city were prepared to surrender, but before Kuan-lan forces reached the county capital peasant bands from other towns had already poured into the walled city. The revolutionary forces, after reestablishing order, left only a few garrison forces there; the main force departed on November 7 for the prosperous town of Shen-chen, some 60 *li* to the east. In exchange for generous donations from Shen-chen merchants, the revolutionary leaders assigned a band of 40 men to police the local market.

Two days later the revolutionary troops started north toward Canton along the Canton-Kowloon railroad. Their first major target was Shih-ma (now Chang-mu-t'ou), a flourishing market town at the junction of the principal roads connecting the Waichow region with the railroad. Before they reached Shih-ma, however, they heard rumors that routed Manchu battalions were approaching from Waichow. The revolutionaries accordingly stopped and concentrated their forces at T'ang-t'ou-hsia (or T'ang-hsia), a big market town on the rail line.

The next morning (November 10), when they found the rumors were false, the bands poured into Shih-ma. On November 11 they occupied the larger market town of Shih-lung, located at the junction of the East River and the railroad to Canton. That same day they received the news that the provincial capital had been taken by other revolutionary forces. The chronicle ends with a very brief account of the Kuan-lan troops' march to Canton, where they joined forces with other revolutionary troops.

The role of market towns. The strategic importance of market towns and their central role in such local uprisings can be seen even in this very sketchy account of events. The two revolutionary chroniclers obviously took the towns rather than the villages as their points of reference. As far as they could recall, it was in the *towns* that various kinds of support were secured; from one *town* to another that the military moves were directed; and over the security or control of *towns* that battles were fought. The chronicle mentions eight towns and the county capital of Hsin-an, but not a single village.

Indeed, individual villages seem to have no identity of their own. The term *hsiang-min*, meaning the people of a community, invariably appears after the name of a market town, not a village: thus "Kuan-lan hsiang min" for participants from the area around the town of Kuan-lan, "Lung-kang hsiang min" for those from around the town of Lung-kang. This suggests that what mattered to our chroniclers was the marketing community, the town and its dependent villages as a unit. Serving as the node of a marketing system in peaceful times, the market town also played the central role in revolutionary operations within that system. Further, as we shall see, the subsequent development of the mobilization process reflected the hierarchy of marketing centers, which was of course not identical with the formal hierarchy of administrative centers. Let us begin with the operations at the market town of Kuan-lan.

The revolutionaries who came from Hong Kong to organize the uprising brought with them only revolutionary ideals, enthusiasm, and a handful of Hong Kong paper currency. Presumably they also had some preliminary contacts with local elements. But they needed men, weapons, and funds, which had to be raised in the Kuan-lan area in the few days following the uprising. A local theatrical troupe made the first donation, and many merchant households in Kuan-lan also contributed. The headquarters of the revolutionary bands was a large store at the market, borrowed from someone who was presumably a clansman of the band commander. Volunteers were recruited from neighboring villages, and a loan of one hundred Mauser rifles was secured.

As the movement developed, Kuan-lan changed from a launching pad for the uprising to a center for revolutionary operations. As soon as a sizable band had been organized, a mass rally was held in the town and brigades were dispatched to occupy strategic points, to attack other towns, and to ambush government troops. News of other uprisings was received and pondered; negotiations with envoys from the county magistrate were conducted there. After the main forces had marched to Lung-kang, Kuan-lan was still retained as a logistical center. As soon as they had won the battle at Lung-kang, the bands returned to Kuan-lan, along with hundreds of captured government soldiers.

Kuan-lan's importance was to diminish after the county capital was taken, however, and especially after the revolutionary troops had moved on to the big and prosperous town of Shen-chen. By then the movement had shifted from the local level to higher levels of the marketing hierarchy. While the revolutionary leaders were busily engaged in planning the march to Canton, many local bands left Shen-chen for home.

To judge from the presence of at least one store large enough to serve as a revolutionary headquarters, from the ability of local merchants to contribute handsomely to the revolutionary coffers, and from the existence of a theatrical troupe in the town, Kuan-lan was evidently a local economic center of some importance. That it was also a natural political center is clear from the revolutionaries' "instant" acquisition of men and weapons from surrounding villages and perhaps especially the loan of a hundred rifles overnight at a time when guns were considered more precious than a villager's life. Whatever form of personal credit may have been involved, it worked effectively: on the eve of the revolutionaries' entering of Canton, the rifles were duly returned.

The Kuan-lan community. As we have seen with the "Sixteen Delta Sands," the alignment of a natural area like the one dependent on Kuan-lan has no necessary relation to the boundaries of formal administrative units. The movement of local bands in the Kuan-lan area during the thirteen-day crisis clearly points to a case of cross-cutting alignments.

Kuan-lan in 1911 was located very near, and possibly right on, the border between Hsin-an and Tung-kuan counties, and was within walking distance of the border of Kuei-shan county (later known as Hui-yang).* At the next level up, Kuan-lan can also be seen to lie near the

---

* An 1892 provincial atlas places Kuan-lan in Tung-kuan county (see Liao T'ing-cheng et al., eds., *Kuang-tung yü ti t'u shuo* [Explanatory notes for the

border of two prefectures, namely Kuang-chou prefecture, which included Hsin-an and Tung-kuan counties, and Hui-chou prefecture,
which included Kuei-shan county. The local marketing community dependent on Kuan-lan naturally fell within the administrative domain of
these three counties and two prefectures. As our chronicle clearly indicates, the administrative authorities took Kuan-lan as part of Hsin-an
county; but trade and commerce in Kuan-lan were traditionally oriented
toward T'ang-t'ou-hsia, a big market town downstream, and, more recently, toward T'ien-t'ang-wei, the nearest railroad station, where a new
market was flourishing. Both T'ang-t'ou-hsia and T'ien-t'ang-wei were on
the Tung-kuan side of the county border. It is obvious that Kuan-lan's
marketing activities could not have been confined to a single county.
Both Hsin-an and Tung-kuan counties (and probably even Kuei-shan
county as well) shared the territory and revenues of this prosperous
marketing community.

The battle at Lung-kang and its aftermath further demonstrate to us,
if further evidence is needed, that the local marketing community
around Kuan-lan and Lung-kang functioned as a natural political unit
regardless of administrative boundaries. Government forces had been
drawn to the area initially by the disturbing news that massive people's
armies were gathering at Tan-shui in preparation for a siege of Waichow. In order to attack the Tan-shui bands from the rear, a battalion
of the *hsün-fang-ying* patrol forces set out from the Bogue (Hu-men),
passing by Kuan-lan en route.

To the T'ung-meng Hui leaders from Hong Kong, the prospective
siege of Waichow by the Tan-shui forces was exciting news; but to their
local followers at Kuan-lan, both Tan-shui and Waichow seemed too
remote to be of any immediate concern. The rumor of approaching
troops, however, was another matter. The Kuan-lan leaders' first reaction was to dispatch a band of one hundred men to intercept the troops.
When they were told that this band was far outnumbered by the invad-
ing forces, they followed up by mobilizing all the fighting bands available from Kuan-lan.

Despite their superior arms, the government troops fought only half-
heartedly. After an initial skirmish lasting about half an hour, the troops
pulled away and raced toward their assigned destination at Tan-shui.

Kwangtung atlas], 1892, ch. 1, p. 20b), as does the Tung-kuan county gazetteer
of 1919. However, an earlier Hsin-an county gazetteer places Kuan-lan in Hsin-an
county, and a provincial survey conducted in 1934 indicates that jurisdiction over
the town was then still disputed between these two counties (see local maps in
Min cheng t'ing, ed., *Kuang-tung ch'üan sheng ti fang chi yao* [A province-wide
survey of local conditions in Kwangtung], 1934).

This move suggested weakness and invited attack from a local mob in the Lung-kang area. Before nightfall the government troops were encircled on a small hill south of the market of Lung-kang. The local people generously aided the fighters from Kuan-lan, providing them with food and bedding, lighting the hillside with an ocean of torches, and finally cutting off the water supply to the hillside where the government troops were encamped. The troops surrendered the next day.

The enthusiastic support given the Kuan-lan revolutionaries by the people of Lung-kang contrasts strongly with their cool and distant attitude toward Tan-shui, even though Lung-kang was in the same county and prefecture as Tan-shui. In spite of the strategic importance of the battle at Waichow, the Kuan-lan and Lung-kang bands made no move to join forces with the Tan-shui bands. Their first concern was with the security of their own community. They were also attracted by the soldiers' weapons, and when the Kuan-lan leaders marched into the government encampment following the surrender, they found that rifles and ammunition had been looted by the Lung-kang mob.

My informants from the area tell me that the Lung-kang dialect is closely similar to that of Kuan-lan, but different from that of the Hakka-dominated Tan-shui area; that old feuds have left lingering hostility between the inhabitants of Lung-kang and Tan-shui; and that the county line was redrawn in the 1950's so as to include the town of Lung-kang in Pao-an (previously Hsin-an) county. The hostility between the two communities may be seen in the above-mentioned incident following the victory at Lung-kang, when a band from Tan-shui attacked the Kuan-lan bands on their way home and tried to take away their government prisoners. The fighting was called off only after the revolutionary leaders from the two sides reached an understanding that the soldiers who were familiar with the Bogue fortress should stay with the Kuan-lan bands to assist in future attacks on the fortress. The Tan-shui revolutionary leaders could not dissuade their followers from attacking until it was clear that the prisoners no longer had their rifles.

The metamorphosis of the revolutionary forces. The Kuan-lan uprising may be divided into two phases. In the initial phase, i.e. during the nine days before the occupation of Shen-chen, it was strictly a local uprising. The insurgents were mainly concerned about establishing control over the local market towns; their ultimate goals extended little beyond taking over the county capital. After the rebel troops moved into Shen-chen, however, the operation shifted to the higher-level urban centers, and the insurgents began to think of occupying the remote provincial capital, Canton. Although the same revolutionary leaders were in command throughout the movement, the major participating forces differed greatly in character during the two stages.

One is struck in the accounts of the first nine days by the predominance of local bands and the mobs with which they were so closely associated. The revolutionary chroniclers understandably praise the idealism and discipline of the revolutionary forces, but the facts they present suggest that the tiny revolutionary contingent under the T'ung-meng Hui leaders' direct command was dwarfed by the local mob. The latter's support had its attractions: the victory at Lung-kang, for instance, would have been impossible without them. But they also posed problems of public order, notably in Hsin-an city and Shen-chen.

In effect, the "revolutionary army" probably differed less from the mob than some chroniclers would have us believe. For instance, certain revolutionary troops from towns other than Kuan-lan who had agreed to confine their operations to Tung-kuan county, leaving Hsin-an county to the Kuan-lan forces, rushed toward Hsin-an city when they heard that the county authorities were ready to hand over the city. The Kuan-lan forces themselves were little better. Three of their leaders and over a hundred troops left Shen-chen for home as soon as they learned that the town was already controlled by an armed police corps. They had no enthusiasm for a "northern expedition" to Canton.

As more and more peasant bands melted away during the expedition to Canton, their place was taken by other elements, among them the newly surrendered regular soldiers, recruits from among the railroad workers, and forces sponsored by the secret societies. Before the troops had reached Shih-lung, for instance, a Triad force of over a hundred men, calling itself the Fourth Army, had taken control of traffic on the East River; after intercepting a navy gunboat carrying rice to the government troops at Waichow, they shared their loot with the revolutionaries. To be sure, some local bands that had personal ties with the revolutionary leaders followed the troops to Canton, but the difference in the character of the main forces at the two stages is clear.

Conclusions

Although any conclusions derived from these two episodes in the Canton delta must of necessity be tentative, certain interesting common themes emerge. First, the two dissident forces—and indeed such forces in all the local uprisings reported throughout the delta during the revolutionary months of 1911—came exclusively from marketing communities that had enjoyed prosperity for a significant period but had recently encountered sharp economic reversals.

Of the many examples of other uprisings that might be adduced here, two must suffice. The decline of the silk trade was no less devastating in the town of Le-ts'ung, south of Fo-shan, than it was in the Lung-tu area. Founded in the early eighteenth century as a center for processing and marketing silk cocoons, Le-ts'ung became a major silk center in the nineteenth century after the introduction of semi-modern machine-reeling techniques. In the years around 1911, after a large number of Le-ts'ung's silk workshops had been closed down, several disturbances and uprisings occurred in the town.

Similarly, the Kowloon-Canton railroad affected not only Shih-ch'i and Kuan-lan but many other cities and market towns. Shih-lung, for instance, which had for centuries been a key transit port for flat-bottomed junks plying their trade along the East River between the Canton delta and the Waichow region, lost much of its trade to Shih-ma with the opening of the railroad. Although both towns were close to the new railroad, Shih-ma was advantageously situated at the junction of the railroad and the principal highways leading directly to the Waichow region. In 1911 the Triads staged an uprising at Shih-lung.

Second, the local uprisings of 1911 clearly reflected the importance of natural marketing systems, and their independence of formal administrative boundaries. Thus although Shih-ch'i, for instance, was the administrative seat of the whole of Hsiang-shan county, the Shih-ch'i uprising attracted no forces from outside the city's western sectoral marketing community. Conversely, the cooperation of Kuan-lan and Lung-kang against government troops suggests a natural political community persisting in the face of an administrative division. Of the towns mentioned above, Shih-lung, T'ien-t'ang-wei, and Shen-chen were all situated close to county or prefectural borders, and the marketing communities dependent on them crossed those borders.

Third, as the prairie fire of revolution spread, the movements of the people's armies closely reflected the hierarchical structure of the marketing systems. We see this pattern not only in the Kuan-lan uprising, but in the way young peasants from the Lung-tu area congregated at the Shih-ch'i market, the way secret-society forces gathered at market towns like Tan-shui and Shih-lung and then jointly laid siege to Waichow, and the way the revolutionary armies that had assembled at Fo-shan, Shih-ch'i, and other cities in or near the Canton delta were ultimately brought by T'ung-meng Hui leaders to metropolitan Canton.

There are obvious reasons why any successful revolutionary movement had to climb this hierarchy. For one thing, the local centers could provide neither the influence nor the resources that such a movement would eventually need; these could come only from higher-level centers, the nodes of larger, higher-order marketing systems. For another, the goal of political revolution is after all to conquer the central places in the formal administrative hierarchy—the county, prefectural, and provincial capitals—and through them to control the territories they administer; and in practice control of the major economic central places in an area facilitates seizure of its administrative nerve center. In these terms the aims of revolutionary activity have long been clear. What the marketing-hierarchy approach adds is a deeper understanding of the mechanisms by which these aims are achieved or frustrated.

Fourth and last, careful attention to the marketing hierarchy facilitates the researcher's task of distinguishing among various kinds of people's armies. Militia forces, "clan-feud" bands, delta defense corps, and the like usually operated at the lowest levels of the hierarchy: villages and small, low-order market towns. As "people's armies," they rose in 1911 to resist, ambush, and rout the government troops that invaded their territorial communities. These peasant bands would attack higher-level urban centers only after they had been aroused. As soon as the revolutionary tide ebbed, they would return to their ordinary life at the lower reaches of the hierarchy.

In order to mobilize such troops for activity extending beyond their local areas, a broader network of communication, organization, and coordination was necessary. It was here that secret societies became prominent.[*] Although lineage ties were not the sole bond of the local forces and secret-society ties were not the only ties operating at higher levels, there is no disputing this general pattern. It reflects a decline in organizational effectiveness as one moves from localized lineages to higher-order lineages and on to clans, and the increasing heterogeneity of kin groups as one moves from villages to standard marketing communities and on to higher-level, more extensive marketing systems. At these higher levels the secret societies, with their own kinds of ties, their far more extensive organizational network, and their own financial bases, seem increasingly to have replaced the lineages as channels of mobilization.

It seems safe to conclude, then, that the stage on which the drama of peasant insurrection unfolded in 1911 was not an undifferentiated platform on which the peasant actors moved at random, but rather a hierarchical structure of nested local economic systems in which urban centers occupied strategic positions. Indeed, perhaps no movement of dissi-

---

[*] For a more detailed discussion of the role of secret societies in local uprisings during the revolution, see the article cited at p. 131n.

dent peasant forces in Chinese history can be fully understood apart from this hierarchical system of marketing centers. At a still higher level of generalization, our findings raise questions about the differential political effects of urbanization in rural China. Why, for example, was revolutionary energy in the Canton delta region heavily concentrated in less urbanized marketing systems that had recently suffered severe economic reversals after sustained periods of commercial and urban growth? Why did the larger and more prosperous urban centers of the region—Canton, Fo-shan, and Waichow—play a passive or "reactionary" role in the struggle of 1911?

School-Temple and City God

STEPHAN FEUCHTWANG

When I started to research the "state cult" I had very little idea what it might have been. I knew that it was centered in the administrative capitals of China, i.e., in cities. Now that I have done some research,* I find it difficult to make my report of it directly relevant to the quality of urban life in traditional China, although it is entirely relevant to the relations between rulers and ruled in traditional China and therefore in some degree to the power structure within cities and to urban-rural relations. The state cult was of course closely related to sociopolitical control, but the objects of control were not so much the populace at large as the bureaucracy and local elites. The use of religion to control the common people may have been legitimated by the state cult, but in manipulating the masses, the managers of society necessarily looked to religious arenas outside the strict confines of official religion.

A second source of difficulty lies in the number of gross misconceptions of Chinese religion that have grown up over the years as a result in part of overcategorization, by which (for example) we have too easily identified Confucianism with state orthodoxy. The official religion as I found it in my research is not the same as the Confucianism we associate with the Confucian classics or with the schools in which they were studied. Faced with the problem of how to describe the state orthodoxy, I decided to focus on documenting the religious attitudes of officials and on discussing the place of the official religion in Chinese religion as a whole. This is not, therefore, a strict account of the rites, deities, and edifices of the official religion, although these are all mentioned in the course of the discussion.

I have translated and studied as the official religion (1) what is written

* The research on which I based this paper was conducted in March and April of 1968, thanks to the generosity of the Subcommittee on Research on Chinese Society.

in the *Ta Ch'ing hui-tien* under the headings "Tz'u-chi" (shrines and sacrifices), "Ch'i-ssu" (sacrifices and offerings), or the combined term "Tz'u-chi-su," and (2) what is contained in local gazetteers in the sections entitled "Ssu-tien" (sacrificial statutes), where official temples are listed before or apart from those of the popular religion and from those specifically Buddhist or Taoist. Official temples were also specified as *t'an-miao*, "altars and temples," whereas all others were called *tz'u-miao*, "shrines and temples"; but it must be remembered that all temples given in gazetteers were listed by their scholarly, not their popular, nomenclature, and that a great many popular temples were not listed in the gazetteers at all. *Ssu-tien*, the official religion, was also the term for rites addressed to deities, and I have of course included them; but the many other official rites not directed to deities have not been considered. The *Hui-tien* was a collection of statutes that was revised several times during the Ch'ing dynasty; I have used the one issued in the K'ang-hsi reign. In the section devoted to the affairs of the Board of Rites (*Li pu*), the whole range of *li* includes not only the official religion but also mourning rites, court etiquette, the protocol of dress at court, enfeoffment, reception of foreign dignitaries, the making and receiving of presentations, and propaganda such as *hsiang-yüeh* (the recital of the Imperial Edict in rural districts). The scope of the Board of Rites follows the example of the *Li-chi* (Record of Rites), only two sections of which—the "Chi-fa" and "Chi-i"—concern the official religion. I mention this here merely as a reminder before I narrow my sights that the official religion was only part of what we would call etiquette, protocol, ceremonial, and propriety.

"Religion" is here confined to communal, not individual, worship. "Worship" may be taken as avowed communication with beings who are not subject to the physical conditions of the known world. There are those who will count Chinese religions as three: Confucian, Taoist, and Buddhist. Others feel unable to include Confucianism as a religion, because the Confucian classics contain passages expressing scepticism over, or dismissing the issue of, the existence of "gods," and drawing attention rather to "spirits": the examples, names, and reputations of men and women who have lived and died. "Spirits," then, are heroes—historical figures whose examples are to be emulated, or one's own ancestors whose reputations are to be maintained, enhanced, or created. To make the contrast clear, we may say that such "spirits" *exist* only as names, whereas "gods" are believed to be agents.*

---

* "Agent," according to the Shorter Oxford English Dictionary, is "The efficient cause, . . . any natural force or substance which produces phenomena."

I do not want to prejudge the question of the religion of the scholar-officials of China, nor do I want to start with undefined categories that may be misleading. I want to offer a view of certain Chinese institutions of symbolic action as they were distributed throughout Chinese society. This view is logically anterior to the labeling of these institutions as Buddhist or Taoist or Confucian, which we may do either according to philological analysis and the history of the texts used in these institutions or according to the way the participants labeled the institutions and themselves. In other words, on principle, I am making a distinction between action (and institution) and interpretation (recording, philosophizing, and labeling). I am aware of the dangers of such an enterprise when it is itself based on documents checked with direct observation only in a much later period (Taiwan, 1966–68). But I have done my best to be sure that what I am reporting was real and not just paper action.

The Confrontation in the City

The establishment of an administrative city was marked by the building of city walls. Other emblems were a temple to the City God (*Ch'eng-huang miao*) and a school-temple (*hsüeh-kung*) within the walls, and at least one of the prescribed open altars outside the walls. This would seem to have been a minimum at the lowest level of administration, the county.[1]

In only very rare cases would a city have been purely administrative. It would have been founded at or next to an already existing economic center, or else it would itself have become the basis for the development of economic functions. Among the institutions almost invariably found in economic central places were temples of the popular religion, some of them centers of cults that were shared by or adopted into the religion of the state. Two such that I will draw attention to were the cults of Kuan-ti, god of trustworthiness and loyalty in war and trade, and T'ien-hou (or, to give her equivalent popular name, Ma-tsu), goddess of seafarers. Both deities were very popular as patrons for merchant associations in the Ch'ing period, T'ien-hou more so in coastal than in inland regions.

In instances where government funds officially raised were sufficient, officials could afford to build separate temples to these gods for their exclusive use, as was the case for example in the administrative walled city of T'ai-pei-fu, built late in the nineteenth century next to the flourishing port of Meng-chia. But even in such instances exclusion of the non-official populace could not last long in the life of the city as it developed its own markets and nonofficial institutions. In the case of T'ai-pei-fu, repair funds for temples came from the pockets of nonofficials. In at least one of the city temples to T'ien-hou or to Kuan-ti—there were often several to each even within the city—officials and nonofficials would mix.

Merchants desirous of converting their wealth into status and moving into the literati class would contribute to the building of official temples. In the absence of official temples, they would sponsor the building of temples to gods or spirits included in the official cults. An example of this face-improving enterprise—an even better one than the building of temples to Kuan-ti and Ma-tsu, who were popular in all classes of the population—was the building of temples dedicated to both Confucius and Kuan-ti, often called Wen-wu miao and often founded in conjunction with the establishment of a private school.*

I hope to show that there was also a counterprocess in which popular cults were incorporated into the official religion (*ssu-tien*). Kuan-ti and T'ien-hou are only two examples of popular cults thus adopted, and in their cases the adoption went so far that temples to them were built by officials throughout China. The scholar's equivalent to the merchant's T'ien-hou cult was the cult of Wen-ch'ang, which also had temples within and without the official religion throughout China. There were other cults that were less widespread, or that were honored by officials but not yet formally incorporated into the *ssu-tien*. These borderline temples were often the largest and most frequented in a city. A case in point seems to have been the Ling-ying miao, in Ningpo, cult center of a deity honored since the twelfth century by tablets with the imperial seal for various acts of protection of officials traveling at sea but not accepted into the *ssu-tien*.

Although the most crowded and striking to look at, these temples were below or at the bottom of the official religious hierarchy, which was organized into ceremonial divisions. Tables 1, 2, and 3 chart this ceremonial hierarchy. All the open, suburban altars (Table 2), except for the altar to the local unworshiped dead, are superior to the mass of the temples in the lowest level. When we move up from this point, we find a sharp distinction from popular religion. It is possible to detect the gradations of exclusion by noting from the relevant sections of the gazetteers who sponsored the building of and repairs to the several shrines. Since in at least half the cases this had not been recorded, our findings must be crude. But it appears that the altars to the land and grain and to wind-rain-thunder-clouds, as well as certain shrines to Hsien-nung (god of

---

* In Taiwan, Hsin-chu, Tainan, Kao-hsiung, and Lu-kang all had Wen-wu miao; and so did Taipo in the New Territories of Hong Kong. All of them were nonofficial temples. Both merchants and local scholars would have joined in such enterprises.

TABLE 1. THE THREE LEVELS OF SACRIFICE IN LATE CH'ING OFFICIAL RELIGION

Level	Description
1. Great Sacrifice (*ta-ssu*)	Rites at this level were conducted at the imperial capital only, either at the open suburban altars or at the temples within the walls. Sacrificial animals were washed three lunar months in advance; there was a three-day fast before the rite; and the emperor in person was the leading participant.
2. Middle Sacrifice (*chung-ssu*)	Rites at this level were conducted at the imperial capital and at lower-level capitals. Sacrificial animals were washed 30 days in advance; there was a two-day fast before the rite; and either the emperor in person (at the imperial capital) or a delegated official of the appropriate administrative rank (at lower-level capitals) was the leading participant.
3. Common Sacrifice (*ch'ün-ssu*)	Rites at this level were conducted at all capitals. Sacrificial animals were washed 10 days in advance; there was a one-day fast before the rite; and an official of the appropriate administrative rank was the leading participant.

agriculture) and Huo-shen (god of fire), were, in the two prefectures I investigated (Ning-po and T'ai-wan), the only ones sponsored exclusively by officials.° In the case of Hsien-nung and Huo-shen, however, there were other temples, not officially sponsored. This leaves the two open altars as the only exclusively official cults.

Other cults occurring in seven or more of the eleven counties are, in order of the increasing involvement of nonofficials, the altar for unworshiped dead (officials and gentry); the school-temple and Wen-ch'ang (officials, gentry, and commoners, with gentry outnumbering commoners); the City God; and T'ien-hou and Kuan-ti (officials, gentry, and commoners, with commoners outnumbering gentry).[2]

Since the *Li-chi* was written, every dynasty has had its version of the official religion, and the changes it underwent as dynasty succeeded dynasty, and reign succeeded reign, were substantial. Even the several open altars (to the land and grain, to wind-rain-thunder-clouds, to mountains and rivers, and to unworshiped dead—all cults directly sanc-

° I have put under the general heading "officials" all persons referred to by office above and including the rank of magistrate. "Gentry" are all those given only examination-degree title or referred to merely as *shih* or *shen-shih*. And "people" are those referred to as *min*, plus merchants, monks, priests, and men named but without degree or title. It is, of course, more than likely that common people contributed either through special taxes or through a special fund in cases where only officials and gentry were actually named.

TABLE 2. MAJOR OFFICIAL TEMPLES WITHIN THE WALLS, CH'ING CHINA

Great Sacrifice (ta-ssu) Level

Rites at this level were held in the imperial capital only, at the T'ai miao (Great Temple).

The objects of worship were the ancestors of the reigning emperor; great imperial predecessors; and great statesmen and warriors.

Worship was held on auspicious days in the 1st month of each of the four seasons; on Ch'ing Ming; and on the birthdays and death-days of the objects of worship.

The color of the silk offerings and notices (petitions) was white with yellow borders.

Middle Sacrifice (chung-ssu) Level

Emperors of previous dynasties were worshiped at the imperial capital only, at the Li-tai Ti-wang miao (Temple of All Former Emperors).

The rite was held on an auspicious day in the 8th lunar month.

The color of the silk offerings and notices was white with yellow borders.

Confucius and his disciples, their respective fathers and most noted followers; famous officials; wise men; and virtuous women were worshiped at the imperial and lower-level capitals, at the Wen miao (Temple of Civil Culture) or the Hsüeh-kung (School-Temple).

Rites were held on the 4th stem day of the 1st hsün of the 2d and 10th lunar months.

The color of the silk offerings and notices was white with yellow borders.

Common Sacrifice (ch'ün-ssu) Level
Rites at this level were held at all capitals

1. Kuan-ti (Imperial Ruler of the Passes, or God of War) was worshiped at the Wu miao (Temple of Military Culture) on the 13th day of the 5th lunar month.	2. Hsien-i (Former Physicians) or Huang-ti, Fu-hsi, and Shen-nung (the Three Emperors of Man, Heaven, and Earth) were worshiped at the San-huang miao (Temple of Three Emperors) on the 1st stem day of the 1st hsün in the 2d and 11th lunar months.	3. Huo-shen (the Fire God) was worshiped at the Huo-shen miao on the 23d day of the 6th lunar month.	4. Lung-shen (the Dragon God) and/or other gods of water, rain, and sea travel were worshiped at the Lung-shen tz'u.	5. Ch'eng-huang (the City God), often in association with military gods and the gods of the North and of the Sacred Eastern Peak, was worshiped at the Ch'eng-huang miao on an auspicious day in the 8th lunar month and on the emperor's birthday.

Sacrificial level and location of altar	Object of worship	Shape of altar	Date of worship	Color of offerings
Great sacrifice, Imperial cap, S suburb	T'ien (Heaven); plus the tablets of WRTC° and of the heavenly bodies (from the agriculture complex)	Round mound	Winter solstice, and (from 1742) New Year's morning (harvest prayer)	Green-blue
Great sacrifice, Imperial cap, N suburb	Ti (Earth); plus tablets of the 5 mountains and of the 4 seas (from the agriculture complex)	Square with a pit	Summer solstice	Yellow
Great sacrifice, Imperial cap, N suburb	She-chi (Land and Grain)	Square with a pit	5th stem day of the 1st *hsün* of the middle months of Spring and Autumn	The 5 colors of the 5 elements
Middle sacrifice, Imperial cap, E suburb	Chao-jih (Sun)	Round mound	Vernal equinox of odd-numbered stem years	Red
Middle sacrifice, Imperial cap, W suburb	Hsi-yüeh (Moon)	Square with a pit	Autumnal equinox of certain branch years	—
Middle sacrifice (after 1726), Imp. and lower-level caps, S suburb	Hsien-nung (patron deity of agriculture); plus, at the Imperial capital only, tablets of WRTC and MR,° and the Great Year Calendar	Round mound	*Hsien-nung*, 12th branch day of the 1st *hsün* of the middle month of Spring; *Great Year Calendar*, the New Year	White with yellow borders
Middle sacrifice, provincial and lower-level caps, N or E suburb	Local Land and Grain; and, on separate altars, WRTC and local MR	Square	*Land and Grain*, 5th stem day of the 1st *hsün* of the middle months of Spring and Autumn; *WRTC and MR*, 6th branch day of the middle months of Spring and Autumn	*Land and Grain*, black; *WRTC and MR*, white
Common sacrifice, provincial and lower-level caps, N suburb	Li (the local unworshiped dead, overseen by the City God)	Square	Ch'ing Ming, Chung-yüan (the 15th day of the 7th month), and Meng-tung (the 1st day of the 10th month)	White

SOURCES: *Ta Ch'ing hui tien*, K'ang-hsi edition (1690), and contemporary local gazetteers.
° WRTC = Wind-Rain-Thunder-Clouds. MR = Mountains and Rivers.

tioned in the *Li-chi*—have been changed in their position around the city, merged, separated, neglected, or rehabilitated, both in the ritual statutes and in practice. The official cults that occurred with greater regularity in county capitals, including those to Confucius and the City God, were only indirectly sanctioned by the *Li-chi* and its criteria for the Five Sacrifices (the *wu chi-ssu*). They all had histories of entitlement as gods and promotion through feudal ranks of nobility, and they were all popular as well as official. Judging from the Ning-po gazetteers, which are continuous from the Sung to the Ch'ing, the cults that survived most steadily and for the longest time were those of the schools (to Confucius) and of Kuan-ti and the City God. Cults to other gods derived from the popular religion were subject to the vagaries of imperial favor; canonization might last only as long as a dynasty.

People without degrees or aspirations to join the scholar-official class did not generally frequent the school-temple for the official worship of Confucius and worthy Confucians, much less the open altars. But even where commoners and officials shared temples, official rituals were distinctive in their ceremonial, in the absence of priests, and in the strict order of participation by official rank and degree.

The county capital was the lowest level of the hierarchy both of yamens and of official temples and altars. In nonadministrative cities and towns, and in all lower places in the central-place hierarchy, temples of popular cults proliferated. It was in administrative capitals that popular religion met with and contrasted with official religion: the theater, noise, color, urgency, and bustle (in short, *je-nao*) of the popular temple contrasted with the dignified and ascetic seclusion of the official shrine; the market contrasted with the yamen.

There were several ways in which popular temples and markets were associated. A temple might have housed the figure of the patron deity of a guild and have been the meeting place for guild members for both secular and sacred business—that is to say, annual worship, feasts, and theatrical entertainment. The open space in front of the temple, the temple yard, might have been the site for regular markets or fairs, as well as for theater; temple dues would then have been collected from the traders. In other cases a popular temple might have produced its own commerce on festival days in ritual goods (incense, spirit money, candles), food, snacks, fortune-telling and so on. The official altars and the school-temple had none of these associations.

City God temples, on the other hand, as much as if not more than any other shrines, were the sites of markets and all other kinds of *je-nao*. The cult of the City God was only partially incorporated in the Ch'ing *ssu-*

tien. Yet because such temples existed only in cities (unlike the temples of other popular cults), they were closely associated with the idea of official government—so much so that officials had to perform certain ritual duties at them. City God temples were linked according to the organizational principle characteristic of the altars of the official religion.

Various aspects of the position of the City God cult as a point of transformation between the official and the popular religions will be developed throughout this paper. Here I want to dwell briefly on some of the marks of distinction between the two, including the organizational principle I just mentioned. Gods in the top and middle ranges of official ritual were represented by narrow upright blocks of wood called *shen-wei* (deity position) or *shen-p'ai* (deity board) or just *chu* (roughly, "host"). These blocks were inscribed with the full title of the being to be worshiped at them, and they resembled in all ways the tablets for ancestors on domestic altars and in ancestral halls. As far as I know there was no special ceremony for the consecration of a tablet, not even the dotting that was done to inject the spirit of the deceased into an ancestral tablet. This contrasts strongly with the elaborate rite for the consecration of images in the popular religion, which was an elaborate version of the dotting rite.

The eyes of a properly made and consecrated image, I have heard it said, should light up when incense is burned in front of them. Such an image is said to contain *ling* (numen, or uncanny intelligence and power). In the ceremony of consecration, the priest inscribes a mirror or an incense pot in front of the image with a charm headed by the character *ling*; he then performs *fa* (magic ritual), in which all the parts of the body, which are a microcosm of the universe, are invoked and an oath written in the air for each. A crude form of consecration involves the killing of a chicken and the dotting of the image's ears (by which the god hears prayers) with its blood. Also dotted with blood are the mouth (by which the *ling* of the god responds to prayer), the eyes (*yin* and *yang*), and the nose (human society), as an expert told me in Taiwan. Into the back of the image are placed the five precious metals, the five viscera, plaited threads in the colors of the Five Elements, and a piece of bread or a living thing—for instance, a bee. To purify the image, Huo-shen is then invoked in some cases, a stretch of burning coals or burning spirit money laid out and the image carried over it.

Ideally, in the regulations of the *Hui-tien*, the official cults celebrated at the open altars and the City God cults were set in a ranked hierarchy that exactly paralleled the administrative one, i.e., the county-level cults were subdivisions of the prefectural-level cults, and so on up to the imperial capital. The regulations were not often put into practice exactly, but their principle was followed. For instance, the tablet at the altar of the land and grain would have inscribed on it "*hsien* land and grain" at a county-capital altar, "*fu* land and grain" at a prefectural-capital altar, and so on. The school-temples were also subdivided. They were ranked according to administrative level and there were rules specifying the rank and position of the chief celebrants—prefect for prefecture, magistrate for county. It is not surprising that the official religion should have been organized in this way parallel to, and indeed dovetailed with, the imperial bureaucracy. In contrast is the principle of organization that was peculiar to popular religion. A temple that had grown up around a peculiarly powerful manifestation of a deity became a center of that deity's cult from which shrines subdivided by a process known, in southeastern China at least, as "division of incense" (*fen-hsiang*) or "division of power" (*fen-ling*). There were, for instance, according to the Republican *Yin hsien t'ung chih*, in the first urban district of Yin *hsien* twelve branch temples of the cult whose center was the above-mentioned Ling-ying miao in Ningpo.[3]

The most important ideological difference between the two principles of organization was that the popular division was of a specific *shen-ming* (god) and his power, or of the *place* where *ling* had been remarkably manifest; official division, in the case of City Gods and official altars, was based on administrative level, independent of the *shen-ming*. The structure of official cults was not subject to the vagaries of supernatural power and its manifestations. As for such borderline cults as that of T'ien-hou (Ma-tsu) on the popular side, continued worship of a *shen-ming* depended on repeated miracles—response to prayers. Once a deity was adopted by the *ssu-tien*, however, worship of it was a remembrance and became a regular spring and autumn duty.

The bureaucratic division of areas into lesser areas of supernatural administration continued down into the countryside below the county level. But the division of power was peculiar to the popular religion; and, in Taiwan at least (and I see no reason in this case why Taiwan should be exceptional), many city temples were and are the centers of networks of local village temples—networks established by the ritual of the division of incense from the city temple's incense burner. At the popular level, the social jurisdiction of a temple—whether that temple is a bureaucratic subdivision of another, a center of a network, a branch temple, or an independent temple—is known as *lu-hsia* (those beneath its incense burner). As far as I know, this expression was never used for official temples. It signifies the absence of the discrimination by rank and class that characterized the official cults. A popular temple's area is defined purely territorially—all those within a given territory, whatever their rank or class, are expected to participate in its major festivals, at least by paying the ritual maintenance tax.

A point I shall develop later is that village temples had the character of being for the village area what the City God temple was for the capital. But it was not these local village temples (very often centers or divisions of *fen-hsiang* networks) that the officials who wrote the gazetteers considered to be subdivisions of their own cults and therefore the only proper temples for the people of the county. The only ceremonies they encouraged for the people were spring and autumn rites at the temples they called *she* or *t'u-ku shen*, or at the altars for *li*. Virtuous local elders, not officials, were supposed to officiate at them. The *she* temples were obviously considered to be subdivisions of the capital's *she-chi* (land and grain) altar, and the *li* a subdivision of the capital's *i* or *hsien-li* (unworshiped dead) altar. What they were calling *she* temples were in fact what the people generally call *t'u-ti* (local territory) temples. What they would have liked to think of as local *li* shrines I think must have been what in northern Taiwan are usually called Yu-ying-kung (Responsive Gentlemen)—a euphemism for those dead that have become malicious, that have to be calmed with offerings of food and money, and that in some cases may reverse their negative power into a positive beneficial one in order to pass out of purgatory.*

The official interpretations were attempts at controlling popular religion. It would appear from a passage in the gazetteer of Fo-shan *chen* in Kwangtung, quoted by C. K. Yang,[4] that this nominalistic control was sometimes converted into practice. It is there described how the rites of the "earth and grain god" in every neighborhood of one hundred households were (or should be?) used for "the reading of the law and the elucidation of the agreements" to help the poor and aged, and for feasting in order of seniority and rank. In this way "officials who are skilled in government use the gods to assemble the people, and use the congregation to demonstrate the rules. This may be a good way to improve the customs and traditions."

Kung-chuan Hsiao in his *Rural China* considered the state religion to be a form of ideological control in nineteenth-century China, putting it after the *hsiang-yüeh* (Imperial Edict) lecture system. I want now to

---

* There are a number of other names for similar types of shrines. Common in other parts of Taiwan is Wan-hsi T'ung-kuei (Ten Thousand Joys for Those Returned [or Gathered] Together), another euphemistic title for shrines containing the bones of those found dead—for example, the bones of the unknown soldier and the unidentified stranger.

sketch out the attitude of officials to the rites as a form of control—how rites were to be used, and what they were meant to encourage and discourage.

Ideological Control

Performing the rites correctly was believed to have lasting effect, to exemplify the order of the universe, and to maintain the correct distinctions. Mencius, whose work (as part of the Confucian classics) was chanted in the school-temples much as sutras were in Buddhist shrines, excoriated as heretics the epicurean Yang Chu and the undiscriminating humanitarian Mo Ti. Lack of discrimination and egalitarianism would lead to cannibalism and bestiality, he wrote.[5] The school-temple, or more colloquially, the Temple of Civil Culture (*Wen miao*), was as its name implies both school and shrine. It was in two parts. One was centered on the main shrine, in which stood the tablets for Confucius and his peers. The other half was centered on the Ming-lun T'ang (the hall in which human relationships are illuminated). Next to it was a small pagoda mainly for Wen-ch'ang, the patron of learning, but often also for tablets in memory of renowned local officials and scholars. Magistrate Chou of Chu-lo *hsien* in Taiwan rebuilt the school-temple in the capital of his county in 1715 and added a Ming-lun T'ang, which to his expressed regret it had lacked. Since the school's establishment, he wrote, the county had had to wait thirty years for a place of ritual, music, and instruction in the teaching of the three ancient dynasties (Hsia, Shang, and Chou), which illuminate the human relationships (ruler-official, father-son, husband-wife, elder brother–younger brother, friend-friend). As the provincial governor of Fukien had written in his memorial for the completion of the Ming-lun T'ang in the capital of Taiwan (present-day Tainan), "Since there have been humans there have been human minds and human principles. Since heaven creates and earth forms, there is a Ming-lun T'ang [to make creation and formation intelligible (*ming*) is the function of man (*jen*) in the San Ts'ai—the Three Powers of Heaven, Earth, and Man]. If the hall is not established then the children of gentlemen have no place to discuss and recite [*chiang-sung*, the process of learning and rehearsing the classics by heart]. This would inevitably lead to the obscuring of human relationships, the destruction of human principles, and the darkening of the human mind. Men would no longer be human."[6]

The rites "are really the responsibility of the guardians of the land [i.e., the county magistrates]," says one of the prefaces to a handbook on ceremonial.[7] "The ritual of all matters of worship [*ssu*] has one root in reverence [*ching*]." "The rites and music and sacrificial vessels are means of reverence and of communication [*t'ung*] with the gods [*shen-ming*]. But now the rites have fallen into disarray and neglect. How can worship be serious or the keeping of the law illuminated?" This preface was written in 1835, shortly before the Opium War and the Taiping Rebellion, the beginnings of the end of the dynasty. An attempt to maintain order ritually was made by distributing the handbook to all administrative capitals so that the official religion should not be neglected. Another preface of the same handbook says that "incense and vessels [that is to say, ritual offerings] can control [keep in place, *ko*] the lower gods and spirits [*kuei-shen*]. Jade, silk, bells, and drums [other offerings and instruments of worship] can reveal the rites and music.... Awe of virtue and the passing on of merit [through worship] civilize the people and form customs."

And in the 1788 gazetteer for Yin *hsien* it is written that the *li* (rites) came down to us from the golden age of Yao and Shun. "*Ssu-tien* rituals are composed on an altar ... in order to grasp the hidden virtue of unostentatious good and spread the transforming influence of the ruler [*yüan-hua*, which also means the beginning of creation]."

There follows a passage on how the people are ruled if they respect the gods. "Gentlemen [*chün-tzu*, the literate and enlightened men] assist government well if they perform the rites and thus illuminate tradition. Prosperity results. Thus it is meritorious and scholarly. Through the secret, pure, and profound ceremony of the *shen*, the universe [*T'ien-ti*, heaven and earth] is aided and benefited and the people protected. Whereas if the altars and rites are allowed to go to rack and ruin, disaster follows."

It is evident that in the ideology of Chinese officials—who wrote the gazetteers and the handbooks on ceremonial, and who set up the shrines of the official cults—the performance of correct ritual was a vital part of man's function in the universe, which was to order what heaven had created and earth completed.[*] If order was correctly maintained, there would be universal harmony and prosperity. This was government by example, the culture of nature and society. More specifically, the rites of the official religion were a form of control, control of both the people and the lower gods.

The *Li-chi* supports the idea of social and spiritual hierarchies, which

---

[*] The gazetteers were organized and introduced by officials, who of course were never posted to their native areas. That they were outsiders writing in their official capacity undoubtedly influenced their work; in their home areas they would have been more bound to local traditions.

are, as it were, the two sides of the same ladder. Its "Chi-fa" section speci-
fies the depth of ancestry to be worshiped for each rank in the feudal
hierarchy, shortening in the climb down from the emperor until in the
last rank no ancestral shrines at all are permitted. As a worshiped ancestor, the deceased is a *shen*. But the dead of the lowest feudal class "become *kuei* as soon as they die." A full discussion of this pair of concepts
shen and *kuei* is impossible here, but a brief outline is necessary. They
are variously used in the sense of spirit and of god (or demon). Any
dead human is a *kuei*, unless he is worshiped as an ancestor or as having
lived a life worthy of commemoration, in which cases he is a *shen*. An
exalted *shen*, one whose life and works are highly respected and have
been for many generations, is called a *shen-ming*. *Kuei-shen* I take to be
a usage that developed after the time when all classes were known to
worship their ancestors; it refers to the spirits of the lowest class, of the
common people whose lives had not shone with any officially noteworthy
merit. The lowest class of spirit given credence in official religion is formally called *li*, the unworshiped dead, otherwise known as *kuei*.

But the institutions of the official religion did not of themselves restrict
interpretation of the category *shen* to the memory of ancestors and
exemplars. If anything, the substantial offerings, even to Confucius, of
cooked and uncooked food and of wine, and the burning of a eulogy
written on silk and addressing him directly, would seem already to imply
a being more active than a mere exemplar. The passage from the handbook, with its talk of communication with *shen-ming* and the control of
kuei-shen, would also seem to imply something more active.

Magistrate Chou in the gazetteer of Chu-lo *hsien* takes an agnostic
position. He recommends, in a detailed guide to the Confucian rites, the
text of a eulogy almost identical with the text given in the 1875 handbook. The one line he omits, however, is the most openly pragmatic line
of all: "You maintain the constancy of the sun and moon." The rest is confined to praise of Confucius's virtue and wisdom. Chou's position meant
discomfort in some of his religious duties as an official: "As to the establishment of the shrine to Wen-ch'ang, former people, considering the
securing of salary and office to be scholar's luck, put the absurd god of
Taoism [i.e., Wen-ch'ang] beside the former master [Confucius]. Most
of the Confucian schools in the empire have borrowed in secret the blessings of the god in order to encourage students. Nor was any of this
abolished by the sage men and sage ways of those who set up instruction.
I record its establishment." The K'ang-hsi emperor had instituted the cult
of Wen-ch'ang as part of the official religion.

The phrase "borrowed in secret" would seem to indicate not a denial of the existence of "the absurd god of Taoism" and other luck-influencing gods, as one would perhaps expect, but rather a sentiment that it is wrong to have truck with them. We shall see later how this ambiguity was acted out in the official religion when the need to apply to gods for practical results in the here and now became urgent, typically in times of flood and drought. The official did not then deny the existence of supernatural agencies, but he avoided dealing with such categories by employing Taoist priests to do the magic for him—thus withholding recognition, as it were.

The official religion, an institution of government, was subject to the wide range of interpretations put on it by the officials who ran it. But as a product of a ruling class and its history, it did set limits of orthodoxy.

Individual officials came to it with various ideological commitments and manipulated it accordingly. There would be officials like Magistrate Chou who would concentrate on the Confucian cult, deemphasize belief in the existence of demonic and supernatural agencies, and stress the enlightening function of ritual. Performance of the correct ritual for them was an exercise in the revelation of immanent reason in the universe, a process of self-enlightenment at the same time as a demonstration of that reason, dispelling confusion from the common people and hence part of the practice of good government.

The officials could believe in a *t'ien* (Heaven) that was the moral nature of the universe,[8] a metaphysical category that was dominant over all other categories, being the arbiter of their and the world's destiny (*ming*). This *t'ien* was not substantial. As Lien, the historian of Taiwan, wrote: "Good and evil depend on *t'ien*. What is *t'ien*? *T'ien* is something that has no voice and no smell, that you can see and yet cannot see, can hear and yet cannot hear.... Its meaning is naturalness [*tzu-jan*].... This cannot be comprehended by the common people, who therefore resort to Shang-ti [supreme emperor]."[9] Shang-ti is the personification of Heaven. But in many texts, despite Lien and those like him, Shang-ti and Heaven are used interchangeably where the sense is "moral arbiter,"[10] and are so used by the emperor himself in worship at the Altar of Heaven as part of the official religion.

The emperor was, after all, *t'ien-tzu*, "son of Heaven," and it was his prerogative alone to worship Heaven directly. There was only one altar to Heaven officially, and that was the one in the imperial capital. Its lower-level equivalent was the land and grain altar, one in every administrative capital. There is thus another side to the ideology of Lien and that is its support for this imperial prerogative—the maintenance of the idea of supreme power in the hands of the sage ruler. On the grounds

that the lower orders in their illiteracy and ignorance cannot understand *t'ien*, this ideology provides for the prosecution of heterodox worship of Heaven. Alternative interpretations, or challenges to the possession of the right to the cult of Heaven, were also challenges to the ruler.

Along with Lien's strictures against popular worship of Heaven went
equally strong disapproval of the use of charms and magic by Taoists,
who in Lien's words, "confused the world and cheated the people like
snakes and scorpions." An Imperial Edict of 1724 had made the point that
Taoism was strictly for the cultivation of essence, Buddhism for the non-
material, and Confucianism alone for social relations. Taoism and Buddhism were corrupt (i.e., heterodox) when they were used to affect, or
worse to organize, social relations.

To refer directly to *kuei* and *shen* for material benefits instead of to
law and order under enlightened government was corrupt. If gods or
spirits were to be worshiped, it was only in recompense for past benefits,
not in hope of future blessings. Yet government funds were spent on
astronomers, geomancers, doctors, herbalists, musicians, dancers, Buddhist monks, and Taoist priests—a nice enumeration of occupations filled
by literates who were nevertheless not part of the official literate class.[11]
Such people constituted a subclass in possession of dangerous alternative
ideologies, interpretations, and religious practices.

Practice

In order to show the limits of the official religion in action, I want now
to take up a number of contrasting pairs of religious practices as in-
dexes of transformations between the official and popular religions. For
the basis of my comparison I shall take for the official religion the annual or biannual ceremony of recompense (*pao*) called *shih-tien*, performed as I saw it in Taiwan for Confucius and prescribed, also for Confucius, in the 1875 handbook already cited. For the popular religion a
comparable ceremony is the *chiao*, which is performed in local temples
at intervals of a year or more.*

In both ceremonies there are ritual experts who guide the rest of the
participants. And in both there are among the participants some who
take leading parts and others who are generally passive. In the *shih-tien*,
the ritual experts are members of the local directorate of education and
teachers at the school. Their role is to stand on either side of the chief

* The following comparison is tentative. My knowledge of the *chiao* and the Taoist
priesthood has been substantially enlarged by discussion with Kristofer Schipper. Use
of the present tense in the following comparison for convenience and clarity should
not be taken to indicate that the official ceremonies occur in Taiwan today exactly
as they did in imperial times.

celebrants and guide them from their appointed places to wherever the rites demand they be—at an altar for instance—there handing them the proper offerings and announcing the proper number of kneels and kowtows they are to undergo. In the *chiao*, the ritual experts are Taoist religious practitioners—priests. They perform all the rites themselves, the leading participants delegating to them even the presentation of offerings and merely standing behind them, holding incense, and bowing and kneeling when signaled by the priests to do so.

The knowledge that the experts in the official religion have is qualitatively no different from that of the rest of the participants. They are set apart from the other participants only to the extent that specialists in one branch of government are from specialists in another. Neither does the ceremony itself remove them from the other participants. The leading participants lead by virtue of their rank, which has been established outside the ceremony. The knowledge of the Taoists, on the other hand, is gained only after a rite of passage that initiates them to a more sacred status than that of the rest of the population. Their knowledge is esoteric, and at points in the ceremony they propitiate those patron deities through whom they have their knowledge—deities whose worship is not shared by the other participants. And the ceremony itself gives the leading participants a more protected and more sanctified status than it gives the rest.

In both ceremonies, then, there is status differentiation; but in the *shih-tien* the statuses are extrinsic, whereas for the *chiao* they are intrinsic, created for and by the religious ceremonies themselves. The final selection of leading participants in the *chiao* is not by code, decree, or law of the land but by the authority of the chief deity of the temple concerned, before whom the candidates are announced and his approval tested for each by divination blocks. For the duration of the *chiao* the temple takes on the character of a government office, its *lu-hsia* area being its administrative region; but its leaders are representatives of its population, not delegated to it as the officials of the official religion are.

All women, and all men without degrees, are entirely excluded from the *shih-tien*, whereas the *chiao* always includes the entire population of the area in the last part of its rites. For the *chiao* everyone in the temple's region has to be ritually clean, whereas for the *shih-tien* only the leading participants need be. Only the leading participants have anything to do with the offerings to the gods in the official religion. In the *chiao* everyone makes offerings outside the temple and in their homes, and the leading participants witness the presentation of offerings in the temple itself.

The precautions for the *shih-tien* fast are read out in ceremony to the leading participants and guides three days before the main ritual: "There will be one communal fast when they [the leading participants] will lodge together in the fasting house thinking of the *shen* [in this case Confucius]. They will think of the *shen's* eating and drinking, the *shen's* residence, the *shen's* laughter and talk, the *shen's* will, whatever the *shen* enjoyed, the *shen's* occupations and tastes. Each will purify his own mind and be the more reverent and discreet and care for the precautions." The climax to this meditation comes on the main day of the ceremony, when the great gate of the temple is opened and the *shen* welcomed to the august rites and the munificent offerings. And this is the nearest there is to a physical presence of a *shen* in the *shih-tien* or, for that matter, in all the official cults where gods are represented only by tablets.

Both the *shih-tien* and the *chiao* are believed by their respective participants to have a generalized good effect. In the case of the *shih-tien* for Confucius and his associates, it is the spread of learning and the maintenance of civilization; and in the case of the spirits of Wind-Rain-Thunder-Clouds and Mountains-and-Rivers, for whom the *shih-tien* is also performed, it is the maintenance of food and shelter for all in the administrative region. But where the official would explain that disaster and confusion are avoided by respect for the proper relationships and the performance of the proper rites to glorify those that exemplified and illuminated them, the people (though not necessarily the priest) would explain that prevention of calamity and assurance of a good harvest are brought about by the protection of a god who is to be propitiated by the proper rites. To the people, then, temple ritual is performed either by officials or by priests, both of whom have ritual knowledge that they, the people, lack. There is a sense in which the god of popular religion is imperial: he sanctions statuses that in the official religion are those of the imperial government. And there is a sense in which priests are the equivalents of officials in relation to these gods.

There is a core ceremony of showing respect that is common to both *shih-tien* and *chiao*, just as the kowtow and other gestures of deference are common to all Chinese culture, and that is the *san-chüeh li*—the triple offering of wine. But the *shih-tien* and the *chiao* differ in their elaborations of this rite, in the contexts in which they set it, in the beings respected, in the wording of the eulogies and texts read and played, and in the fact that the *chiao* is a manipulation of the forces of the universe (magic, if you like) involving a great number of other rites, all of them absent from the *shih-tien*.

Within the official religion itself, elaboration of the *san-chüeh li* differed according to the being addressed. There were minutely specified differences in the amount of offerings, music, and obeisance required and, of course, in who constituted the proper worshipers. The official pantheon was divided largely into three levels of ritual importance, which I have charted in Tables 1, 2, and 3, indicating a few of the ritual distinctions between them. Within these levels the gods were again kept distinct by finer ritual prescriptions, such as those for the measurements of their altars, the positions of their tablets on the altars, and the number of steps up to the altar. When there was more than one god in a single temple or ceremony, the gods were ritually ranked by whether they were housed in the back or front shrines, or by whether they received as animal offerings *shao-lao* (which was without an ox) or *t'ai-lao* (with an ox). These and many other kinds of prescription were what constituted the *ssu-tien*. They defined which gods were to be worshiped by whom and at what time and place.

The *chiao*, in contrast, means the setting up at the center of the temple region of a ritual area that is movable and the same wherever the priests take it. It consists of the Taoist pantheon of cosmic forces and deities superimposed on whatever the *shen-ming* and *kuei* of the local temples happen to be. In other words, it is the whole structure every time and not an exclusive part of it. The *chiao* is a purification of the region: the gods are called upon to protect it and to act as mediators to greater powers, and the ghosts are fed to keep them away from it. *Shih-tien* is rank-specific, whereas *chiao* is place-specific. Both evoke a universe, but that of the *shih-tien* is of rank in a hierarchy; that of the *chiao* is of a place as microcosm of the macrocosm.

A lesser form of *shih-tien*, called *shih-ts'ai*, was performed on the 1st and 15th of the month at the school-temple. According to the handbook, it was also performed in weddings at the visit to the bride's family, and in funerals at the viewing of the dressed corpse. Worship in ancestral temples is also, as I have observed it, a lesser form of *shih-tien*. There appear, then, to be two sets. The one is kin ritual, memorialism, officials, and tablets. The other is god ritual, magic, priests, and images. Nevertheless, they share a cosmology and interpenetrate in several ways, some of which we shall now examine.

The emperor's birthday was celebrated with rites very similar to those for Confucius, rehearsed, as were Confucius's rites, in the Ming-lun T'ang and performed in a Longevity Hall that was in all respects like a temple. On New Year's Day (lunar) and at the winter solstice the emperor himself in the imperial capital worshiped *t'ien* and his own ancestors, while simultaneously in the provinces the same rites as those for the emperor's birthday were performed in the Ming-lun T'ang. Receiving the orders of the emperor in the provinces involved going out into the eastern suburb to welcome them much as spring was welcomed in the same suburb at the vernal equinox. "We must welcome the spring in the eastern suburb because the people rely on it, and present the military banners in the west drillyard so that confusion and evil can be suppressed before it rises. It cannot be said that the rites [*li*] were invented today. We are following ancient practices," says the introduction to the "Chi-ssu" in the T'ai-wan *hsien* gazetteer of 1721.

At the Altar of Heaven, as the gods and spirits were welcomed, the tablets of the gods and the imperial ancestors were brought from the temples where they were stored to the open altar where they were to be worshiped.[12] The tablet of Huang-t'ien Shang-ti, God of Heaven, was put on the top terrace of the circular altar, flanked by those of the imperial ancestors. At the emperor's own flanks but on the second terrace were put, to the left and superior side the Sun and then all together the Northern Dipper, Five Planets, the Twenty-eight Lunar Mansions, and the Three-hundred-and-sixty Stars of the Heavenly Circumference. These astrological bodies were common to all Chinese religious institutions. They were used by the Directorate of Astrology for making up the ritual calendar, and by diviners for making up the annual almanac of the days propitious for weddings, opening shops, or visiting the sick, or dangerous because of monsters and *kuei*. And they were part of the cosmology used by Taoists in the *chiao*. To the emperor's right on the second terrace was the Moon and Wind-Rain-Thunder-Clouds—the latter worshiped in spring and autumn throughout the capitals of the land together with local mountains and rivers and the City God. The emperor himself sat on the second terrace, opposite and facing Huang-t'ien Shang-ti. He, like the gods, had been preceded to his place by his own tablet carried by his ceremonial guides to mark where he should stand for every movement in the rites. On the third terrace, behind the emperor, sat princes of the first, second, and third ranks, plus dukes. The gods' and ancestors' tablets had been taken up the sacred way—the time was predawn and the way was lighted by red lanterns—through the central opening of the gates leading to the altar, while the emperor, princes, and dukes passed through their side openings. They were guided by the presidents and officials of the Boards of Rites and Music and of the Censorate. All other officials were excluded, just as the common people were excluded from the provincial rites. The imperial progress through the city from the palace to the altar area was masked from all those not taking part. The street was cleared and the side alleys screened at their entrances by green-blue (the color of Heaven) cloth hangings. During the rites only the emperor and his guides moved. He was the sole leading participant.

As the officials claimed, the rites ordered both natural and social classes. As we move down the ranks of the *ssu-tien* from altars to temples, and from the highest to the lowest levels of ceremonial (see Tables 1, 2, and 3), there is an increasing personification of natural bodies and forces, and an increasing tendency to attribute to the spirits of those who have had a personal existence the power to effect events in the here and now. The lower the deities the more they conform to a bureaucratic image of the universe, namely the filling of its parts as offices with the spirits of the worthy dead as officials. At the top level, Land and Grain, Heaven, and Earth have no title but their very names. On the second level, Wind-Rain-Thunder-Clouds each have titles; the first Earl (*po*), the others Master (*shih*). At the lowest level, Ch'eng-huang (literally "walls and moats," the City God) is clearly a spiritual office. It is noteworthy that Ch'eng-huang was represented by a tablet when worshiped at the open altar and by an image when worshiped in his own temple.[13]

The City God temple was within the walls. But the tablets of the Land and Grain were kept in his temple and taken out to their altar—with the City God's own tablet—on days of worship. Similarly the tablets of Wind-Rain-Thunder-Clouds were kept in the Hsien-nung temple when one was built. In the many cases where the prescriptions for the directional position of the altars were not kept, the altars for the Land and Grain, Wind-Rain-Thunder-Clouds and Hsien-nung (plus his temple) were often built all in the same place.

The City God had another side. He was thought to be the otherworld (*yin*) equivalent of the chief of the administrative capital, the this-worldly (*yang*) ruler. It was the rule that an incoming magistrate, before taking up office, first seclude himself in the City God temple and report himself to the god, swearing an oath: "If I govern disrespectfully, am crafty, avaricious, get my colleagues into trouble, or oppress the people, may the *shen* [you] send down retribution upon me for three years."[14] As *yin* administrator, the City God was welcomed as chief deity at the official rites for the unworshiped dead at their altar. He was believed to be in charge of all the spirits of the local dead, but the *li* were his special responsibility and were his underlings in the detection of good and evil among the living (the magistrate resorted to him in cases that he could not decide) and in the discovery of injustices in the lives of those already dead.[15]

When it came to officially still lesser rituals, the populace joined the officials and the City God's image was used. For instance, worship of the City God for himself was not part of the statutory official religion. His annual birthday celebration was largely a popular ceremony. Yet Gray[16] reported that in Canton on the City God's birthday the prefect in the name of the government presented for the image a new suit of silk with which wealthy families had vied to supply him, and he produced the god's jade seal which had been in his keeping for the year. This jade seal was the mark of rank by administrative level ordained by imperial decree in the Ming dynasty. It was turned by the populace into a magic implement, the stamp of which, on a charm or the garment of a sick person, could cure.

The local administrator was the emperor's delegate to the people. The City God, as his *yin* complement, was Heaven's delegate to the people and to their dead. Here the official either pandered to or really subscribed to the beliefs of the people. We can see how close official religion and popular beliefs are when it comes to an occasional rite such as a rain ceremony, as the following account from the 1788 gazetteer for Yin *hsien* shows.

The ceremony is abundant and the power of the god [*shen-ling*] magnificently manifest. Pray and he responds throughout the year or when it rains too much and the people grieve to him. The *shen* [i.e., the City God] blesses the people munificently. Now, the year after Prefect Lu [of Ning-po] took up office there was drought. He prayed to the *shen* and *t'ien* rained. Again there was drought and again he prayed to the *shen* and *t'ien* rained. He [the prefect] illuminated the people of the prefecture. From the *chin-shih* [degree-holder] to the head of a Board, when they had virtue toward men shrines were built for them. How, too, can the officials for whose virtue the fathers of Yin *hsien* were grateful be forgotten for even one day? The official takes benevolence to govern the people and the *shen* takes sincerity. So the *shen* controls [*ko*] and the people have good faith [*hsin*]. Therefore the people of the whole prefecture asked for an image [*shen-hsiang*] to be made for the temple and they bought it gowns and a crown. The temple's appearance was suddenly new and awesome, uncannily [*ling*] brilliant. The civil and military offered congratulations. Gentry all looked upon it with reverence. That was in 1445, on the tenth day of the eleventh month. The next year Prefect Lu went to make presentations at the Imperial Court and the magistrate of Yin *hsien* asked [him to relay a request to] Marquis Yang to compose a memorial to be engraved for the beautification of the temple in the name of gentry and people.

The order of the provincial rain ceremony, as detailed for Taiwan in the *Fu-chien t'ung chih, T'ai-wan fu*, 1830–69, was that there should be worship first at the altar of Mountains and Streams, and then at the altar of the Land and Grain. The ceremony was to be the same as that of the regular rites, with the addition of a petition prayer for rain. All officials were to take part. Next, all were to go to read the prayer and burn incense to the City God and then to the Dragon God, in their respective temples. The Dragon God was included in the official rites only for rain ceremonies, not for the regular ones.

The officials wore court dress to the altars, but after the plea for rain had been read they changed into plain linen, as for mourning, which they continued to wear as they went to the two temples every day until rain came. In addition to the usual fast, there was a general taboo on the slaughter of animals, and thus the common people were involved. They were even more involved if sufficient rain did not come within seven days. In such a case a committee of officials was formed that went again—after a repeat of the rites at the two altars—to pray and burn incense in the City God and the Dragon God temples. If the drought was severe, the officials had to burn incense and pray in public as they walked, without parasols in the blazing sun, to the temples through the streets. In Tan-shui *t'ing*, Taiwan, there was a shrine to a virtuous magistrate who had died of exposure while praying for rain.

The wearing of mourning and the exposure to the elements were a penitence and an effort to move heaven; the fast was a purification. If the plea was still not successful, Taoist and Buddhist priests were ordered to plead in their ways, which for the Taoists was the *chiao* in the City God temple. The gazetteer qualifies this by saying that it used to be done thus in the old days, but de Groot[17] at the end of the nineteenth century observed this stage of officials and priests praying for rain. If rain still did not come, then the image of the City God was taken out into the sun, stripped of his headgear, and sometimes chained to experience the drought himself and to move Heaven to rain. Similar events were reported for Canton by Gray on personal observation at the Dragon God temple. When rain came, the officials retreated to the exclusive altars and tablets to give thanks, dressed now in embroidered robes.

It was common practice for degree-holding scholars of literary repute to write the preliminary address to the deity for rain read in the *chiao*. After the address came the more esoteric Taoist rites. A Taoist handbook of the 1870's listing documents to be prepared for a number of ceremonies includes such an address (called *su-i*) written by a *chin-shih* degree-holder. Both the address and the document that follows it—an announcement text (*piao-wen*) that we may attribute to the Taoist compiler of the book—appeal to Heaven and all the spirits (*chu shen*) to put an end to the misery of drought. But the *chin-shih* leaves the relationship between the supernatural and the living vague. He goes so far as to call

Heaven "imperial Heaven" (*Hao-t'ien*) and to say that it would not order living things to be lost and that the spirits who protect the people would not leave them with no support. In the Taoist's document the relationship is much more specific. Heaven has strength, earth has achievements; Heaven and earth have virtue, and the empyrean (*shang-tsang*) has mercy. The spirits have love for the people and have power (*ling*). Appeal is made to a list of entitled deities in this order: Hao-t'ien Chin-kuan Yü-huang Shang-ti (the full Taoist name of Yü-huang Shang-ti—the supreme *shen-ming*); Duke of Thunder; Mother Lightning; Earl Wind; Master Rain; the forces of the five quarters; the rain Dragon God and the spirits of the dragon kings of the five lakes; the four seas; the spirits of the mountains and streams and of the land and grain. They are all besought to use their power (*ling*) to drive out the drought demon (or star influence—*k'uei*). The *chin-shih* never mentions the drought as a demon or as star influence, nor does he mention *ling* once in his prayer.

Another *chin-shih's* prayer for rain[18] addressed to the City God does, however, go further than the above *su-i*. This prayer refers to the *ling* of the City God, to his virtue as guardian of the territory, and to the *shen* of rain and the *ling* of such broad natural categories as the ocean. He implores the City God to take his appeal to the gates of Heaven. But the *ling* categories all occur in couplets paired with references to Buddhist concepts.

The Taoist priest who lent me the handbook wrote out another plea for rain for one of his pupils to learn. It is a combination of the *su-i* and the announcement text. Features not found in either of the *chin-shih's* prayers are references to the cause of the drought as a *k'uei* and to the *ling* of the sage strength of the spirits of Heaven and earth, of empyrean Heaven, and of the thunder god, who is to open the gates of Heaven with his peals. Most importantly, this plea states the intention to establish communication with Heaven by means of a *fu*, a document that is a cross between a memorial and an order (and is usually translated as charm) and that is held by the Taoist during the prayer.

With the concept of malignant influences to be expelled by the use of charms we have moved completely out of the realm of official religion, for only Taoists use charms. A glimpse at some of the oaths, or commands, and the movements prescribed to accompany the burning and brandishing of the charms takes us beyond the bureaucratic universe of the announcement text mentioned earlier. For these more esoteric rites refer to less anthropomorphic forces of the universe, such as the spirits (*ch'i*) of the four quarters, of the Five Elements, and of *yin* and *yang*. A new imagery of cosmic forces and of alchemy is here introduced into the rain ceremony, and into all occasions when the *chiao* is performed. The Taoist priest seeks to concentrate in himself as a microcosm forces of the universe sufficient for him to realign things that have gone out of balance and to counter malignant forces that have come into play.

One can move from popular religion into the Taoist as well as into the official religious traditions. The two shared a common ground of metaphysical speculation. But it is in Taoism and not in the official religion that the metaphysical categories of this cosmology are applied as real forces. In the official religion, the notion of a hierarchical structure in the moral universe is consistently displayed. This notion is anthropomorphized as it approaches popular religion, for the metaphor of bureaucracy becomes increasingly elaborate as the spirits of men who have died take on greater and greater powers and the representations of gods are themselves treated as having power.[19] The distribution of this power is through a hierarchy, that is to say by *delegation* through ranks from the top. The image of bureaucracy is applied to the universe in Taoist religion, too, and with it the attribution of substantial powers to the spirits of the dead—again as Taoism approaches popular usage. But between Taoist religion and popular religion—the former in its application of transcendental metaphysical categories; the latter in the use of the concept *ling*, in particular—an alternative relationship is added to that of delegation. It is the diffusion and concentration of power from a center. In Chinese metaphysical tradition this is the concentration of power in any spot of time or space as a center appropriately oriented to the greater arrangement of power on a transcendent plane. The ultimate center at the most transcendent plane is known as the great unique (*t'ai-i* and its synonyms). One may call this a process of *identification*, and it is common to Taoist religion, alchemy, and geomancy.

Popular religion is pragmatic religion; metaphysical categories are latent in concrete phenomena. Power is immanent, manifested in extraordinary phenomena and events, and tapped from them. At the same time *shen* and *kuei* can become gods and demons of this immanent power and can be brought under control through the officials of a supernatural bureaucracy. Taoist priests perform rites in the name of these gods and demons; officials do not.

Bureaucratic Control

By a regulation promulgated in the first year of the Ch'ing period, the state sponsored the building of shrines to celebrated officials and local worthies. Candidates for canonization were to be recommended to the emperor, who would authorize their enshrinement. The criteria for canonization were contained in five statutes of the *Li-chi*. Now it is true that almost all popular temples were also dedicated to former humans, many of whom had lived in or administered the localities where they were enshrined. In Ningpo, a number of popular temples not included in the *ssu-tien* or else crossing the line between official and popular (having been built by officials but having no official rites performed in them) were dedicated to past officials posted to Ningpo—many of whom had relieved the people by reducing taxes in times of hardship.

There was certainly an overlap between the official and the popular religions, and there was an exchange of gods, or rather a transformation of each other's gods, between them. It was characteristic of the popular and not of the official religion that the former official had to manifest his power as a god if he were to continue being worshiped. To be worshiped officially, a candidate must have been worthy by official standards of virtue—loyalty to the emperor, and so forth—and recommended by the appropriate officials. Like the degree system, this was open to corruption. Hsiao has shown how local gentry bribed the appropriate officials to recommend their ancestors for canonization.[20]

The principle of judging a *shen* by his life as a human was often abandoned, however, especially where the *shen* had become very popular. Canonization of the latter into the official religion was a form of control. More direct means of control have been documented by others,[21] but we can mention here the bureaus in every administrative capital for the registration of Taoists and Buddhists, and for the commissioning of one of their number for such official services as the rain ceremony. This had the effect of creating an orthodoxy under official control. At its highest point was the head of the Cheng-i sect, the so-called Taoist pope, who was given the task of appointing jointly with the emperor former officials and worthies who should fill the posts of the City Gods of the empire.

There are many examples of popular cults that were adopted into the *ssu-tien* because the *shen* had been officially recommended for saving emperors' or officers' lives (e.g., Ningpo's Hsieh-chung miao to the six generals who died defending Sui-yang city against the forces of An Lushan), or for producing rain (e.g., Ningpo's Pai-lung-wang miao, a Dragon God temple to two Sung-period brothers who lived in the mountains). Kuan-ti, the various gods of Wen-ch'ang, and T'ien-hou are examples of the most thoroughgoing adoption, for they were recommended so many times from so many different places that in the Ch'ing period it was ordered that official temples to them be built—in all capitals for Kuan-ti and Wen-ch'ang, and in all coastal capitals for T'ien-hou.

It was characteristic of this class of beings that they were reputed to have led unorthodox lives, or not to have fulfilled their allotted span, or to have met violent death. Kuan-ti was supposed to have died in battle without blood descendents. T'ien-hou to have died a virgin. It was this extraordinary aspect about them that manifested *ling*. As *kuei* their unspent force was dangerous. They chose to use it positively, to bring prosperity to those who prayed to them. With their incorporation in the *ssu-tien*, an official interpretation of their deeds and function was imposed and an orthodoxy dictated by the Board of Rites.[22]

The school-temple and the City God are both the oldest and the most constant features of the county-level cities I have investigated. There is a case to be made for their being the two most essential features of the official religion: the City God was the focus of a religion based on natural forces and ghosts, and thus was the god for the control of the peasantry, as it were; the school-temple was the center for the worship of sages and exemplars of official virtues, for the spirits of bureaucracy. The school-temple was the center of the cult of literacy. For Confucians the spirit was in the written word, not in any object or image or natural body. The written word was enough: it was the vehicle of tradition, the trace of the sages and of the golden age. In most Wen-ch'ang temples there was an incinerator for the respect of the written word. It was, in theory, the only place where scraps of paper containing writing could be destroyed, since it was a shrine to the inventor of writing.

To scholars, skill in writing was the way up the official ladder. Worship of Wen-ch'ang was only one of many ritual observances by which members of the scholar-official class "borrowed in secret" blessings for scholars' luck. To the illiterate people, writing meant statutes and decrees, on the one hand, the means by which their rulers governed them, and secret charms, on the other, known only to the initiated and effective as cures for sickness or ill-luck.

There was a dialectic in which officials adopted deities from popular religion and bureaucratized them, while the people worshiped gods that were like magic officials or that were magic official deities. Gods that in popular religion were fluid, whose identities flowed into one another, whose functions were potentially universal, and who were magic in their ability to metamorphose and to fuse man and nature in themselves, were in the official religion standardized and classed, minute distinctions and the separation of rites and cults keeping them apart.

Taoism offered confirmation of an alternative to the official type of power structure. To place the official religion in a completed context it would be necessary to show how Buddhism offered a third tradition out of popular religion.

As a last point, let me make it clear that what I have described as the official religion did not constitute the religion of all those who were, or who aspired to be, officials. In his home county before he became an official, in his nonofficial capacity while he was an official, and when he retired, a scholar-official might well sponsor nonofficial temples and take part in nonofficial rites. At the very pinnacle of the hierarchy, the Ch'ing emperors had their nonofficial religion in the inner palace.[23] The official religion with the office of emperor at its head was an institution of government; and, like the examinations, possession of it and the content of it could be disputed and changed. On either side of the official religion, so to speak, were on the one hand the *shu-yüan* and on the other the secret societies. Outside the city were the places of Buddhist and Taoist retreat. All of them were places where the institutions of government and the official religion could be disputed. The walled cities of administration stood for official power. The power of nonofficial religious institutions and the governed lay beyond the walls in the countryside and in unwalled central places.

Gods, Ghosts, and Ancestors

ARTHUR P. WOLF

In the rural areas along the southwestern edge of the Taipei Basin, conservative families burn three sticks of incense every morning and every evening.[1] One of these is placed in a niche outside the back door for the benefit of wandering ghosts; one is dedicated to the Stove God, whose image resides above the large brick structure on which all meals are prepared; and the third is placed in a burner before the tablets of the family's immediate ancestors. The purpose of this essay is to examine the significance of these three acts of worship. I will argue that this significance is largely determined by the worshippers' conception of their social world. The reader should therefore note at the outset the limited scope of this exploration. My informants have been farmers, coal miners, and laborers, as well as a few shopkeepers and petty businessmen. Thirty years ago the homes of many of these people were constructed of mud bricks and roofed with straw thatch. Thus my social perspective is that of a poor and politically impotent segment of the society. It is also that of the layman rather than of the religious specialist. Were we to look at the same acts of worship from the perspective of government officials, wealthy landlords, or the Taoist priest, we would find they had very different meanings. The most important point to be made about Chinese religion is that it mirrors the social landscape of its adherents. There are as many meanings as there are vantage points.

[1] The first draft of this paper was written in 1965, for a seminar conducted at Cornell University by Maurice Freedman. The paper has since been revised several times to take account of new information and the comments of friends and colleagues. I am particularly indebted to Maurice Freedman, Margery Wolf, Robert J. Smith, Emily M. Ahern, and C. Stevan Harrell, all of whom have commented on earlier drafts. I am also indebted to Freedman, Ahern, and Harrell for permission to report data drawn from personal correspondence and unpublished field notes.

The geographic scope of my study is most appropriately defined with reference to the Ch'ing Shui Tsu Shih Kung temple in San-hsia. In 1895, when Taiwan was ceded to Japan, this god was regarded as the supernatural governor of much of the Taipei Basin. The area of his jurisdiction extended from the outskirts of Shu-lin in the north to just beyond Ying-ke and Chung-chuang in the south, embracing the entire valley that is bounded on one side by the Kuei-lun Hills and on the other by the lower reaches of the central mountain range. In cultural terms the boundaries of Tsu Shih Kung's domain were coterminous with the limits of an area dominated by the descendants of eighteenth-century immigrants from An-ch'i. To the west T'ao-yuan and Ta-ch'i were controlled by Chang-chou people, while to the east Tsu Shih Kung's subjects faced Ting-chiao and T'ung-an people at Shu-lin and Chang-chou people in the direction of Pan-ch'iao and T'u-ch'eng. Until the Japanese administration brought an end to years of internecine strife, An-ch'i people worshipped An-ch'i gods and married An-ch'i women. Although Hsia-ch'i-chou, the site of my first fieldwork, is only fifteen minutes' walk from villages controlled by Chang-chou people, it was not until 1918 that the first Chang-chou woman married into the community.

This is not to say that Tsu Shih Kung's domain existed as an isolated, self-sufficient kingdom. At the turn of the century at least half a dozen families in Hsia-ch'i-chou made their living as boatmen, and San-hsia's position as the area's leading commercial center depended on its role as a riverport. The area sent camphor, tea, coal, and wood down the river to Wan-hua and Tamsui, and received in return cotton, paper, and tobacco from Amoy, sugar and sweetmeats from Hong Kong, and occasionally flour and kerosene from the United States. Recognition of the area's position as part of the Chinese empire is clearly reflected in the natives' conception of their supernatural governor. The most enthusiastic of Tsu Shih Kung's subjects would never have claimed that he was an autonomous ruler. It was universally understood that his authority was delegated by a higher power, responsible for a much larger community. Tsu Shih Kung is but the local representative of a vast supernatural bureaucracy, headed by a deity whose every characteristic marks him as the spiritual equivalent of the human emperor.

I have probably given the reader the impression that my subject is a community that disappeared shortly after the turn of the century. There is a sense in which this is true. The bandits who used to parade through the streets of San-hsia shouting, "You trust the mandarins; we'll trust the mountains," have long since been dispersed (MacKay 1895: 159–60). The river that once carried the burden of all commerce was supplanted by the railroad seventy years ago. By the time I began my research in the area in 1957 many residents were commuting to jobs in Taipei City, and by 1970 the area's leading employers included Sony and Motorola. Everything has changed, and yet nothing has changed. Even new houses have ancestral altars and a Stove God as well as a television set, and I have seen a fire-walking performed on a baseball diamond. The reader will have to exercise some historical imagination to understand the conditions that gave rise to the beliefs I discuss, but he must not forget that these beliefs endure and will influence the future.

II

The Stove God, Tsao Chün, is not a god of the culinary arts, nor is his location above the stove a matter of convenience or coincidence. In northern Taiwan the large brick cooking stove on which most meals are prepared stands as a substantial symbol of the family as a corporate body. Possession of a stove identifies a family as an independent entity. The new independent segments of a recently divided household often share many of the facilities of a single house, including, occasionally, the kitchen, but independent families never share a stove, not even when the heads are brothers. When brothers divide their father's household the eldest inherits the old stove, while his younger brothers transfer hot coals from the old stove to their new ones, thereby inviting the Stove God to join them. For this reason, family division is commonly spoken of as *pun-cau*, "dividing the stove." In the view of most of my informants, the soul of a family, its corporate fate, is somehow localized in their stove. When a shaman informed one family that there were "ants and other things" in their stove, they demolished the structure and threw the bricks into the river. A neighbor explained, "There was nothing else they could do. A family will never have peace if they don't have a good stove."

The association of Stove God and stove is thus an association of god and family. The character of the relationship is essentially bureaucratic. The family is the smallest corporate unit in the society, and the Stove God is the lowest-ranking member of a supernatural bureaucracy. In the Yangtze delta village of Kaihsienkung, Stove Gods were viewed as the spiritual remains of foreign soldiers forcibly billeted in the houses of the region to act as spies and informers (Fei 1939: 99–102). In San-hsia the god is usually described as "a kind of policeman." The metaphors chosen to describe the god vary from one area of China to another, possibly as a result of political experience, but the god is everywhere looked upon as representing a supernatural bureaucracy. The glutinous rice cakes offered him at the New Year are explained as a means of forestalling. an unfavorable report on the family. According to one of my informants in Hsia-ch'i-chou, "You have to give the god something so that he won't say things about your family and cause you a lot of trouble."

The prototype of the many gods in the Chinese pantheon is, in my view, Fu Te Cheng Shen, commonly known as T'u Ti Kung. This "earth god" is often introduced as the Chinese god of agriculture, but this is only partially accurate. "T'u-ti" is better translated as "site" or "locality" than as "earth" or "soil." T'u Ti Kung is a tutelary deity, the governor of a place, concerned with agriculture, to be sure, but no more so than any official responsible for the welfare of a rural community. T'u Ti Kung are just as common in the towns and cities of Taiwan as in the villages. Older residents of Tainan City claim that in former times every neighborhood had its own T'u Ti Kung, and evidence gathered by Kristofer Schipper appears to bear them out. A Taoist manuscript dated 1876 lists all of the city's divine agents from whom one must request forgiveness in time of disaster. Among the 138 cults mentioned in the list, 45 are devoted to T'u Ti Kung (Schipper 1977).

T'u Ti Kung is seen as having two functions, one of which is to police the *kui* (*kuei*), the "ghosts," the supernatural equivalent of bandits, beggars, and other dangerous strangers.[2] The association between T'u Ti Kung and the earth is in part a consequence of this role. The kui are creatures of the soil, spiritual residues of the most material part of man, often represented in experience by bones uncovered in digging a foundation or plowing a field. It is T'u Ti Kung's task to protect the living from the depredations of these unhappy, wandering spirits. Although the god thus serves the best interests of the human community, he is not that community's agent. His other role is to spy on the affairs of his human charges, keep records of their activities, and report regularly to his superiors. Commenting on H. A. Giles's view that T'u Ti Kung are worshipped "for anything that can be got out of them," Clarence Day (Day 1940: 65) notes, "Not only that, but all local events and proceedings must be duly reported to them: births, marriages, misfortunes, deaths." Most people in the San-hsia area report vital events to their neighborhood T'u Ti Kung as well as to the local police station, and in many villages people customarily ask the god's permission to build a new house or demolish an old one.

In imperial China every local official was responsible for a discrete ad-

[2] Place names and the names of familiar gods are romanized with their Mandarin pronunciation. Otherwise, all terms are given in Hokkien. Where Hokkien terms have a familiar Mandarin equivalent, I sometimes give the Mandarin in parentheses following the Hokkien.

ministrative district, and this was as true of the supernatural bureaucracy as it was of their human counterparts. Until only recently the jurisdiction of many T'u Ti Kung in the San-hsia area was defined by means of a circulating plaque, a piece of wood about twenty inches long and eight inches wide, inscribed on one side with the name of the god and on the other with the name of the community.[3] This token of the god's authority was passed from family to family, day by day, moving through the community along an irregular but exhaustive route. The family holding the plaque on any given day was responsible for making an offering of incense, fruit, and tea at the T'u Ti Kung temple. This it did in the morning after receiving the plaque and again in the evening before passing it on to a neighbor. In this way every family participated in honoring the local T'u Ti Kung and in so doing identified itself as part of the community.

This practice implies a conditional relationship between the god and his subjects. The family that moves from one community to another should see themselves as leaving the authority of one T'u Ti Kung and entering that of another. And so it is. R. F. Johnston's description of Weihaiwei at the turn of the century is entirely applicable to the San-hsia area in the 1960's. After describing a procession of mourners "wending their way along the village street in the direction of the shrine of T'u Ti to report the death of a relative or fellow villager," Johnston continues: "It is noteworthy . . . that no village in Weihaiwei, or elsewhere as far as I am aware, possesses more than one T'u Ti, though there may be two or more 'surnames' or clans represented in the village; moreover, when a man migrates from one village to another he changes his T'u Ti, although his connection with his old village in respect of ancestral worship remains unimpaired" (Johnston 1910: 372–73).

Johnston's point is that T'u Ti Kung serve localities, not kinship groups. This is right and explains why farmers in San-hsia who own land in more than one locality worship more than one T'u Ti Kung. However, Johnston makes an avoidable error when he observes that no village ever has more than one T'u Ti Kung. The library of the School of Oriental and African Studies contains Johnston's copy of Arthur Smith's *Village Life in China.* The book is inscribed "R. F. Johnston, Government House, July 6th, 1901," a year or two after Johnston's arrival in Weihaiwei and nine years before he published his *Lion and Dragon in Northern China.* Had Johnston consulted Smith on the T'u Ti Kung, as he did on many other sub-

[3] Sung Lung-sheng, recently returned from field research, tells me that one of the T'u Ti Kung plaques in the San-hsia area also lists the names of the heads of all households that receive the plaque. Thus the plaque makes explicit the relationship between the god, the community, and the residents who worship the god.

jects, he would have found this passage: "If the village is a large one, divided into several sections transacting their public business independently of one another, there may be several temples to the same divinity. It is a common saying, illustrative of Chinese notions on this topic, that the local god at one end of the village has nothing to do with the affairs of the other end of the village." (Smith 1899: 138.)

Smith, too, errs in implying that T'u Ti Kung temples are always thought of as independent of one another. In fact, many T'u Ti Kung are the delegated representatives of other T'u Ti Kung. This is sometimes made explicit in the ritual process by which a new temple is established or an old one refurbished. During my most recent trip to Taiwan, in 1970, the people of Chung-p'u on the west side of San-hsia decided to rebuild the residence of their local deity. On the day the old temple was to be demolished, the head of the village bent six long strips of bamboo into circles and tied them together with red string to form a large hoop. Before the god was invited out of the temple for the duration of the repairs, this bamboo hoop was lowered over the roof and thus made to encircle the entire building. I was told that the hoop represented the boundaries of the district governed by the god. The purpose of encircling the temple was to keep the god from deserting the community while his home was under repair. "This is the god of this place. We do not want him to leave and take up residence somewhere else."

This step of the ritual identified the god with the district for which he is responsible. The next made it clear that he is not conceived of as a sovereign ruler, but as the local representative of a higher authority. Once it had been ascertained by divination that the god agreed to leave the temple, the village head took a spoonful of ashes from the incense burner and wrapped it up in red paper. This packet was then conveyed to the town of San-hsia, where it was deposited in the incense burner of what is known as the Big T'u Ti Kung temple. The village head explained that this was done because "our temple in Chung-p'u is only a substation of the big temple in town." He also told me that upon completion of the new temple, he would get ashes from the temple in town and deposit these in the new burner in Chung-p'u. "This is like asking the god in the big temple to send someone to live in our temple and protect us."

The view that the T'u Ti Kung temples in villages and neighborhoods are substations of larger temples is not an unusual one. There are fourteen other temples in San-hsia and its immediate environs that are commonly regarded as branches of the Big T'u Ti Kung temple on the main street. Until the changing character of the town led to a reorganization in 1947, these relationships were given explicit recognition on

T'u Ti Kung's birthday. The puppet shows provided for the entertainment of each of the fourteen neighborhood gods were always organized and paid for by the individual neighborhoods. The responsibility for the far more expensive opera performed to entertain the Big T'u Ti Kung was rotated among the fourteen neighborhoods on an annual basis. Even today the special status of the Big T'u Ti Kung receives occasional acknowledgment. When families invite gods to their home for some special occasion, they usually include the Big T'u Ti Kung as well as their neighborhood T'u Ti Kung. "It's the same as inviting both the mayor and the head of your village."

In considering the implications of this equation of god and bureaucrat, it is important to remember that one side of the equation is objective, the other subjective. A T'u Ti Kung and the administration he serves do not partake of the same reality as the human bureaucracy. People with different perspectives can interpret the supernatural hierarchy in different ways. An interesting case in point is provided by the T'u Ti Kung temples in Ch'i-nan, across the river from San-hsia. The community comprises four hamlets, each of which is dominated by a single lineage and its ancestral hall. At one time all four hamlets were united under the jurisdiction of one T'u Ti Kung. One T'u Ti Kung plaque circulated from family to family and then from hamlet to hamlet, and the four hamlets rotated the responsibility for the show presented to the god on his birthday. Then, sometime in the late 1950's, the hamlet dominated by the Ong lineage decided to build its own T'u Ti Kung temple. Residents of the Ong hamlet continued to take their turn in sponsoring the show for "old T'u Ti Kung's" birthday, but stopped accepting the plaque from the old temple and began instead to make daily offerings at the "Ong temple."

According to a member of the Ong lineage who now lives in the town of San-hsia, this decision was prompted by the Ongs' fear that the old T'u Ti Kung was neglecting them. "All our pigs and chickens suddenly died, and so someone called a geomancer who told us that it was because the old temple faced away from the Ong settlement. The god couldn't see us." Emily Ahern has since discovered that there were other reasons for the Ongs' dissatisfaction, but I will leave that story to her.[4] The important point for my purpose is that the present situation in Ch'i-nan is reflected in differing accounts of the Ong temple's origins. My Ong

[4] A detailed account of the four Ch'i-nan lineages and the problems that led to the construction of the Ong temple is now available in Ahern's *The Cult of the Dead in a Chinese Village* (1973: 64–66). Readers who want another perspective on the topics discussed in this paper are urged to read Ahern's book and Wang Shih-ch'ing's paper (1974). All three studies are based on fieldwork in San-hsia *chen* and its neighbor, Shu-lin chen.

informant claims that the incense used to found the temple came from the Big T'u Ti Kung temple on the main street of San-hsia. A senior member of the Lou lineage in Ch'i-nan insists that the incense came from the old T'u Ti Kung temple in Ch'i-nan. The disagreement reflects the social perspectives of the two informants. The Ong lineage would like to put their settlement on an equal footing with the rest of Ch'i-nan. The other three lineages put the Ongs down by insisting that their temple is only a branch of the Ch'i-nan temple.

I emphasize the influence different social perspectives have on what is said about T'u Ti Kung temples in order to underline my primary thesis. People would not argue about the age of temples or the source of their incense if they did not see this as a question of the relative rank of the gods in question and hence the relative status of the communities they govern. Conflicts are expressed in these terms because everyone thinks of the gods in terms of a bureaucratic hierarchy. John Shryock reports that the followers of a certain Tung Yo in Anking advanced his claims for godhood by claiming for him the governorship of the entire province. Skeptics countered by arguing that the god's activities were confined to the East Gate suburb. Even Buddhists and Taoists expressed their perennial opposition in the same idiom. A Taoist monk told Shryock that the Ch'eng Huang responsible for Anking prefecture was a Taoist deity, while the god responsible for the hsien, who differed from the prefecture god in no way except for the smaller size of the district he governed, was Buddhist (Shryock 1931: 87–88).

The view of the gods as bureaucrats is so pervasive that evidence to the contrary is itself explained away in bureaucratic terms. The picture of the pantheon with which many families decorate their ancestral altar has the Stove God in the lower left-hand corner and T'u Ti Kung in the lower right-hand corner. The reason for this has to do with the ritual specialist's view that the left side is the *iong* (*yang*) side and the right side the *im* (*yin*) side.[5] One of T'u Ti Kung's tasks is to escort the souls of the dead to the underworld, the im world, so he appropriately appears on the im side of the picture, the right side. But since etiquette makes the left superior to the right in seating guests, this positioning of the gods conflicts with the laymen's view of their relative status. T'u Ti Kung should be at the left and the Stove God at the right because Tu' Ti Kung

---

[5] I am following the Chinese convention of taking the ancestors' perspective in designating right and left. If one asks a native how he seats guests at a home banquet, he will almost always turn his back to his ancestral altar and say, "The guest of honor sits this way (with his back to the altar, facing the door), while the second guest sits at the left and the third at the right." Thus, right is stage right; left, stage left.

governs a community while the Stove God is responsible only for a single family. I first noticed the contradiction while attending a feast in San-hsia, and immediately raised the problem with my fellow guests. One of the older men present explained that the T'u Ti Kung and the Stove God are not comparable. "T'u Ti Kung is like a policeman who wears a uniform. He can only report to lower gods like the Ch'eng Huang. The Stove God is more like a plainclothesman. He reports directly to T'ien Kung [the supernatural emperor]." I asked: "But how is it that a little god like the Stove God can report directly to T'ien Kung?" Another old man answered: "The Stove God is not a small person like T'u Ti Kung. He is T'ien Kung's younger brother." The apparent departure from bureaucratic principles is thus explained away as nepotism.

Popular mythology in northern Taiwan as in other areas of China has it that T'u Ti Kung's immediate superior in the supernatural bureaucracy is Ch'eng Huang, the so-called City God, a deity posted to govern the spirits residing in each of the major administrative districts of the empire. When a small T'u Ti Kung temple in a mountain village near San-hsia was enlarged in 1967, the village head obtained incense from the Ch'eng Huang temple in Taipei City as well as the Big T'u Ti Kung temple in San-hsia. He felt this was necessary "because the Taipei Ch'eng Huang is overseer of all the T'u Ti Kung in Taipei hsien. There is no point in building a new temple if you do not ask the Ch'eng Huang to send someone to live in it." The residents of Hsia-ch'i-chou also obtained incense from the Taipei Ch'eng Huang when they built a new temple to replace the one destroyed by a typhoon in 1962. They were afraid that if they did not inform the Ch'eng Huang, he might post a new T'u Ti Kung without recalling the old one. Two gods in one temple might quarrel and thereby bring the village further misfortune.

As his relationship with T'u Ti Kung implies, Ch'eng Huang is also conceived of as a scholar-official. The god's image is always dressed in official robes and usually appears on a curtained dais flanked on either side by secretaries and fearsome lictors; his temples are laid out on precisely the same lines as a government yamen, even to the details of red walls in the courtyards and flagstaffs at the entrance. In most cities the god appeared in public three times a year to *ke-kieng* (*kuo-ching*), "tour the boundaries," or, as other informants put it, "to inspect the frontiers." Preceded by heralds carrying his gold boards of authority and his banners, the god passed through the streets in a covered sedan chair, accompanied by hundreds of young men dressed as servants, soldiers, secretaries, and lictors. By all accounts, the procession was awe-inspiring. Shryock says the tour in Anking commenced about nine in the morning and did not return to the temple until after midnight, the god visiting every street whose inhabitants had made known their desire to welcome him in the proper manner:

The parade took more than an hour to pass my point of observation. There were hundreds of ghosts like the wildest nightmare visions, their faces painted and lined with every colour under heaven, their robes bright with embroidered silks, beads, and tinsel glittering in their high head gear and banners streaming from their shoulders like wings. Soldiers with gags in their mouths, lictors bearing staffs of office, secretaries, giants and dwarfs passed two by two down the narrow, crowded street, until finally, to a continuous roar of firecrackers exploding under the feet of the marching men, and a deafening clash of cymbals and drums, came the god in the sedan chair of an official, curtains drawn for fear pictures might be taken. I caught a glimpse of his dark, impassive face, and he was gone. (Shryock 1931: 105.)

A somewhat subtler indication of the god's assimilation to the imperial bureaucracy is his loss of individual identity. Although some tales of the god's origins give him a specific identity, most people now treat Ch'eng Huang as a position rather than a person. For example, deceased notables are commonly assigned the status of Ch'eng Huang. Ch'ü T'ung-tsu identifies the Ch'eng Huang of Lou hsien in Kiangsu as a former magistrate, Li Fu-hsing, who died there in 1669 (Ch'ü 1962: 311), and, according to Florence Ayscough, the god governing Shanghai is a former member of the Hanlin Academy, Ch'in Yü-poi, who was assigned to his present position by the founder of the Ming dynasty (Ayscough 1924: 140–41). This is a particularly interesting case because it led commentators on the Shanghai gazetteer to recognize that the term Ch'eng Huang is nothing more than a bureaucratic label. Ayscough quotes one commentator as asking, "How is it that we know nothing of a former P'usa [bodhisattva]? Did the seat of Spiritual Magistrate wait for Ch'in Yü-poi?" Another commentator she cites comes to the conclusion that officials in the im world are moved around just like those in the iong world (1924: 141).

Ritual specialists and people who take more than a casual interest in temple affairs commonly distinguish two types of deities. On the one hand, there are the *su* (*shih*), the "officials," the most notable of whom are the T'u Ti Kung and the Ch'eng Huang; on the other, there are the *hu* (*fu*), the "sages" or "wise men," a category represented in the San-hsia area by such gods as Tsu Shih Kung, Pao Sheng Ta Ti, Shang Ti Kung, and Ma Tsu. The former are explicitly compared with the imperial bureaucracy and are often treated as administrative positions that can be occupied by different people. The latter are usually thought of as particular deified persons with saintly qualities, the emphasis being on the deity's moral character and good works rather than on his bureaucratic functions.

Most laymen, though aware of this distinction, do not trouble much about it. From the point of view of farmers, coal miners, coolies, and the keepers of small shops, all gods are bureaucrats. Whereas the managers of San-hsia's Ch'ang-fu Yen, the residence of Tsu Shih Kung, insist that the god is hu, "a wise man like your Lincoln," the great majority of the population think of the god as their supernatural governor. Local legend says that many years ago a god named Ang Kong saved San-hsia by warning its inhabitants of an impending raid by head-hunting aborigines. To thank the god for this timely warning, San-hsia now sends a delegation every year to invite Ang Kong to attend a festival in his honor. The god is brought from his home temple in Hsin-tien on a sedan chair, and is met at the San-hsia border by Tsu Shih Kung, riding in another chair. Asked why Tsu Shih Kung goes to meet Ang Kong at the San-hsia border, people explain that it is because "Tsu Shih Kung is the god in charge of this place and so must meet Ang Kong and show him the road." The custom is precisely parallel to that by which a hsien magistrate greeted a visiting colleague and escorted him to the yamen.

Wang Shih-ch'ing's account (1974) of the history of the Ch'i-an Kung temple in Shu-lin provides another example. Although the god enshrined in the temple, Pao Sheng Ta Ti, is classified as hu by ritual specialists, the populace treat him as the town's chief bureaucrat, comparable in many ways to the Ch'eng Huang found in administrative centers. He makes an annual inspection tour and is looked upon as the official responsible for the many T'u Ti Kung temples in the area. When a village or neighborhood decides to build a new temple or enlarge an old one, they usually invite Pao Sheng Ta Ti to choose the temple's site and orientation. There is even a legend to the effect that Pao Sheng Ta Ti was once an official in Ch'üan-chou *fu* and that he was deified in recognition of meritorious service.

The same habit of thought molds the views of people whose gods are not responsible for communities as large as San-hsia and Shu-lin. The small village in which I initiated my research in Taiwan is one of five hamlets that together constitute a rural community known as Ch'i-chou. The local gods are two T'u Ti Kung, one for each half of the community, and Shang Ti Kung, who is considered the supernatural governor of Ch'i-chou. The five hamlets rotate the responsibility for Shang Ti Kung's annual inspection tour on the occasion of his birthday. Preceded by the village band and the clatter-bang of firecrackers, the god visits the four landmarks that define the boundaries of Ch'i-chou, stopping along the way to exchange incense with the head of every family that resides in the community. The whole affair is a country version of the grand tours undertaken by the Ch'eng Huang of important towns. The only difference is in the number of people involved and the magnificence of the god's equipage, a matter of magnitude rather than meaning.

Shang Ti Kung's bureaucratic character is most evident in his relationship to the local T'u Ti Kung. Although the T'u Ti Kung are always invited to witness a play or puppet show performed for Shang Ti Kung, people are careful to place Shang Ti Kung in the center of the viewing platform with the two T'u Ti Kung at his right. Shang Ti Kung is thought of as a proud, somewhat arrogant official, who would take offense were he denied the seat of honor. A person can use the same foodstuffs to make offerings to the two gods, but he must present the offering to Shang Ti Kung before he presents it to T'u Ti Kung. A series of misfortunes that befell one family was widely blamed on a careless daughter-in-law, who thanked T'u Ti Kung before she thanked Shang Ti Kung. I was told that on one occasion Shang Ti Kung refused to leave his temple for his annual inspection tour because only two men were assigned to carry his chair. A god of his status would not deign to sally forth in a sedan chair carried by fewer than four men.

The relative status of the two gods is also apparent at the fire-walking that is held every year "to cleanse the gods and make them efficacious." Riding in sedan chairs carried by young men chosen by lot, the various images of the two gods are carried two or three times across a bed of hot coals. Every year some of the men carrying the chairs occupied by Shang Ti Kung are possessed by the god and carry on as though he were in complete command of their senses. The chairs charge the crowd and one another, sometimes meeting in violent collisions, causing bloody if not very serious injuries. This display of energy is looked upon by the villagers as evidence of Shang Ti Kung's great vitality. It therefore says something about their conception of T'u Ti Kung that the men carrying his chairs are never possessed, despite their exposure to the excitement of the occasion and the example of Shang Ti Kung's bearers. I think it is simply that people consider T'u Ti Kung "a little god," who lacks the strength and authority to take command of a person's body.

The greatest power the peasant can imagine does not escape the impress of the imperial bureaucracy on his thought. Yü Huang Ta Ti, Pearly Emperor and Supreme Ruler, the mightiest god in the peasant's pantheon, is but a reflection of the human emperor. Although there are temples for Yü Huang Ta Ti in some parts of Taiwan, there are none in San-hsia or Shu-lin. People say this is because "Yü Huang Ta Ti is a long way away and cannot be spoken to directly." All communication with the god must be by way of another god, who must himself be one of the higher-ranking deities. Lowly deities like the T'u Ti Kung cannot approach Yü Huang Ta Ti any more than a district magistrate could approach the emperor. As the Rev. Justus Doolittle puts it on the basis of his observations in Foochow, "In strict theory, the great gods, the divinities of high rank, may worship him, while the gods of lower rank may not properly worship him, in accordance with the established practice that only mandarins of high rank may wait upon the emperor in person and pay their respects, while officers of lower grade may not approach into the emperor's presence" (Doolittle 1865: II, 257).

In traditional China not all officials were assigned to territorial posts. Some served as general inspectors, traveling from one area to another and reporting their observations to the central government. The same practice is followed by the supernatural government. In her brief account of religion in a fishing village in southern Taiwan, Norma Diamond describes "two wandering inspector gods" who visit the village periodically. Their visits are announced through a shaman, who cries the news through the village streets. During their stay in the village the gods are housed in the village temple, where each household worships them in the morning and again in the evening. Diamond notes that there is some disagreement about what the gods do while they are present, but the opinions expressed by her informants suggest that most people think of them as carrying out bureaucratic functions:

One informant was of the opinion that the god came only to bring protection, to prevent illness, and to help people earn more money, and that he did this of his own volition during a pleasure trip. Another felt that he was specifically sent by the Jade Emperor to investigate men's activities, parallel to the secret police being sent by the government. A third informant explained that while the god himself was benevolent in his intentions, the troops that followed him were a mixed breed, some of whom would bring misfortune and harm. And some felt that illness or misfortune would strike evildoers shortly after the god reported back to his superiors. (Diamond 1969: 94.)

It is not only bureaucratic organization that is replicated in the world of the supernatural; the gods also display many of the most human characteristics of their worldly counterparts, including their fallibility. A temple history translated by Shryock (1931: 113–14) tells the story of a Ch'eng Huang who allowed an innocent boy to be identified as a thief. The boy, knowing he was innocent, wrote a report condemning the god and burnt it. The report was picked up by one of the wandering inspector gods mentioned by Diamond and brought to the attention of the Jade Emperor, who "immediately issued a decree banishing the City-God 1,115 *li* from his city for three years." Thus castigated, the penitent Ch'eng Huang testified on the boy's behalf and thereby managed to get his sentence reduced to 15 *li.* "So the City-God has a temple in San K'ou Cheng, because that place was just 15 *li* from the city. Anyone who does not believe this may go to San K'ou Cheng and see the temple."

In this case a culpable deity is punished by his superior in the supernatural bureaucracy. In other instances irresponsible gods are punished by human officials. The bureaucracy of the other world is not thought of as superior to the human bureaucracy with authority over it. Rather the two are parallel systems, in which the higher-ranking members of one bureaucracy have authority over the lower-ranking members of the other. When drought strikes part of a province, the governor does not appeal to the local gods to bring rain. Instead, he orders them to see to their duty, treating them with as little ceremony as he would treat one of his county magistrates. Gods who failed in their duties could be tried and condemned to a public beating. Shryock writes: "A year or so ago, at Nanling Hsien during a drought, a god was publicly tried by the magistrate for neglect of duty, condemned, left in the hot sun to see how he liked it himself, and finally, after enduring every kind of insult, was broken in pieces" (1931: 97).

Like their human counterparts in the imperial bureaucracy, the gods are far more powerful than ordinary men. They can quell rebellions, check epidemics, apprehend criminals, dispatch ghosts, cure illnesses, control the weather, and otherwise intervene in natural and social processes for the benefit of their subjects. One of the T'u Ti Kung in Ch'i-chou is credited with the important capacity to control the market price of pork. Yet the gods are far from omnipotent. Like the capacities of powerful human bureaucrats, those of their supernatural counterparts have limits. One day while I was attending a shamanistic session an elderly woman appeared and asked the god to save her seriously ailing husband. The shaman, speaking with the authority of the god, told her that although her husband's fate was due, his death could be postponed one year. My assistant happened to be present when the woman returned a little over a year later. Again her husband was seriously ill, and again she appealed to the god. This time the shaman refused to hear her appeal, bluntly informing her that nothing could be done. "Your husband's time is up. He will die no matter what I do. If I were to tell you that he will live, he would still die, and then what kind of a god would people think I am?" Although this answer may have been the shaman's way of saving himself from an almost certain loss of credibility, the idea that the god was powerless was accepted without surprise by everyone present.

The resemblance between the gods and their human counterparts extends even into the realm of their personal lives. The temples of the gods often include living quarters for their families as well as the hall in which they conduct their public business. Behind the main hall of the Ch'eng Huang temple in Shanghai is a room for the god's father and mother and an apartment occupied by his wife and four daughters (Ayscough 1924: 147). Even the lowly T'u Ti Kung is usually provided with a wife, and some take it upon themselves to add a concubine. On inquiring why a T'u Ti Kung in Weihaiwei was accompanied by two female images, R. F. Johnston was informed that "the lady on his left (the place of honour) was his wife and the lady on his right his concubine. . . . Two explanations were offered as to why this particular T'u Ti Kung had been allowed to increase his household in this manner: one was that he had won the lady by gambling for her, the other was that the T'u Ti Kung had appeared to one of the villagers in a dream and begged him to provide him with a concubine as he had grown tired of his wife." (1910: 374.)

In sum, what we see in looking at the Chinese supernatural through the eyes of the peasant is a detailed image of Chinese officialdom. This image allows us to assess the significance of the imperial bureaucracy from a new perspective. Historians and political scientists often emphasize the failure of most Chinese governments to effectively extend their authority to the local level. Certainly many governments had difficulty collecting taxes, and some allowed this function and others to fall into the hands of opportunistic local leaders. Judged in terms of its administrative arrangements, the Chinese imperial government looks impotent. Assessed in terms of its long-range impact on the people, it appears to have been one of the most potent governments ever known, for it created a religion in its own image. Its firm grip on the popular imagination may be one reason the imperial government survived so long despite its many failings. Perhaps this is also the reason China's revolutionaries have so often organized their movements in terms of the concepts and symbols of such foreign faiths as Buddhism and Christianity. The native gods were so much a part of the establishment that they could not be turned against it.

III

When we turn to the other two acts of worship, we must shift our perspective. All people worship the same gods just as they live under the same government, but people do not all stand in the same relationship to the two other classes of supernatural, ghosts and ancestors. Whether a particular spirit is viewed as a ghost or as an ancestor depends on the point of view of a particular person. One man's ancestor is another man's ghost. A young man in Hsia-ch'i-chou was returning home late one night and saw "a white thing floating across the fields" near the village. He told me he had seen a ghost. When I appeared skeptical he assured me that in this instance there were solid grounds for identifying the object as a ghost. It had been moving in the direction of Lim Bi-kok's house, and the next day was Lim Bi-kok's mother's deathday. Surely, then, the object must have been Lim Bi-kok's mother on her way home to receive her deathday offerings. "The ancestor, though dead, is a person with rights and duties" (Freedman 1967: 99); the ghost, also dead, is a person with neither rights nor duties. The one is usually a kinsman; the other is always a stranger.

In a world in which every person married and produced at least one male child, it could easily be argued that the rites of ancestor worship are a function of descent. In such a world every male child would take his descent from his father, and every woman would, on marriage, become a member of her husband's line of descent. Under these conditions men would worship their parents, their paternal grandparents, and their remote lineal agnatic ascendants; women would worship their father's ascendants before marriage and their husband's ascendants after marriage. From the point of view of any living person, the dead would fall into two mutually exclusive classes. On the one hand, there would be those dead represented by the tablets on one's family altar, all of whom would be lineal agnatic ascendants and their wives, people who would have the right to receive regular deathday offerings; on the other, there would be those dead enshrined on altars in other people's homes, the deceased members of descent lines other than one's own, outsiders to whom no obligation was owed.

With the important recent exception of Emily Ahern's *The Cult of the Dead in a Chinese Village*, this is the world assumed by most analyses of Chinese ancestor worship.[6] It does not exist. Many people die as children or before marriage, and many of those who survive to marry fail to produce male descendants. When we examine what happens to these people we discover that descent is only one of a wide range of relation-

---

[6] And I must now note a second exception, having just received a draft of a paper by Wang Sung-hsing entitled "Ancestors Proper and Peripheral." The essence of Wang's argument is that Chinese on Taiwan classify ancestors into two categories: those who are patrilineal forebears and those who are not.

ships that create an obligation to care for the dead. Instead of two mutually exclusive categories made up of agnatic ascendants and everyone else, we find a finely graded continuum that extends from those people to whom one is obligated by descent to those toward whom one owes no obligation at all. At one end of this continuum are ancestors whose tablets are placed in the position of honor at the left of the altar; at the other, we find the despised ghosts whose offerings are set outside the back door. Between the two are people who contributed to one's line but were not members of the line, and people who died as dependents of the line and have no one else to care for them. The tablets of the latter are placed on the right of the altar and are treated as ancestors; the tablets of the former are placed in a corner of the kitchen or in a hallway and are almost ghosts.

The one class of dead neglected as a matter of course are those who die as infants or small children. In Taiwan as elsewhere in China, an infant's death is assumed to prove that the child was really an evil spirit or "someone from a previous life coming back to dun you for a debt." As Mary Bryson puts it in her account of life in Wuchang in the 1890's, "The very fact of a baby's death convinces the parents that the little one was not a precious gift to be treasured, but possessed by some evil spirit, and only a source of anxiety and misfortune from the first, and the sooner they forget about it the better" (Bryson 1900: 22). Mrs. J. G. Cormack claims that in Peking a child whose death seemed imminent was "stripped and placed on the floor just inside the outer door of the room. The parents leave it there and watch what takes place. If the child survives this treatment, it is recognized as a true child of their own flesh and blood; but if it dies, then it never was their child, but an evil spirit seeking to gain entrance to their family in order to bring trouble on them." (Cormack 1935: 243–44.) She also notes that small children are never buried in the family graveyard "as that would mean adoption, and to adopt an evil spirit into the family would be the height of folly" (1935: 244). On the Shantung Peninsula children were buried without a coffin, just covered with sufficient dirt to hide the body from sight. The result was that at night the bodies were dug up and eaten by dogs. According to Robert Coltman (Coltman 1891: 77), the parents intended it thus, "For they say, 'An evil spirit inhabited the child's body, otherwise it would not have died so young. If the dogs eat it, the bad spirit enters the dog and cannot again enter another child who may be born to the same parents.'"

The idea that children who die young are really strangers is a consequence of the Chinese view that ancestor worship is an act of obeisance that can appropriately be performed only by a junior for a senior. If a man dies as a young adult, he will be worshipped by his own children, but never by his parents. On the contrary, his father will usually beat the coffin to punish his son for being so unfilial as to die before his parents. Consequently, if a person dies as a child, there is no one who can appropriately provide for his soul. His parents must either deny that the child was their own offspring, or live with the disquieting thought that a member of their family is now a hungry, homeless ghost. The only way the person who dies as a small child can achieve security as an ancestor is to "return" a generation or two after his death. If a shaman or fortune teller suggests that some misfortune is due to the anger of a neglected forebear, the family may then "discover" an ascendant who died as a child, and in this case the solution is to erect a tablet and initiate regular propitiatory offerings. The person who died as a child is now grandfather's older brother, and can therefore be accorded a place on the family altar and worshipped as an ancestor.

Although the Chinese kinship system demands that younger children defer to their older siblings, an older child can appropriately worship a younger brother or sister. People say that "the child who dies first is the eldest" and ignore the reversal of roles. This means that the great majority of people who die after early childhood but before marriage can be provided for, despite the fact that they have no descendants of their own. But it does not mean that they are all enshrined as ancestors on a proper altar. The fate of the person who dies before marriage depends on whether that person is a son or a daughter. Because a son who survives the first years of life is automatically recognized as a member of his father's line, he is entitled to a place on his father's ancestral altar. A daughter can never be accorded this privilege because women acquire membership in lines only through marriage. From her father's point of view, a daughter is an outsider. She can achieve the right to a place on his altar only by marrying a man who agrees to reside uxorilocally. Were a family to place the tablet of an unmarried daughter on their altar, they would risk the possibility of ancestral punishment. As one elderly informant put it, "The ancestors would surely be angry if you put an ugly thing like that on the altar."

The souls of unmarried girls can be disposed of in any one of several ways. At most of the funerals I have observed in San-hsia the soul is represented not by a tablet but by a small red sachet of incense ashes. After the funeral this is placed in a little basket to which is attached a section of bamboo that serves as an incense burner. In Ch'i-nan, where lineage organization creates a stronger sense of agnatic solidarity than elsewhere in San-hsia, many people insist that this basket and its contents cannot remain on lineage property.[7] In most villages in the area the basket can be hung anywhere in the house except in the *kong-thia:* (*kung-t'ing*), the hall where guests are received and the honored dead are worshipped. The preference is for "someplace where it won't be seen"—a dark passageway, behind a door, the corner of a storeroom. Asked why the souls of daughters are discriminated against in this way, some people say it is because these things are ugly and hateful. Others explain that it is because "women are meant to marry out and don't belong to their father's family." Ahern's informants told her (Ahern 1973: 127) that the soul of an unmarried girl could not be seated on lineage property because "she does not belong to us. From birth on, girls are meant to belong to other people. They are supposed to die in other people's houses."

The view that the souls of unmarried women should not come to rest in their natal home is not unique to San-hsia or to Taiwan. In his colorful description of ancestor worship in Shun-te hsien in Kwangtung, P. Alfred Fabre notes that a woman of marriageable age is not allowed to die in her father's house. Instead, she must breathe her last in a tent set up outside the house. And, Fabre adds (1935: 114), the same applies "a fortiori to the old unmarried aunt." In San-hsia the sachet of ashes that serves as the seat of an unmarried woman's soul often remains indefinitely in some dark corner of the house, but it appears that in Shun-te the soul was either removed by means of a ghost marriage (to be discussed shortly) or sent off to the care of a Buddhist monastery. At least Fabre does not mention the possibility of the soul's remaining in the care of its natal family. He only notes (1935: 114) that while awaiting removal the soul is not placed on the family altar, but is temporarily shut off in an area near the back door to the parents' house.

In his paper for this volume, Jack M. Potter reports that in the New Territories of Hong Kong people are afraid to put the tablets of unmarried daughters in the house "because they might haunt the family." One solution is to pay a spirit medium to care for the soul in her *pay-dhaan* (Cantonese), the shrine in which she communicates with the dead. In San-hsia families that want to rid themselves of an unmarried daughter usually deposit the ashes that represent her in what is known as a *ko-niu-biou,* a "maiden's temple," an example of which can be seen in Lung-p'u

---

[7] By "lineage property" people in Ch'i-nan mean both corporate land held by the lineage and land owned by families who are members of the lineage. I suspect that this usage reflects the fact that lineage members once enjoyed preemptive rights with respect to one another's landed property.

on the west side of town. This particular temple was built as a community project and now houses the souls of 32 unmarried girls. These girls receive occasional offerings from their natal families but derive most of their support from prostitutes, who take their collective soul as a kind of patron deity. These women go to the ko-niu-biou with requests they would not dare take to a representative of the supernatural bureaucracy.[8]

Elderly people in San-hsia say that in "the old days" a girl's parents could rid themselves of the responsibility for her soul by trapping a husband for her. The girl's name and horoscope were written on a piece of red paper, which was concealed in a purse or some other attractive bait and placed beside the road. The girl's brothers then hid nearby and waited until some unsuspecting passerby discovered the purse. The fact that he picked up the girl's horoscope was taken as evidence that he was fated to marry her, and so he usually did, in return for a small amount of money offered as a dowry. It did not matter if the man who discovered the purse was married. Indeed, I think married men were preferred because they would have children who would be obligated to worship the soul as a mother. Local custom made the soul the man's first wife, and thereby gave her the right to be worshipped by all her husband's children.

People in San-hsia no longer attempt to trap men to marry the souls of their deceased daughters, but a more elaborate form of ghost marriage still occurs. I heard of three such marriages in the San-hsia area in less than a year, and was invited to attend one of them as a guest. The groom was a young married man with two children who had recently suffered second-degree burns at a fire-walking in which he had participated despite his father's warning that he was polluted as a result of attending a funeral the day before. This experience convinced the young man that his father might also be right in insisting that his son had a "two-wife fate," which is to say that his first wife would die. Because a ghostly wife becomes her husband's first wife whether the marriage is his first or second marriage, the obvious way of forestalling the untimely death of the young man's living wife was for him to marry a woman already dead. He therefore agreed to let his father arrange a ghost marriage. The go-between was his father's sister, whose neighbor had a daughter who had died fifteen years previously. I did not have a chance to interview the bride's family, but was told that they had been trying to arrange a marriage for their daughter for some time.

[8] A woman who feels indebted to the maidens in the ko-niu-biou will usually leave a pair of children's shoes at the temple as an offering. People say they offer children's shoes because women in the im world still have bound feet.

The first step in the marriage procedure was to prepare a contract, which identified the groom and stipulated that his two living children would become the bride's children. This document was then submitted to the bride for her approval. "Had she refused, that would have been an end of the matter," but she agreed. The two families then exchanged a series of gifts, the groom's side sending to the bride's wedding cakes and NT $120 as a bride-price, receiving in return a dowry consisting of a gold ring, a gold necklace, several pairs of shoes, and six dresses, all fitted for the use of the groom's living wife. On the morning of the wedding day the dead bride's family held a feast for her benefit, "feeding her the same as if she were alive." The bride's brother and the go-between then placed the girl's tablet in a taxicab and conveyed it to the groom's home, where his friends and relatives had gathered for a second feast. On leaving their own home the bride's brother invited her to get into the cab, and on arriving at the groom's home informed her of their arrival and invited her to descend. The bride was always treated as though she was alive and participating in the proceedings. During the wedding feast her tablet sat on a chair next to the groom, and after the feast it was put in his bedroom. Local belief has it that a ghostly bride has sexual relations with her husband on their wedding night, and that as a result the man is always exhausted the next day. One of the guests told me that a man who sleeps with a soul "doesn't ejaculate just once or twice, but many times so that he cannot work the next day. A soul is im and so it is very *li-hai* [severe]." I asked if the soul ever returned a second time but was assured that this was impossible. "The next day the tablet is put on the ancestral altar and becomes a *sin* [*shen*, deity]. It cannot return to sleep with the man after that." It appears that once a soul is installed as an ancestor, it loses many of its human appetites.[9]

Although much of the talk at a ghost marriage is about the sexual prowess of female souls, the purpose of these weddings is not to provide dead girls with sexual partners, but to give them children who will be obliged to worship them. The point is made strikingly by the case of a woman I will call Ong A-mui. One day on her way home from the school where she taught, A-mui was struck down by a young man on a motorcycle and suffered such a severe concussion that she died a few hours later. She was forty years old, unmarried, and a member of a household that included her elderly mother and two married brothers. I inquired

---

[9] It appears that the form of ghost marriages varies considerably. In south-central Taiwan, David K. Jordan found that the groom was usually the bride's sister's husband (Jordan 1972: 152–53); in San-hsia most ghost marriages join unrelated families and thereby create new affinal ties. I was told that the groom in the marriage I describe was urged to visit his wife's parents frequently and treat them "like a father and mother."

into the case because I was interested to learn how much compensation her family would demand and how they would press their claim. Much to my surprise I discovered that rather than demanding compensation, her family was offering the young man all Ong A-mui's savings if he would agree to become her son. A neighbor explained that A-mui's mother feared that her sons would divide their sister's savings and neglect her soul. She had therefore spent a night in Mu-cha's famous Hsien Kung temple in the hope that the god would appear in a dream and tell her what to do. The god told her that the young man was an orphan, and said that the accident was a sign that he was fated to become her daughter's son. Because the young man agreed, there was no need for Ong A-mui to marry.

It is important to understand that daughters are not excluded from their father's altar because they are young and female. They are excluded because they are outsiders without a place in the descent line. Before World War II the great majority of all families in the San-hsia area gave away their own female children and adopted in their place "little daughters-in-law" (*sim-pua*) as wives for their sons. Although sim-pua did not enter into a conjugal relationship until they had reached puberty, they were considered married at the time they joined their future husband's family. Consequently, they were members of their husband's line and entitled to all the rights of a married woman. Whether she died as an infant or as a young adult, a sim-pua had a right to a seat on her foster father's altar. The girl's intended husband was responsible for her soul and could not marry without obtaining her permission, which required a promise that one of his sons would worship the girl as his mother. My older informants say that this promise had to be submitted to the deceased in the form of a written contract signed by the girl's foster father, her intended husband, and the woman he wanted to marry. "You had to promise that she would get one of the children or her soul would come back and cause trouble."

Although people often say that "you have to do something for the soul of a daughter or she will come back and cause trouble," it is my impression that serious misfortunes are more likely to be attributed to wives of the line than daughters of the line. Because married women have more rights than unmarried women, there is more likely to be understandable grounds for indignation on the part of a deceased wife. One of the most common sources of trouble is the failure of a second wife to respect the rights of her predecessor. In addition to the right to a place on her husband's altar, a married woman also has the right to expect her replacement to treat her "like an older sister." The second wife should pay a formal visit to the first wife's home immediately after her marriage and thereafter observe all of the duties of a daughter with respect to her predecessor's parents. She should also prepare special foods for the first wife on her deathday and say, "I hope older sister will protect me and help take care of the children." One of my most reliable informants told me that his father's sister had died shortly after marriage and that her husband's second wife had not visited their family. "Her children were sick all the time until she did this, but then everything was all right. The first wife was happy."

It is also important to recognize that the rights women attain through marriage depend on their continued association with their husband's line. If a woman's husband dies and his parents arrange a second marriage with a man who agrees to reside uxorilocally, she retains all her rights vis-à-vis her first husband's line. But if she divorces her husband or marries out of his family as a widow, she forfeits all claims on members of her first husband's line, including the right to expect her sons to worship her after death. It is said that Confucius worshipped his mother despite the fact she had divorced his father, but his grandson Tsu-ssu told his disciples that he could not expect his own children to worship their divorced mother. "My grandfather was a man of complete virtue. I cannot aspire to his level. For me, so long as the deceased was my wife, she was my son's mother. When she ceased to be my wife, she ceased also to be his mother." (Giles 1915: 116–17.)

Although married women who remain identified with their husband's line have a right to a place on his altar, this right does not extend to members of their natal family. If a woman should bring her parents' tablets with her at marriage or be forced by a brother's death to assume responsibility for them later in life, these guests in her husband's home are relegated to an altar in a back room of the house or at best a subsidiary altar located at the right of her husband's altar in the kong-thia:. They are granted a place on her husband's altar only if the wife's responsibility entitles her to inherit a share of her father's estate. Property makes unwelcome visitors honored guests. In such a case the husband must treat his wife's parents with respect, and must assign one of his children to act as their heir and descendant.

In addition to the tablets of unmarried daughters and those introduced by women who married into the family, one occasionally finds in a back room the tablets of dead who are cared for "because they died here and had no one else to provide for them." A good example can be seen in a kitchen in the Song compound whose residents worship the dead of five descent lines. The eldest member of the compound is a woman named Song Suat, whose father and husband both married uxorilocally. Their tablets are located on the main altar in the kong-thia:, alongside the tablets of the original Lim line of Song Suat's grand-father. The remaining two sets of tablets belong to a Ti: line and a Tiu: line and are located on a small shelf in the kitchen of Song Suat's second son. Song Suat insists that these tablets cannot be allowed on the family altar in the kong-thia: "because these are people who just came back here to die." Her story is that one of her mother's sisters married a man named Ti: and bore one child, a daughter. When her parents died the daughter married a man named Tiu: who died a few years later, leaving his wife with one child, an adopted daughter, and the responsibility for both the Ti: and the Tiu: tablets. At this point Song Suat adopted the adopted daughter to raise as a wife for her second son, and the girl and her mother came to live with Song Suat's family. The death of the adopted daughter, and shortly thereafter the death of her mother, left Song Suat's family with two sets of tablets belonging to unrelated lines. They felt they could not abandon them "because they had no children of their own," and so they put the tablets on a shelf in the kitchen, where they are now cared for by Song Suat's son.

We have so far identified two classes of dead. First, there are those dead who are not worshipped because no one has an obligation to care for their souls. They include strangers and children whose deaths are taken as evidence that they are in fact strangers. Second, somewhat closer to the core of the family, is the class of dead best described as dependents of the line. This class includes unmarried daughters, rela-tives of women who married into the family, and dead who are cared for because someone feels sorry for them. These dead are not worshipped on their individual deathdays, and their tablets cannot be placed on the family altar in the kong-thia:. The best they can hope for is a shelf in some corner of the house and occasional offerings on such calendar holi-days as the lunar New Year.

Until recently most homes in the San-hsia area were built in a style that allowed the house to expand into a large U-shaped compound as the family itself was expanded by the marriages of the founder's sons and grandsons. Approaching one of these homes by way of the open end of the U, one faces heavy double-leaf doors that lead into the kong-thia:, and beyond these doors, facing them from the opposite wall, a high, dark wooden table—the ancestral altar. The altar is more than just a table for tablets and an incense burner; it is the seat of the head of the family's line and is generally regarded as the exclusive property of the line. The tablets of other lines may be placed on the altar, but only with the permission of the dead who own the altar. Some people say their ancestors would punish anyone who placed a guest tablet on the altar without first obtaining the ancestors' permission, and everyone agrees that if other tablets are added, they must be placed in the inferior position to the right of the owners' tablets. People also feel that the tablets of different lines must be separated from one another. Altars with guest lines always contain an incense burner for each line, and on many of these altars the lines are separated from one another by a small wooden partition. Some people say that the purpose of these partitions is to save the owners the embarrassment of eating in the presence of guests; others insist that if the dead of different lines are not kept apart, they will quarrel and bring disaster on their descendants.

We can therefore add two further classes of dead to the two already identified. The first occupies the position of honor on the altar located in the kong-thia: and consists of deceased members of the family head's descent line, typically his lineal agnatic ascendants and their wives. The second occupies the inferior position at the right of the altar and consists of a heterogeneous class of dead whose one common characteristic is that their line somehow contributed to the welfare of the host line. Lou Hok-lai's father-in-law qualifies because he gave Lou a share of his estate. Probably because he was too poor to afford a bride price, Lou married a woman whose father was looking for a son-in-law who would help him support his family until his own sons were old enough to cope. Although men who marry in this way sometimes demand a small piece of land as well as waiver of the usual bride-price, this was not part of the agreement Lou reached with his wife's father. It therefore came as a pleasant surprise when his father-in-law gave him a small piece of property "to thank me for helping him raise his children." The result was that when his father-in-law died, Lou made a tablet for him and placed it on his altar next to that of his own parents. He told me that he does not have to worship his father-in-law, "because he has sons of his own," but added that he felt that he ought to "because he was very good to me and gave me a share of his property."

Since inheritance of landed property ordinarily follows descent, it is unusual to find people obligated to worship the dead of other lines as a consequence of inheritance. The only other case I have encountered in San-hsia is that of Tan Thian-lai, whose altar contains the tablets of four lines. In addition to his own parents and grandparents in the Tan line, Tan Thian-lai worships three people surnamed Hong, a man named Ng, and three people who bear the surname Yu:. By his own account, Tan Thian-lai's obligation to these people derives from his inheriting property from Yu:, who had inherited it from Ng, who had in turn inherited it from Hong. Tan told me that the land in question once belonged to a man named Hong Hue-lieng, whose only child was an adopted daughter. To perpetuate his line and provide for his old age Hong married his daughter to a man named Ng Jong-kuei, who agreed to reside uxorilocally and assign some of his children to the Hong line. Unfortunately, Ng Jong-kuei and his wife died childless, at which point the Hong estate and the responsibility for the Hong and Ng dead passed to a man named Yu: Chieng-cua, "the manager of the Hong land." When Yu: Chieng-cua also died without descendants, his wife "called in" as her second husband Tan Thian-lai's father, who brought with him the tablets of his own forebears. The result was that Tan Thian-lai inherited what had once been the Hong estate and an ancestral altar that contained the dead of four lines. He told me that he has to worship the Hong, Ng, and Yu: dead as well as his father and his Tan ancestors "because all of the land we have used to belong to them."

A more common reason for worshipping the dead of another line is that one's father belongs to it. Although the Chinese ideal is for all a man's children to take their descent from him, in practice a large percentage of all children take their descent from someone other than their father, most commonly their mother's father. When a family has no sons who survive to marry, they ordinarily must arrange an uxorilocal marriage for a daughter or an adopted daughter. Occasionally a man can be found who is willing to resign his place in his own line and allow all his future children to take their descent from his father-in-law. But most men who marry uxorilocally insist on retaining their own surname and the right to name some of their sons to their own line. One arrangement is to name the first-born son to his maternal grandfather's line and all other children to their father's line; a common alternative is to alternate the children's descent without regard to their sex.

Those children of uxorilocal marriages who take their descent from their father must worship their mother as well as their father and his forebears, but this obligation does not necessarily produce a mixed ancestral altar. They can simply ignore the fact of the uxorilocal marriage and worship their mother as their father's wife. For example, if a man surnamed Lim marries into an Ong family, those children who take their descent from him usually worship their mother as Lim Ma, Ancestress Lim, ignoring the fact that their brothers worship the same woman as Ong Ma. But this solution to the problem of uxorilocal marriages is not available to those children who take their descent from their mother's father. They are obligated by descent to worship him and his forebears, from whom they inherit their property. But they are also obligated to worship their father. "You have to worship your mother's father because he gave you his property, but you also have to worship your father because he raised you. How could you not worship your father?" Since it is inconceivable that a man should be treated as his wife's husband rather than as a representative of a line, these obligations always produce mixed altars.

When a man marries into his wife's family he contributes labor and children to their line, while they provide him and his children with a home and the use of land. The result is a strong sense of mutual obligation that often endures for several generations. If the marriage produces enough children to carry on both lines, these obligations are not expressed in ancestor worship beyond the first generation. But if one of the two lines should lack descendants, the other is required to care for their dead. The inevitable result is that many ancestral altars contain tablets devoted to the remote dead of guests' lines as well as tablets representing the worshippers' parents and the senior members of their own descent line.

Ong Hok-lai's altar is unusual only in that it contains the tablets of two guest lines. Ong's maternal grandmother was an only child whose husband, a man named Lim, married uxorilocally, bringing with him his parents' tablets. Had this couple produced enough children to represent both lines, the responsibility for the Ong and Lim dead would have been divided when Ong Hok-lai's parents died. But his parents were even less fortunate than his grandparents. Their only child was an adopted daughter, who was assigned to the Ong line. Because she was an only child, she had to worship her father and his parents as well as her mother and her ancestors in the Ong line; and, for the same reason, she also married uxorilocally, to a man surnamed Tan, who brought with him his foster parents' tablets. Consequently, by the time Ong Hok-lai was born the family altar contained representatives of three lines. At the left, in the position of honor, were the tablets of the original Ong line; at their right, the Lim tablets brought by Ong Hok-lai's maternal grandfather; and, at the right of the altar in the lowest position, the Tan tablets introduced by his father. Ong Hok-lai's parents proved more fertile than his grandparents and his great-grandparents, bearing six sons and three daughters. Ong Hok-lai was the eldest son and was assigned to the Ong line; his second and fourth brothers were given to the Lim line; and his third and fifth brothers, to the Tan line. Unfortunately for the dead, Ong Hok-lai was the only filial son in the lot. His brothers all tired of the hard life of upland farmers and moved away to the city, deserting the tablets on the family altar. By descent, Ong Hok-lai is obligated only to his mother and her ascendants in the Ong line, but in fact he worships all the dead represented on the altar. These include, in addition to his deceased wife, his mother, his maternal grandmother, this woman's parents, grandparents, and great-grandparents; a man Ong identifies as his mother's mother's grandfather's younger brother's son; Ong's father and his foster parents; and Ong's maternal grandfather and his parents: a total of sixteen people. When I asked Ong Hok-lai how he could remember the deathdays of sixteen ancestors, he showed me a notebook that lists the names of the dead in one column and their death dates in another.

Ong Hok-lai's case is also interesting as an example of a tendency to divide the dead into classes representing degrees of obligation. The Ong tablets at the left of the altar are divided from the Lim and Tan tablets by a partition, but the Lim and Tan tablets are not separated from one another. Thus, whereas the altar contains tablets belonging to three descent lines, these are presented as divisible into two classes: those dead to whom Ong Hok-lai is obligated by descent and those to whom he is obligated as a consequence of uxorilocal marriages. The difference between these dead and those to whom Ong owes little or no obligation is shown by the location of a set of tablets introduced into the house by Ong's second wife. These have been relegated to a little shelf in the corner of a storeroom behind the kitchen. Ong Hok-lai insists that they could not be placed on the family altar or even in the kong-thia:. "These people didn't marry into the family. They aren't really members of the family."

Although Ong Hok-lai's arrangement of his ancestral tablets is a common one, it is by no means universal. The degree to which the various classes of dead are separated varies with the size and corporate solidarity of the group that owns the altar. One seldom finds partitions on domestic altars that serve a single household. These appear only later, when the house has grown into a compound occupied by several agnatically related families who worship their common ancestors at what I call a communal altar. If further growth does not destroy the residents' solidarity, they may even bar the tablets of other lines on the altar in the kong-thia:. The tablets of guest lines are then relegated to subsidiary altars in the private quarters of those people who are responsible for their care.[10] The extreme case in San-hsia is Ch'i-nan, where communal altars have been replaced by true lineage halls. Although the altars in

[10] In the course of our work in the San-hsia area, C. Stevan Harrell and I have examined 33 altars whose owners worship guest lines in the same house. Twenty-two of these were domestic altars belonging to a single family; eleven were communal altars serving two or more families living in one house. In eleven of the 33 cases the tablets of the guest lines were divided from those of the host line either by a partition on the altar or by removal of the tablets of the guests' lines to subsidiary altars. The difference between domestic altars and communal altars is evident in the

these halls admit the recent dead as well as the remote dead and serve as domestic altars for weddings and funerals, they are rigidly exclusive, admitting only lineage members who have given all their sons to the lineage (Ahern 1973: 121–25). The result is a situation in which the dead of lines that belong to the lineage are worshipped in halls at the center of the community; the souls of in-marrying men are worshipped only at private altars in the homes around the hall; and the souls of un-married daughters are entirely excluded from the community. The order is the one found throughout the San-hsia area, the difference being that in Ch'i-nan more rigorous distinctions are drawn between the three classes of dead.

My thesis is not that people in San-hsia classify the dead into three or four mutually exclusive categories, but rather that they recognize a con-tinuum of obligation and arrange ancestral tablets in a way that expresses their relative degree of obligation to particular people. After her husband died Lim Chun-ki lived for a number of years with a man named Tan Tsui-ong, who helped her raise her four sons. When Tan died Lim felt obliged to worship him "because he helped me raise my children," but she did not want to place his tablet on her family altar, probably because she and Tan had never married. On the other hand, she felt that she could not relegate his tablet to a back room "like someone who didn't matter." Her solution was to locate Tan's tablet on a small shelf next to the family altar in the kong-thia:. The important point is that however they arrange their tablets, people in San-hsia recognize a continuum of obligation that runs from those dead to whom the living are obligated by descent to those to whom they are hardly obligated at all. The dead at one end of the continuum are true ancestors; the dead at the other end are almost ghosts.

IV

In China ancestor worship is by nature an act of obeisance. Many people make regular offerings to dead who are not members of their line, sometimes even to quite distant relatives. But no one would con-sider worshipping a child or grandchild. Although people are under-standably reluctant to contemplate the possibility, all agree that parents will abandon the soul of an adolescent son rather than worship him them-selves. "Parents can never worship their own children. Children are supposed to worship their parents."

The offerings made to the gods also express obeisance, but the mo-

---

fact that hosts and guests are separated by one or the other of these devices in eight (72.7 percent) of the communal altars as compared with only three (13.6 percent) of the domestic altars.

tives are entirely different. A person worships his ancestors because he is obligated to do so as an heir or descendant; he worships the gods in the hope of gaining their sympathy and good will. Since a man is no more obligated to worship a god than he is to make gifts to an official, there is no thought that a god might punish a person for neglecting him. But neglect of worship is the most common reason given for misfortunes attributed to the agency of the ancestors. A man who used to live in Hsia-ch'i-chou married and moved out of the village, leaving his sister and her husband to care for his parents' tablets. A few years later his wife fell ill, and then one of his children. Frightened by these events and a doctor's inability to cure the illnesses, he consulted a shaman and was told that they were caused by his father, who wanted his son to care for his tablet. The shaman explained the essential difference between the gods and the ancestors in these terms: "A man is free to believe in the gods or not believe in the gods, but he has to believe in the ancestors. If he doesn't, they will come back and cause him trouble."

People ordinarily worship the god under whose jurisdiction they live because worship is often a community activity and because it is prudent to maintain good relations with such powerful figures, but it is clear that the average man does not feel morally obligated to make offerings to any god. If a particular deity is uninterested in his subjects or lacks the authority to be of any use to them, they turn to another god who is more sympathetic and more powerful. According to stories now told in Hsia-ch'i-chou, there was a period in the late 1930's and early 1940's when Shang Ti Kung was less efficacious than he is at present. During this period the god and his temple were neglected. The roof of the temple leaked; the garden in the courtyard filled up with weeds; and the god himself sat unconsulted and unhonored on a dirty altar. It was not until Shang Ti Kung was credited with predicting the political troubles of the late 1940's that his temple was repaired and interest in the god revived. What I think is the essential attitude toward the supernatural bureaucracy is revealed in the advice an old woman claims to have given Shang Ti Kung during the period of his decline. In her words, "I went to the temple every day, and every day I said to the god, 'You are a god with great ability, so why do you sit here and say nothing? You ought to show what you can do and let people here know what kind of a god you are. It is because you don't show what you can do that people all go elsewhere to worship. If you would do something to make your ability known, the people would all come here to worship.'"

When people encounter misfortunes it is usually to the gods that they appeal for help, but occasionally the aid of the ancestors may also be solicited. Because the ancestors are not so powerful as the gods, one cannot expect as much of them. They may even choose to ignore requests made of them, and if they do their descendants have little ground for complaint. A person's ancestors are his parents and grandparents, and parents and grandparents have no obligation to heed every request of a child or grandchild. But even though the relationship favors the ancestors as seniors, there is still an assumption of reciprocity. The ancestors may ignore many of their descendants' requests without endangering the relationship, but they cannot consistently ignore urgent and repeated supplications. If they do, their descendants may forswear their obligations. This is an extreme step, comparable to a man's abandoning his aged father, but it is not unheard of. Conversion to Christianity is often attributed to the failures of the convert's ancestors, and one man I know destroyed his ancestors' tablets in a rage at what he took to be their indifference. When Lim Bun-iek's wife became seriously ill, Lim appealed to his ancestors to help her recover. Unfortunately, and much to Lim's distress, she died. Two years later Lim's mother became ill; again he appealed to the ancestors for aid, and again without success. His mother also died. For a man with a temper as violent as Lim Bun-iek's this was more strain than his bonds with his ancestors could bear. He seized the ancestral tablets, chopped them into small pieces, burnt the pieces, and then threw the ashes into the river, telling his neighbors that he was henceforth a Christian. When I asked him why he no longer worshipped his ancestors, he replied, "What use are your ancestors? You spend money making offerings to them all the time, and then when you need their help they don't do anything for you."

In making the point that a son does not have an absolute obligation to worship his father, Ahern notes (1973: 155) that if a man has more than one son and fails to leave one of them property, the man who is disinherited need not worship his father. "Most of the people I asked about this replied, 'Why would that son want to worship his father if he didn't get any property?'" But some of Ahern's informants added that although "a son was justified in not making offerings to his father under these conditions, he still risked his father's anger; an angry deceased father could easily bring sickness or misfortune on him. No matter how strained a son's relations with his father, he may be held accountable to his father anyway simply for the gift of life." Although the obligation a son owes his father is not absolute, then, this evidence suggests that it is very nearly so. That a man could be disinherited and still be held accountable for "the gift of life" argues that the burden of obligation favors parents and gives them the right to demand unquestioning loyalty.

Although revolutionaries in China have destroyed images of the tutelary deities as symbols of the establishment, most Chinese would not blame a god for failing to answer a petition. Because the gods are not conceived of as having obligations to their subjects, there would be no cause for indignation. When a man appeals to an ancestor he appeals to a kinship relationship involving a certain degree of mutual dependence, but when he appeals to a god he negotiates for his good will just as he would in attempting to secure a favor from a magistrate or a policeman. He makes a small sacrifice and promises a larger one if the god will grant his petition. If divination reveals that the god is not inclined to grant the petition, he then promises a more substantial gift, repeating the process until the god finally agrees. The god is always treated with all the courtesy owed someone of such high status, but the larger gift is not produced until after the desired outcome has been obtained. Having promised a pig's head if a child's illness is cured or the price of pork raised, a person does not actually sacrifice the pig's head until the child has recovered or he has sold his pigs at a profit. As is always the case in negotiations with officials and petty bureaucrats, small gifts and respect are offered in promise of larger gifts to come, but the larger gifts are not delivered until the results are safely in hand.

Although neither the gods nor the ancestors are conceived of as essentially malevolent, both are considered capable of inflicting misfortunes on the living. These misfortunes are always interpreted as punishment, but very different motives explain the penalties attributed to the gods and those attributed to the ancestors. Like their counterparts in the human bureaucracy, the gods are thought of as proud and exceedingly jealous of their prerogatives. Any derogation of their high status is likely to bring a quick and angry response. A few years ago a man in Hsia-ch'i-chou fell at a fire-walking and was so badly burned that he later died of his wounds. Some of his neighbors now say that the god was punishing him for having failed to observe three days of sexual abstinence prior to the event. "The god was angry because that man came there dirty." Another man in the same village suffers from severe palsy, which people say is a consequence of his having made fun of a god he saw at a procession when he was a child. That this view of the gods was widespread in traditional China is suggested by Mrs. William L. Pruen's comments on the death of one of her neighbor's children in Chengtu: "At another home in this compound a little fellow, about eleven years of age, was suddenly taken dangerously ill. The poor boy was very worried because he had in some way insulted an idol shrine and thought he was being punished for his fault. He died the next day." (Pruen 1906: 101–2.)

The gods are sensitive to insult and may punish a man for personal reasons, but they are also officials who promote the general welfare. They are said to reward those who lead virtuous lives and to punish anyone who violates the moral code. An elderly man in Kan-yüan told me that a typhoon had washed away his neighbor's field and not his own "because the gods were punishing that man for always stealing other people's water. He was a bandit who took whatever he wanted." Several people in Ch'i-pei, on the other side of San-hsia town, claim that one of their neighbors used a potion to make her husband impotent (because she was a sim-pua and didn't like her husband), and that as a result the gods punished her with a protracted illness. Any particularly striking death is likely to be interpreted as supernaturally administered punishment. One day Hsia-ch'i-chou was struck by an unusually violent electrical storm. As one villager described it to me six years later, "There was lightning everywhere. The rice stalks in the kitchen looked like they were about to burn." Ong Hok-hin, returning from his fields, stopped to rest in front of the village store. "After watching the storm for a while, he said, 'I wonder who the lightning will kill today.' Then he got up and walked toward home. He was killed just as he was entering his house." Although Ong Hok-hin was generally thought of as a man of good character, the manner of his death was taken as evidence of some unsuspected crime. "He always seemed to be a good man, but he must have done something very bad that no one knew about or the gods wouldn't have punished him that way." A more sophisticated informant made the same point about a relative who had been killed by a truck, adding that "this is the reason people say it is better to die of an illness than to die a violent death."

Most people in San-hsia say that the gods only punish people "who are really bad," but the belief that the gods do administer punishment leads a few people to assume that they can be induced to avenge private wrongs. When Li A-hong's uxorilocally married son-in-law persuaded his wife to move out of her mother's home, Li A-hong was furious and "asked the gods to let him be crushed to death in a mining accident." "A year later when I heard that his shoulder had been broken in an accident, I was very happy. But then he recovered, and so I told the god that if he would let that man be killed, I would burn a hundred sticks of incense in an open field." When her son-in-law was killed in a second accident in the mines, Li A-hong was delighted. "My neighbors came and told me that that man had been crushed beyond recognition in the mines, and I was so happy that I laughed and laughed and laughed."

Just how punitive the ancestors are is the subject of sharp disagreement. On the basis of his extended experience as the British magistrate of Weihaiwei, R. F. Johnston concluded (1910: 286–87) that "ancestral spirits are regarded as beneficent beings who never causelessly use their mysterious powers to injure the living; but if their descendants lead evil lives, or neglect the family sacrifices, or treat the sacred rules of filial piety with contempt, then the spirits will in all probability exercise the parental prerogatives of punishment. . . . The father does not, by the mere accident of death, divest himself of his patriarchal rights of administering justice and inflicting punishment on his sons and grandsons." Essentially the same view is expressed by J. T. Addison (Addison 1925) and by Maurice Freedman, who summarizes his view of "the characteristic behaviour imputed to Chinese ancestors" as follows (Freedman 1967: 92–93): "While they will certainly punish their descendants if they suffer neglect or are offended by an act of omission which affects them directly (chiefly, the failure to secure for them a firm line of descent), they are essentially benign and considerate of their issue. Before taking action against their descendants they need to be provoked; capricious behaviour is certainly alien to their benevolent and protective nature."

In his study of West Town in Yünnan and in his generalizations about China as a whole, Francis L. K. Hsu argues (Hsu 1963: 45) not only that the ancestors are benevolent, but that they do not punish at all. "It can be stated unequivocally that ancestral spirits, in every part of China, are believed to be only a source of benevolence, never a source of punishment to their descendants. This is shown by the fact that when the Chinese is suffering some misfortune, such as sickness or fire or flood or the lack of male progeny, he will suspect that the fault lies with any of a variety of deities or ghosts, but never with the spirits of an ancestor." Emily Ahern, on the other hand, challenges the view that the ancestors are "essentially benign" and offers impressive evidence of their occasional capriciousness and malevolent intent. Her informants told her that the ancestors sometimes inflict misfortunes just because they are "mean" or have "a bad heart," and that even when a person makes regular offerings to his ancestors, he cannot be certain that they won't come back and cause trouble (Ahern 1973: 199–200).

In the version of this paper written in 1965, after my first field trip, I characterized beliefs about ancestral punishment in much the same terms as Johnston and Freedman. Since then I have returned to the field twice, and on each occasion have come away convinced that the ancestors are more punitive than I had previously thought. Ahern notes that many people in Ch'i-nan refused to tell her their version of a story that reflects hostility between the dead and their surviving descendants (1973: 207). This seems to me only one manifestation of a conflict between an ideal that says the ancestors are always benevolent and a fear that they are in fact punitive. Asked if they believe that their ancestors would punish them for neglect, people usually insist that they would not. But when they suffer a series of misfortunes, most people give serious consideration to the possibility that the ancestors are responsible.

I cannot cite here all the evidence that led me to this conclusion, but the following excerpts from my field notes should suffice to make the point that ancestors are not always benign and considerate:

1. The wife of a doctor in the town of San-hsia married out of her natal family despite being an only child. When her children suffered a series of illnesses, this was widely interpreted as punishment inflicted by her neglected ancestors. Apparently she and her husband accepted this interpretation, for they named one of their children to her father's line and now worship her forebears as well as her husband's.

2. Tan Kim-hok told me that if one of three brothers dies without children, the survivors have to give him one of their sons in adoption. "If they didn't, the man who died would come back and cause trouble." He explained that this is why he and his sons worship his younger brother even though he died after the family was divided.

3. I asked Li Chieng-cua if a man's sons have to have their father's permission to divide the family. He insists that they do, and that the ancestors would punish anyone who talked about dividing the family when their father was unwilling.

4. A man whose registered name is Ong Kok-hua told me that his real name is Ong Ng Kok-hua. He was given the second surname as a child, when it was discovered that an illness was caused by "an early ancestor" named Ng who wanted him to be his son. He also told me that two of his four children died because he did not give them the Ng surname, and made a point of noting that the two who survived had been given the surname Ng.

5. The wife of a farmer for whom Tan So-lan picked tea mistreated her sim-pua so badly that the girl committed suicide. To get revenge the girl's parents pulled an edge of her clothing out of the coffin before it was buried. "That girl came back all the time to scare her [foster] mother. When the mother's son married, the daughter-in-law was very aggressive and fought with her mother-in-law. Their quarrels made the son feel so bad that he ran away to the mainland and became a bandit. All this was because that woman treated her sim-pua so badly."

6. Hong Hai-a told me that the ancestors will punish anyone who dis-

turbs their tablets. He says nothing will happen if a cat or dog disturbs a tablet because the ancestors understand that animals do not know any better.[11]

7. One of Ui A-chan's neighbors told me that when Ui's grandmother died, the family arranged a *kong-tik* (a "merit" ceremony) for all their ancestors. Unfortunately, they wrote the wrong name for one ancestor, writing A-hok, the name he was always called by, though his real name was Thiam-hok. When they discovered the mistake they asked a shaman to intervene, but he said it was too late. By that time someone else had received all the money they had burned for Thiam-hok. The neighbor claims that Ui A-chan's family is so poor because of this unwitting slight to their ancestor.

8. Ong Lai-ho used to live next to a family who made their living as wood cutters. Because it was inconvenient for them to worship their ancestors on their individual deathdays, they decided to worship them all together on the ninth day of the ninth lunar month. "After that the husband and wife were sick all the time. The husband even lost one of his eyes."

9. Ong Lai-ho also told me that one of her neighbors inherited his brother's land and built a house on it, but did not bother to worship his brother. "His family was very troublesome until he went to see a god and found out the reason. After he began to worship his brother, the trouble stopped."

10. Lou Mui-mue told me that when her husband was about ten years old, his parents went to ask a god why he was so often sick. The god said it was because his mother's first husband wanted the boy to worship him. After his death this man's wife had married out of his family and left his tablet in charge of an adopted daughter. This girl worshipped her foster father and took his tablet with her when she married, but he was dissatisfied because his tablet was placed on a subsidiary altar in a back room. He wanted his wife's son to worship him and place his tablet on the main altar.

11. Ong Cin-tik's daughter says that an American missionary persuaded her mother's brother's son to throw away his ancestral tablets and become a Christian. "He died a few months later, and his father the following year. It's not a good thing to become a Christian and neglect the ancestors."

[11] Hong Hai-a's attitude is not unusual. Ahern (1973: 201) quotes one of her informants as follows: "Several years ago a Ui man accidentally bumped and moved the incense pot for the ancestors in the hall. As a result, another man in the lineage died shortly thereafter. When they opened the box to insert the man's tablet, two more people died."

12. I asked Lou Kim-lan if the gods would punish a mother-in-law who mistreated her daughter-in-law. She agreed that the gods would punish a woman who mistreated her daughter-in-law, adding that the ancestors would punish a daughter-in-law who mistreated her mother-in-law.

13. When his younger brother died, Li Ai-cu's neighbor drove his sister-in-law out of the house and claimed all the family's property for himself. Li Ai-cu says that as a result the man still cannot use the rooms that were once occupied by his brother's family. "Anyone who tries to live in those rooms sees that man who died and gets scared."

14. A former head of the Lou lineage in Ch'i-nan told me that Lous never marry their neighbors the Uis. "The Uis tried to steal our land and we told our ancestors we would never marry anyone named Ui." He also told me that when a Lou family broke this pledge and gave a daughter to a Ui family as a sim-pua, the girl died before she was old enough to marry her foster brother. He attributes the girl's death to the anger of his lineage ancestors.[12]

15. After fathering one son Lim Iu-chan was killed by aborigines, and his wife called in as her second husband a man named Ti: Cin-cai, who fathered three sons. When Ti: died the family prepared a gravestone that indicated he had four sons, counting Lim Iu-chan's son along with Ti:'s three. When several members of the family fell ill shortly thereafter, everyone agreed that this was because Lim did not want his son counted as one of Ti:'s sons. Neighbors say the sick members of the family did not recover until the gravestone was changed.

These cases and those mentioned earlier should not be taken as evidence that everyone in San-hsia fears their ancestors or attributes most misfortunes to their agency. Even when confronted with examples provided by their neighbors, many people insist that the ancestors do not ordinarily punish their descendants. At the same time, the fact that many people do not attribute misfortunes to their ancestors does not necessarily mean they consider them benign. When I asked Tan A-bok if she thought the ancestors would punish their descendants for neglecting them, she replied, "Oh, no, that wouldn't happen. Wouldn't everyone be rich if their ancestors were so powerful?" I think that Hsu is right in saying that Chinese never attribute such major disasters as epidemics to their ancestors, but I feel he is wrong in taking this as evidence that the ancestors are essentially benevolent (1963: 45–46). In my view the ancestors are

---

[12] Similar instances involving the same two lineages are mentioned by Ahern as evidence that people attribute serious illness and even death to their ancestors (1973: 201).

not propitiated as possible causes of major catastrophes because people do not think them powerful enough to affect the living in such a dramatic fashion. Freedman has argued that ancestors are not feared in China as in some West African societies because the living are not conscious of having displaced their ascendants from coveted positions of power (1966: 143–54; 1967: 90–102). A simpler explanation might be that Chinese ancestors are not feared because they are not conceived of as powerful beings. The African societies Freedman discusses are stateless societies in which the senior men of the lineage dominate the social landscape. In traditional China the authority of senior kinsmen was overshadowed by the far greater power of the imperial bureaucracy. People did not attribute great events to the spiritual remains of kinsmen because kinsmen were not capable of controlling the course of events. Great events were more appropriately attributed to gods, gods who were modeled on the imperial bureaucracy.

The essential difference between the gods and the ancestors is not that the former are punitive while the latter are essentially benevolent. It is, rather, that while the gods are powerful and represent public morality, the ancestors are relatively weak and concerned only with their own welfare and that of their descendants. The gods often punish people for crimes against society at large, the ancestors never. Quintessentially members of kinship groups, they remain identified with their best interests. When I asked people if they thought their ancestors would punish them for stealing from a stranger, they seemed genuinely surprised by the question. "Why should they want to punish you for a thing like that?" one of my more outspoken informants replied. "Aren't your ancestors your own parents and grandparents?"

This difference between the gods and the ancestors is evident in the way the two are supplicated. When a man asks the help of a god he must accompany his petition with an offering to gain the god's attention and assure his good will. Without an offering, there is no reason to expect the god to hear and respond to his plea. But when a person appeals to his ancestors, he need not make an offering then and there. Insofar as senior kinsmen are obliged to heed the requests of their juniors, they are under a general obligation to do so, just as juniors are under a general obligation to provide comfort and support for their seniors. Where relations with the gods must be continually renewed with offerings and shows of respect, any favor being dependent on an exhaustible good will, a man's relations with his ancestors are general and permanent, involving an assumption of a common welfare and mutual dependence. One is a kinship relationship; the other a political relationship.

V

Although the gods and the ancestors differ in many important respects, they also have a great deal in common. The extreme contrast, from the Chinese point of view, is between the gods and the ancestors on the one hand, and ghosts on the other. The gods and the ancestors are granted the respect due social superiors; ghosts are despised, "like beggars." Where the gods and the ancestors can be appealed to for protection and help, ghosts offer men nothing but misfortune of every kind. The terms used to refer to the two forms of the supernatural denote the sharpest spiritual and moral opposition. The gods and the ancestors are sin, "gods" or "deities"; the generic name for ghosts is kui, "demons" or "devils." In Chinese metaphysics the positive, immaterial, and celestial aspect of the human soul is termed sin; the negative, material, and terrestrial side of the soul is called kui. Philosophers associate sin with growth, production, and life, and hence with light and warmth; kui is identified with decline, destruction, and death, and, by extension, with darkness and cold.[13]

The catalogue of human misery attributed to ghosts is a lengthy one. Accidents, barrenness, death, and all varieties of illness are laid to their agency, as are crop failures, business losses, bad luck in gambling, and the wasteful and disruptive habits of individual men and women. One woman in Ch'i-chou blames ghosts for her husband's frequent visits to wine houses and prostitutes, and another sees their malevolent influence at work in her son's lack of enterprise and her daughter-in-law's stubborn independence. Any contact with ghosts, however brief, is likely to result in misfortune. One night Tan Chun-mui was returning home late from the market town and saw "something black" ahead of her on the path. Frightened by the apparition, she stopped, thinking it might be wise to return to town and spend the night with friends. While she hesitated, "the black thing flipped over into the field and was gone." Tan Chun-mui was so shaken she had to crawl all the way home to the village, and she and her friends now say the encounter resulted in an illness "lasting for months and months."

Some ghosts are purposely harmful, "like a man who is mad at you," whereas others are only passively dangerous, "like a hot stove." In the view of most of my informants the character of a ghost depends upon his

---

[13] C. Stevan Harrell (1974) discusses cases in which ghosts acquire a reputation for great power and come to be regarded as gods. The important point with respect to my thesis is that powerful spirits become gods and are then clothed in bureaucratic trappings. It is as though the peasant cannot imagine great power that is not essentially bureaucratic.

social and economic circumstances. Most dead people have descendants obligated to make offerings for their benefit, and their souls are therefore supplied with all the means of a comfortable existence in the next world. The spiritual remains of these people are content and bear no malice toward the living. The malicious ghosts are those discontented souls who are forced by their circumstances to prey on the living. They include the neglected dead—those who have no descendants because they died childless or as children, and those who died away from home and were forgotten—and also those hateful souls who receive no sacrifices because they remain at the scene of death seeking revenge—murder victims, suicides, and the unjustly executed. Some are angry because they are hungry and homeless, and some are hungry and homeless because they are angry. The weaker of these unhappy beings gather outside temples to beg for a living like the derelicts of this world, while the more powerful among them roam the countryside like so many bandits.

Although people in San-hsia differ on how one should deal with these malevolent creatures, they agree that dealing with a ghost is like dealing with *lo-mua:*, the gangs of young toughs who use threats of violence as a means of extortion. According to Ong Thian-co, "You have to make offerings to ghosts. They are just like the lo-mua:. If you don't give them something so that they will go away, you will never have any peace." Ong Zi-ko also views an offering to a ghost as comparable to paying off a lo-mua:, but he takes a more defiant attitude toward the use of such offerings. In his view it is a mistake to make an offering to a ghost "because the more you offer them the more often they come. They are like the lo-mua:. If you give a lo-mua: something when he comes to your house, he'll come back every day." As poor men with little means of defending themselves, Ong Thian-co and Ong Zi-ko fear both the ghosts and the lo-mua:. Their affluent and politically powerful neighbor, Li Bun-tua, fears neither. One day at a funeral Li told me that his relatives would not have to burn spirit money to keep the ghosts from harassing his soul on its journey to the underworld. "The next world is just like this one. If you are a strong man like me, big and fat, no one will bother you, but if you are old and weak, the ghosts will bully you just as the lo-mua: bully the old and weak in this world."

When pressed to explain their conception of ghosts, most of my informants compared them to bullies or beggars. Why do you have to make offerings to ghosts? "So that they will go away and leave you alone. They are like beggars and won't leave you alone if you don't give them something." Why is it that people usually call ghosts "the good brothers"? "Because they would be angry if you called them ghosts. Calling a ghost kui is like calling a beggar 'beggar.' " Ghosts ordinarily appear to the living as evil, formless objects, seen lying next to an irrigation channel or lurking in a dense bamboo grove. The one exception in Hsia-ch'i-chou was a creature who was said to walk through the village every night "beating two bamboo sticks just like a beggar." The dozen or so villagers who claimed to have seen this particular spirit agreed that it was the spiritual remains of a former beggar. "He used to come here all the time before he died. That was a long time ago now, but he still comes every night. He didn't have any children, so there is no one to make offerings."

The association of the destitute of this world with those of the next is also clear in the Reverend Doolittle's description of funeral customs in Foochow in the 1860's: "When burials connected with wealthy families take place on the hills, or the regular sacrifices to the dead are about to be performed in the spring at their graves, beggars often interfere for the purpose of getting food or money. . . . Oftentimes a considerable sum of money is distributed on such occasions among the beggars before they will allow burial or the sacrifice to proceed without interruptions, and with the desirable solemnity and silence." (1865: II, 262.) Just as the mourner must bribe the beggars to keep them from interfering, he must also pay their supernatural counterparts to save the deceased from similar annoyances. After the coffin has been lowered into the grave, "an offering is also made to the distressed and destitute spirits in the infernal regions, such as the spirits of lepers and beggars. . . . According to the general supposition, they, on receiving what the friends of the dead are disposed to bestow upon them, allow the sacrifice to the dead to go on without interruption." (Doolittle 1865: I, 206.) Each year when people return to the grave to make offerings to the deceased, they must also offer something to the ghosts. This, Doolittle says, is "in order to prevent departed friends from being molested by the importunity of beggars and lepers in the unseen world" (1865: II, 49).

In the Chinese view a beggar's request for alms is not really begging. It is a threat. Beggars are believed capable of laying terrible curses on anyone who ignores their entreaties. The man who sends a beggar away empty-handed risks the possibility of illness or damage to property. Beggars are thus like bandits and ghosts in that they are feared, and bandits and ghosts are like beggars in that they are socially despised. The social identities of the three are so similar that bandits and beggars are sometimes treated like ghosts. It was once the practice in northern Taiwan for every village and town to make a massive offering to the ghosts during the seventh lunar month. A high bamboo structure was erected in some central place, a market or a village square, and then hung with firecrackers and a wealth of food: chickens and ducks, both dead and alive, slices of pork and pigs' heads, fish of every kind, rice cakes, bananas, pineapples, melons, etc. This great feast was first offered up to all the wandering spirits who had answered the summons of the gongs, and then, after the ghosts had had time to satisfy themselves, the entire collection was turned over to the destitute humans who had gathered for the occasion. The Rev. George MacKay witnessed one of these festivals in Taipei City in the 1880's:

It was a gruesome sight. When night came on and the time for summoning the spirits approached, the cones were illuminated by dozens of lighted candles. Then the priests took up their position on a raised platform, and by clapping their hands and sounding a large brass gong they called the spirits of all the departed to come and feast on the food provided. "Out of the night and the other world" the dead were given time to come and gorge themselves on the "spiritual" part of the feast, the essence, that was suited to their ethereal requirements. Meanwhile, a very unspiritual mob—thousands and thousands of hungry beggars, tramps, blacklegs, desperados of all sorts, from the country towns, the city slums, or venturing under cover of the night from their hiding-places among the hills—surged and swelled in every part of the open space, impatiently waiting their turn at the feast. When the spirits had consumed the "spiritual" part, the "carnal" was the property of the mob, and the mob quite approved of this division. . . . At length the spirits were satisfied, and the gong was sounded once more. That was the signal for the mob. . . . In one wild scramble, groaning and yelling all the while, trampling on those who had lost their footing or were smothered by the falling cones, fighting and tearing one another like mad dogs, they all made for the coveted food. (MacKay 1895: 130–31.)

All ghosts are like bandits and beggars, but not all ghosts are the spiritual remains of bandits or beggars. The reader will remember the case of the young man who saw "a white thing" moving across the paddy. His argument for labeling this apparition a "ghost" was his belief that it was the soul of another man's mother. This woman had not been a beggar during her lifetime, and she was not destitute in the next world. She was on her way to her son's house to receive deathday offerings made in her honor. I suggest that the category "ghosts" includes the souls of all people who die as members of some other group. They are not all malicious because the great majority are cared for by their living descendants, but they are all potentially dangerous because they are all strangers or outsiders. The malicious among them are malicious for the same reason some strangers are malicious. They are souls who have been insulted or injured in this life or the next, or souls who can support themselves only by begging or banditry. The crucial point is that the category "ghosts" is always a relative one. Your ancestors are my ghosts, and my ancestors are your ghosts, just as your relatives are strangers to me, and my relatives strangers to you.

This is not a point one can prove by asking people if the ghosts they see are their neighbors' ancestors, or, worse yet, by asking them if their own ancestors are ghosts to their neighbors. The two categories are polar opposites, like day and night, good and bad, and iong and im. Hence it is impossible for people to seriously consider the idea that what is an ancestor from one point of view is a ghost from another. The few informants on whom I tried such questions replied, "How could your ancestors be ghosts? Your ancestors are your own people and help you. Ghosts make you sick and cause trouble." Only the rare informant can look at his own society from a vantage point other than his own. Tan Cin-chiong was such a man because of his education and his academic interest in Chinese folklore. In his view kui is the generic term for all spirits or souls of the dead. "Sin is just a polite name for kui. Your ancestors are sin to you, but they are kui to other people. It just sounds better to call them sin."

Most people realize that their ancestors are other people's ghosts only when unusual circumstances make them look at their own dead from another point of view. One of my best examples was recorded by Ch'en Cheng-hsiung, who worked as my field assistant for a few months in 1967. A woman named Peq A-mui was telling Ch'en that her mother had once quarreled over water with one of her husband's cousins. "That man went to see a famous *hu-a-sian* and got something and put it in my mother's tea. Ten days later a red stripe appeared on my mother's neck and she died. Exactly one year later his neighbors heard that man scream, saying that someone was squeezing his testicles. When the neighbors ran to see what was happening, they saw my mother coming out of the house." Ch'en then alertly asked his informant if her mother was a ghost to that man. She seemed surprised by the question, but agreed that her own mother was a ghost from the other man's point of view. "If he wanted to make an offering to my mother, he would have to do it outside the house rather than in the house."

Maurice Freedman has kindly allowed me to report another striking case in point, which he collected in Hong Kong. Talking to a man who had grown up in Kwangtung province, Freedman asked him about the difference between *shan* and *kwai* (the Cantonese equivalents of sin and kui). "He was horrified at the suggestion that the ancestors were other than shan; kwai are evil, ancestors never are, they help. But when I got him on to the festival of the hungry ghosts in the seventh lunar month, it occurred to him that other people's ancestors could be kwai and therefore harmful." A few weeks later Freedman asked the same informant to explain the use of the term kwai in the context of female mediums who are hired to call up customers' ancestors. One term of these mediums in Cantonese is *man kwai p'o*, "old women who talk to ghosts." "My informant patiently explained that everybody else's dead are kwai to you: the word kwai in such expressions as *man kwai p'o* . . . refers to the fact that the customer's ancestors are not the medium's ancestors. Your own ancestors cannot possibly be kwai to you; kwai means (implies) stranger."

The essential point that ghosts are the supernatural equivalent of feared strangers need not rest on contemporary evidence alone. Thanks to the careful work of Shen Chien-shih, we have a detailed account of the evolution of the character *kuei* (the Mandarin equivalent of kui and kwai). Drawing on both paleographic and documentary evidence, Shen (1936–37: 19) reconstructs the character's history as follows:

1. *Kuei*, like *yü*, was originally the name given to some strange anthropoid or simian creature.
2. From the name of an animal, *kuei* was extended to denote a people or race of alien origin.
3. From the abstract idea of an animal, *kuei* was extended to express the abstract ideas of "fear," "strangeness," "large size," "cunning," etc.
4. *Kuei*, the name of a corporeal creature, was "transferred" to represent the imagined appearance of a spiritual being, i.e., the ghost of the dead.

One could argue that the meaning of the character kuei has not changed at all. The term still refers to strange creatures who are regarded as aliens and are feared. The only difference is that whereas kuei once referred to real beings, it now refers to their supernatural counterparts. As the horizons of the Chinese world expanded, aliens became fellow citizens, making it impolite and impolitic to refer to them as kuei. But from the point of view of the average villager, people who are nothing more than fellow citizens are still strangers, and still to be feared. Consequently, their souls become kuei.

Until the Japanese occupied Taiwan and established an effective police system, the average village was a small community surrounded by a largely hostile social environment. The mutual animosity of the various racial and ethnic groups occupying the Taipei Basin made it a cauldron of internecine strife. The Chinese settlers fought the aborigines; Hokkien-speaking Chinese fought their Hakka neighbors; while among the Hokkien, people from Chang-chou and Ch'üan-chou competed bitterly for land and control of ports. In the hills surrounding the Basin, law and order gave way entirely to the rule of bandit chiefs and fugitives from the mainland. Under these conditions much of a peasant's contact with strangers was with bandits, beggars, bullies, and equally rapacious ya-men hirelings. When a man left his village it was usually to visit relatives in a neighboring community, and the only outsiders welcomed in the village were those recommended by ties of kinship. The world beyond the bamboo walls that encircled each community was dangerous be-cause it was inhabited by strangers, and strangers were feared because they were represented in experience by bandits and beggars. The ghosts are the product of this experience. They are dangerous because they are strangers, and strangers are dangerous because experience has proved them dangerous.

The conception of the supernatural found in San-hsia is thus a detailed reflection of the social landscape of traditional China as viewed from a small village. Prominent in this landscape were first the mandarins, rep-resenting the emperor and the empire; second, the family and the lin-eage; and third, the more heterogeneous category of the stranger and the outsider, the bandit and the beggar. The mandarins became the gods; the senior members of the line and the lineage, the ancestors; while the stranger was preserved in the form of the dangerous and despised ghosts. At a more general level the ancestors and the gods, taken together as sin, stand for productive social relationships, while their spiritual opposites, the kui, represent those social forces that are dangerous and potentially destructive.

As an example of the Chinese peasant's "singular and unscriptural sentiments" concerning the soul, the Reverend Doolittle observes (1865: II, 401–2) that people in Foochow believe "each person has *three dis-tinct* souls while living. These souls separate at the death of the adult to whom they belong. One resides in the ancestral tablet erected to his memory, if the head of a family; another lurks in the coffin or the grave, and the third departs to the infernal regions to undergo its merited pun-ishment." The soul enshrined in the ancestral tablet clearly represents the dead in his role as kinsman, while the soul subjected to judgment in the underworld is just as obviously the dead in his role as citizen of the empire. Although the Chinese peasant's conception of the underworld was inspired by the Buddhist imagination, it has long since become a multi-layered yamen staffed with supernatural bureaucrats. The great amounts of spirit money transmitted to the Bank in Hell at the end of a funeral are only partly intended for subsistence expenses. Everyone knows that most of it will be expended to bribe officials who might otherwise subject the deceased to his merited punishment and perhaps some unmerited punishment as well.

This leaves for identification the soul that goes into the coffin and the grave. In Freedman's view the rites performed at the grave are the reverse of those performed before the ancestral tablets in homes and lineage halls. Where the soul represented by an ancestral tablet is involved in a moral relationship with its descendants, the soul associated with the bones in the grave is the source of an amoral power that can be manipulated by impersonal means. The former is iong; the latter, im (1966: 140–42; 1967: 86–88). I am inclined to extend this interpretation, and to argue that the soul in the grave represents the social role of the stranger. Division of the social world into strangers, bureaucrats, and kinsmen means that every man plays the role of stranger as well as the role of kinsman and citizen. At death the kinsman takes his place on the ancestral altar, where he continues to perform many of his rights and duties as an ascendant; the citizen is conducted to the underworld by a representative of the supernatural bureaucracy and is there judged and punished; while the stranger goes into the grave and becomes the source of an amoral and impersonal power.

VI

In China, as in most societies, eating and the exchange of food are socially significant acts. The family is commonly defined as "those people who eat together," and it is often in terms of food that a family expresses its relations with other people. While most families give a bowl of rice or sweet potatoes to a beggar who stops outside their door, they never invite the beggar into the house to eat. He squats outside the back door and leaves his bowl on the threshold when he is finished. The only people invited to eat a meal as guests are the family's relatives, friends, and other persons of approximately equal social status. A family will invite a schoolteacher, a policeman, or a petty bureaucrat to dinner, but they would never invite a senior official such as a hsien magistrate or one of his principal secretaries. When I naively invited the heads of several of Hsia-ch'i-chou's more prominent families to dinner with the magistrate's secretary and another senior official, my guests from the village all found reasons to absent themselves. Eating together implies intimacy and a certain degree of social equality, and it is therefore impossible for a farmer or a coal miner to eat a meal with a ranking official. If a farm family wishes to curry the favor of an official, they often use food as a means of establishing a relationship, but it is presented through a go-between as a gift rather than in the form of an invitation to dinner.

The offerings of food made to the various forms of supernatural express the same social distinctions. As kinsmen and people with whom one is on intimate terms, the ancestors are offered food in very much the same form as a family's guests. The table in front of the altar is set with chopsticks, rice bowls, soup spoons, and a selection of common spices and condiments: salt, soy sauce, vinegar, and perhaps a hot sauce. The food is presented in the form of fully prepared dishes, hot from the stove, and always includes cooked rice. The offerings to the ancestors are meals, in both form and intent. By means of these offerings the living support and succor their kinsmen in the next world just as they supported them during their last years in this world. The intimate nature of the relationship is reflected in the efforts many families make to respect the personal tastes of individual ancestors. When an ancestor is known to have been particularly fond of certain dishes, these are commonly included in the offerings made on the anniversary of his deathday. One woman told me that she always makes rice cakes to offer to her father-in-law and something made from flour for her mother-in-law "because my father used to like rice cakes very much and my mother loved things made of flour."

The offerings prepared for a god's birthday also include the elements of a meal, but this meal is intended for the god's soldiers and attendants rather than the god himself. Despite their considerable power, a magistrate's personal attendants and other members of his staff had very little status in traditional China. During most of the last dynasty they were officially designated *chien-jen*, "mean people," and excluded from competition in the civil service examinations. It was therefore conceivable for a farmer to invite these people or their supernatural counterparts to a meal, but it would have been presumptuous for him to issue an invitation to either a magistrate or a god. The offerings for the gods usually consist of what is known as *sieng-le*, i.e., three or five kinds of meat—for example, a duck, a large slice of pork, and a fish, or, alternatively, a chicken, a duck, squid, a slice of pork, and liver or kidney. Except on the occasion of special offerings to the supernatural emperor, T'ien Kung, these foods are cooked, but they are never seasoned or sliced as for a meal. The only items on the table aside from the offerings themselves are three cups of wine and perhaps a bowl of fruit. There are no eating utensils, no spices or relishes, and, most significantly, no rice. The ancestors are dependent on their living descendants and must be sustained. The gods, on the other hand, are in no way dependent on their subjects, and their high status makes it inappropriate for them to eat in the home of a farmer or coolie. The offerings to the gods are essentially gifts, presented in the same spirit as a gift of food to a magistrate. As one of my informants in Hsia-ch'i-chou explained, "The gods don't really eat the things you give them. These are just to show them that you respect them so they will help you and protect you."

The form and manner of offerings to the gods also reflect their relative status in the supernatural bureaucracy. When people worship T'ien Kung, the offerings for the god and those for his soldiers and attendants are placed on separate tables. The table with the meal for the soldiers and attendants stands on the floor, but the table with the offering for T'ien Kung must be raised by being placed on four stools. T'ien Kung's status is infinitely higher than that of any of the subordinate officials in his empire. If a rooster is included among the offerings made to such deities as Shang Ti Kung or Tsu Shih Kung, the tail feathers must be plucked. Only T'ien Kung can command a rooster with both a "head" and a "tail."

The ranks of the various gods are also expressed in ritual protocol. While they are not ordinarily observed in practice, there are rules on the number of prostrations to which each of the gods is entitled. If the deity is the lowly Stove God, at the very bottom of the hierarchy, a petitioner need only prostrate himself twice. The much higher ranking Shang Ti Kung, comparable to a hsien magistrate, is accorded one hundred prostrations, while, ideally at least, a person who approaches the supernatural emperor, T'ien Kung, should prostrate himself a thousand times.

The content of offerings made to ghosts varies more than that of offerings made to the gods or the ancestors. Although everyone agrees that the spirits inhabiting the little Yu Ying Kung temples are ghosts, it is customary to offer them sieng-le just as one would a god.[14] The shopkeepers in the San-hsia market also offer whole ducks and chickens and large pieces of cooked meat to the ghosts during the annual festival for hungry ghosts. In many villages, however, the offerings made on this same occasion consist of fully prepared dishes of food laid out in the form of a meal. Aside from the fact that offerings to ghosts often consist of masses of food "because there are so many of them," their only characteristic feature is a wash basin and towel. People say that the gods and the ancestors "don't need these things because they have homes of their own." Many families also set next to the wash basin a pack of cigarettes and occasionally a bottle of beer. As one man explained, this is because

---

[14] The name Yu Ying Kung refers to an inscription found over the doors of most of these temples: *yu ch'iu pi ying*, "a request gets a response." A common alternative name is Pai Hsing Kung: the honorific *kung* plus the most common Chinese term for "the people." This suggests that from the point of view of any particular person, the people are ghosts as well as strangers.

ghosts are like lo-mua:—"They all smoke and drink." Another man said that "you have to treat the ghosts as you would treat a policeman who stopped at your house." I am confident that his point was not that the ghosts represent law and order, but rather that like the police, ghosts are demanding and dangerous. In the peasant's view the modern police-man, the traditional yamen runner, the bandit, the beggar, and the ghost all belong to the same category. "You have to give them something so they will go away and not cause trouble."

Although ghosts are sometimes offered sieng-le like the gods and some-times meals like the ancestors, the location of offerings to them shows that they form a distinct class of supernatural. Whereas offerings for the gods and the ancestors are always presented in the house (facing out-ward in the case of the gods and inward in the case of the ancestors), offerings for ghosts are always presented outside the house. If the object of the offering is a single spirit who has been identified as the cause of an illness or some other misfortune, the offering is usually placed on the ground outside the back door, "the same as for a beggar." The great mass of ghosts placated during the seventh lunar month usually receive their offerings on tables set in front of the house. But no matter who the spirit is or what the occasion for the offering, ghosts are never served in the house. They are despised and disreputable strangers, not guests. "It would be dangerous to invite them into the house." The bowls used to offer food to a ghost are turned upside down and left in the yard for three days to protect the family from pollution. Anything that has come in contact with ghosts is contaminated and dangerous.

The offerings made to the various forms of supernatural usually in-clude several types of "spirit money" (*gun-cua*), as well as food and incense. The different categories of spirit money reflect the division of the supernatural world into spirits modeled on senior kinsmen, on strang-ers, and on the imperial bureaucracy. Confused by the various kinds of spirit money I had seen for sale in San-hsia, I once asked an elderly man with some reputation as a geomancer to explain their use. He kindly prepared for me a chart that divided the supernatural into categories, and listed for each category the appropriate monies for their worship. Because this was the first time we had met and I had not yet discussed with him my own view of the Chinese supernatural, I am confident that his chart lists native categories and not artificial ones prompted by my questions. All I have added, for the convenience of the reader, is the numbers.

1. For Yü Huang Ta Ti, colloquially known as T'ien Kung: *thi:-kim, gou-ci:, siu-kim, hok-kim,* and *kua-kim.*

2. For Ch'ing Shui Tsu Shih Kung and T'ien Shang Sheng Ma, colloquially known as Tsu Shih Kung and Ma Tsu: siu-kim, hok-kim, and kua-kim.

3. For Fu Te Cheng Sheng, colloquially known as T'u Ti Kung: hok-kim and kua-kim.

4. For worshipping the souls of dead people (i.e. the ancestors): *tua-gun, siu-gun,* and *kho-ci:.*

5. For begging peace of the *gua-sin* (i.e., ghosts): kua-kim, hok-kim, siu-gun, *kieng-i, kim-ci:, ka-be, tai-lang, ngo-kui, peq-ho, thi:-kau,* and *pun-mia-ci:.*

On completing the chart my informant placed parentheses around the hok-kim and kua-kim listed under T'ien Kung. "These," he explained, "are not for T'ien Kung himself, but for his followers—his secretaries and his soldiers." Thus, the gods are divided into three ranked classes, as one would expect given the fact that they are conceived of as bureaucrats. At the bottom of the hierarchy is T'u Ti Kung, whose offerings are the same as those made to T'ien Kung's soldiers and secretaries. Above T'u Ti Kung are Tsu Shih Kung and Ma Tsu (and my informant agreed that one could add to this class such gods as Shang Ti Kung and Pao Sheng Ta Ti). Their offerings include the hok-kim and kua-kim offered T'u Ti Kung, but also one of the three types of money offered T'ien Kung. Finally, at the top of the bureaucracy but still part of it, is T'ien Kung. He, like such middle-ranked gods as Tsu Shih Kung and Ma Tsu, receives siu-kim, plus two types of money that are reserved for his exclusive use.

My informant also explained that kho-ci: is offered only to the recent dead, the typical offering for ancestors whose tablets are established on an altar being tua-gun and siu-gun. We therefore find that where the gods are usually offered *kim,* gold, the ancestors are usually offered *gun,* silver. The use of gold money for the gods and silver for the ancestors divides these supernatural into two classes and at the same time suggests that the gods are superior to the ancestors. We need make only the obvious assumption that Chinese think of gold as superior to silver. The one problem is that both T'ien Kung and the recent dead are offered a form of *ci:,* "copper cash," or more generally "money" and "wealth." Since ghosts also receive two forms of ci:, kim-ci: and pun-mia-ci:, it appears that ci: alone is not a diacritical mark. What is crucial in this case is the form of ci:, which is different for each of the three classes of supernatural.

The fact that hok-kim and kua-kim are listed as offerings for ghosts as well as for T'u Ti Kung and T'ien Kung's retainers appears to conflict with the assertion that money offerings separate the supernatural into three categories. But in fact this is not the case. When questioned on this point my informant explained that offerings to ghosts always include an offering to T'u Ti Kung, "because he is the god responsible for policing ghosts." The hok-kim and kua-kim are intended for T'u Ti Kung, not for ghosts. Thus, there is only one type of money that is used for more than one class of spirit, i.e. siu-gun, which is listed as an offering both for the established ancestors and for ghosts.[15] We are thus offered some support for Stephan Feuchtwang's contention (1974) that the fundamental opposition is between the ancestors and ghosts on the one hand and the gods on the other. But it is nonetheless clear that by the most obvious criteria, the supernatural are sorted into three classes. While ghosts are sometimes offered siu-gun, "little silver," they are never offered tua-gun, "big silver." And while the ancestors and ghosts share one form of money, they are distinguished by the use of nine or ten others. Perhaps the most important point to note is that the ancestors are never offered kieng-i, "contributed clothing," the one form of spirit money that is almost always included in offerings to ghosts. Although it is considered a form of gun-cua, kieng-i is not actually imitation money. It consists instead of rectangular sheets of paper, each of which is printed with pictures of such common apparel as pants, shirts, and shoes. This suggests that where the gods get gold and the ancestors silver, the ghosts get a handout—like beggars.

Both the use and the interpretation of gun-cua vary considerably. One man who made his living recovering children's lost souls told me that the "money" offered to the gods is not money at all, but is more "like the petitions people send to the government." He scoffed at the idea that the gods would be interested in money. On the other hand, Ahern's informants in Ch'i-nan gave her monetary equivalents for many of the various types of gun-cua offered to the gods, for example, NT $100 for the siu-kim burned for Tsu Shih Kung, Ma Tsu, and T'ien Kung. She also discovered that on special occasions, the monies normally reserved for the higher spirits can be offered the lower spirits. Such ritual escalation occurs, for example, when people in Ch'i-nan kill pigs for Ch'ing Shui Tsu Shih Kung. On this occasion the ancestors are offered kua-kim; T'u Ti Kung receives siu-kim in addition to hok-kim and kua-kim; Tsu Shih Kung gets siu-kim, gou-ci:, and thi:-kim; while T'ien Kung is honored with the usual offerings plus a special form of money known as *ciok-pik-siu-kim*. But Ahern's evidence indicates that whatever the occasion, the

---

[15] Michael Saso tells me that in Hsin-chu the souls of unmarried daughters are offered siu-gun, little silver, but never tua-gun, big silver. This appears to support my argument that the souls of unmarried daughters are almost ghosts.

monies offered always divide the gods into ranked classes and distinguish them both from the ancestors and from ghosts.[16] The idea that there are gods, ghosts, and ancestors is expressed differently in different contexts, but it appears that whenever peasants think about the supernatural, they think in terms of these three classes.

[16] Personal correspondence.

Developmental Process in the Chinese Domestic Group

MYRON L. COHEN

The notion that most Chinese lived in "joint" or "large" families has been thoroughly discredited by now. Certainly, it is not necessary to again confirm the point here. But if we agree, using Lang's definitions (1946: 13), that simple and stem families greatly outnumbered those of the joint type, we may add that the discussion as it has been presented so far has obscured aspects of Chinese domestic organization that are both intrinsically interesting and relevant to the study of family size and complexity. In this paper I argue that the property-holding unit known in Chinese as the *chia*—which has generally been identified as the "family"—was actually a kin group that could display a great deal of variation in residential arrangements as well as in the economic ties that bound its members together. These variations could appear within the history of a given *chia* in such a way as to make it equivalent at certain times to what is usually regarded as a family; but the *chia* could also exist as a social unit in the absence of a single family-like arrangement of all its members.

Some of the material introduced in this essay was provided by sixteen months of fieldwork during 1964–65 in a southern Taiwan Hakka-speaking community, which I will call Yen-liao. With a resident population of 746 in May 1965, Yen-liao is located in the *chen* (township) of Mei-nung, which in turn forms one of the administrative subdivisions of the *hsien* (county) of Kaohsiung. The argument that I develop in this paper derives for the most part from my interpretation of the Yen-liao data. Nevertheless, I also use evidence from other parts of China, in the hope that my remarks and conclusions may be more generally applicable.

The *fang* and the *chia* are the smallest units defined within the Chinese kinship system. Though the term *fang* may be used in reference to patrilineal groupings of varying size and genealogical depth below the lineage level, it is also used to designate the conjugal unit consisting of husband, wife, and children. (For the use of the term *fang*, see Hu 1948: 18; Fried 1953: 31.) As for the *chia*, it has been defined as "the economic family, i.e., a unit consisting of members related to each other by blood, marriage, or adoption and having a common budget and common property" (Lang 1946: 13). A *chia*, of course, may vary in size, in generational depth, and in the degree to which there is extension (more than one *fang*) in each generation. It is only when there is more than one *fang* within the *chia* that the *fang/chia* differentiation has force. Thus it is obvious that if a multi-*fang chia* is localized to the extent that at least two *fang* are co-resident in the same household, an "extended family" of one sort or another is visible to the observer.

A *fang*, however, is more than a unit of reference. In many, if not most, cases the marriage that established the *fang* also made it an autonomous unit with respect to property rights and economic resources. In theory, the bride had exclusive rights over parts of her dowry, which might have included cash; this confirmed her as an independent property-holder. (See McAleavy 1955; Cohen 1968.) In fact, her husband as well as she might use these rights to develop an economic subsystem on a *fang* basis distinct from the larger system of the *chia*. (The custom of adopting a "little daughter-in-law" into the household to eventually marry the son may have produced modifications in the position of the *fang* vis-à-vis the *chia*; see Fei 1939: 54f.) Elsewhere (Cohen 1968), the *chia* has been treated primarily as a unit localized within one household, and the *fang* has been viewed from that perspective. For our present purposes the existence of the *fang* and its distinguishing features, by and large, may be taken for granted; I will, however, refer to a few situations in which the distribution of *fang* members sheds light on the organization of the *chia*.

Like *fang*, *chia* is a term of many uses. In the course of my own fieldwork I often heard agnates who shared a common ancestor many generations removed refer to each other as "people of the same *chia* (*t'ung chia jen*)." Even people with identical surnames who were in no position to trace their actual genealogical ties (if such existed), would use similar phraseology. Needless to say, closer agnates would not hesitate to count themselves as members of the same *chia*. I do not know the extent to which this wide range of usage was found in most of China. Certainly it has been most common to think of the *chia* as a family arrangement of some sort, although there has been some confusion over the term, as was noted in a recent summary of work on the subject: "At the base of our hierarchy is the family or *chia*. Exactly what the term means has never been agreed upon and perhaps it is a variable which is subject to local variations" (Osgood 1963: 355).

It is of some interest that one of the earliest efforts to identify and describe the *chia* involved the use of data gathered in a community that had sent many of its members abroad. Within Phenix Village, Kulp distinguished four kinds of "families" (Kulp 1925: 142f). Of these, two—the "conventional-family" and the "religious-family"—are of no concern here, for they refer to agnatic groupings not at the domestic level. (See Freedman 1958: 33.) The "natural-family," which consists of "father, mother (wife or concubines), and children" (Kulp 1925: 142), clearly refers to the *fang*. One or more "natural-families" may be found within the "economic family," which "is a group of people who on the basis of blood or marriage connection live together as an economic unit. It may be a natural-family or a number of natural-families which have not divided the ancestral inheritance" (Kulp 1925: 148). But Kulp on the same page then indicates that the "economic-family" may not necessarily be a co-residing unit:

Members of the economic-family may all live under one roof, under several roofs joining one another, in houses somewhat separated in the village, or far apart as in Chaochow, Swatow, or the South Seas [Southeast Asia]. So long as there is no distinction between the income and outgo of funds and so long as the whole group is administered by a certain head or *chia-chang*, the persons living under these arrangements belong to an economic-family.

Kulp's "economic-family," then, is defined on the basis of both a common estate and a common budget. This, surely, is a *chia*; he refers to its leader as a *chia-chang*. But the terminological looseness I noted in Yen-liao must also have been found in Phenix Village: the "religious-family" also has its *chia-chang* (Kulp 1925: 149). There is yet another difficulty in Kulp's description; according to his account, the only way a new "economic-family" is created is "by the division of property and the declaration of separate finances" (Kulp 1925: 149). To what extent was the considerable out-migration from Phenix Village tied in with the formation of new "economic-families" in this fashion? Though Kulp provides no direct answer to this question, he indicates in his description that some "economic-families" might very well include persons who had departed for Southeast Asia. So if at least some of the out-migration did not involve the formation of new "economic-families," can it be that in such circumstances the migrants remained in a situation where there was "no distinction between the income and outgo of funds" and where the entire "economic-family" was still "administered by a certain head or *chia-chang*"? The answer seems to be no. Those who had left, Kulp tells us (1925: 50), accounted for "as many as one-third of the total men in the village population."

[Yet] not more than one-tenth of the emigrants return successful. Many of them, while in foreign lands, are barely able to send back enough money to keep their families alive. Not a few persons are forced to live from hand to mouth, finally returning broken in productive efficiency, a charge upon their families, or dying miserable deaths away from home with none to burn the candles. (Kulp 1925: 53.)

What emerges from Kulp's description is a sociological no-man's-land found between the establishment of discrete "economic-families" on the one hand, and the existence of an integrated economic unit (perhaps spanning the ocean) on the other. Ch'en Ta, in the English edition of his book, refers to the latter arrangement as the "dual family system" (Ch'en 1940: 121). However, he really means one "family" residentially separated into two (or more?) units, and in the earlier Chinese text he uses the phrase " 'dual family-head' system," i.e., *"liang t'ou-chia" chih-tu* (Ch'en 1938: 126). The circumstances leading to the *"liang t'ou-chia" chih-tu* are similar to those described by Kulp. From Ch'en's book it can clearly be seen that emigration is often an aspect of "family" activity rather than a process to create new families. Referring to one sample of emigrants, Ch'en (1940: 136f) noted that "at least two-thirds, and more probably three-fourths, of the emigrants leave home at an age when . . . they are not heads of households, though many of them may be married." Furthermore, the young emigrant "remains subject to the head of the family" (Ch'en 1940: 137). New "families" are formed through the division of property (Ch'en 1940: 130f).

Neither Kulp nor Ch'en explicitly states what I suggest can be drawn from their writings: that the "family" or "economic-family" might continue to exist as a unit in the face of both the physical and economic disengagement of its members. The way the emigrant ultimately related to the group he left behind depended, in addition to other factors, on his achievements, or lack of them, overseas. From Kulp and Ch'en it can be gathered that although there were various possible relationships, all were encompassed by the "family" unit. The migration to Southeast Asia is but a better-known example of a process that occurred over wide areas of China. I say "better-known" because physical dispersion is more pronounced in the context of migration from one country to another and the Overseas Chinese presumably had a greater chance to succeed than did persons who sought their fortunes within China. Furthermore, the overseas migration of the Chinese became an object of great interest in itself, so the role played by the "family" in the process received a commensurate share of attention.

Some of the problems encountered in dealing with "family" units might be clarified if first the corporate and developmental features of the *chia* as such are understood. Having said this, I must add that it is easier to deal with the partition of a *chia* than with its development. The *chia* is a group of persons who not only have kin ties to each other, but also have a series of claims of one sort or another on the *chia* as an estate. I have already noted that use of the term *chia* may vary in scope of reference. Nevertheless, its meaning in at least one terminological context is quite precise: it applies to a specific, bounded, kin group acting in terms of an equally well delineated body of holdings. This type of action is referred to in *fen-chia*, "to divide the *chia*." There is nothing vague about this; *fen-chia* has or has not taken place. If it has, two or more *chia* exist where before there was only one, and the estate of the original *chia* is distributed accordingly.

There are thus at least two broad areas of inquiry regarding the development of the *chia*. The first concerns the variety of arrangements to be found within the pre-*fen-chia* context; the second deals with pre-*fen-chia*/post-*fen-chia* contrasts. The tendency among scholars has been to lump these two together by viewing the development cycle only as culminating in the dismemberment of previously integrated households. But there are indications that the life and death of a *chia* might involve much more. If Levy's generalizations about Chinese "family" type in "traditional" times are accepted, then the movement of Chinese abroad may be seen as an extension of a very common pattern. During that period, he states, "the average Chinese" must have lived in the *famille souche*, "a family in which one of the sons marries and continues to live with the parents, while the other sons and daughters marry and go out of the family unit" (Levy 1949: 55f). How did the *famille souche* operate in the face of the equal rights to the *chia* estate held by brothers? These rights, he says,

could not have been meaningful to peasants living in areas where the average family's land was just sufficient to support life. Under such circumstances . . . only one son could feasibly remain. Whether given a cash settlement or not, the other sons had to go elsewhere or find alternative employment in the locality. . . . When holdings had reached a bare subsistence level, the assumption by one son of the total responsibility for the support of the parents . . . would often be accepted by the other sons as adequate reimbursement. (Levy 1949: 56f.)

According to Levy, then, there were ways by which claims to *chia* holdings could be adjusted. He cannot be sure, however, to what extent such adjustments, which the Chinese call *fen-chia*, actually took place. He does briefly indicate one alternative: "These excess sons sometimes left the family only temporarily and sent their wages back home for the economic betterment of the family. . . . Such sons were at best only peripheral family members" (Levy 1949: 52n).

Lang presents evidence that alternatives to *fen-chia* were quite common. Speaking of traditional China, she notes that "sons . . . seldom left their homes. If they did so without formally separating themselves from their family, they sent their earnings to their parents" (Lang 1946: 17). At the time of her research, members of the "working class and lower middle class in Peiping" were still part of the "tradition bound group," and this was reflected in their family life: "They send money to their rural homes, leave their wives and children with their old folks, and regard their sojourn in the city as temporary, even when they spend their entire lives there" (Lang 1946: 82).

As a contrast to the Peiping group with traditional occupations, Lang (1946: 86) also discusses the "new industrial workers" found in Shanghai. In spite of certain differences, the Shanghai workers still seem to be very much involved in traditional *chia* arrangements:

Thus 28 textile workers (out of 44) and 13 employees of public utilities (out of 43) still owned land. With the majority of them this ownership was purely formal: they derived no income from it (they left the land to their brothers and other near relatives), only retaining title as security against possible unemployment. Some of them rented their land. Several workers expected to inherit land from their fathers. (Lang 1946: 87.)

I would suggest that differences between the Peiping and the Shanghai workers may have involved something more than tradition and modernization. Unfortunately, the extent to which the ties of the Shanghai workers to their home regions were qualified by *fen-chia* or the lack of it is not clear. Lang's problem, like Kulp's, is that she is talking about families but dealing with *chia*. Her solution, also identical to Kulp's, is to use the concept of the "economic-family" to sort out what she regards as functional domestic units (Lang 1946: 13). Yet Lang is fully aware of the existence of the *chia* in the sense in which I have been using the term, and she must grapple with the problem in the part of her research that involves the enumeration of families on the basis of type and size. What seems to be the cause of concern is that the "economic-family," like the *chia*, can display variations in the distribution of its members:

One cannot . . . refuse to regard as family members those who do not reside with the family. . . . A young man may work at a place very distant from his family's residence, yet remain a member of his father's or brother's family. For example, he may send money home, he may return to marry a girl his parents or brothers have chosen for him, and later may leave his wife and children with them. (Lang 1946: 135.)

Lang's solution is to incorporate features of both the "economic-family" and the *chia* in the demarcation of family units. Residence is considered the paramount criterion, however, if the dispersion of a *chia* is on a *fang* basis, regardless, apparently, of the *fang's* possible inclusion in a larger "economic-family." A son is taken to have established a new family if he lives with his wife and children apart from his father (Lang 1946: 136).

If the sources I have cited above indicate nothing else, they certainly show that there may be more to domestic units than meets the demographer's eye. In the face of both the *famille souche*, which may have been quite prevalent, and the dispersion of conjugal units, the *chia* could survive. Before discussing the extent to which this survival could have significance in terms of the interaction of *chia* members, we must pay attention to the variety of forms the *chia* could assume.

Dealing with the structural variability of the *chia* is both a descriptive and an analytic task. For descriptive purposes, I first discuss the *chia* as it could be found at a moment in time. To simplify matters somewhat, I reduce the relevant components of the *chia* to three: the *chia* estate, the *chia* group, and the *chia* economy. The *chia* estate is that body of holdings to which the process of *fen-chia* is applicable. The *chia* group is made up of those persons who have rights of one sort or another to the *chia* estate at the time of *fen-chia*. Division, of course, is on the basis of male members of the *chia* group; but the process may also be conceptualized as division on the basis of the *fang* or *fang* segments (surviving members of a *fang*) found in each of the generational levels comprising the *chia* group. The *chia* economy refers to the exploitation of the *chia* estate (and the benefits derived therefrom) as well as to other income-producing activities linked to its exploitation through remittances and a common budgetary arrangement.

The connections between the three components can assume a variety of forms. To simplify matters once more, I assign each component only two possible alternative characteristics. The *chia* estate is either concentrated or dispersed; if concentrated, the members of the *chia* group exploiting it are from one household only; if dispersed, exploitation is by members of the *chia* group residing in two or more households. Similarly the *chia* group may be either concentrated in one household or dispersed in more than one. The *chia* economy is either inclusive or non-inclusive. An inclusive economy is one in which all members of the *chia* group participate. Participation need not necessarily be productive: dependents (the aged, the ill or disabled, children, students) may also be involved. If some members of the *chia* group do not participate in the *chia* economy, it is non-inclusive.

The Chinese family has by and large been described in terms involving or assuming the existence of a *chia* in which the estate is concentrated, the group is concentrated, and the economy is inclusive. (To anticipate later remarks, it can be noted that such an arrangement of the three components can occur at varying times during the history of a given *chia*.) I will choose, somewhat arbitrarily, to view a *chia* newly formed through division. The new *chia* consists of a man, his wife, and some unmarried children. They derive their income from land they own or rent. All live together in one household, and if there are secondary sources of income, these are combined with that derived from working the land. Let it be further assumed that the estate remains sufficient to provide for the rearing and livelihood of the younger generation. These children, all still at home, enter their adulthood; the daughters marry out and the elder of the sons—there are two of them—obtains a wife. Shortly thereafter, the second son also marries. The sons' wives are absorbed into the economy and contribute labor in the performance of domestic and productive tasks, and they also have children of their own. The group is now complex, consisting of two *fang* in the second generation. The parents die, but the two *fang* continue to live together for a period of time. Finally, each demands complete control over its share of the estate, and the *chia* divides.

The above, of course, is a sketch of the maximal developmental cycle of the Chinese family as it has been frequently described. (See Freedman 1961–62: 327.) A simple family develops into one that is stem, as that term has been defined by Lang (1946: 14), which definition does not necessarily imply the existence of the *famille souche* pattern described by Levy (1949: 55–56); and after the marriage of the second son the family becomes joint and then, with the death of the parents, fraternal-joint. For the purposes of this discussion it is essential to note that the three components have remained in unchanging relationship with each other throughout the developmental history of this *chia*.

However, the connections between the components can vary. An inclusive economy can be found in association with a dispersed estate and, of necessity, a dispersed group. In *The Golden Wing* (1948), Lin Yueh-hwa describes at one point in the story how Dunglin entered into a partnership with his sister's husband and established a shop in a town near his home village. Dunglin's share of the shop actually belonged to his *chia* as a whole, as did some land in the village. Though Dunglin lived and worked in the shop (frequently coming home), his wife lived in the village with his mother and the *fang* composed of Dunglin's brother, his brother's wife, and their children (Lin 1948: 11f). The economy certainly was inclusive: "As the family had not been officially divided, the capital and money income of the store, as well as family lands and their produce, were still common property, belonging to both brothers. Thus the two men took an interest in each other's work and planned together for the good of the whole family" (Lin 1948: 13).

Dispersion on a somewhat greater scale was found in a group distributed between the village of Nanching and the nearby city of Canton:

Wong Han was a wealthy landlord with considerable landholdings in the village and an import and export firm in the city of Canton. A man in his early sixties, he lived with his wife, two concubines, two married sons and their wives, one unmarried son and two unmarried daughters, and three grandchildren, all as one household with common property. Although the married sons and their wives spent most of the time in their common city residence, family unity was effectively maintained among the fourteen members. (C. K. Yang 1959b: 17.)

For a final example of this particular *chia* form, I turn to my own field data. The case I describe is extreme in regard to the size of the group and the extent of its dispersion. The group was one of the largest (and wealthiest) in the region where the study was carried out. Yet it is one of a kind with the previous cases cited.

In May 1965, the group of which Lin Shang-yung was the *chia-chang* consisted of forty-two persons. In the oldest generation only Lin himself survived. In the second generation the marriage of each of his three sons had led to the formation of as many *fang*. The first of these had twenty-two members: in addition to the father and mother it included five sons and two daughters, the wife and seven children of the first son, and the wife and four children of the second. The second *fang*—twelve persons in all—consisted of a father, a mother, four sons, four daughters, and the wife and child of the first son. In the third *fang*, with the father and mother there were five young children. The Lin *chia* had established four households, each associated with a part of the estate. There were the buildings and fields that had been obtained (and later expanded) by Shang-yung when he separated from his brother. In an adjoining village (Yen-liao) the *chia* owned a rice mill, and in yet another nearby settlement it operated a shop selling fertilizers and animal feed. About twenty-five miles to the south, additional land and buildings had been purchased. In the management of all these holdings, a common budget was maintained. Funds and goods were transferred as needed, and expenditure by the manager of a given enterprise was scrutinized by other group members. Shang-yung continued to live at the site of the original holdings. With him were some members of the first and second *fang*: the two daughters of the first *fang*, the oldest married son, and two of his children, the father and mother of the second *fang*, their seven unmarried children, and their married son's wife and child. The married son had lived there prior to his induction into the army (and even he still participated in the economy, for he continued to receive money from home to supplement very low soldier's pay). Part of the first *fang* —the second married son, his wife and four children, and the two youngest unmarried sons—resided at the rice mill. Living in the south was another unmarried son of the first *fang*, and the wife and remaining children of the first married son. The mother of the first *fang* also lived there, and the father divided his time between the south and the rice mill. The entire third *fang* was quartered at the shop.

So far we have described situations in which the *chia* economy is inclusive and the group and the estate are either both concentrated or both dispersed. But an inclusive economy and a dispersed group can also be found together with a concentrated estate. In such a case only group members in one of the households exploit the estate; other members of the group receive remittances from or send them to the estate. Most of those receiving money from the estate were, in traditional times, dependents such as students studying for the examinations or a small minority of apprentices who might pay their masters some sort of "tuition" or who might continue to get additional spending money from home. Remittances to the estate by officials, merchants, craftsmen, salaried workers, etc., were much more common. In his description of the rise and fall of gentry families, Ho gives many examples of the remittance system among the gentry and wealthy merchants (Ho 1962: 292, 312). For less prestigious groups, relevant data from Lang have already been cited. I am unable to find much evidence from mainland China about the residential variations that were possible in such circumstances, but generalizing from observations made in Taiwan, I can say that although remittances were commonly from single men or married men whose wives and children were still residing with the other members of the group, there were also cases of remittances being forthcoming when dispersion was along *fang* lines.

Though this discussion has not covered the entire range of variations possible within the inclusive economy, the main patterns have been set forth, and we now turn to the non-inclusive economy. It is, of course, always associated with a dispersed group; one or more members of the group are economically independent and residentially separated from the rest. The remaining members can exhibit varied residential and economic connections with the estate identical to those found in the context of an inclusive economy.

Though examples of such situations could be cited here, these may be left to the reader's imagination or experience, for it is now pertinent to ask if a *chia* group with a non-inclusive economy is, indeed, worthy of consideration as a discrete social unit. As a group of kinsmen is it any different from one constituted along identical genealogical lines in which *fen-chia* has taken place one or more times?

The very fact that all members have claims to the estate gives the group at the very least a sort of terminal cohesion. It can be expected that the group will either reassemble or in some fashion have dealings with each other at the time of *fen-chia*, or even prior to *fen-chia* if the death of a member leads to a realignment of the rights to the estate enjoyed by the survivors. The existence of a dispersed group with a non-inclusive economy has been observed by Moench among the Overseas Chinese (mainly Hakka) in Tahiti. This unit he calls the "dispersed family": "The dispersed family is that group of persons who maintain residual claims to shares of an undivided patrimony. This dispersed family is seldom a production group and is thus irrelevant in a discussion of production: its relevance is to problems of exchange, succession and family division" (Moench 1963: 72).

Although under the conditions of life in Tahiti the "dispersed family" may have been the end of the line as far as significant interaction among members of the group was concerned, this was not necessarily the case in China. The connections between the components of the *chia* could change. To see this requires that they be considered diachronically and developmentally. In a post-*fen-chia* situation similar to that described earlier, in which the estate and group are concentrated and the economy is inclusive, the possibilities for various kinds of development were many. Simon's account of the history of Ouang-Ming-Tse's "family" illustrates some of these (Simon 1887: 209f; this source was used by

Freedman 1958: 23f). Simon records Ming-Tse's description of the successful development of the *chia* headed by his paternal grandfather:

At that time my grandfather was far from rich. . . . When the number of children was found to be on the increase, it was decided that the boys should learn trades, and go to town to add to the common weal. My father was the one to begin. He had six brothers and sisters younger than himself, and chose the trade of carpenter. His apprentice fees were paid for three years, and his wants provided for until he was able to maintain himself. He was soon, however, able to save something to bring home to the fortnightly meetings. Three other sons followed his example, and my father increased the size of his field with their savings, pushing back the boundaries, and as soon as he could give employment to one of them, he recalled him. Only one, the youngest, remained at Fou-Cheou, and became one of the first merchants in the town. (Simon 1887: 226f.)

Of his father's two older brothers, one was already established as a mandarin, and the other had remained on the farm throughout (Simon 1887: 226). How the mandarin achieved his success is not made clear, nor is it indicated why the youngest brother never returned. During many of the years that it existed, then, this group was dispersed. While they were apprentices, the boys remained *chia* dependents. Next came a period of self-support, which meant exclusion from the economy, followed by a re-inclusion into the economy, first through remittances sent home and then through participation once more in the exploitation of the estate. No information is provided about the presence or absence of economic ties between the estate, on the one hand, and the mandarin and the merchant, on the other. If there were no such ties, these two remained members of the group only insofar as they demanded their shares at time of division (Simon 1887: 230).

Though this is a success story not duplicated by the majority of *chia* in China, it does illustrate some of the more important junctures that must have characterized the development of many of them. The first of these is the initial dispersion of the group, most often occurring on the basis of managerial decisions taken by the senior generation—usually in the person of the *chia-chang*—and affecting the junior members of the group. In situations where there was one son only—and this may have been quite common (see Lang 1946: 10)—dispersion might occur only in the face of extreme poverty (see Fei and Chang 1949: 272), natural calamities, or war, for in ordinary circumstances, the primary concern was the continued exploitation of the estate. For the poor with more than one son, dispersion was often a grim necessity forced on them by the inability of their land to support many people. Nevertheless, dispersion was tied in with the notion that diversification of the economy into nonagricultural activities was one means of achieving success, and there are good indications that the advantages in such an arrangement were recognized by poor and rich alike. The poor often made the attempt, or wished they could, and the rich frequently owed their favorable position to successful implementation of diversification schemes. (See Cohen 1967 for a brief discussion of economic diversification within the traditional framework of Chinese society, and its carry-over into contemporary Yen-liao.) In a rural setting an effort to diversify often, if not usually, meant leaving one's parents and home community for a length of time (Fei and Chang 1949: 271f; Chow 1967: 117). The physical mobility associated with such attempts to diversify the *chia* economy must be kept distinct from that possibly resulting from *fen-chia*. My own work in Yen-liao brought to light several cases of brothers at the time of *fen-chia* converting their portion of the estate into cash and leaving the village to seek their fortunes elsewhere. These men had participated in the dismemberment of the *chia*; those who leave while still belonging to the original *chia* group might very well be concerned with promoting *chia* survival and advancement.

Following the dispersion of the group, the issue then became one of success or failure. Here, of course, the rich had advantages over the poor, for unless he was supported by a lineage or some other source of non-*chia* funds, a youth leaving the farm was unlikely to get a chance to compete in the examinations. For the very rich, even if a career outside officialdom were intended, the influence that could be brought to bear by powerful members of a group would probably assure success in most cases. Apprenticeship was a common means of effecting the dispersion of the group. Within this category some positions were more desirable than others, so here prior ties and influence also played a part. (See Fried 1953: 165f.)

In terms of the *chia* economy, success meant the onset of remittances, and there are good reasons to believe that most persons did send home a portion of their earnings. Yang has spoken of this in general terms:

Most of the villagers who seek work in the city . . . send their earnings back to their homes to be used to buy land and build houses for the family. If they are married, the wives and children remain in the family home. If they were single when they left the village, they usually return to marry a girl chosen by the family. (M. Yang 1945: 228.)

Though this passage perhaps overstates the case, it does provide some clues about why this tendency could be so prevalent. A son could and did sometimes establish economic independence (*fen-chia*) from his parents as well as from his brothers. (Fei 1939: 66f provides one of many examples.) However, this rarely, if ever, occurred before his marriage. In all probability, most sons who went out to work did so at an early age; if they were apprenticed, they certainly did. In general, the younger the son was, the greater the managerial authority exercised over him by the *chia-chang* (C. K. Yang 1959a: 139). Yet when he left, he still had the support of the *chia*: to the extent that the value of its holdings permitted, the *chia* economy was geared to ensuring that the son be provided a wife (C. K. Yang 1959a: 25). Furthermore, he still had rights to the estate.

Before marriage, paternal authority might in itself be sufficient to ensure that a young man working outside faithfully remit home a portion of his earnings. And there were compelling reasons for the *chia-chang* to see that the youth living away from home turn over to him as much of his earnings as possible. Matters of support aside, if the *chia-chang's* son had married brothers working the estate, there was already the possibility of *fen-chia*. The sons remaining at home also were quite anxious that the *chia-chang* continue to obtain remittances from their younger brother, for if these did not enable them to expand the estate, at least it would reduce the burden of rents or other expenses. The additional source of income, contributing to the maintenance of the estate as a whole, served to counter divisive tendencies that might develop between the *fang*.

After marriage, the situation would be somewhat different. The person working outside was now in a position to assert his own rights to the estate. The situation was now one of cooperation among equals, for if the man living outside was earning money for the estate, his brothers were exploiting it for all. Although it is certainly true that in general and ultimately "the rights of brothers to more or less equal shares of property ... entailed a constant pressure against unity"' (Freedman 1958: 27), in the context of the diversified *chia* economy this pressure could be lessened. (See Cohen 1967, 1968. M. Yang 1945: 238 gives an example of a highly interdependent *chia* economy.)

Finally, with increasing wealth a dispersed group might be formed (or maintained) by the expansion of the estate to different locales. In effect, the *chia* group might follow the estate and set up new households. Ouang-Ming-Tse noted that his younger brother living in Foochow had bought some land in the village, "which is cultivated by his eldest son." He added that "when he gives up his business to two of his sons, as he soon will do, he will return here" (Simon 1887: 227). It cannot be determined from the text if this simply meant a shift from one to the other of the two households containing the *chia* group, or if *fen-chia* is implied. Similar dispersed estates and their associated households were observed in Taiwan, where mobility was pronounced. In Lin Shang-yung's *chia*, discussed earlier, there were from 1949 to 1965 four different conjugal units that occupied the rice mill sequentially for periods ranging from three to five years. In such *chia*, it may be added, the interdependence of the various *fang* is so complex as to present real obstacles to early *fen-chia*.

Of course, it is probable that a great many, if not most, of the persons who went out looking for work were failures. Failure did not necessarily mean an inability to survive. The critical standard was whether survival was accompanied by remittances. Failure, indeed, might sometimes have the same result as success—a return to the original *chia* household. (See Lang 1946:16.) This could also occur during times of war or other disturbances. In Nanching, before 1933 for instance, there were about one hundred "families" with "long-term" emigrants. By 1948–51, war and economic depression had forced many of the emigrants to return, so the number of such "families" had been reduced to forty or fifty (C. K. Yang 1959b: 71).

The *chia* group, then, was distinguished by the potential of its membership to rejoin the *chia* economy, as well as by the possession of an estate. The circumstances through which *chia* members might once again come to participate in a common residential or budgetary arrangement were varied, as were those associated with the development of the economy in its non-inclusive form. The possibility arises that a good deal of the movement of persons in Chinese society, movement connected with "horizontal" or "vertical" social and economic mobility (Ho 1962), or with efforts to achieve such mobility, in fact occurred within a *chia* framework. To be sure, there were obvious exceptions. The number of potential *fang* within a *chia* could be reduced through the sale or adoption out of children, or through a man's marrying into his bride's *chia*; marriage in any event involved transfer of a person, in most cases a woman, from one *chia* to another. Again, as I have noted, men leaving their natal homes might do so following *fen-chia*. Nevertheless, it is likely that most men seeking employment and opportunities away from their birthplace remained members of their original *chia* group. *Fen-chia* was a very different matter. It was a jural act of fragmentation; together with partition of property there was termination of many kinds of actual or potential cooperation and mutual support. On the other hand, *fen-chia* also meant ending the obligations that tied *chia* members together. In the final analysis, the responsibilities of kinship in a post-*fen-chia* situation were quite contingent: the separate *chia* headed by brothers could suffer or enjoy very different fates. (See Smith 1900: 328.)

Factors leading to early *fen-chia* were associated mainly with membership in a common household. It was under one roof that conflicts of interest were likely to emerge quickly; when members of a *chia* group lived together, dissatisfaction over distribution of *chia* resources or other situations increasing tension between the *fang* could appear most rapidly and with greatest force. In general, it may be that *fen-chia* was delayed by circumstances involving an inclusive or non-inclusive economy associated with a dispersed *chia* group. Such situations, perhaps, also increased the chances of success (an improvement in economic circumstances) or prolonged its enjoyment.

The *chia* was the crucial domestic unit in China, one in which ties between persons were associated with common ties to an estate. The estate could vary in size and value; at one extreme it could consist of a humble home, a few agricultural tools, and a small area of farming land, rights to which might only be those of tenancy. Although great poverty could deprive the *chia* of the minimum endowment for corporate cohesion, what evidence there is suggests that even in comparatively recent times such a situation prevailed only in a minority of cases. (See Tawney 1932: 33f.) In any event, a contrast stressing the presence or absence of a *chia* estate is more useful than one emphasizing gross differences in domestic organization, as between wealthy and poor or gentry and peasant, for at least prior to the establishment of the present government on the mainland, the bulk of China's population was organized on a *chia* basis, and it is precisely in the *chia*'s adjustment to many different social and economic situations that the variability of arrangements possible within the *chia* framework can be seen.

The relationships among *chia* members, then, were quite flexible; one might even say that the *chia* as a social group was highly adaptable. Likely parallels in other aspects of Chinese social structure provide an area for future investigations that may considerably increase our understanding of Chinese society and behavior.

The Sociology of Irrigation: Two Taiwanese Villages

BURTON PASTERNAK

Our approach to the study of Chinese culture and society, long marked by an over-reliance on casual observation and easy generalization, is at last becoming more systematic and more specific. Chinese cultural phenomena are being observed in particular times and places as Sinologists try to learn how sociocultural variants arise and how they are integrated into the larger culture.

This paper considers only one very limited aspect of Chinese society: the management of a single natural resource, water, in two Chinese villages of southwestern Taiwan. The general question involved is how a community's handling of its essential resources affects its sociocultural adaptation. The specific question—and the subject of this paper—is how a community's irrigation system influences such cultural patterns as conflict and cooperation, labor supply and demand, and even family size and structure. Data from a Chinese village on the Chia-nan Plain will be presented in some detail and compared briefly with data from a village on the Ping-tung Plain.*

* The village of Chung-she on the Chia-nan Plain is inhabited by 1,115 Hokkien-speaking people in 194 households. Twenty surnames are represented, but three of them account for half of the village households. The village is compact and nucleated, with each surname group tending to concentrate in a particular portion of the village. The village of Ta-tieh on the Ping-tung Plain is a nucleated, multi-surname, Hakka-speaking community with a resident population of about 1,600 people in 265 households. There is no marked tendency for people with a single surname to concentrate in one part of the village. Neither the ethnic difference (discussed later) nor the difference in physical grouping of the population between the two villages is highly significant for purposes of the comparison to be presented here, and the villages are otherwise quite similar. The Chung-she data were collected in the course of a community study undertaken in 1968–69 with the support of the National Science Foundation. The Ping-tung data, collected between 1963 and 1965 with the aid of a Foreign Area Fellowship, have appeared elsewhere (Pasternak 1968), and are presented here only for purposes of comparison.

Considerable attention has already been given to the social correlates of irrigation, particularly at the level of the State (Eisenstadt 1958; Geertz 1970; Leach 1959; Orenstein 1956 and 1965; Pan-American Union 1955; Pasternak 1968; Steward 1955; and Wittfogel 1957). Most familiar, perhaps, is the work of Karl Wittfogel who, in his monumental work *Oriental Despotism*, investigates the sociopolitical concomitants of particular technological environments. Wittfogel believes that dependence on integrated irrigation systems tends to generate despotic states and elaborate bureaucracies. These bureaucracies develop, he argues, because so much labor is required first to construct and then to maintain irrigation facilities—labor that must be recruited and coordinated—and because considerable planning, supervision, and authority are required to keep such a complex system running. I do not intend to discuss the first part of this argument except to note that integrated irrigation systems may be constructed piecemeal and without benefit of the elaborate bureaucratic forms Wittfogel describes (see Leach 1959: 2–25) and that even if a complicated bureaucracy evolves while a system is being built, it may be abandoned once construction is complete. I will be concerned from time to time, however, with the second part of Wittfogel's argument—that the distribution of water and the adjudication of conflicts over water require a managerial presence, specifically of a bureaucratic sort.

There is a threshold of complexity in irrigation systems at which cooperation* must give way to coordination; at which those served by the systems relinquish their decision-making power and their direct role in settling disputes. Authority and responsibility for these vital functions are then transferred to managerial structures of one sort or another. This is not to say that cooperation is then absent, but rather that it is no longer the dominant pattern of operation. The transfer to managerial coordination is not simply dependent on the size of the irrigated area. It is also—and more directly—dependent on the number of farmers drawing water *from a single source*. Where so many farmers are involved that face-to-face relations break down, management of some kind becomes necessary. Otherwise, the system may be disrupted by constant conflict, and much of the community may be deprived of water.

Conflict and Cooperation

In any densely populated rice-growing community, frequent conflicts over water would certainly not be surprising, if indeed they were not

---

* This word as used here and elsewhere in this paper denotes joint activity jointly decided upon.

taken for granted. What might be surprising on first thought, however, is the precise and almost paradoxical relationship between such
conflict and the means developed to manage it. For the very existence
of feuding seems to stimulate the emergence of both cooperative networks and managerial structures to preclude or at least restrain overt
expressions of hostility. And the greater the danger of such hostile out-
breaks, the more extensive and powerful the networks and structures
seem to be.* Exactly what they will be like in a particular case will be
influenced by the character of the factors that generate them—that is,
by the nature of the specific irrigation system involved.† Changes in the
system will, of course, cause changes in the kind and intensity of conflict
prevalent in the community and, consequently, in the means of dealing
with it.

With this in mind, let us consider a specific irrigation system and a
specific community, the Chia-nan Irrigation System and the village of
Chung-she on the Chia-nan Plain of southwestern Taiwan. The plain,
which includes the *hsien* of Tainan, Chiayi, and Yunlin and the city of
Tainan, has a total area of approximately 4,884 sq km, or virtually one-
seventh that of the island. Rainfall on the plain is unevenly distributed
throughout the year (roughly 80 percent of the mean annual precipita-
tion of 3,000 mm falls between May and September), and underground
water is not abundant, but the region is otherwise well suited to agriculture. About two-thirds of it is flat and fertile, and the temperature
does not normally fall below 17° C. except in January. The area is often
referred to as "the granary of Taiwan."

Chung-she Village lies in the southeastern portion of the plain. According to my census in 1968, 174 of its 194 households cultivated land,
104 of them as full owners (161 households owned at least part of the
land they farmed). Its total cultivated area was 249 hectares in 1968.
The principal crop has always been rice.

Before the Chia-nan Irrigation System was built, a small part of
Chung-she's farmland drew water from public or private ponds scattered about the landscape. The farmers dependent on each pond functioned as a group to obtain "common water," and to manage disputes
arising over it. The larger ponds had radiating canals. When the water
in such a pond was sufficient, the canals drew water in a scheduled
sequence, with farmers at the shallow end operating foot-treadles or

---

* Arend Lijphart (1968) has made a similar point with respect to the accommodation of pluralism at the national level.

† For a discussion of the various irrigation systems on Taiwan, see Chen 1963:
140–71.

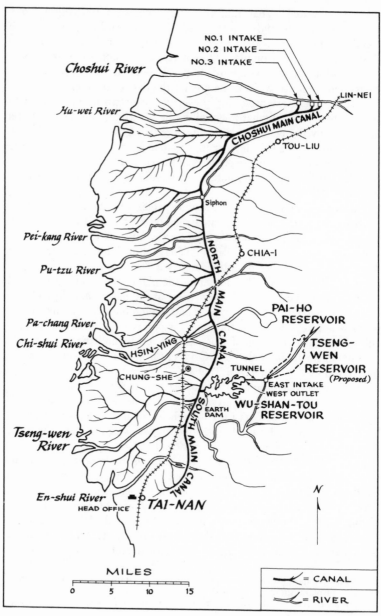

FIGURE 1. THE CHIA-NAN IRRIGATION SYSTEM

opening gates before those at the deep end. The drawing period for each farmer was determined by the area of his fields, and measured by burning incense sticks. When water in the pond was low, however, each canal might draw water without regard to schedule. The only rule was that water would be taken only by foot-treadle. Farmers located at the deep end of a pond sometimes broke this rule. While pretending to pedal, they would covertly open a gate, forcing farmers at the shallow end to pedal furiously, and causing conflict. Farmers who were caught at this trick were denied access to the water in the canal. The smaller ponds were usually capable of supplying water only to the fields immediately surrounding them. So few farmers were involved that there was no need for schedules; each field-owner and his family simply treadled at will. Cooperation was not necessary.

Most of the fields cultivated by Chung-she villagers during this period depended exclusively on rainfall, and were referred to as *k'an-t'ien t'ien*, or "fields that depend on the heavens." Generally speaking, then, either all farmers had water, or no farmers had water. Before 1920, cooperation and conflict in irrigation were minimal and involved only individuals. Households needed to cooperate for only a few purposes, such as providing drainage for each other's fields, or equalizing the supply of water by passing it from one field to another. Theft of water was rare, and usually involved farmers cultivating fields irrigated by ponds. There was a saying that "a good field is made by a good field-neighbor; a good house is made by a good house-neighbor."

Some canals were built on the Chia-nan Plain early in the Ch'ing period.[*] These were mostly small, private canals that drew water from nearby rivers to irrigate the owners' lands. The total irrigated area at that time has been estimated at only 5,000 hectares. The great change came when Japanese authorities bent on extending the cultivation of sugarcane devised a plan to irrigate and provide drainage for 150,000 hectares of farmland on the plain (expanded by the Nationalists to over 160,000 hectares). The canals constructed under this plan between 1920 and 1930 constitute the largest integrated irrigation system on the island, the Chia-nan Irrigation System (see Figure 1). It has over 10,000 km of irrigation canals, nearly 7,000 km of drainage canals, and over 300 km of sea and river dikes.

[*] The following general introduction to the Chia-nan System is based on numerous documents, the most important of which are: Chen 1963: 160–66; Hsieh 1964: 168–71; *Brief Introduction of Chia-nan Irrigation Association*, 1967; *Report on the 1964 Irrigated Land Survey of Irrigation Associations in Taiwan*, *The Republic of China* 1965: 325–50; *Tai-wan Sheng t'ung chih Kao* 1955: 200–211; *Tai-nan Hsien-chih kao* 1960; and *Chia-nan ta-chün hsin-she shih-yeh kai-yao* 1921.

Most of its water is drawn from two sources, the Tseng-wen and Cho-shui rivers. Water from the Tseng-wen is led into the Wu-shan-tou Reservoir, which covers some 6,000 hectares. From there, water is conducted into the south and north sections of the main canal. At the northern end of the system, water is drawn from the Choshui River at three intakes, combined, and then conducted into the Choshui section of the main canal. A large diesel facility called a siphon connects the Choshui and north sections of the canal so that a deficiency in one can be remedied by drawing water from the other. The main canal feeds lateral canals that in turn provide water to lesser canals and to farm ditches throughout the plain.

The water supplied by the Chia-nan System is not sufficient to allow the cultivation of rice every year throughout the entire region. For this reason, a three-year rotation schedule has been established for about 75 percent of the system (122,167 hectares), including the area cultivated by Chung-she Village.[*] The rotation area is divided into *hsiao-ch'ü*, or "small areas," of about 150 hectares each, which are in turn divided into three roughly equal sections. In any one year only one section is to be planted to rice, while the second is to be planted to sugarcane, and the third to a crop that requires even less water, perhaps none at all from the system. The intent of this plan is to give every farmer equal access to the available water.

Putting the plan into effect is a complex matter, as the operation of the Wu-shan-tou portion of the system (serving Chung-she) may illustrate. Water is furnished to the main canal every day from June 1 to October 10.[†] All the water in the canals during this period is intended for the rice-growing areas. During December, all gates are opened for a period of approximately twelve days. Water supplied during this period is intended for the irrigation of dry crops. For fifteen days in February or March, the canals are again filled to supply water for the cultivation of sugarcane. When newly released irrigation water has reached the terminal points of the main canal, and when water levels have been determined to be correct, all gates exiting from them are simultaneously opened. Two or three times a day while these gates are open, the water level is checked at various points along the canal and adjustments are made to keep it constant. As water is led into each

[*] *Report on the 1964 Irrigated Land Survey*, pp. 328–29. There are two other basic irrigation patterns on the plain. A so-called combined irrigation pattern, using additional sources of water such as pumps and ponds, allows one or even two crops of rice each year on 12,246 hectares. And 26,371 hectares of farmland are independently irrigated by small streams, ponds, and lakes.

[†] All agricultural dates used here and elsewhere in this paper are solar dates.

lateral canal, gates exiting from it are partially opened, starting from the top gate and working down to the last one, as water passes each gate. When the water has reached the end of the line, the level of water at various points along the lateral canal is checked and adjusted accordingly. Thus, all gates in the system are actually kept open at the same time, and their apertures are adjusted as necessary.

The preceding description illustrates the integrated nature of the irrigation operation and the high degree of coordination that is required. The coordinating body is the Chia-nan Irrigation Association.° Below the system level, however, cooperation prevails. The local irrigation station hires one or two villagers each year and assigns them to manage water distribution in a "small area." In fact, however, these men do little more than make ritualistic patrols. The actual channelling and distribution of water is handled by the farmers themselves.

In fact, it would probably be fair to say that cooperation in the handling of water resources is more prevalent in Chung-she today than it was before the irrigation system was built. Most village households own from two to four fields located in different places. When fields were watered by rainfall, as already noted, households needed to cooperate in only a few ways, such as providing drainage or equalizing the supply of water by passing it from one field to another. Theft of water was rare, and usually involved farmers cultivating fields irrigated by ponds. For the most part, either all farmers had water or no farmers had water. Since completion of the Chia-nan System, water is supplied to fields on a schedule and from a localizable source. Since each field has to be filled and drained several times during the growing season, and since not all fields border on canals, it is clear that a farmer must articulate his activities with those of other farmers. Not only must he cooperate with the owners of adjacent fields, but he must also arrive at understandings with farmers farther up the line on the canal, who receive water first.

In addition to cooperating in the day-to-day operation of the irriga-

° The twenty-six irrigation associations of Taiwan are approved and supported by the government, but self-administered. Empowered to levy workers, to acquire land, and to collect fees from farmers within their jurisdictions, they are administratively responsible for maintaining local irrigation systems and for arbitrating irrigation disputes. The irrigation association of a district lying entirely within the jurisdiction of one *hsien* or city is supervised primarily by the government of that *hsien* or city and only secondarily by the Water Conservancy Bureau of the Provincial Department of Reconstruction. Just the reverse is true where a district involves more than one local jurisdiction. The members of each association elect representatives to a representatives' congress. The congress in turn elects a supervisory committee and a president, who appoints a general manager and who serves as the association's *de facto* representative to the Joint Council of Irrigation Associations.

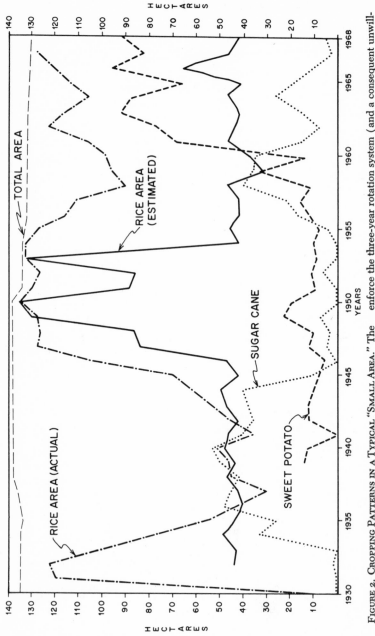

FIGURE 2. CROPPING PATTERNS IN A TYPICAL "SMALL AREA." The sharp increase in both estimated and actual plantings of rice that occurred after 1945 may reflect the removal of Japanese controls. The sharp drop in estimated plantings that occurred about 1954 enforce the three-year rotation system (and a consequent unwillingness to give permission for farmers to grow rice out of turn) in the face of increased overall demand for water from the system. SOURCES: Shui-tao tso-fu kwan-hsi shu-lei (1930–37): Pao-kao

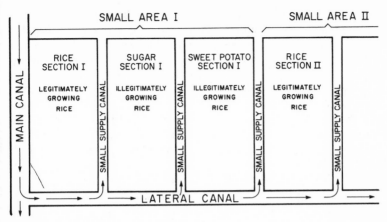

FIGURE 3. AN IRRIGATION MODEL FOR A "SMALL AREA." Arrows indicate direction of water flow.

tion system, many farmers cooperate to steal water (see below). They even establish complicated rotation schedules among themselves. Figure 2 suggests the extent of water-theft in one typical "small area" in Chung-she. Actual plantings of rice during much of the period since 1930 have far exceeded official estimates (the forty-five hectares scheduled to grow rice plus those areas given special permission to grow rice out of turn). This excess area could have been watered only with water illegally diverted from the irrigation system. It should be noted that the mean hectarage cultivated by individual households in this area has steadily decreased since 1935, and that the smaller a farmer's holding, the more likely he is to feel compelled to plant rice every year rather than sugarcane, in order to be sure of feeding his family.[*]

The potential for conflict in Chung-she has obviously increased greatly since the Chia-nan System was built. Yet conflict over water in the village has not increased in the proportions that might have been expected —except possibly for disputes arising from thefts of water. And means have evolved for managing even these, as the following actual cases will illustrate.

Case 1. As noted above, "small areas" like the one schematically represented in Figure 3 are subdivided into three sections of about 50 hectares each. According to the rotation plan, each of the three sections

[*] There are other reasons for the persistent preference for rice that can be seen in Figure 2: sugar prices have not always been stable; rice produces a crop in four months, whereas sugarcane takes eighteen; and the cultivation of rice allows more effective use of family labor during the year.

should be cultivating a different crop as the diagram shows, but all three are in fact growing rice. When a farmer in the section scheduled to grow sugarcane needs water, he will watch the fields. Each farmer in the legitimate rice-growing section will come to his field shortly before his turn to draw water, so there will usually be at least one farmer there at any given time. The would-be thief will ask him whether he needs all the water he is entitled to, or whether he needs the entire period of his turn. If he does not, a small part of his share can be diverted through small ditches and drainages. When water is plentiful, the legitimate rice-growers may not even bother to come to their fields early. In this case, the thief will simply divert water to meet his needs. Relations between farmers within the "small area" are face to face.

Case 2. Problems sometimes arise between "small areas." Suppose, for example, that many farmers scheduled to grow sugarcane in "Small Area" I draw water out of turn. This will cause shortages farther down the line in "Small Area" II as the level of water in the lateral canal falls below that of the exit gates. Such a situation brings large blocs of farmers into opposition and might lead to violence. But the customary way of handling the situation avoids violence by avoiding the direct expression of hostility. One or more of the legitimate rice-growers being deprived of water will complain to the irrigation station. The clerk at the station will then telephone the clerk at the nearest canal-management station, who will consult his counterparts at higher-level canal management stations. Water levels at each station—closely watched in any case to guard against theft—will be checked until the diversion is located and corrected. The relations between "small areas" are therefore indirect. Face-to-face encounters occur between agents of the irrigation association rather than between the two groups of farmers themselves. A potentially hostile situation is managed by taking it out of the hands of those directly involved in it.

Case 3. One night a certain Mr. Huang diverted water from an adjacent section of his "small area" into the supply canal leading to his field. Before it reached his field, however, this stolen water was diverted again, by a canal block placed by one Mr. Ts'ai. When Mr. Huang discovered the block, he went to work at once to remove it. Mr. Ts'ai saw him and came over to stop him. Mr. Huang complained that this was *his* stolen water. After some pushing and shoving, they finally agreed to take turns using the water. Mr. Huang was allowed to draw first.

Case 4. In one case there was a potential for conflict between larger areas, i.e. between areas dependent on separate laterals. One year, about eighteen farmers owning seven or eight hectares of land in a single section of the East Chung-she "Small Area" met informally in the fields and in front of village shops. These farmers were all growing rice out of turn and needed water. Not enough water was available in their immediate vicinity, so they agreed to cooperate in drawing water illegally from a lateral canal to the north. At the specified time, designated farmers brought a gas pump, a siphon, and hoses. The owner of the pump received a fee from all other members of the group.

The diversion was accomplished as follows. A siphon was set up at Point A on the Lin-feng-ying Lateral Canal (see Figure 4). Water was lifted from the canal and led through a small drainage canal to the medium drainage canal indicated on the map. The medium canal was blocked at Point B so that water south of the block would rise and flow southward (the reverse of normal flow in this canal). All who were to benefit from the diversion helped build the canal block. The gas pump was installed at Point C to lift water from the medium drainage canal into a small drainage canal that ran along the edge of the area to be watered. At Point D the water was diverted by another cooperatively constructed block into the first field to be watered. From there it was led to the other thieves' fields in a sequence previously agreed upon

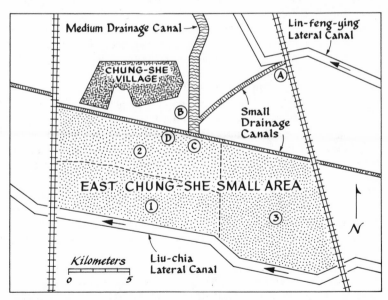

FIGURE 4. A CASE OF WATER THEFT IN THE EAST CHUNG-SHE "SMALL AREA." Arrows in lateral canals show direction of water flow.

by all. The pump used in this operation was left in place and watched by one of the group members day and night. Only the siphon was removed after each night's use.

Farmers dependent on the medium drainage for irrigation noticed that water had suddenly vanished from it. They immediately reported the fact to clerks of the irrigation association, who eventually located the block and had it removed. Thus was averted a conflict that might eventually have involved farmers in several villages and might even have disrupted a large portion of the system.

The Chia-nan Irrigation Association has taken several steps specifically designed to reduce conflict over water. The various farm ditches served by a single small-supply canal initially drew water simultaneously. But the water flowed so slowly that much of it seeped away, and it took a long time to irrigate the area supplied by each ditch. Farmers with fields located at terminal points had to wait a particularly long time. Besides, farmers whose ditches were higher on small-supply canals were in a position to draw water faster at all times and to draw more water in times of shortage. Water passed their ditch entries first, and the openings could be widened to let in a greater quantity of water. Conflicts therefore arose between the owners of ditches fed by a single small-supply canal.

A year or two after the Chia-nan project was completed, however, a plan was devised whereby each ditch received water by rotation. The time allotted for each ditch depended on the type of soil and the total area to be watered, and was measured by burning incense sticks. All the water in the small-supply canal could now legally pass into the entitled ditch. The water flowed faster, and less of it seeped away.

When conflicts arose because certain farmers sheltered their incense sticks to make them burn more slowly, alarm clocks were introduced to standardize timing. The first farmer on a ditch would open it and draw water. Because conflicts over timing arose between farmers along a single ditch, the irrigation station devised rotation schedules for each ditch. When the last farmer on the schedule had drawn his share, he passed the clock to the first farmer on the next lower ditch, who opened its entry and closed that of the upper ditch. If anyone claimed that the clock was running slow, it would be checked against the one in the local train station.

In a further attempt to reduce conflict over water, the irrigation station created the water patrol a few years after the Chia-nan System was completed. Steam-powered tillers used in the planting of sugarcane worked very deep, causing the soil to absorb great quantities of water during a short period. Simultaneous drawing of water from a small-supply canal, such as was still being practiced in rice areas, was no longer possible. Rotation among ditches in the sugarcane areas was therefore established early, and the patrol was set up to supervise it and to watch for flooding in the canals. It was later extended in modified form to rice areas as well.

In summary, then, the extension and integration of irrigation that occurred when the Chia-nan Irrigation System was built required a parallel expansion of the cooperative and managerial networks previously developed by the farmers of the Plain. Bernard Gallin has described the same sort of expansion in Hsin-hsing, another Taiwanese village. In that village, as in Chung-she, the extension of canal irrigation during the Japanese period made water available to a greater number of farmers, extended the area of interdependence, and broadened cooperative networks (Gallin, 1966).

The experience of Chung-she and Hsin-hsing contrasts sharply with that of Ta-tieh Village on the Ping-tung Plain farther to the south (Pasternak 1968). Before 1956, the 220 hectares of farmland cultivated by Ta-tieh farmers were tied into an integrated irrigation system. Conflict over water in this area, already sharp because of population pressures and ethnic rivalry, was intensified early in the twentieth century when subsurface dams and new canals built upstream for the benefit of a new sugar factory deprived the system of much of its water.

Beginning in 1956, pumps designed to tap underground water were installed at various points along the canals in Ta-tieh and the rest of the Ping-tung system. These pumps were intended to counterbalance the drying up of older sources and to ensure more equitable and timely distribution of water for irrigation. An unintentional effect of introducing the pumps has been to split the system into more or less independent units, each drawing most of its irrigation water from a single pump, and there have been noticeable sociocultural adaptations to this change. Conflict over water has significantly diminished, and cooperative networks have contracted. The irrigation association still functions, and a small-group chief is still elected every three years to collect irrigation fees, to disseminate information passed down from the irrigation association, and, theoretically, to help arbitrate water disputes arising within each large-canal system. But the real authority lies in the hands of natural groups consisting of the twenty to twenty-five farmers who draw water from a single pump. It is within and between these groups that rotation and other forms of cooperation mainly occur.

Each pumping station is assigned a watchman by the irrigation association, but the selection usually follows the recommendation of pump-group members. The watchman is responsible to the members of the group he serves for the day-and-night security of his pumping station. During the dry season, especially during periods of severe drought, a pump group may also employ one or two field watchmen to ensure an equitable distribution of water day and night. Such watchmen are paid directly by the owners of the fields they guard. Once a rotation schedule has been agreed upon, usually by drawing lots at a group meeting, these watchmen must see that it is followed. They cannot change it without unanimous prior authorization from the group. During periods of really severe drought, farmers stay in their fields all night to double-check the watchmen.

Where local groups of farmers request it, the irrigation association may investigate the feasibility of and arrange loans for the construction of special pumping devices. The association then assumes responsibility for the maintenance of these facilities, passing both construction and maintenance costs on to the farmers. The irrigation association also assumes responsibility for major water projects such as dikes along the river, but its presence is rarely felt in the areas of water distribution and conflict resolution at the local level. These activities are normally regulated and managed on a face-to-face basis within and between pump groups. Major decisions are enforced by public opinion.

Labor Supply and Demand

Before the Chia-nan Irrigation System was built, the labor supply in Chung-she consisted of the farmers and their grown sons.° Only a few wealthy families had permanent laborers attached to their households or living elsewhere in the village. The demand for labor was characterized by brief but intense peaks followed by relative lulls. Rainfall, unevenly distributed throughout the year and lasting only barely long enough at certain critical points in the rice cycle, had to be taken advantage of when it came. Every farmer was reportedly ready to begin preparing his rice fields (about 2.5 hectares in the second cropping season) as soon as the rains began. During the few days when the fields were actually wet enough to allow proper preparation, he and his sons and their buffalo would work as hard and fast as they could. But work as they might, they would sometimes not finish in time and would have to plant a faster-growing but lower-yielding strain of the native *tsai-lai* rice.

° Before the second World War, Hokkien women did not work in the fields.

When rice seedlings reach the proper stage of development, they must be transplanted within a certain period of time (see below), or they will be lost. Even if rainfall was adequate, the farmer and his sons had to work steadily to finish the job in time. Obviously under these circumstances there was no labor available for exchange or for hire within the village. Nor was there labor that could be brought in at these crucial times from villages just to the north, south, or west. As in Chung-she, farmers in these areas were under pressure to prepare their fields and plant their crops with the rains. Labor could not even be imported from areas farther away where the planting and harvesting times were different, because transportation was so expensive. In 1920 a round-trip train ticket from the city of Tainan to Chung-she, for instance, cost the equivalent of 50 catties of rice. The average yield per hectare at that time was only 1,000 catties. The only hired labor in the village of Chung-she consisted of a few work teams from the western coastal areas brought in to help with the second-season harvest of rice.

The Chia-nan Irrigation System has changed all this. More land is irrigated and can therefore be more intensively cultivated. Yields per hectare are higher. Fields are no longer perpetually flooded, and each rice crop must be weeded at least three times, instead of once as before. The total demand for labor has accordingly increased. However, the prolonged availability of water has spread this demand over a longer period of time. Farmers do not all have to carry out the same operation at the same time, and the peaks in demand are considerably less sharp.

Exactly the opposite happened in Ta-tieh (Pasternak 1968). In a system where farmers once received water in sequence, water was suddenly available to most villagers at about the same time of year, so that households were in a position to prepare, transplant, and harvest their fields almost simultaneously with everyone else. Peak periods of demand for labor (when rice is transplanted or harvested and when beans are planted) were therefore contracted.

Interestingly enough, these opposite patterns of demand for labor have not produced opposite patterns of labor supply: both villages began to hire far more labor than before. An increase in the hiring of labor would be predictable in Ta-tieh, where peak periods of demand were suddenly created. In Chung-she, however, where these peak periods were considerably eased, it might be thought that the villagers would begin to exchange labor. On the contrary, they began to hire workers for transplanting, for routine care of plants, and for harvesting. Brokers even appeared in some villages in the area to accommodate the new demand for hired labor. Perhaps the best explanation for this similarity is that in both villages the irrigational changes I have been describing brought substantial increases in annual income for most residents.

Family Form

By blunting and extending peak periods of demand for labor, the Chia-nan Irrigation System may have removed an important impediment to family division in Chung-she. Let us consider this possibility more closely.

Rice nurseries are seeded from mid-May to mid-June (solar). The seedlings are ready for transplanting thirty days later, by mid-June to mid-July. It is important to remember that once the seedlings are ready, they must be transplanted within twenty days. It should also be remembered that before the Second World War, field labor in this Hokkien area consisted exclusively of males. This custom placed an important limitation on available labor, one not present in Ta-tieh, for the Hakka traditionally have had no such restriction. With these facts in mind, and considering only the amount of labor needed to plant rice on each holding, let us now look at a model joint family and weigh the advantages and disadvantages of dividing it.*

The family contains three males capable of field labor: two married brothers, A and B, and A's son. Like other such families in the village, it owns two buffalo and cultivates about two hectares of land. If the water supply is adequate, two of its three workers using its two buffalo can prepare the two hectares for transplanting in twelve to fifteen days. Three workers can transplant the entire holding in seven days. At worst, if they wait until their entire holding has been prepared before beginning to transplant, the family can prepare the land and transplant the seedlings in nineteen to twenty-two days.

If the brothers set up separate households, Brother A would now have one buffalo, two workers, and one hectare of land. One man and one buffalo could prepare the land in twelve to fifteen days, and two men could complete the transplanting in five days. Brother A and his son could therefore get their crop planted. Brother B, however, could not quite make it alone. He would need twelve to fifteen days to prepare the soil plus an additional ten and a half days to transplant. He would actually have to wait until his entire holding had been prepared before

---

* A joint family is one in which there are two or more married siblings. A nuclear family consists of one married couple and their children. Where a family contains members not normally associated with a nuclear family, but does not meet the criterion for a joint family, it is referred to in this paper as an enlarged family. For purposes of this discussion it will be assumed that neither hired nor exchanged labor is available.

transplanting, and the total period required could by no means be less than twenty-three to twenty-six days.

Obviously it would be easy to lose a rice crop at this stage. If during the allowable twenty days for transplanting there are fewer than fifteen days with sufficient water for preparing fields, all farmers will lose their crops. If there are between sixteen and twenty days of rain, the amount of labor available will determine the outcome. According to my informants in Chung-she, rice crops were often lost at transplanting time before the Chia-nan System was built. Even more risky is the period just before and just after the rice forms heads. If there is not a single substantial rain for ten days before or twenty days after heading, the crop will be ruined. Lack of rain at this time, according to my informants, was an even more frequent cause of crop failure before the Chia-nan System was built.

A farmer who lost his crop of rice would have to plant a crop of sweet potatoes immediately to tide him over until the next year's rice harvest. Since clay soils, particularly under drought conditions, are far from ideally suited to the cultivation of sweet potato, most village families kept about 0.3 hectare of sandy soil within their holding as insurance against just such drought conditions. Upland rice could be planted on this area in March and harvested in August (i.e. in time to plant a crop of sweet potatoes).

It is when a farmer loses his rice crop because of prolonged drought that the disadvantages of family division become most apparent. Let us assume that the model joint family just discussed has lost its crop of rice because of insufficient rainfall. Since 0.3 hectare of sweet potatoes would be barely enough to sustain the family until the next harvest, it is imperative that the entire area be planted. Two men using two buffalo can prepare 0.3 hectare for ridge construction, manuring, and planting in four and a half days.* Three workers can build ridges in the field and spread the manure in one day, and can then do the planting in two afternoons. The soil will therefore have to be moist enough for this work for at least seven days.

Should the brothers divide their family and their holding, each would now have one buffalo and 0.15 hectare of land suitable for such an emergency planting. Brother A could use his animal to prepare the land in four and a half days. He and his son would need an additional day for

---

* Labor requirements were determined by interviewing villagers. If these requirements appear higher for the same task in one instance than in another, this is because the number of laborers available determines whether everything must be done in sequence (one laborer) or whether parts of certain tasks can be done simultaneously (two or more laborers), and therefore determines the amount of time needed for any step in cultivation.

ridging and manuring and three afternoons for planting, a total of at least eight moist days. In what informants called a dry year, a farmer dependent on rainfall could rarely hope for more than seven sufficiently moist days between mid-August and the end of September. There might even be fewer than seven. Brother A would thus be hard pressed to plant his entire holding within the allotted period, and Brother B would find it impossible (he would need at least eleven moist days). If they remained members of a joint family, on the other hand, their chances would be considerably improved.

If Brother B's wife whispered her displeasure at having to feed and support the sons of her husband's brother, therefore, her husband might well reply, "And who then would work in our fields when the year is dry?" Whereas in good years a younger brother might have more to gain from an early division of the family, in dry years he would have more to lose.

A more reliable water supply, the introduction of the power tiller, and the increased availability of wage labor (and of the means for hiring such labor) have all served to remove these obstacles to family division. Rice has become a reliable crop, and the sweet potato is no longer a crisis crop. Before the Chia-nan Irrigation System was built, the noontime earth was so hot and dry that sweet potato stems had to be planted in the afternoon to survive; today, the continuously moist earth allows planting in the morning as well. Also, the soil can be prepared much more rapidly now. One man with buffalo and plow needed thirty days just to get one hectare ready for ridging and manuring. With a power tiller he can do it in twenty-four hours. There are, essentially, no more dry years. Thus it is not surprising that in Chung-she today the younger brother usually initiates the division of a joint family.

We have been dealing with a model family, but one of a type that was fairly well represented in the village before 1930. To be sure, there were families with more or fewer working males; but there were also families with more or less land (and a proportionately greater or lesser demand for labor)—and years with more or less rain. The illustration suggests the adaptive advantage of joint families prior to the completion of the irrigation system.

Another of the system's consequences has been a dramatic decline in the number of *ju-chui*, men who marry matrilocally and allow one or more of their sons to adopt the surname of their wives. Though now uncommon in Chung-she, such marriages were formerly even more common than male adoptions. Since *ju-chui*, unlike adopted sons, enter their new families as adults capable of field labor, and since many are known to have entered families that already had a male heir, it seems clear that the main motive of families taking a *ju-chui* was to obtain labor—not only or even primarily for day-to-day needs, but for the sort of need that might arise in a crisis. Indeed, in virtually all cases known to me, *ju-chui* entered families deficient in adult male labor; and in some cases *ju-chui* marriages resulted in joint families.*

Although I cannot demonstrate beyond any doubt that families in Chung-she Village deliberately put off dividing in order to have enough labor for times of crisis, the evidence points that way. A preliminary examination of Japanese household registers dating from 1905 indicates that before the Chia-nan project was completed in 1930, most village families, tenants as well as landlords, with two or more adult sons achieved the joint form before dividing.† Although the data await finer quantitative analysis, it appears that families divided at a much slower rate between 1905 and 1930 than they did after 1930.

This suggestion is supported by Japanese census figures. As Table 1 indicates, the number of resident households in Chung-she rose much more gradually between 1920 and 1935 than between 1935 and 1968. The table indicates no comparable disparity between the two periods for Ta-tieh Village. Households in Chung-she thus apparently proliferated more slowly than in Ta-tieh during the first period, but considerably faster than in Ta-tieh during the second. Note also the dramatic drop in the percentage of joint families in Chung-she for a comparable period, shown in Table 2.‡

* Such marriages have always been rare in Ta-tieh, and contracted strictly for the purpose of acquiring a male heir to carry on the family line.

† Great care must be exercised in using household registers as a source of information on family form in Taiwanese villages. One difficulty is that their recording of migration is incomplete. This deficiency is greater today than it was during the Japanese occupation, when people usually moved only from one village to another and registers were maintained by local police officers who knew everyone in the villages under their charge. In recent years people have tended to move to large cities, and the registers are now maintained by the township office, which is ill equipped to keep up-to-date records. Another difficulty in using the registers is that false reporting of family division—both registering divisions that have not taken place and failing to register divisions that have taken place—has been common from the beginning of the Japanese period to the present. My own censuses in Ta-tieh and Chung-she have indicated considerable error in the data on family form in contemporary household registers of both villages.

‡ My copies of the household registers for Ta-tieh prior to 1946 are incomplete. Thus I am unable to compare the two villages before that year. A simple arithmetic mean obtained by dividing total resident population by number of households would not be satisfactory, since the actual distribution curves would probably be skewed differently in the two villages by the presence of unknown numbers of very large or very small households.

TABLE 1. CHANGES IN POPULATION AND NUMBER OF HOUSEHOLDS IN
CHUNG-SHE (1920–68) AND TA-TIEH (1920–64)

Village and category	1920	1935	Percent change since 1920	1964	1968	Percent change since 1935
Chung-she						
Households	78	87	11.5%	—	194	122.9%
Population	364	565	55.2	—	1,115	97.3
Ta-tieh						
Households	148	189	27.7	265	—	40.2
Population	809	1,051	29.9	1,602	—	52.4

SOURCE: Figures for 1920 and 1935 are based on the Japanese censuses for those years. Figures for 1964 and 1968 are based on my own censuses and apply to units comparable to those of 1920 and 1935.

That Ta-tieh is a Hakka village and Chung-she a Hokkien village is seemingly no help in explaining their differences in family form. There is no reason to suspect, for example, that the Taiwanese Hakka as an ethnic group are any more or less prone than the Hokkien to live in joint families. Whereas in Ta-tieh joint families have constituted about 5 percent of all households for at least a generation, Cohen finds that in Yen-liao (another Hakka village on Taiwan) they constitute about 32 percent of all households (Cohen 1967: 638); and Gallin's figure for Hsin-hsing, a Hokkien village, is 5 percent, the same as Ta-tieh (Gallin 1966: 138).

Some years ago, Karl Wittfogel noted a propensity for nuclear as opposed to joint families in societies with large-scale irrigation (1935: 42f, 48f, and 1938: 7–8). More recently, using data on fifty-nine Indian villages, Henry Orenstein found a significant negative correlation between availability of large-scale irrigation and percentage of joint families (1956: 317). He was not entirely successful in explaining this correlation, but he attributed it primarily to the "immediate economic consequences" of irrigation (Orenstein 1956: 318–19).

Irrigation often accentuates the importance of cash crops and a money economy. Where income is primarily for direct consumption, the joint family stores its produce in one unit and uses it when needed. But when a large part of income is in cash, its joint use becomes complicated, and it is a fact that a number of joint families are divided because of quarrels over the disposition of money income.

For Taiwan, a comparable focus on cash income would probably be too narrow. Cohen, for example, found the joint family thriving in Yen-liao, where tobacco is an important cash crop. He ascribes the persis-

TABLE 2. FAMILY FORM IN CHUNG-SHE AND TA-TIEH

Family form	Chung-she				Ta-tieh			
	1946		1968		1946		1964	
	Number	Percent	Number	Percent	Number	Percent	Number	Percent
Joint	10	9.2%	3	1.6%	10	4.8%	13	4.9%
Enlarged	43	39.4	51	26.4	80	38.5	94	35.6
Nuclear	53	48.6	135	69.9	110	52.9	147	55.7
Other	3	2.8	4	2.1	8	3.8	10	3.8
Total	109	100.0%	193	100.0%	208	100.0%	264[a]	100.0%

SOURCE: Household registers and my censuses.
[a] The household made up of residents of the village temple has been excluded from these calculations, since the members are in no sense related.

tence of joint families in Yen-liao to "the interdependent nature of the various economic activities undertaken by different family members." Specifically, a joint family is less likely to be divided where "the limited possibilities remaining to each unit would not bring total returns as great as those derived from the total investments of the family as now constituted," or where "division would also mean a reduction in total income from present enterprises" (Cohen 1967: 642–43). The persistence of joint families in Chung-she before 1930 would appear to be explainable in exactly these terms.

If this explanation has merit, it may help resolve long-standing disagreements over the conditions under which "Chinese families" achieve joint form during their developmental cycle. If, for example, we could compare the dynamics of family development in areas dependent on rainfall and areas dependent on irrigation, we might find that, other conditions being equal, families in rainfall areas are more likely to achieve and retain joint form than those in irrigated areas. At a minimum, I have shown that changes in local irrigation patterns can lead to significant sociocultural adaptations. A proper understanding of this relationship in its many forms and aspects should throw light on sociocultural differences not only in Chinese society, but in all societies that practice irrigation.

Child Training and the Chinese Family

MARGERY WOLF

The Chinese family has been examined in many contexts—from its place in the economy to its role in ancestor worship. Only in passing has it been considered in terms of the family's basic function: the training of future adult members. The accumulation of data about socialization processes is essential to our understanding of human behavior and personality development, but even the researcher whose interests are confined to more specific problems may find that such information yields unexpected insights into areas of culture seemingly unrelated to children. The cooperation, or at least interaction, of the entire domestic group is required to one degree or another in the preparation of the family's children for future responsibilities. Adult attitudes and approaches to the job of socialization suggest a great deal about their attitudes toward one another and their evaluation of their own positions in the family.

Generalizations about the Chinese family in this essay are drawn from the experience of a two-and-a-half-year field study of child-training practices in a small village of Hokkien-speakers in northern Taiwan. The research, designed by my husband, Arthur Wolf, had a dual purpose: to carry out a conventional anthropological village study and to replicate the work of the Six Culture Project. The Six Culture Project, under the direction of its senior members, John W. M. Whiting, Irvin L. Child, and William W. Lambert, sent field teams to six different societies to collect systematic information on child rearing, carefully timed observations of child behavior, child interviews, and comparable ethnographic data (Whiting *et al.* 1966). Their methodology included techniques traditional to anthropology as well as those confined until then to psychological laboratories. To their elegant design we added, among other things, some homemade projective tests, informal parent observations and interviews, questionnaires administered in local schools, and, in collaboration with W. W. Lambert, a biochemical analysis of the epinephrine and norepinephrine levels of our sample of 64 children.

In the process of observing and interviewing parents, we found that we were being given information beyond that asked for in our specific questions—information that told us much about the dynamics of the family. A Chinese woman's assumptions about the behavior of close kinsmen, assumptions she may be neither willing nor, in many cases, able to express, were often clearly delineated in her responses to questions about who was responsible for feeding and disciplining her child. Although our questioning was nearly always directed toward adult interactions with the family's children, the responses frequently contained spontaneous information about adult interaction with other adults in the family, a type of information, incidentally, that is extremely difficult to elicit by direct questioning. In a sense, our study of child-training practices produced quite accidentally a projective test of the dynamics of the Chinese family. More simply, it provided another perspective from which to examine the Chinese family and the nature of the interactions of its members.

In Taiwan there remains an old and stable laboratory of traditional Chinese culture. Between 1895 and 1945 Taiwan was under the control of a Japanese colonial government, but Japanese influence over such institutions as the family was superficial at most, and in many rural areas nonexistent. Moreover, the isolation Japan imposed on her colony protected the traditional culture from the Western influences that provoked so much of the social upheaval in China during the 1920's and 1930's. The comments made by Wusih factory girls interviewed by Olga Lang in the 1930's (Lang 1946: 266ff), so full of uncertainty about their new status and new rights, are strikingly similar to those made now by the girls working in Taiwan's factories. Change is coming to Taiwan and will continue with increasing speed as the younger people declare their independence and use it to experiment with new ideas and new ways.

The village of Peihotien (a fictitious name) is located on the edge of the Taipei basin, a fifteen minute walk from the railroad and a half hour from there by train to the city of Taipei. Although the majority of the families in the village own land, few obtain their sole income from the land. Nearly every family has one member who brings in wages from a job outside the village. Peihotien's proximity to an urban center seems to strengthen rather than to weaken family ties. The market town of

Tapu (a fictitious name) has, besides a railway station, several small factories that can and do employ the young people of Peihotien. From Tapu it is only fifteen minutes by train to a small city with many employment opportunities. It is feasible in terms of time and it is economically advantageous for the young men and women of the village to remain a part of their parents' domestic units and commute to employment elsewhere. Few young people, including those without obligations to parents in Peihotien, leave the village to be closer to work opportunities.

Although my observations are based on information obtained from Hokkien-speakers in Taiwan, I refer to my informants as Chinese or as Taiwanese, both of which they are. I am nonetheless aware of the dangers of implying uniformity across a culture that is so full of variation. Strictly speaking, the term "Taiwanese" includes the Hakka, about whose family life I know very little, and the term "Chinese" includes people as disparate as the wealthy bureaucrat in Peking and the poor peasant living hundreds of miles away on the Yunnan plateau. It is tempting but dangerous to generalize that the family tensions reflected in the child-training practices of Peihotien are found within other social classes and linguistic groups. It is tempting because many of the conclusions reached in the following analysis are familiar to those who have observed the Chinese family in other provinces, centuries, and social classes; it is dangerous because the data on socialization in other areas of China are so limited, and our assumptions about uniformity of customs across such a vast country have in the past proved so erroneous. I will, however, venture a conservative assertion: as long as power is vested in the senior generations of a family (i.e., the grandparents) child-training practices will change more slowly than other aspects of culture. Older people, in particular older females, are less exposed to and less vulnerable to innovative ideas. And, until the Communist movement, new ideas were both less available and less appealing to the lower classes. Given the strong tendency toward hypergamy in Chinese marriage, the conservative attitudes of lower-class women probably travel fairly high up into the social hierarchy. In other words, it seems reasonable to assume that child-training practices among the Chinese are not particularly open to Western influences and are likely to accurately reflect traditional goals and values—as long as those goals and values are maintained. In Taiwan, the authority is just beginning to pass from the hands of the grandparents to those of the parents.

Just as current research has made us aware of the unexpected frequency and broad geographic distribution of alternative forms of marriage in China, it is probable that further research will find more variation in the nature of relationships within the family. It would be foolish to assume that the particular tensions and the particular socialization techniques discussed in this paper are typical of China as a whole. The variations that occur in conjunction with alternative forms of marriage in Peihotien are enough to discount this. Undoubtedly the economic base of a community, the status of its women, the importance of matrilateral kin ties, and any number of other factors can affect the style of interaction among family members *and* the techniques they use to train their children. The child-training practices in a remote village in Kwangsi province may vary greatly from those of Peihotien, but they will nonetheless be related to the tensions afflicting the families of that particular village.

Mothers and Fathers

Both the mother and the father of a Taiwanese child share the same broad goals in the training of their son. They want him to become a strong healthy adult who is obedient, respectful, and capable of supporting them in their old age. They want a son who will not embarrass or impoverish them by his excesses, who will maintain if not increase their standing in the community, who will handle relations with outsiders skillfully but at the same time keep them at a polite distance. No matter how alienated man and wife may be from each other, they nonetheless share these common aims in regard to their children. The techniques they use to implement these goals differ considerably and, more importantly, so does the intensity of their desire for any particular result in their sons.

A father's relationship with his son is both affectionate and informal until the boy reaches the age of six or seven. In the evenings the small boy accompanies his father on errands about the village, and falls asleep on his father's lap as the older man chats with neighbors and friends. Although fathers do not play games with their children, they are apt to play with them in the manner that an American adult plays with a kitten or puppy. Fathers of young children are usually fairly well prepared with the sweets or pennies that dry the tears resulting from scraped knees and bumped heads. In return a father expects very little. A toddler is too young to understand what his father wants when he asks the child to bring him a packet of cigarettes, and a four-year-old is too young to understand that he must obey his father's command. The child's disobedience is treated with either amusement or tolerance, depending on his age and his father's mood. If the child's infantile behavior becomes annoying, or if, as so often happens with Chinese children, he falls into a kicking, screaming rage over some small (though conclusive) frustration, he is simply turned over to his mother or older sister with little or no paternal comment.

The age of reason has been established by Taiwanese parents at about six years, coinciding in modern times with the child's beginning school. Since this age is unmarked by any ceremony (other than that of starting school), the father's subsequent change in behavior must seem to the child abrupt, bewildering, and drastic. Social pressure and the father's own understanding of "what is right" force him to create a social distance between himself and his son. The sleepy child no longer finds a haven on his father's lap but is told to go to bed. If he decides to shoot one more marble before complying with his father's request to fetch him cigarettes, he hears his name called in the stern, icy voice of the feared schoolmaster. He may still accompany his father about the village for a while, but the behavior expected of him in his father's presence tends to turn the outing into an ordeal not to be repeated if avoidable. As their interaction becomes more and more formal and their conversation deteriorates into paternal lectures, the father's dignity becomes more impressive and more impregnable.

Taiwanese fathers say that it is only from this aloof distance that they can engender in their sons the proper behavior of a good adult. "You cannot be your son's friend and correct his behavior." A child will not take seriously the friendly suggestions of an obviously loving adult, but he will obey the commands of a stern feared parent. This philosophy, of course, reflects (or is reflected in) the educational techniques of Chinese schools even today. Be it unintentional or simply concomitant, this remoteness also builds the supports necessary to maintain the senior male's position of authority over his adult sons. The weakening powers of an aging father, both mental and physical, provide the all-important social justification for a young man desiring independence and/or control of the family destiny. The increasing indecision and faltering that might be revealed in the camaraderie of an informal relationship can be concealed for a considerably longer time when the son is faced with an austere, aloof figure of authority toward whom society demands he show respect and obedience. All fathers are aware of this potential problem, but whether it actually motivates their behavior is another question, and one not within the scope of this paper. For whatever reason, fathers believe that if they are to teach their sons at all, they must first teach them obedience and respect.

Long before they have learned to fear their father, children are aware

of his power in the family. On several occasions I have heard a three-
or four-year-old imperiously warn his mother to stop interfering with
his (usually dangerous) activity lest he summon his father to beat her.
Although the father's wrath may not yet have been directed toward him,
the child has observed its effect on his mother or his elder siblings.
Children with older siblings may not find their father's change of behavior toward them as abrupt or as unexpected as do first- and second-
borns. The mother, intentionally or not, provides considerable assistance
to her husband in building his image of authority. The recalcitrant child,
or the child who has committed a serious misdeed, may be threatened
with all sorts of dire punishments, but if he has reached the "age of reason," or has siblings who are six years of age and older, the threat of
paternal punishment is one of the most effective. If the mother's threat is
actually carried out and the father beats his son, the strokes may be far
lighter than the mother's would have been, since the punishment is administered with cool forethought; but perhaps for the same reason the
emotional effect on the child is far stronger.

A male is born into a community and grows up there, learning almost
unconsciously the idiosyncrasies of his physical environment and of the
temperaments of his neighbors and relatives. By the time he reaches
adulthood, there is little in his everyday social world that is so surprising
or uncertain that he cannot deal with it automatically. His own pecu-
liarities of temperament or behavior have long been accepted (or rejected) by his neighbors and are hardly worthy of comment. He is a
member of a family that considers all non-kin as outsiders and of a community that similarly considers all non-residents. Not so the wife of this
man. Growing up in a similar social environment in a distant village, she
enters a community of outsiders to live with a family that until the day
of her marriage has been classified by her as outsiders. Whereas security
and familiarity are givens to her husband, to her they are completely
absent and may be for many years to come, if not (in her frightened
young eyes) forever. In her first few years of marriage, her own children
will seem more a part of this new community than she can ever hope to
be. Under these conditions, it is not at all surprising that she should give
precedence over the inculcation of respect and respectability in her sons
to a different set of values. Her concern in her isolation is more with her
own personal well-being than with the vague expectations of the somewhat alien world of her husband and his family. To them, her infant son
is the next link in a long chain of descendants carrying their name and
their future. To her, he is the source of the first bit of security she has
felt since she entered the family. He is her defense against her mother-

in-law and her sisters-in-law. His birth, providing an object of shared concern, may change her somewhat ambiguous relationship with her husband into a more satisfactory commitment, but if it does not, the dissatisfactions of that relationship will not matter as much. She may simply endure her present situation and build toward a future family environment that will not be hampered by mothers-in-law or be dependent on husbands. No matter what is involved in her current status, the whole quality of her future life depends on the strength of the ties she develops with her son.

The salient difference between what a Chinese mother and a Chinese father hope for in their relations with their sons can best be described in slightly exaggerated terms. A Chinese father wants respect and obedience even at the price of fear or dislike. If he is to maintain his authority over the household when his sons are themselves adults, he must have their respect if not their admiration, their obedience if not their affection. He is aided in his endeavors by the sanctions of his culture, the example of his neighbors, and the teachings of the schools. A Chinese mother would certainly appreciate her son's respect and obedience, but not at the price of his affection. Her marriage into a family of strangers has forced her to depend entirely on herself in constructing working relationships. The degree to which she can depend on those ties is less related to the sanctions of society, the examples of neighbors, or the teachings in the local school than to the intangibles of affection, spontaneous gratitude, and goodwill. Chinese culture extracts from a son the obligation of supporting his mother and showing her a minimum degree of respect; but a woman's experience with social sanctions has usually been that they have operated against her position rather than in any way promoting it. Far more dependable are the ties of affection and gratitude that she weaves in the years of her son's childhood.

Chinese society has given a father both the power and the authority to manage his adult sons. A mother's authority is not so clearly stated, and so she must establish her power in a more subtle fashion. For her, the father's method of withdrawal into formality would be both difficult and dangerous. When her son is six years old, she may expect more of him in terms of obedience and chores, but her menial services to him are still a necessity and will be for some time. These services are often extended considerably longer than is necessary, and are referred to again and again when the child is being punished. "Why are you so bad? Do you want me to die? Then who will feed you and take care of you?" Mothers seem to be as convinced as fathers that learning does not take place without physical punishment, but mothers administer beatings in a very different atmosphere. The father's beating is usually preceded by a stern lecture on the expectations of the family and administered with a cool temper; the mother's beating usually grows out of the frustrations of the day and is administered in fury (and often as not interrupted by a relative or neighbor). Once her anger has passed, she may comfort the crying child, explaining why she *had* to punish him, or if he has run away before she managed to strike him, she may just let the whole matter go with a few words of warning when he returns. Impending punishments by a father do not blow over. Paternal punishment of a child or of his siblings occurs just often enough to make it a useful threat, one which mothers employ frequently. As mentioned previously, this threat serves to establish more firmly the father's position of familial superiority, but it also has an interesting side effect on the mother's position. She appears in the role of go-between. Each time she makes the threat and does not carry it out, she becomes the child's go-between rather than the father's, the child's ally rather than the father's. An adult son fuming under the continued dominance of his father is far more likely to recall these "interventions" by his mother than the beatings he received at her hands.

Village mothers state, as do the fathers, that you must not let a child know you love him or you will not be able to correct his behavior, assuming of course that if you love him you will forgive anything. The open expression of affection toward an older child is considered not only in bad taste but bad for the child. One must not praise children for accomplishments or they will feel they have done well enough and will stop trying to do better. Superficially these dicta do seem to be observed. Upon presenting an essay or school report to his father for his chop (to assure the teacher that it has been seen by the parent), a child who has placed second in the class is admonished to reach first place by next year, and if he has placed first he is warned to do as well the following year or expect a beating. The father may swell with pride as he discusses the matter later with the child's grandmother or mother, but he will show no pleasure in the child's presence. If other adults comment on the achievement, the father counters with deprecating remarks about the child's other, bad, characteristics, concealing his pride from no one, except perhaps the child. The mother's reaction to the child's accomplishment will be somewhat the same, but her pleasure will be less carefully concealed from the child; the extra ten cents to buy sweets or the choice piece of food swiftly stuffed into his mouth before the dish goes on the table will not go unrelated to her pride in him. Like his father, his mother rarely pets or hugs him, but unlike the father, she has many other means available to her for expressing her affection: cooking his favorite dishes, granting privileges, or simply listening to childish prattle about the day's happenings at school. The constant interaction between mother and child provides far more opportunity for the mother to influence her child's attitudes than does the briefer more formal interaction of father and son. Most mothers make good use of their opportunities.

The inferior status of female children is not as pronounced in times of prosperity (the present situation in Taiwan) as it is during periods of economic hardship. Sons are of course preferred, but most families want at least one daughter if they can afford her. In general, the treatment of a girl is not dramatically different from that of her brothers. The attitudes her parents hold toward her, however, are quite different. The expectations and consequent behavior of father and mother toward their son are almost reversed when they deal with their daughter. As an adult the daughter will be nearly irrelevant to her father. Very little of his future prestige or his physical comfort in his declining years will depend on anything she does or does not do. The rigid standards of respect and obedience her brother must adhere to as an adult are of less value in her, since she will be in another household. As long as she does not become wantonly immoral while a member of her father's household, she is a luxury he can enjoy. Fathers who are acting against their natural propensities in the treatment of their sons, find considerable satisfaction in a relaxed informal exchange with their daughters. As long as he maintains the general rules of propriety (i.e., does not openly express his affection for her or allow her publicly to disobey him), he is safe from the criticism of his neighbors. Should she turn out to be a poor wife and daughter-in-law, criticism would not be directed at him, her father, but rather at her mother as the person responsible for her training in the domestic arts. Ultimately, the hardship would fall on the girl herself.

An adult daughter will have no more opportunity to add to her mother's comfort or status than she will to her father's. If she turns out to be an excellent mother and daughter-in-law, she will by definition see less of her mother and relegate her to a position of minor importance in the demands on her time and affection. Publicly, or even privately, the mother will receive little credit for having trained her so well. Should the daughter fall short of adult standards, criticism will eventually be directed at her mother's laxness and incompetence. This potential criticism, however, has little influence on the mother's everyday attitude toward training her daughter. Until one of her sons marries and provides her with a daughter-in-law, the services of her daughter are needed.

She can afford to smile on the disobedience and arrogance of her son as on interest accumulating on a loan, but the misbehavior of her daughter threatens daily operating expenses. If she has a family of any size at all, she must have someone to help her wash the vegetables, mind the younger children, hang out the clothes. If the mother does not establish early at least the minimum standards of obedience in her daughter, she will suffer for it several times each day. If some degree of responsibility has not been internalized, the mother will not dare leave the girl in charge of infants and toddlers, send her on errands, or depend on her to have the rice washed in time for dinner.

Taiwanese mothers believe that no children can be expected to understand much during their first six years of life. This is not to say that all training is delayed until their sixth birthday, but rather that not much is expected to result from it until after that age. Nonetheless, by the time they are five, most little girls are doing a few chores regularly and certainly are minding their slightly younger siblings. Before this time, the mother's treatment of her sons and daughters is not noticeably different except in one aspect. The techniques the mother employs throughout are essentially the same, but the intensity of the training for girls is considerably stronger. I doubt that there is any conscious intent involved in this; the girls as potential errand-runners and baby-sitters are kept closer to home and thereby receive a larger dose of the medicine administered. Even in behavior not immediately relevant to their mother's requirements for helpers, girls are found to socialize earlier and better than boys. Their performance on a variety of quantitatively measured variables is usually more consistent with the stated adult values at a considerably earlier age.

The warm intimate relationship that mothers desire with their sons they more frequently achieve with their daughters. As the daughter begins to worry about how she herself will fare at the hands of an unknown husband and mother-in-law, her mother's complaints about the behavior of her husband and his relatives fall on a more sympathetic ear. Her father's indulgence does little to increase his stature in his daughter's eyes, and often serves to damage it, since he is unlikely to defend to her his usually harsher public behavior toward her mother. She may retain a real though slightly cynical affection for her father, but the more frequent interaction plus their increasing similarity of interests and anxieties will involve her sympathies more deeply with her mother. The contrast between her mother's worried fretful questioning of the matchmakers and her father's calmer financial evaluations of a proposed match cements the emotional ties between the women. Her father may be, and often is, even more concerned than his wife about the treatment his daughter will receive at the hands of her husband's family, but as a man he must pretend to consider it irrelevant, and never having experienced this traumatic change himself, he truly is unaware of many of its more painful aspects. It is on her mother's good judgment that the girl must depend. The tears ritually required of bride and mother when the former leaves the home on her wedding day may fall for different reasons, but they rarely are forced.

As young men sons may fear their fathers, but they nonetheless emulate them, rejecting the open intimacy desired by their mothers in favor of a more manly stance. Even so, the mothers' efforts have not, in most cases, been in vain. As age gradually erodes and reverses the relationship between son and father, that existing between son and mother erodes little and reverses only in the way the mother desires. Should her relationship with her husband be antagonistic, the mother may begin early to isolate him by referring decisions about the household economy to her son rather than to the head of the household. As her son's earning capacity increases and his wages come to her for the purchase of daily requirements, she may also discuss with him the advisability of this or that major purchase or the advantages of joining this or that cooperative loan association. This show of trust and increasing dependence both strengthens their relationship and erases any lingering resentment the young man may have of the punishments received at her hands in his youth. Should, on the other hand, the relationship between husband and wife be a happy one, the wife can act as peacemaker between the older man, fearful of losing his hard-won authority, and the younger, impatient to test his own abilities. She can flatter and in many ways train the younger man by referring to him the minor domestic decisions (decisions she might have made herself without consulting her husband) and by discussing the larger decisions with both men, allowing each to feel that his was the decision acted upon. Eventually, however, the two must meet head-on in conflicts outside her domestic sphere, and the inevitable change in authority will proceed either speedily or gradually, depending on the personalities and abilities of the two men. The external pressures of his world demand that the son treat his aging father with respect, but the internal pressures of his socialization demand that he repay his mother with more than respect.

Grandparents

By the time she is a grandmother, a Chinese woman usually has come to regard her husband's family and community as her own. To her daughter-in-law it is inconceivable that the older woman was ever any-thing but a representative of the interests of that family. Most women are delighted when their son marries and a daughter-in-law enters their home. Unless the marriage is a love-match, the older woman has chosen the girl herself and investigated her qualities and faults as carefully as possible. Because of the exaggerations of go-betweens, she expects a great deal of her daughter-in-law. The girl's mother, her peers, and her own observations have taught the bride what is expected of a daughter-in-law, and she usually enters her husband's family determined to do her best to fulfill these expectations. For the first few months, or perhaps only weeks, after the marriage, there exists between mother-in-law and daughter-in-law that amiable relationship that in the West is supposed to exist between husband and wife during what is called the honeymoon period. Village women laugh at new mothers-in-law singing the praises of their sons' wives, saying, "We'll wait a while and then see." Indeed, they usually have a very short period to wait. The two women's good feelings quickly sour after a series of disagreements about how to pickle radishes, when to wash clothes, how much to spend on excursions, and when to have the evening meal on the table. Regardless of the merits of her position, the older woman is likely to be the victor in any conflict for a good many years to come.

No matter how antagonistic the young wife may feel toward her mother-in-law or how confident in her own abilities, at the birth of her first child she finds herself in need of the older woman as she will at no other time. The child should be born in its father's home, but if this proves impossible, almost anywhere would be preferable to the natal home of its mother. The young woman's mother is sometimes called to be with her during her first delivery, but even if she should arrive in time to help her daughter during her travail, propriety and her own responsi-bilities prevent her from staying longer than a day or two. During those first few weeks when the infant seems so fragile to the new mother and each act in its care so fraught with disaster, it is to her mother-in-law that she must turn for reassurance and advice. In the months and years that follow, the young mother may come to regret this early dependence and to resent her mother-in-law's continuing advice, but by then the pat-tern is set. Even with later births, she will need assistance if not ad-vice, and the two seem to be indivisibly joined in the aging Taiwanese female.

I suspect that the influence the grandmother exercises over the child-training practices of her daughter-in-law with her first two or three children makes this area of culture highly resistant to change. Young women, particularly with the increased literacy of modern times, may approach motherhood with some new notions about the proper way to care for and train children. Their attempts to implement these notions are likely to find little support from their mothers-in-law. The older woman's resistance may not be directed against change in and of itself but simply against taking chances with something so valuable as her grandchild. If she has been fortunate enough to raise several children to a respectable adulthood, she will be convinced of the splendid efficacy of her methods; if she has had the misfortune of losing a number of children, she will be convinced that raising children is far too hazardous an enterprise to allow unknown techniques introduced by an inexperienced young woman. Considering the lowly status she occupies in the household and the absence of friends or supporters in the community, it would be a rare young woman who could maintain enough independence to raise her children in an unconventional way. She could not expect much support from her husband, who would likely look to his mother as the family expert in this area of life. At best the young mother must compromise, and since she is usually only one of many caretakers, her efforts at innovation are likely to be wasted or so watered down as to be unnoticeable. By the birth of her third or fourth child, when she is more apt to have a freer hand in its upbringing, she will be far too busy to start something new and her zeal may well have faded anyway.

A grandmother may wish to supervise her daughter-in-law in the care of her son's child and may even feel required to intervene when the job is not being done in a way she deems proper, but in general she would prefer to enjoy her grandchildren without any of the painful responsibility of molding them into good sons and responsible daughters. Of course, she does not want them to grow up in such a way as to disgrace the family that has now become *her* family, but when she sees an exasperated mother disciplining her grandson more harshly than she thinks necessary, she has no qualms about interfering and moderating the punishment. Nor need she feel any anxiety about granting what the mother has denied, giving money for sweets that the mother has refused, ignoring misdemeanors that the mother judges crimes. A grandmother's physical comfort and security depend on the strength of the relationship she has built with her son, but her grandsons need only exist to fulfill her hopes in regard to them. She can enjoy their affection without any restraint, and cherish the knowledge that there will be at least two generations to follow her coffin to the grave and burn incense before her tablet.

In the first few years of her grandchildren's lives, the grandmother may be regarded by her son as the final authority and the expert on raising children, but as she begins to enjoy the children more, and as her daughter-in-law gains confidence in herself and in the eyes of her husband, the grandmother's position as expert weakens. For many Taiwanese women this shift to the side is graceful and happy, the grandmother finding she takes more pleasure in nurturing and spoiling her grandchildren than in competing with their mother. Depending on her age, the grandmother may at the same time be turning over more and more of the household responsibilities to her daughter-in-law, but more likely she still has quite a few more years of power to control the domestic organization. If, however, the older woman feels really threatened by her daughter-in-law, fearing, for example, that her son may be induced to move to the city for employment or set up a separate household, the tension between the women is felt in all their interactions. The poor grandmother must again take up arms in the battle she thought she had won—the battle for the prime position in the affections of her son. Both grandmother and mother then compete for the children's loyalty and affection, the former to tighten her ties to her son and the latter to build toward her own future security. Both set up incidents in which the adversary appears in the worst possible light to the bedeviled son-husband, and in which, incidentally, the children are given sound practical training in manipulating human relationships. Most of the children in Peihotien could tell us which adult in the family particularly favored him and who favored each of his siblings, parental favoritism being freely discussed by the family in the children's presence. It is not too farfetched to suggest that in those families in which favoritism follows lines of factionalism in the family, the seeds of antagonism between adult brothers are sown.

No matter how well fought the battle, the outcome of any long conflict between mother- and daughter-in-law is as inevitable as the shifting of authority from a father to his son. If she has raised her son well, he will not desert her, but with age her influence in the kitchen and over the family budget will gradually diminish and eventually disappear. If she has not treated the daughter-in-law more outrageously than is considered normal in village life, the position of the aged mother in the family of her children is usually enviable compared with that of the aged father. The life expectancy of women on Taiwan, as in most other countries, is considerably longer than that of men, but from the situation of the few elderly men we observed in the village, it is clear that the women's efforts to ensure a comfortable secure old age are more effective than those of their spouses. To be sure, a few old women spend their last years being shuffled from the home of one son to another, never allowed to stay longer than a prescribed period; more commonly they live quietly in the home of the son who stays on the land or who is financially more capable of caring for a larger family.

By the time their first grandchildren have reached the age of reason, most grandfathers are beginning to feel serious threats to their authority in their sons' growing competence and income. By the time the last-born grandchildren reach this age, the grandfather's authority in the family is either completely gone or in a state of sham. Either the old man decides, as did his wife, to forget the forms and enjoy this next generation, or he realizes the futility of assuming the mask of aloof dignity in order to correct behavior. To the children, he is a source of pennies for sweets, an occasional place of solace when the rest of the childhood world turns against them, and a good place for stories when nothing else is doing. The truly aged man no longer able to work at much of anything in the midst of a busy household is a pitiful sight. His physical needs are usually met (although some old men complain that they are not), but busy mothers cannot prevent children from teasing and cannot or will not punish children for disobeying even simple commands an old man might issue. His son sees that all the forms of filiality are observed for the public eye, but his ambivalence toward his aged father often allows for little more. Old women, however, even those who made the lives of their daughters-in-law miserable in earlier years, usually find life considerably more comfortable. Until completely senile or physically incapacitated, they can perform functions in the household that even a revengeful daughter-in-law finds valuable. Sewing, nursing sick children, rocking fussy infants to sleep—these are minor but time-consuming occupations not suitable to old men or half-grown children, but they suit an old woman very well. And when she is beyond even this, if she has trained her son well, his affection will see to it that his wife cares for her with a gentleness that an old man might never experience. The funeral of the father will, nonetheless, be more elaborate than that of the mother.

Sisters-in-law

Rural Taiwanese children, particularly those born early in their mother's child-bearing career, enter a world teeming with adult relatives. Theoretically, these adults should consist of the father's parents, his brothers, and his brothers' wives—adults toward whom and from whom certain behavior is expected by tradition. Father's older brother should be like father only a bit more awesome; father's younger brother should be like father only a little less formal; the wives of both these men should be like second mothers. Actually, few children grow up with a paternal uncle and his family in their home, although many children do

have such relatives in their immediate neighborhood. Moreover, few children consider their father's brother's wife in any way similar to their own mother, and very few women would, under any circumstances, consider treating their husband's brother's children in the way they would treat their own children. If the brothers and their wives are on good terms, they do not want to endanger these good relations by disciplining one another's children; and if, as is more common, their relationship is brittle but still operative, nothing could more quickly open (or reopen) hostilities than a fracas between the wives over the misbehavior of a child. During the few years that the two couples are members of the same joint family and during the briefer period in which the family property is divided, all manner of antagonisms and jealousies are raised that will color their relations with one another for many years to come.*
The exact role played by the wives during these trying years varies with their personalities and with the quality of their relations with other family members, but it is almost never that of peacemaker. It would seem reasonable to expect a daughter-in-law to welcome her husband's younger brother's new wife into the family as an ally against their traditional foe, the mother-in-law, but other factors seem to operate against this. For one thing, the first daughter-in-law and her children have undergone the financial strain and parental tension that exists in a household accumulating the money and negotiating a marriage settlement for a son. Moreover, when this expensive troublesome commodity arrives, she is often given preferential treatment for a period of time or, if nothing else, is the source of much attention and interest. When the household settles down again, the older daughter-in-law is likely to take advantage of the younger's inexperience in the family's routines to shift both duties and blame for errors onto her head, at the same time, of course, shifting the mother-in-law's hostility. This behavior does little to endear older brother's wife to younger brother's wife, and though deposing the mother-in-law might have some advantages for the older daughter-in-law, it would have little for the younger, producing merely an exchange of tyrants. Nevertheless, the sisters-in-law have and work toward, albeit separately, a common goal, that of separate *chia*. Their husbands are fully and emotionally informed of each incident of preferential treatment from the senior generation, the bad habits one man's children are learning from his brother's poorly trained wretches, and the opportunities his children will surely miss because he is forced to make up the deficit in the family budget caused by his brother's insufficient income.

---

*In my book (Wolf 1968) I have described in considerable detail the difficult years that precede the division of a joint family.

The fact that very few joint families in Peihotien survive the marriage and fatherhood of a second son indicates the success of the sisters-in-law. The relationship between brothers in Taiwanese society is both weak and strained by inconsistent dicta concerning proper behavior toward each other. As children, the elder is required to yield to his younger brother's demands in all things, some of which are outrageous when the younger is still small. If the younger child desires some prize possession of the older and when denied it proceeds to beat the older boy with a stick or rock, the elder has no choice but either to give him the object or to leave the scene with it before adult attention is attracted. If, out of a mixture of pain and frustration, he slaps his younger brother, he can expect punishment for himself and special favor for his little brother. As they grow older and the elder brother is no longer a caretaker but still responsible for his younger brother, the latter continues to hold the strings of power. If elder brother does not like his behavior, in a particular instance, the younger can easily and often does provoke a quarrel, knowing full well that the parents will punish the elder automatically without giving him a chance to explain his actions as an attempt to correct younger brother's aberrant behavior. Younger brothers learn very early and very concretely that older brothers yield to younger brothers, and yet as adults the expectation is exactly the reverse—the younger is expected to yield to his older brother's decisions and guidance, a situation for which he has been poorly prepared. The comparative ease with which sisters-in-law can manipulate the brittle relationship between their husbands is not difficult to understand. Although some students of Chinese society suggest that the wives merely capitalize on the brothers' competition for the parental wealth or property, this seems quite a minor factor in their conflict, since the equality of their shares is clearly prescribed by the culture. Far more explosive is the emotional content of their relationship and the inadequacy of their training, in particular the younger brother's, for their adult roles of dominance and submission. Unless he is extraordinarily tolerant, the elder will retain some degree of resentment over the troubles his younger brother has caused him for so many years, and he may be just a bit heavy-handed in wielding his at last consistently approved authority; unless he is exceptionally adaptable, the younger brother will find his position untenable. If left to themselves, adult brothers might be able to overcome the strains built into their relations with one another, but most men marry before any compromise can be reached and often before the conflict between them has become fully apparent. Their wives are not motivated toward effecting such a compromise. In view of the fact that the brothers are given wives during the same period of time that they are adjusting their adult roles toward one another, it is understandable that the Taiwanese so often place the blame for the break-up of the family on "the narrow hearts of women" rather than on the contradictory demands the society makes upon their husbands.

The intensity of the hostility between brothers and brothers' wives lessens considerably after the family property is divided and each unit is established as a separate household, but their mutual distrust never disappears completely. Much as they might like to pursue a policy of complete noninvolvement, their housing usually makes this difficult. In many cases they will continue to share the same courtyard and the same guest hall, and their children will grow up playing more often with one another than with other village children. To prevent trouble or perhaps just for spite, a mother will warn her children not to go into the other part of the house or even not to play with their father's brother's children, but it is not a very practical order. The children nonetheless are influenced by their parents' distrust and are more wary around these adults than around others—less cheeky and somewhat more self-conscious.

The adults' attitude toward aggressive behavior in their children and their handling of fights between children reflect quite sharply the tensions within the family and the weight the various family members give to relations with one another and with other adults in their environment. All adults state emphatically that a child must not aggress against another no matter what the provocation, even if it is to defend himself or his property. Fathers point out that quarrels between children can draw in adults and endanger the good relations between relatives whose economic or social assistance may one day be essential. A grandmother condemns aggressive behavior because of its disruptive influence within the family. The escalation of a squabble among the children can be the final act that precipitates the family division. With time the perimeters of her world draw in, and the activities within the family become more significant to her than ever before. Even after her sons set up separate homes, a grandmother will want their relations at least to appear harmonious, since they are the source of her prestige and her pleasure. Her daughters-in-law are just as eager to prevent children's quarrels. During her first years as a resident outsider in the community, the young mother's only relief from the pressures of her husband's relatives is in the casual friendships developed with unrelated village women in like situations. These friendships, both because they develop in a time of great need and because they continue to provide a channel through which any injustice can be placed before the social jury of the village, are too important to a young woman to risk in a children's quarrel. Quarrels amongst her own children will be handled with a severity that depends much on her tolerance for noise and turmoil, but quarrels with unrelated children will not be countenanced. To a certain extent, the mother will also share her husband's attitude toward quarrels involving the children of relatives, but her handling of these children may well depend on just who the parents are. If her child reports that a village child struck him, she may scold or spank her own child for even being in a situation that led to aggression, studiously ignoring the actual transgressor or making light of his act should it come to his parents' attention. If, however, her child reports that his cousin attacked him, she is more likely to let his grandmother, the cousin's mother, the men of the family, and most of the village know that her sister-in-law's children are slyly dangerous and likely to strike at any time. Her own child could expect at least a cursory scolding for playing with undesirable companions. If her own child is clearly and obviously responsible for a fracas with a cousin, woe be unto him because his mother will be overconscientious about letting the family and the larger world know that she will not stand for such behavior on the part of her children, punishing the child with a severity that he may have neither expected nor deserved.

Village children have developed a technique for taking revenge on an attacker that is both safe and rewarding. They report the transgressor to his parent, a strategy obviously safer than reporting to their own. The mother of the naughty child then either beats her own child in the presence of his victim or promises to do so when she finds him. If the offending child has his wits about him and avoids his home for a few hours, the beating may never take place, his mother either having forgotten about the matter or having decided to settle for a scolding, since the victim is no longer there to observe the outcome. It seems quite likely that this ingenious technique of retaliation is first learned and most consistently reinforced in the context of the family. By reporting a cousin's misdeeds to his mother, a child places her in a situation in which she can do nothing but punish her child severely, no matter how long he stays away from home, since she is under the constant critical observation of the family of his victim.

Taiwanese children are aware almost from birth of the latent or perhaps active hostility between their parents and their father's brothers' families. That these people and their children must be treated with more circumspection than others they learn early and, as we have just seen, painfully. Their paternal cousins, nonetheless, will be their most frequent playmates. It is here, long before they are old enough to conceive

of it in the abstract, that they learn the intricacies of kin behavior—
the obligations it imposes and the penalties it extracts. As adults these
paternal cousins will be the very people to whom a man turns when he
needs a peacemaker, emergency funds, a job for his son, an introduction
or letter of credit, or sympathetic advice in the quarrels between his
brothers and himself. It will be to preserve their goodwill that he pun-
ishes his own children harshly for aggression. Yet in his childhood his
parents will have ingrained the proper style for their interactions for
almost the opposite reasons, reasons ostensibly relevant only to their
own generation.

Variations

The preceding generalizations have assumed, as do most studies of
the Chinese family, a "typical" family in which wives for the sons are
brought in from "outside" as adults, and adult daughters are married
into other "outside" families. This is undoubtedly the most common situation in China, but there is a large body of evidence from all over
China indicating that these are not the only means of providing men
with wives and ancestors with descendants. A sizeable proportion of the
marriages arranged in Peihotien before 1930 departed from the normal
pattern. Some families chose for one reason or another to bring adult
males of another surname into their families as husbands for their daughters and fathers of their grandchildren; other families chose to adopt and
raise female children who would become their sons' wives upon adulthood. The children resulting from these marriages grew up with a set of
family relationships quite different from those of children born into more
"typical" families. Since many of these differences provide contrasts to
some of the relationships previously discussed, it may be useful to examine them briefly.

In the past, a good many families on Taiwan, both poor and wealthy,
solved the social and financial problem of providing their sons with
wives by adopting an infant girl (*sim-pua*, little daughter-in-law) who
was raised as a sibling but married to the son when the two reached an
appropriate age. For a variety of reasons this custom has almost completely disappeared in the past generation, at least on Taiwan. There
are still, however, many adult *sim-pua* and many children and adults
who grew up in families with *sim-pua*. In theory, a *sim-pua* was to be
treated as a daughter of the family until the time of her marriage, but
in practice she was often treated as something slightly lower than a
daughter. She was expected to do more work earlier and was frequently
the victim of harsh punishments, punishments resulting more often from
her adoptive mother's unhappiness at her own lot in life than from the

sim-pua's behavior. By the time she was married to her brother, she and her adoptive mother had worked together in the house for many years. Her training in the domestic arts was far more thorough than that of a daughter. If a daughter proved inept in some task, the mother would simply push her aside and do it herself. Not so the *sim-pua*. Even though still a child, her adoptive mother would be conscious of the fact that this was not a daughter she was training for someone else, but a daughter-in-law with whom she herself would have to live. In some families, the relations between the two were almost as warm and as affectionate as that between any mother and daughter, but even in those where they were not, the *sim-pua* was habituated to submission, both as a means of avoiding pain and as behavior appropriate to her status. No matter how personally distasteful she might find the physical aspects of her marriage to a former brother, she was at least spared the many adjustments required of other newly married women. Her loyalties to the family in which she was reared were not disrupted, and her obedience and respect continued to be to the parents of her former brother and now husband. Nothing new outside her husband's bed was required of her. From the mother's point of view, the situation must have been a comfortable one. The young woman in her son's bed was more completely under her control than her son would ever be. There was no need for the older woman to assert her authority over a newcomer and no risk that her grandchildren would be raised in any way other than as she wished. The girl carried no threat to her security and had been, moreover, carefully trained over the years to make her mother-in-law's old age even more comfortable.

Unfortunately, for the purposes of this study, parents were no longer adopting *sim-pua* when we were in Taiwan, and I had no opportunity to evaluate any differences the presence of such a girl might have made on the parents' general child-training practices. It is possible that a young mother with a son and a *sim-pua* might feel more confident about her future security and be less consistent in her attempts to weave the complex emotional ties with her son that other Taiwanese mothers feel essential to their future well-being. This seems unlikely, though, in terms of the general orientation toward males; ultimately, it is the son on whom the mother must depend. Until recently sons have dutifully married the *sim-pua* their parents raised for that purpose, but there is considerable evidence that they find these marriages unsatisfactory, at least sexually. Men who married *sim-pua* are much more likely to visit prostitutes regularly and to arrange a semipermanent source of sexual satisfaction outside the family with a female over whom the mother has no control whatsoever.

From comments made by adult *sim-pua*, it seems that the adoptive father's behavior toward *sim-pua* was more similar to his behavior toward his sons than to his behavior toward his daughters. Rather than enjoying informality and affection in his relations with her, he tended either to ignore the girl or treat her with the distance and reserve that was his son's lot. This seems reasonable in view of the fact that her future behavior and her loyalty are more relevant to his future and the family's than those of his own daughter who leaves the family to marry. Although we were assured repeatedly that *sim-pua* were just like daughters until their marriage, it may well be that the relationship was nonetheless tinged in the father's mind with the semi-avoidance behavior expected toward a daughter-in-law. Whatever the cause, *sim-pua* tended to speak of their father/father-in-law with great respect but little warmth.

It is also unfortunate that at the time of our visit to Peihotien there were no families that contained two or more brothers married to *sim-pua* and in which all partners were living. (There were cases in which remnants of their families were living together and others in which they lived in the same compound, but we neglected to inquire whether the former had recombined after a crucial death or in which generation the latter had set up separate households.) I think it is safe to assume that the presence of *sim-pua* would have little effect on the development of the brothers' relationship with one another. As adults, however, the brothers marry women whose primary loyalty is to their joint family and parents—women who are also joined (presumably) in the warm relationship of sisters. A few well-documented cases of more than one *sim-pua* marriage in a sibling order might well provide a crucial test of the relative weight of the internal strains within a family that leads to its division.

Not a few families on Taiwan have found themselves required to make an uxorilocal marriage for one of their daughters, either because of the lack of an adult son when an urgent need is felt for additional income or because the complete absence of sons in a generation threatens the line of descent. Like the *sim-pua*, the young woman who marries uxorilocally is not required to leave the family in which she has been raised and toward whom her loyalties have been due up to the time of her marriage. There the similarity ends. During her childhood her parents are unlikely to consider the possibility that *she* might be their source of support and the family's source of continuance, constantly hoping that a son would either be born or adopted to fulfill the family's needs. As such she would be raised like any other daughter: less used to submission than a *sim-pua*, less belabored about her reasons to be grateful and loyal to her parents, and certainly less well trained in the domestic arts. Since uxorilocal marriages are more common amongst girls high in the sibling order, she probably had special consideration from her grandparents simply by being first on hand. She may for the same reason, although with less certainty, also be a favorite of her father. Compared with a *sim-pua* of her age, she may seem arrogant, willful, and unfilial; compared with a daughter born later in the sibling order she may seem slightly more assertive and somewhat more inclined toward independent attitudes.

The man who makes an uxorilocal marriage could be of the highest moral standards, of unusual intelligence and strength, and have an exceptional earning capacity. He would be nonetheless not quite the equal of other men, by virtue of his willingness to enter his wife's family. All girls are aware to some degree of the traumatic adjustments they must make when they leave their natal families at the time of their marriage, but they are also aware of the propriety and respectability of this move. No matter how delighted a girl may be to avoid these trying experiences, few young women who are party to uxorilocal marriages feel that its advantages in comfort are worth the disadvantage of being married to a man who is by definition inferior. Such a woman will comply, having little other choice, but both she and her parents are aware that they have done slightly less than right by her. The socialization process she has experienced increases the likelihood of her dissatisfaction and the likelihood of its being communicated to her parents.

Parents are even more thorough in the investigation of the qualities and capacities of an uxorilocal groom than they are with a prospective daughter-in-law, but when the man enters his future home, he is greeted with far more suspicion. His mother-in-law is constantly on the watch for any signs of growing intimacy with her daughter which might lead her to suspect that he is trying to "take her away from the family." His father-in-law is in the extremely ambiguous position of being suspicious, dependent, and, if the daughter happens to be a favorite, suffering from a mixture of guilt at forcing her into a "bad" marriage, delight at keeping her at home, and perhaps a tinge of Freudian jealousy. When grandchildren are born, the family often becomes more strained, not less. The grandmother, perhaps in collusion with her daughter, consciously undermines her son-in-law's position with his children, interfering with any discipline he may impose, and encouraging his children to believe that their primary loyalty is to the family of their mother. The young father finds himself in a position strikingly similar to that of the young mother in the customary form of marriage. His authority over his children is not clearly stated, and he must use exceptional means to establish it. He cannot use the father's traditional tool of aloof dignity, or his children will be lost to him forever. Because of this, and perhaps also because of their own isolation in the family and the village, men who have made an uxorilocal marriage seem to spend considerably more time in their children's company than do fathers in a normal family. Grandmothers of children from uxorilocal marriages are careful to make even fewer demands on their grandchildren than other grandmothers, but they have far fewer chances to relax and enjoy them.

If in time the daughter's loyalties do shift to her husband, or, as is so often the case in recent times, she chose the man herself, the parents' worst fear may come true—the younger couple leaves the family. The social reproach, although present, is never as strongly voiced against a daughter's abandonment as against a son's, and the break is consequently less difficult to make. Few daughters literally abandon their parents but simply put some geographic distance between them, continuing to provide financial support and insisting that at least one of the children bear the maternal grandfather's surname. If the uxorilocal marriage was simply a stopgap until a younger brother was old enough to assume responsibility for the family, the break is a natural one and may even have been formally arranged in the marriage contract. Whatever the circumstances of their departure, if the children are of school age, their father is going to have a ticklish resocialization job to do if he hopes to insure his future and found a normal family. His success may depend as much on the quality of his relations with his wife as on his own capacities. Needless to say, there are families in which uxorilocal marriages are very successful. One family in Peihotien was a model of domestic harmony, with the son-in-law behaving and treated as an unusually filial son rather than as a doubtful son-in-law. There was another family in Peihotien, equally atypical, who had maintained themselves for three generations without ever having a permanent adult male in residence. It is interesting to note that this family has in the present generation of women finally managed to produce a son by way of a long since dismissed son-in-law. At the age of sixteen, the boy is so utterly lacking in the virtues of filial respect and obedience as to have kicked his crippled grandmother. From the experiences of this family, the establishment of a successful matriarchy seems highly unlikely.

Conclusion

In the preceding pages the Chinese family has been examined in terms of the basic function of families everywhere: the raising of children. The attitudes various family members bring to the job of socialization throw a new light on familiar problems. The husband-wife relationship has been deemed of secondary importance both by the Chinese and by the scholars who study their customs. Insofar as the interaction between husband and wife is not overly charged with either positive or negative emotions, it is indeed a secondary relationship in the context of the family. The wife who does not despise her husband is not likely to raise her children to treat him as an outsider in his own family; the husband who does not reveal an unusual attachment to his wife is not likely to motivate his mother to an anxious competition with the younger woman for the loyalty of his children. When either the personalities or the behavior of husband and wife threaten to intensify the relationship with extra warmth or extra tension, it becomes disruptive to the more important parent-child relationship—in one generation or the next. This disruption, whichever direction it takes, is reflected in the attitudes of various members of the family toward the children of the family.

The brittle relationship between adult brothers is an important facet of Chinese kinship, from its role in the dissolution of joint families to the inherent weakness it brings to the lineages. When such a crucial relationship is also such a fragile one, when the society values a close relationship, and when its fracture causes intense and lasting hostility, it cannot be explained simply in terms of adult problems. A review of child-training practices suggests that the failure of the relationship originates in the inconsistent preparation of the brothers for their adult roles. This background makes credible the sudden disintegration of their relationship when they come into conflict over income and property. Had the younger brother been trained from infancy to submit to the elder, the Chinese joint family might be less of a myth.

The subtly different definitions of filiality that seem to be held by mothers and by fathers, and the strikingly different techniques they use to realize their definitions, say a great deal about the anxieties and the defenses of women in an androcentric society. They also give us a useful basis for comparison between families continuing their descent through the patrilocal form of marriage and those coping with a lack of male heirs by "marrying in" a son-in-law. The young man who makes an uxorilocal marriage finds himself in a situation quite similar to that of his sister. His rights over his children, like his sister's rights over hers, are not clearly stated, and, again like his sister, he forms ties with them that are individualistic and not dependent on the children's acceptances of cultural mores and values.

It would be satisfying to be able to conclude this paper with an outline for the systematic use of socialization techniques as predictive instruments in the study of the Chinese family. Obviously, that is out of the question. One of the thoughts selected for restatement in this concluding section suggests that the socialization process *reflects* a set of tensions within the family; another argues that child training seems to be the *source* of tension; the third example points out that a particular pattern of socialization is found useful as a basis for comparing two marriage types. There *is* an intimate relationship between the way in which a family trains its children and the dynamics of that family, but the exact nature of that relationship and its predictive value, if any, are yet to be discovered. In time the social sciences may reach a level of sophistication that will allow a quantitative analysis of small groups such as the family. Until that time, those of us interested in things Chinese would do well to cast a speculative eye at the way Chinese are raised. We may find evidence of change, of conflict, or of an error in analysis; at the very least, we will gain further evidence of what the Chinese want of family life.

Marriage Resistance in Rural Kwangtung

MARJORIE TOPLEY

For approximately one hundred years, from the early nineteenth to the early twentieth century, numbers of women in a rural area of the Canton delta either refused to marry or, having married, refused to live with their husbands. Their resistance to marriage took regular forms. Typically they organized themselves into sisterhoods. The women remaining spinsters took vows before a deity, in front of witnesses, never to wed. Their vows were preceded by a hairdressing ritual resembling the one traditionally performed before marriage to signal a girl's arrival at social maturity. This earned them the title "women who dress their own hair," *tzu-shu nü.* The others, who were formally married but did not live with their husbands, were known as *pu lo-chia,* "women who do not go down to the family," i.e., women who refuse to join their husband's family. Such women took herbal medicines to suppress micturition and set off for their wedding ceremonies with strips of cloth wrapped, mummy fashion, under their bridal gown to prevent consummation. Three days after the wedding ceremonies they returned to their natal villages for the traditional home visit, which they prolonged for several years. Some women subsequently returned to their husbands, presumably to consummate their marriage and bear children. Others took the further decision to stay away until they were past childbearing age, and never consummated their marriage.

Most Cantonese grew up knowing something of this resistance, but were it not for a few brief, mostly anecdotal references, chiefly by Westerners, it might have passed unnoted by the outside world. The reasons for this are not difficult to guess. These were not the sort of customs traditional Confucianists would be inclined to write about. The customs arose at a time when marriage and childbearing constituted the only

socially valued way of life for a woman; they thus incurred the displeasure, sometimes active displeasure, of the State. Nor were they the sort
of customs that would commend themselves to modern reformists. The
women who eschewed marriage or cohabitation were not interested in
marriage reform or in converting women elsewhere to their cause.
Throughout the hundred years of the resistance, these practices never
spread beyond a relatively small area. They were confined to those parts
of the Canton delta engaged in sericulture: Shun-te hsien, particularly
the eastern part; a small part of Nan-hai hsien, adjoining northern Shun-
te and including the Hsi-ch'iao foothills; and a small part of P'an-yü, to
the east of Shun-te.

Under what conditions did this unorthodox but nonreformist resistance emerge? How did it manage to persist for a century? And why did
it eventually decline? Most sources stress fear of marriage as the wom-
en's principal impetus. A few refer to their unusual economic status:
women in the area had worked outside the house in the domestic sericulture for centuries, and by the first third of the nineteenth century
they were earning cash in filatures and other industrial establishments
connected with silk production. These factors must have been very important, but we must bear in mind that women all over Kwangtung
traditionally worked outside their home, and by this century women in
other provinces were also working in cash-earning occupations. Yet
marriage resistance remained unique to one small area. Was there, then,
something special about the area itself, something that might have made
the status of unattached women relatively more attractive than it was
elsewhere, or the status of married women relatively less attractive?
Was there anything particularly favoring female solidarity, or the obvious local acceptance of such heterodox behavior? Why was it that
some members of the resistance married while some did not, and what
implications did the two forms of resistance have for the women, their
natal families, and their in-laws?

Unfortunately, though the few published accounts we have provide
us with some insights into the area that occasionally can be followed up
in the wider literature, questions of the kind I have raised are neither
asked nor answered by these accounts. And none of them seem to be
based on firsthand evidence from the women involved. In the last twenty
years, however, a few social scientists have interviewed women from
the resistance area who had emigrated to Hong Kong and Singapore.
The interviews conducted by Ho It Chong, a former social work student
at the University of Singapore, have been of particular value in this
study. These firsthand data do not permit firm answers to the questions

raised earlier, or allow us to make wide generalizations. First, like the earlier material, it comes almost exclusively from Shun-te and Hsi-ch'iao. Second, it comes from only a small fraction of the women involved and is derived in most cases from interviews that were not specifically oriented around the marriage resistance.* Third, the immense task of researching the Canton delta has just begun,† and many as yet undiscovered facts about the area will affect our ultimate assessment of the evidence gathered so far. Nevertheless, significant variables may emerge if all material now available is assembled and analyzed.

Was there anything unique about the area? I will begin by describing the physical environment and its effect on the local economy and culture. I will then try to isolate local factors that helped generate the resistance, encouraged the particular forms it took, and perpetuated its existence. Finally, I will look at changes in the area and elsewhere that may have contributed to the movement's decline, and see briefly if the local ecology and the resistance itself have left any visible mark on the status of women living in the area today.

Environment, Society, and Culture

P'an-yü is the largest of the three hsien involved, occupying about 1,800 square kilometers; Nan-hai and Shun-te are some 1,360 and 750 square kilometers. Nan-hai has the largest population (about 680,000 in 1947), and Shun-te the smallest (417,000 in 1947). But population densities have been highest in Shun-te; indeed, they are the highest in all Kwangtung province.

Much of the land is flat and criss-crossed by rivers. Shun-te, in the heart of the Pearl River delta, is mostly floodplain. The numerous waterways intersect in a spiderweb pattern, making communications relatively easy, but numerous hills rise up from the plain throughout much of the area. On the hills' outer rims—the highest are in Hsi-ch'iao—lie the large villages and market towns. Outside the hilly area, settlement was relatively dispersed.[1]

The wet, sandy soil, often affected by tides, is not everywhere suitable for rice. But it is suitable for both fish breeding and mulberry raising. These activities, together with other phases of sericulture, were the

* My own interviews were conducted in the early 1950's in connection with a study of women and religious institutions in Singapore, and in Hong Kong in 1973 for this essay. Ho It Chong's interviews were part of a study of domestic servants' organizations undertaken in Singapore in the late 1950's.

† The multidisciplinary Canton Delta Project is headed by Winston Hsieh, of the University of Missouri at St. Louis.

economic mainstays of the area. Fishponds and mulberry groves went together. Fish were fed on nightsoil and cocoon waste, and mulberry groves were fertilized with silt from the fishponds. When pits were dug to form ponds, the excavated earth was heaped over the rest of the farmer's land to raise it sufficiently above water level for the mulberry groves. A farmer wishing to increase his output would install additional ponds and groves; the characteristic scene was one of densely planted fields of mulberry shrubs, intersected by narrow canals and dotted with ponds scattered irregularly over the fields.[2]

In 1939 approximately 70 percent of Shun-te's land area was devoted to this economy, and about 90 percent of the population was engaged in one or another aspect of sericulture. Nan-hai had close to one-half the mulberry acreage of Shun-te; a little less than half its population was engaged in sericulture.[3] I have no figures for P'an-yü. I was told that much of the land in Shun-te had been reclaimed by wealthy lineage groups, who in many cases lived elsewhere and rented their land to tenant farmers. Some relatively large lineage villages flourished in the area, alongside many smaller multisurname villages, which were inhabited by tenant farmers. Some of these farmers were described as newcomers by informants, although by the nineteenth century they had been living in the area some time.

Because of the area's subtropical climate, everything grows rapidly. Silkworms produce six or seven broods a year, in contrast to the usual two broods of the Yangtze Valley—another area dissected by waterways. Indeed, throughout Central China, mulberry trees yield at most two pickings a year, which will support only one large brood of worms in spring and another in summer. In this delta area, six to eight leaves could be picked from a plant each month, thus feeding more abundant broods.[4]

Much labor was needed in every phase of sericulture, and a considerable proportion of it was performed by women. Women in Kwangtung did not have bound feet, and female infanticide in the silk area reportedly was relatively rare. B. C. Henry, a nineteenth-century traveler in Hsi-ch'iao, described the scene when the first crop of leaves was ready: "thousands of boys, women, and girls are employed to strip them and pack them in baskets. Hundreds of men in little boats propelled by paddles dart back and forth along the canals carrying these baskets . . . to the market-places, where they are . . . purchased by the owners of silk worms."[5]

There appears to have been a distinct division of labor between men and women. Men and boys were the exclusive rearers of fish: boys helped with the breeding and feeding, men took charge of the fully grown specimens. Catching the fish meant standing in waist-deep water and manipulating heavy nets. This, I was told, was too heavy a task for boys or women. Women cultivated the mulberry groves and together with young boys and girls picked the leaves. Adult men took charge of what was described to me by informants as the first "inside" phases of silkworm raising: the hatching and early care. Later the worms were transferred to matsheds, and this "outside" aspect of rearing was entrusted exclusively to women. Finally the worms were brought inside again, when they formed cocoons and needed extra warmth; women took charge of this phase. When the cocoons were ready, women plunged them into hot water to loosen their silk threads. Reeling and spinning were exclusively women's work, although in some places men wove all the cloth.

Married women were less likely to be involved in sericulture than unmarried women. This was due in part to the time they expended on other household tasks, and in part to notions of pollution and female physiology. Women were considered unclean at certain times, notably during pregnancy and childbirth, when, it was believed, they could harm immature living things, such as young children and silkworms. (According to Winston Hsieh, a similar notion prevailed among silkgrowers near Shanghai.) In Shun-te, married women were usually excluded from worm rearing and the care of cocoons. They were also excluded from the thread-loosening process because, my informants explained, this was "wet work": constant association with water was believed to interfere with menstruation and hence fertility.

There seems also to have been a spatial division of labor. Farmhouses were built not near the villages, but near groves and ponds. Glenn Trewartha, writing in 1939, observed that "nowhere else in Kwangtung ... do most of the farm houses stand alone and isolated outside the villages." He describes the farmhouses as being made of mud plaster mixed with straw, contrasting these obviously more impermanent dwellings with the tile-roofed brick houses in the village.[6] According to informants, men spent much of their time at the farms, looking after the fish and the worms in their initial inside phases, but women usually lived in the villages. The married men visited their wives in their village, where they usually had a more permanent abode, and the women went out to the farms to pick mulberries and care for the worms in the matsheds. Reeling and spinning were done in the village; Henry observed hundreds of Hsi-ch'iao women sitting by their doors winding the gossamer threads from the cocoons.[7]

By the second third of the nineteenth century, however, the picture was beginning to change. Industrialization had gained a foothold, largely in response to outside competition. Large cocoonaries, some of them owned by lineages, were built in the bigger mulberry plantations. Filatures were set up, the first ones using foot-driven machinery. These industrial concerns employed women because women traditionally had worked with cocoons and at reeling and spinning. They used mainly unmarried women because unattached women had fewer family commitments and were believed to be more reliable in their attendance. By 1904, eleven market towns in the Hsi-ch'iao–Shun-te part of the area had filatures, some employing 500–1,000 women.[8] Weaving factories were also established, and at first they employed both men and women (men, we saw, had traditionally done the domestic weaving in some localities).

Steam-driven machinery was first introduced in the mid-nineteenth century. It was bitterly resented by the local population because it supplanted human labor. Henry reports that when machinery was introduced into one of the silk factories near Hsi-ch'iao, the place was twice mobbed and the owners were compelled to remove the machines. Steam machinery was associated with foreign influence, and as Henry remarks, "turbulent and bitterly anti-foreign" feelings were prevalent in the silk areas.[9] Nevertheless, there was no turning back.

One of the first effects of steam-driven machinery was to eliminate male labor in the silkworks. Some of the men may have joined the local militia, which the gentry was then organizing to fight British troops. Others may have returned to their farms. But the domestic economy had been seriously affected by the mechanization of industry. The labor supply necessary to some phases of sericulture was depleted by the exodus of unattached women to the towns. Both the scale and the range of occupations decreased, and in the rural areas both married women living at home with their husbands and married and unmarried men had a harder time finding gainful employment. Agnes Smedley, writing in the 1930's, contrasts the local weaving factories, which employed only women, with silk-weaving factories in other parts of China. She speculates that men were scarce because of heavy farming duties or because of emigration. As the domestic economy declined, men had begun to emigrate in large numbers to Singapore, Malaya, and Hong Kong. Smedley observed that "thousands of peasant homes depended for a large part of their livelihood upon the modest earnings of a wife or daughter."[10]

As a result of industrialization, village populations began to consist largely of women and children. But nubile girls formed a separate group, for another distinctive feature of the area was the "girls' house" or "girls' room," *nü-wu* or *nü-chien*. From my own evidence, and that of Mr. Ho in Singapore, it appears that many parts of Kwangtung had such houses and rooms, as well as similar houses for unmarried boys. There is only one publication on these houses—on boys' houses in a village in Chung-shan hsien, Kwangtung.[11] Clearly, such establishments differed from one another in important ways, but several features of the boys' houses, as described in the article on Chung-shan and by the informants of Mr. Ho and myself, seem to me directly relevant to our subject.

The bachelor houses of the Chung-shan village were owned by the ancestors, i.e., were part of the ancestral trust. Each lineage in the village had such a house, adjacent to its ancestral hall or shrine. Their functions were to provide (a) a sleeping place and recreational center for unmarried men, (b) temporary quarters for married men, (c) a guest house for visiting men, and (d) relief of household congestion. Residence was not compulsory, although it proved on careful investigation that if a household included daughters or other nubile young women, adolescent boys invariably slept in the bachelor house. Married men stayed there from the fifth month of their wives' pregnancies until 100 days after their child's birth[12]—the traditional Chinese period of childbearing pollution. In the Chung-shan village there were no girls' houses. But their function in villages where they were found in conjunction with boys' houses has been described by informants as follows: to provide (a) a sleeping place and recreational center for unmarried women, (b) a guest house for visiting women, (c) relief from household congestion, and (d) "modesty." Nightsoil buckets were kept in the sleeping quarters, where they could be used at night and also secured against theft (a valuable fertilizer, nightsoil was used in Shun-te to feed fish). I was told that it would be "inconvenient" for boys and girls to use the same bucket, in full view of members of the opposite sex.

It is not easy to see why, in that case, *both* boys' and girls' houses were necessary. However, a further explanation I was given for Tung-kuan hsien was that girls' houses were needed because girls could not be married straight from home: a girl who married from home made the house inauspicious; it became "empty," which affected the luck of her brothers who would later bring wives into the household, making it "full." According to informants, the girls' house in Shun-te served the same purpose. Separate houses for boys were not needed, my informants said, because they already lived apart—with the men on the farm. The girls' houses were found in the village, where again they were sometimes part of an ancestral trust. They were organized entirely by women, and in contrast to such houses elsewhere, were separated by some distance from the sleeping abode of the men.

Girls lived in these houses in Shun-te until they married or took their vows of spinsterhood. The older girls there, my informants said, were fond of visiting temples and other religious establishments and attending theatrical performances. Henry also observes that the women of Hsi-ch'iao "show their independence" by going "in large numbers" to theatrical performances associated with large religious festivals, with a separate gallery reserved for their use.[13] The hills of Hsi-ch'iao, which, as he noted, had been "peopled . . . with spirits and deities of various kinds" by the inhabitants, provided an ideal environment for temples and monastic institutions, as did the other hills that dotted the area. The hilly area around Ta-liang, the hsien capital of Shun-te and a filature center, was noted for both its Buddhist nunneries and its other celibate institutions, which allowed members not to shave their heads and to live in their own homes.[14] The latter type of institution was a vegetarian hall, or *chai-t'ang*.

Vegetarian halls were residential establishments for lay members of the Buddhist faith, and for both lay and clerical members of several semisecret sects fragmenting from a syncretic religion called Hsien-t'ien Ta-tao: The Great Way of Former Heaven. These sects appear to have had connections with the famous White Lotus rebels.[15] According to leaders of these sects living in Singapore and Hong Kong, the sects entered Kwangtung from the north in the mid-nineteenth century, as a result of their suppression by the government in more populous areas and the exiling of their leaders.[16] Tucked away in the hills girding the delta, the sectarian halls escaped hostile attention by disguising themselves as Buddhist establishments.[17]

The syncretic Hsien-t'ien religion is messianic and millennial. Its sects stress the Chinese notion that natural and social disorders arise when earth is out of phase with Heaven; this happens when the country's leaders lack virtue. The sects thus appealed to people who felt threatened either by the social disorder resulting from the introduction of steam machinery, by foreign influences, or by the constant possibility of flooding in high-water-level areas. Several informants said their fathers and mothers had belonged to a Hsien-t'ien sect. The sects held a particular appeal for women. The highest deity is a "mother goddess" to whom many local children who had "bad fates" reportedly were bonded. Moreover, the religion stressed sexual equality, and men and women sat together in prayer (a practice earning it official displeasure). One local sect was run entirely by women.[18]

Both temples and monastic establishments printed and sold religious literature, including "good books" (*shan-shu*) written to convert people to the religious life. Aimed expressly at women was the "precious volume" (*pao-chüan*), which contained biographies of model women, usually recounted in ballad form. One such story, about Kuan Yin, the Goddess of Mercy, who is popularly believed to have been a princess who became a nun over her parents' objections, points out that she had no husband to claim her devotion, no mother-in-law to control her, and no children to hamper her movements.[19] Many of my informants had "precious volumes" they acquired in their homeland which further emphasize that refusing to marry is not morally wrong and even that religion can help those brave enough to resist; that men cannot be trusted; and that suicide is a virtue when committed to preserve one's purity.

The need for purity and chastity is explained in terms of pollution. Childbirth is a sin, for which women are punished after death by being sent to a "bloody pond," filled with birth fluids, from which they can be rescued only by ritual.[20] One pao-chüan says that women "taint Heaven and Earth when [they] give birth to children. . . . When you are a man's wife . . . you cannot avoid the blood-stained water . . . and the sin of offending the Sun, Moon, and Stars (*san-kuang*).[21] The only way a woman can improve her fate in life—after death she can go to the Happy Land (the Buddhist paradise) or be reborn as a man in another existence—is to remain celibate. Some of Ho's informants suggested that a person marries the same partner over and over again in many incarnations.[22] Occasionally, my own informants explained, a woman is born with a "blind" or "nonmarrying" fate: her predestined partner is not alive at the same time, not of suitable marriage age, or not of the appropriate sex. In these circumstances, a woman should remain unwed.

Many women in the Shun-te area were able to read this kind of literature. Dyer Ball observes that Shun-te women were considered "more intelligent than others," and "notwithstanding the want of schools for their instruction, those of the middle classes are generally able to read ballads."[23] My informants said numerous local women from farming families received instruction in reading from a tutor who called at the girls' house; also that they read pao-chüan stories in groups in the girls' houses. Ho talks of such women reading the classics.[24]

Tracts were distributed that pointed to more immediate incentives for a celibate woman who joined a Hsien-t'ien sect: an administrative appointment in a vegetarian hall, possibly even complete authority over a hall; permanent residence if desired (some halls were residential), but more freedom to come and go than Buddhist nunneries allowed; no requirement that members shave their heads or, except for ceremonies, wear religious garments; and the opportunity to be worshiped as an "ancestor" by religious "families" (a "master" and her or his disciples), a privilege not granted unmarried or childless women in secular society.[25]

Women visited religious establishments in groups. Members were often sworn sisters (*shuang chieh-pai*, "mutually tied by oath"). Several features of the local ecology encouraged the formation of such sisterhoods: teamwork in various phases of silk production; residence in girls' houses; membership in the same sectarian "family"; and the ties between girls who were bonded to the same deity because of their "bad" (often nonmarrying) fates and who worshiped the deity together on ceremonial occasions.

The term used by both my own and Mr. Ho's informants for sworn friendship between pairs of individuals or groups was *chin-lan hui*, Golden Orchid Association. An 1853 edition of the Shun-te gazetteer notes in its volume on customs that women's Golden Orchid Associations had long been a feature of the district.[26] Informants were not certain why this term was used, and the gazetteer does not enlighten us. James Liu of Stanford University has suggested to me that it may be derived from the following passage in the *I-ching*: "When two persons have the same heart its sharpness can cut gold; words from the same heart have a fragrance like the orchid." Winston Hsieh has suggested that the term may be a metaphor referring to structure—i.e., that such associations may "bud" or divide into subgroups as they enlarge, just as orchids bud into several flowers on one stem. Certainly Cantonese sometimes refer to societies as budding (rather than branching), although my informants said this happened to their sisterhoods only when members went elsewhere to work. Golden Orchid implies a semisecret association; it is used by the Triads for the name of a branch.[27] The women's sisterhoods were indeed semisecret; Dyer Ball talks of groups of girls in the area who used "an emblematical, or enigmatical, method of communication with each other."[28]

Several sources refer to lesbian practices in connection with sisterhoods in Shun-te and P'an-yü.[29] My own informants agreed that they sometimes occurred. One woman gave me a religious explanation. As we saw, a woman may be predestined to marry a certain man over and over again in different incarnations; even if her predestined husband should in one incarnation be born a female, she is nonetheless attracted to her predestined partner. Informants called lesbian practices "grinding bean curd" (*mo tou-fu*);[30] they also referred to the use of a dildo made of fine silk threads and filled with bean curd. A Hong Kong doctor of forensic medicine told me in the late 1950's of a similar type of dildo, filled with expandable raw silk.

Ho, writing about domestic servants in Singapore, says that some of his informants from the Shun-te area discussed sisterhoods that originated with married women who banded together to stop their husbands from taking concubines, promising to tell one another anything "not in order" they heard about the other women's husbands.[31] Concubinage was part of the system of marriage in many parts of China, and marriage for a woman in the Shun-te area had much in common with marriage for a Chinese woman elsewhere. Yet some features of the Chinese marriage system received particular emphasis in the resistance area; some found elsewhere were missing; and some local practices were peculiar to the area. Concubinage appears to have been widespread among tenant farmers as well as wealthier landowners. Children were wanted in large numbers because of the labor requirements of the domestic economy, and even when a wife had borne both sons and daughters (here daughters, too, were wanted for their labor), a concubine might nonetheless be taken to produce still more. In contrast to other parts of China, it was not the practice locally to adopt "little daughters-in-law," i.e., very young girls adopted into other families to be brought up as future brides for their foster-brothers. But girls might be adopted before a married couple had any children of their own, to "lead in" or encourage the birth of sons.*

In some parts of the area, as in many other parts of China, it was the custom for the eldest son to be married first. In some villages, I am told, the girls then had to marry before the rest of their brothers. By the beginning of this century it had become customary to marry girls to younger bridegrooms: the girl was typically about sixteen years old, the boy thirteen or fourteen. Concubines were usually recruited from the contingent of "bonded servants" (*mei-tsai*) who were daughters of poor, usually landless peasants, sold to families needing extra labor. Poor peasants took such girls as wives, but matchmakers specializing in concubines would inquire of families with mature bonded servants about the girls' availability for secondary unions (families taking mei-tsai were obliged to see them married at maturity).

It was not uncommon in the resistance area for girls to be married off to grooms who were on the point of death, or even already dead. The original object of these kinds of marriages was to ensure the continuance of the groom's family line; a son would be adopted for the post-

---

* On this practice see the following paper in this volume, "The Women of Hai-shan," by Arthur P. Wolf.

humous husband, and his living spouse would rear the child.* Girls were also married to men who were working overseas. In a proxy ceremony, the absent husband was represented by a white cock.[32]

Local Culture and the Resistance

Arthur Smith believed that the marriage resistance movement demonstrated "the reality of the evils of the Chinese system of marriage."[33] From both his own vivid nineteenth-century descriptions and Margery Wolf's descriptions of rural Taiwan in recent times, we can see that many women indeed bitterly resented the system.[34] But in many parts of traditional China, the life of a married woman was not so very much grimmer than the life of an unmarried daughter. As Smith and others observe, a Chinese girl was likely to be unwelcome from the moment of her first appearance in the world. She was "goods on which one loses" (*she-pen huo*), of little value to her natal family except perhaps as a partner to a marriage contract aimed at binding two kinship groups. The inferiority of women was supported by an ideological superstructure that equated them with the *yin* cosmic element: dark, empty, negative, and, in Confucian interpretations, inauspicious.[35] This idea seems to underly the notion already observed that girls cannot be married from home because that makes it empty and inauspicious. In the silk area, however, a girl was relatively more welcome: because of her labor potential, she was not "goods on which one loses." Girls did not have their feet bound, and infanticide was rare.

In many other parts of China, as Smith remarks, girls "never go anywhere to speak of, and live . . . the existence of a frog in a well."[36] Again there was an ideological justification: it was appropriate for girls, as "inner" beings, to stay inside. But in the silk area girls traveled freely around the countryside; they visited temples, vegetarian halls, and theaters. And, as we have seen, they even did "outside" work. Like other girls in Kwangtung, they had the companionship of other residents in the girls' houses. In addition, however, they had the companionship of other girls in their economic tasks, and they had sisterhoods. Unlike other peasant girls, they were taught to read. Together they read ballads that stressed the unpleasant aspects of marriage and even the equality of the sexes. By contrast, the local married woman who lived with her husband was of less economic value—after the establishment of filatures her value as a home spinner declined—she went out much

---

* Such practices were harshly condemned in the marriage-reform propaganda for South China put out by the People's Republic. *Hsin-chiu hun-yin tui-pi t'u* (Chart comparing old and new marriage; Canton, 1952).

less, had fewer opportunities for female companionship, and, doing only "inside" work, was kept busy producing and rearing children. In many cases she had also to accept a concubine into her home.

In discussing marriage in general, informants of mine who participated in both the marrying and the nonmarrying forms of resistance contrasted the status of married women unfavorably with that of single women. Many of them stressed the independence of an unmarried woman—her freedom from control by parents-in-law and her ability to move about and do what she liked. Ho's informants stressed their fear of becoming a "slave of man," of being a "human machine of propagation," and of marrying the "wrong type" of man.[37] Several of my own informants were daughters of concubines; they stressed the domestic disharmony arising out of quarrels between different consorts and their children. Many of them also stressed the loneliness of marriage and the lack of economic independence.

Several informants expressed a distaste for heterosexual relations and childbirth. Smith observed that women in the resistance believed "that their married lives would be miserable and unholy."[38] Informants talked of the pollution of childbirth, the punishment in purgatory awaiting women who had children, and the limitations that pregnancy and childbirth, because of their polluting effects, imposed on women in the domestic economy. Some of my informants belonged to Hsien-t'ien sects; a few of them managed vegetarian halls in Hong Kong. These women emphasized the religious advantages of celibacy: a celibate woman could assume a high rank in a sect and have many disciples; she could learn esoteric practices to protect her in her journeys about the countryside (e.g. against rape); and she could assure herself of a better fate in the next life. In other areas Buddhist nunneries provided one socially acceptable alternative to marriage, but our informants contrasted the restricted movements of a nun with the freedom of a vegetarian who was not obliged to reside in a religious institution.

Some women said their fears of sexual relations with men were exacerbated by tales visiting married women told in the girls' houses. One woman Ho interviewed said she had heard "weird stories about childbirth." She married at seventeen and became a pu lo-chia.[39] Some spoke of the frigidity that sometimes marred the wedding night and might last for several months, the consequent anger of the mother-in-law, and the bitter medicines a "stone girl" or frigid woman was forced to swallow. Other women said they had formed close friendships with girls in the girls' house or their work group and did not want any man's "affections." Some pointed to the very real possibility of dying in childbirth, which, they believed, brought even greater punishment after death. Several women said they had nonmarrying fates. They had learned this either from fortunetellers or from their own parents. This brings us to the question of local acceptance of the resistance, including the role of parents.

The local economic system was clearly a major factor in the development of the resistance. We saw how it led to striking contrasts in status between married and unmarried women. The local economy also provided an unmarried woman with a means of supporting herself—a rare option in traditional society. Elsewhere the only alternatives to marriage were religious orders or occupations connected with sex and procreation: prostitution, matchmaking, midwifery.[40] A married woman could sometimes supplement the family income and improve her status by engaging in cottage industry,[41] but it was unlikely that a separated wife could earn enough to support herself by such means. An unhappily married woman who returned to her natal home was not entitled to her parents' support.[42] Finally, an unmarried daughter could not live at home and take in work because of the Chinese conviction that "mature girls cannot be kept in the midst" of the family: *nü-ta pu chung-liu.*

As the silk economy industrialized, there were further inducements for women in the resistance area to remain single. As we have seen, unattached women were preferred by employers of female labor because of their freedom from family ties. And since an unmarried girl working in a silk factory could support not only herself but also her younger siblings and parents, the latter also had an incentive to keep her unwed. Of the women Ho interviewed in Singapore, not all, he notes, remained unmarried "because of a wish to abstain. Some felt they had a duty to provide extra income for their natal families."[43] What if they did not wish to abstain?

One Chinese description of unmarried girls in P'an-yü mentions their "sexual freedom" and "debauchery among the mulberry trees," adding that "they will neither marry the man chosen [by their parents] nor practice proper celibacy; they merely use the concept of celibacy as a pretext for promiscuity." The source goes on to moralize about the dangers of free love, saying that if an unmarried girl becomes pregnant, she has no recourse but the "inhuman device of abortion." It then describes the case of a girl who had been having an affair in the fields for whom a marriage was arranged by her parents; as it turned out, they had arranged for the girl to marry her lover.[44]

One cannot of course rule out the possibility that a girl who formally renounced heterosexual relationships might have done so not out of a positive commitment to celibacy, but out of economic necessity or out of resentment of the traditional marriage arrangements rather than of men as such. But my informants considered it most unlikely that a girl who had taken tzu-shu vows would enter into a forbidden relationship with a man. These vows were said to be absolutely binding—they were made before gods—and in violating them both the girl and her lover would risk terrible punishment from Heaven. I was also told that a girl who had gone through the hairdressing ritual could not be married off by her parents. The ritual meant that her parents had no further rights over her person, i.e., that she was socially mature. Indeed, it was added, it was precisely to avoid the risk that a daughter who did not want an arranged marriage might form a liaison with a man that parents made her take tzu-shu vows. If she did form such a liaison, particularly while away working in a town, her parents might lose an important source of income. The hairdressing ritual gave them further security: once the ritual had been performed, the girl had no further claim to parental support. Whether, as the Chinese source suggests, many tzu-shu nü risked Heaven's "terrible punishment" is difficult to say; no other available source mentions "free love." Moreover, Ho comments that a girl who becomes a tzu-shu nü in Shun-te "is respected . . . ; her parents may gain prestige through having [such a] daughter."[45] This seems unlikely to have been the case if illicit relations were common.

The Decision to Marry or Not

Some parents did not want their daughters to take vows of celibacy. Often betrothals were kept secret from the daughter to forestall objections and even suicide. We have seen that religious literature emphasized the merit of suicide committed to preserve chastity. Several sources mention mass suicides in which sisters of a betrothed girl who did not wish to wed joined her in death.[46] Some girls are said to have obtained magical charms from religious groups that they used to dissuade the other party to a marriage contract. According to Dyer Ball, "they were taught by the nuns" and vegetarian women "to kill their husbands by saying certain charms or incantations."[47] My informants said that a woman who intended to leave her husband without consummating the marriage tucked charms in her underwrappings to ward off his advances. Why were some girls encouraged by their parents to remain single and others married off against their will?

According to my informants, by the beginning of the century most families in the area tried to keep one daughter as a tzu-shu nü. Early signs of an aversion to marriage or of marked intelligence might be interpreted as indications of a "nonmarrying fate." If a horoscope-reader confirmed this view, the daughter's future was set. Daughters adopted to "lead in" sons might also be selected; they would be older than their oldest brother when his time came to marry, and possibly too old to make a good match when their turn came.[48] A girl might even be adopted with this purpose in mind. So-called daughters who were really mei-tsai might also be selected.

Some girls had to marry against their will, I am told, because it was believed that a family who sent out no daughters in marriage would get no wives in return. Once a girl had been betrothed, she could usually not withdraw, betrothal being actually the first step of the marriage ritual. The only course open to her was to refuse to cohabit. Just as not all girls became tzu-shu nü out of a positive desire for celibacy, not all pu lo-chia opposed eventual cohabitation. A girl might object to marrying a stranger or a very young boy, or to having many children. Some girls followed the custom of staying away three years, which gave them time to get to know their husbands (they returned for ceremonial visits) and very young husbands time to mature. In-laws often accepted this arrangement and in some cases even encouraged it, because during her time away the girl worked to support her husband and his family. Indeed, I was told, families began to find brides for younger and younger sons so they could be supported by their daughters-in-law.[49] A girl might, however, strike a bargain with her in-laws: when she returned, she would bear no more than two or three children, afterward being free to abstain from sexual relations.

During their time away, such women did not usually live in their natal homes, but in the cockloft of the girls' house (girls also slept in the cockloft for four days before they married). Usually they worked locally as hired labor. If after a few years they further decided not to return until past childbearing age—perhaps they found their husband or in-laws uncongenial or had resolved to remain celibate—they had to leave the village and buy a mei-tsai to act as their husband's concubine. They then had additionally to support the concubine and her children. According to Ho, "to maintain chastity and support a husband and his children . . . were acts admired and respected."[50]

Both the tzu-shu nü and the pu lo-chia who did not intend returning until old age usually had long-term economic obligations to their natal or conjugal families. Moreover, unattached women of either category could not stay in their natal homes, but had to find somewhere else to live. Let us now see what arrangements they made.

The tzu-shu nü. The nonmarrying woman's hairdressing ceremony, like the bride's, was a prerequisite to leaving home. As for the marriage ceremonies, an auspicious day was chosen for the ritual.[51] Whereas the bride was assisted at the hairdressing ceremony by an elderly woman with many sons, the nonmarrying woman was assisted by an elderly celibate female. Like wedding ceremonies, the tzu-shu ceremonies were followed by a banquet, and like the bride, the nonmarrying woman received red packets of money from her relatives, as well as from her "sisters" and friends. If she was lucky she also received money saved for her dowry, or against her departure if her parents had decided earlier that she would not wed. The peasant woman would eventually use the money she was given on this occasion to pay for residence in a special house for tzu-shu nü, known as a "spinsters' house" (*ku-p'o wu*) or "sisters' house" (*tzu-mei wu*), when she grew too old to work.

Spinsters' houses were found throughout the Shun-te area, usually adjoining a plot of farmland with which the elderly inmates helped support themselves.[52] Like some of the girls' houses, some of the spinsters' houses appear to have been built by lineages as retirement homes for their unmarried women, and perhaps also as residences for unattached women working in an economic operation of the lineage. Some gentry families allowed a daughter to remain unwed without requiring her to work, which enhanced the family's prestige, and in many instances built a house for the girl to live in.

Many women, however, had to finance their own house, or alternatively pay into a vegetarian hall when they retired. Spinsters' houses were in many cases practically indistinguishable from vegetarian halls. They had an altar for a patron deity, usually Kuan Yin, and on festival days they invited priests to officiate at religious ceremonies. But vegetarian food was not required at the spinsters' houses, and there was far less focus on religious activities in general.

During her active years the tzu-shu nü usually shared a rented room with her "sisters" in a town near the filature that employed them. Such residential groups often had elaborate arrangements for saving money. They ran death-benefit clubs, to which members made monthly payments against funeral expenses of one of their number or a parent's postmortuary ceremonies; in some groups women put a fixed percentage of their monthly earnings into a fund for festival celebrations; they contributed to funds for emergency assistance to the families of the "sisters"; and they saved for the retirement home they eventually would build. If they could save enough, they retired early—around forty—and adopted a mei-tsai, whom they brought up in their "faith."

The pu lo-chia. The pu lo-chia who did not return to her husband until old age usually had greater economic burdens than a tzu-shu nü. The nonmarrying woman supported her siblings and parents, but the separated wife had to support not only her in-laws and husband, but also her husband's concubine (for whom she paid) and their children. Expected to return eventually, she did not save for a retirement home. While she was working, however, her life followed much the same pattern as that of the nonmarrying woman. She, too, rented a room with other separated wives—her "sisters"—and with young widows and grass widows whose husbands were overseas, for they, too, in many cases left home to work for their in-laws. Whether the separated wife ever returned depended on many circumstances: whether she had made sufficient financial contributions to win acceptance by her husband's concubine and her children (who were technically the wife's); whether an overseas husband returned; or whether she was called back to care for an adopted child.

Many separated wives and young widows never returned. In the 1920's the silk industry began to decline, at first because of outside competition and later because of the worldwide depression. Earnings decreased, and many a woman's hard-pressed conjugal family refused to take her back. Olga Lang describes her visit to women's residences in and around Canton in the late 1930's, which the Kwangtung authorities had had to erect for women who "had no real contact with their husbands, thus becoming helpless in old age."[53] She also reports that some occupants were women who had lost all contact with their father's families—presumably tzu-shu nü who could not save enough money to build themselves a house or buy into a vegetarian hall.

Decline of the Resistance

By 1935 the slump hit bottom. Writing during the period, Smedley reports that the collapse of industrial life had forced all the filatures in some areas to close down.[54] I am told that some tzu-shu nü and separated wives retired early to spinsters' houses and vegetarian halls; those still young enough to seek employment elsewhere found work as domestic servants in Canton and other cities.

Malaya and Singapore, similarly affected by the depression, began to restrict male immigration. The cost of a man's passage increased as a result of competition for the limited number of quota tickets available. At first there was no immigration quota for women, and their tickets were therefore cheaper. To fill their ships, ticket brokers would sell lodging houses and local ticket agents a quota ticket only if they bought three or four nonquota tickets at the same time. Parents, brothers, and in-laws therefore encouraged their daughters, sisters, and young daughters-in-law to emigrate. I am told that more girls were urged to become tzu-shu nü so they would not marry overseas, and it was impressed upon newly married women that noncohabitation was an honorable practice. From 1933 to 1938, when a quota of 500 females a month was introduced, shiploads of Cantonese women entered Malaya and Singapore. A large contingent came from Shun-te.[55]

Some women left the area in anticipation of the Japanese occupation of Canton and the consequent social and economic dislocations. When the Japanese took Canton in 1938, many young unattached women escaped sexual exploitation by taking up residence in vegetarian halls. After the Japanese left, life scarcely had time to settle down again before the Communists came to power. The People's Republic was sympathetic to the plight of these women who were described as suffering "terrible hardships . . . and [leading] sad and lonely lives."[56] But it considered their resistance essentially negative, and disapproved, I am told, of the "exploitative" custom of purchasing mei-tsai as concubines. The spinsters' houses were gradually phased out. Many women were forcibly removed to the homes of kinsmen. Only those with nobody to take them in were allowed to remain.[57]

Most of the unattached women who migrated to Singapore and Hong Kong from the Shun-te area worked as domestic servants. Many never returned to their homeland. While working they made arrangements similar to those of the silkworkers: they rented workers' rooms, or *kongsi* as they are called in Singapore, and ran several kinds of loan clubs.[58] Some are said eventually to have married and had children,[59] but it is noticeable that with the influx of unattached women in the 1930's, vegetarian halls, particularly sectarian ones, sprang up in large numbers. My own investigations in the 1950's showed that much of their membership was drawn from the nonmarrying and noncohabiting women of the resistance area.[60] Some of these women adopted daughters with the intention of having them follow in their footsteps, but such plans usually went awry. A film made for the female Cantonese audience in the early 1950's in Hong Kong, entitled *Tzu-shu nü*, tells the story of one such adopted daughter and her foster-mother. The girl refuses to take tzu-shu vows, telling her foster-mother that it is old-fashioned and superstitious to reject marriage, that nowadays marriage is much better for women than it was in the past, and that women should work to further improve their marital status.

In Hong Kong today, unmarried women are in demand in factories, offices, and commercial establishments. Demographic data show that many girls are postponing marriage, and one demographer, Janet Salaff, argues that this may reflect the significant contributions they make to their parents' and siblings' support and the higher status they enjoy as a result.[61] But most women in Hong Kong marry eventually. The resistance has not attracted women brought up in a society, economy, and culture that differ so markedly from those of prewar Shun-te.

The Legacy of the Resistance

I have argued that a particular local economy and settlement pattern, tied to a particular physical environment, raised the status of the unmarried or unattached woman considerably above that of the conventionally married woman; and further, that with the industrialization of the economy, women wishing to remain unwed were financially able to act on their preferences. Although unmarried women apparently had already participated to a greater extent than their married sisters in the domestic economy, once industrialization took hold, unattached women were almost the only class of labor in demand. The emigration of thousands of men who could not find work at home made parents more dependent than ever on the earnings of their unattached daughters and their daughters-in-law, which gave them a strong incentive to encourage marriage resistance.

In other parts of China where unattached women were in demand as factory labor, the traditional marriage arrangements were undercut. Fei Hsiao-t'ung, for example, cites the case of an illicit union between a married but detached factory worker and a man in Wusih. The woman's parents-in-law eventually decided to treat her as before because of her earning capacity.[62] One source on P'an-yü also talks of disruptive effects—"debauchery," free love, and abortion—but the overwhelming evidence is that in the resistance area, traditional values relating to premarital chastity and marital fidelity were preserved, and that the system of marriage, though modified, remained more or less intact. Many women remained celibate, but concubines, of whom there was a plentiful local supply, assumed the responsibility of bearing children. The women who chose celibacy were influenced by the high local valuation of chastity, which stemmed in large part from dissident religious groups with whom local inhabitants sympathized. These groups, driven from other parts of China but safely entrenched in the relatively isolated hilly regions around Shun-te, reached the relatively large numbers of literate or semiliterate women in the area with anti-marriage propaganda. In most of industrializing China, families had to balance the financial gain from an unmarried daughter or noncohabiting daughter-in-law who worked away from home against the risk of losing her, and hence her earnings, to another man. In the resistance area, however, the system of sanctions and beliefs surrounding institutionalized celibacy made such defections unlikely. It is not surprising, then, that many parents supported the commitment to celibacy once it was made or even encouraged their daughters and daughters-in-law to make such a commitment.

None of the features I have discussed appears unique to the resistance area, but their combination does. The Yangtze Valley, for example, had a similar terrain, practiced sericulture, and apparently had similar notions of female pollution and silkworm production; but because the climate supported only two broods of silkworms a year, less domestic labor was needed and women played a less important role in the village economy than they did in the resistance area. In the Yangtze Valley, moreover, there were no girls' houses and no sisterhoods, and by the mid-nineteenth century the Hsien-t'ien sects had been driven out or effectively hamstrung. Elsewhere in Kwangtung province there were girls' houses and girls working in the domestic economy; furthermore there was a significant male out-migration, as there was not in the Yangtze Valley. Outside the resistance area, however, women were seldom able to work for cash, at least cash enough to support themselves and their kinsmen, and nowhere else does sectarianism appear to have been so strong. Sectarianism also flourished in parts of Fukien province,[63] but a higher proportion of girls there had bound feet, and they did not work outside. There were no girls' houses in Fukien, so far as I know, and educational opportunities for women were rarer.

Clearly we do not yet know enough either about village-to-village variation in the resistance area or about other superficially similar areas with no history of marriage resistance to assess the relative importance of the variables discussed in this paper.

What about the resistance area today? Has the resistance, or the ecology that produced it, left a legacy discernible even under the People's Republic? Graham Johnson, a sociologist who visited the delta region in 1973, writes that on the average women there participate in collective work only slightly less than men, and that they constitute slightly over 50 percent of the labor force. He contrasts this pattern with that of a village in Honan, described by a recent observer, where there is a low level of female involvement in many aspects of collective production and where few women are rated as fully able-bodied members of the workforce.[64] In Shun-te the silk-and-fish economy persists, although other crops have been introduced or brought under more intensive cultivation. As a result of collectivization, fishponds and mulberry groves have been enlarged, and isolated farms are less in evidence. According to my own informants, there are no active celibate establishments in Shun-te today, although recent interviews recorded by China specialists working in Hong Kong suggest that girls' houses may still exist in some villages, and that there may still be women who do not join their husbands immediately after their wedding ceremonies. Women, moreover, are still the main workers in silk production. Unmarried girls are in exclusive charge of the outside phase of silkworm breeding and predominate in filatures. In a private report, Johnson says that one filature he visited employed nearly 1,300 workers, of whom 1,100 were women.

Johnson also contrasts Shun-te with Tung-kuan, another hsien in the Canton delta but outside the resistance area. In Shun-te there were, in 1973, 2,600 nurseries for workers' children, an average of one per work team. In Tung-kuan there were very few nurseries; instead, women work in the fields with young children on their backs. Family-planning propaganda appears to have been far more successful in Shun-te. Between 1965 and 1972 the birthrate in Shun-te is said to have fallen from 3.4 percent to 1.8 percent (0.9 percent in Ta-liang, the hsien capital), whereas in Tung-kuan the birthrate for the hsien as a whole remained at 2.2 percent, with higher rates in the rural areas. In Tung-kuan, though, abortion is widely practiced, whereas in Shun-te it is rare. As Johnson remarks, traditional notions concerning family and household are "presumably critical."[65] In a private report he writes that with respect to family planning, "it is openly admitted that the major problems stem not so much from parents as grandparents." In Shun-te many former members of the marriage resistance must now be members of the grandparent generation. One imagines that the high value they have always placed on freedom of movement for women—on their being unencumbered by children—and the low value they place on procreation might today find their expression in the distinctive work patterns and extraordinary population statistics of the former resistance area.

The Power and Pollution of Chinese Women

EMILY M. AHERN

In many societies women are considered ritually polluting and unclean. This means in part that a woman's sexual parts and their emissions are regarded as potentially harmful to others. When women are in a state considered unclean, therefore, they must carefully abstain from certain activities, and other people must take precautions before coming into contact with them.

In Chinese society women are regarded as both ritually unclean and dangerously powerful, and they are barred from certain activities because of the harm they threaten to inflict on others.* In the following analysis I explore from three different approaches the question of why Chinese women should be considered unclean or polluting: the first looks to the nature of allegedly unclean substances and their connection with birth and death; the second views the ascription of pollution to women as a reflection of their social role; and the third sees women's putative pollution as part of a system of ideas relating pollution to breaking the boundaries of social groups. In the conclusion I assess the relative merits of the three approaches.

I. Unclean Substances

In *A Daughter of Han* Lao T'ai T'ai declares, "Women were not considered clean."[1] What has made Chinese women unclean, and what other

* The material used here was gathered from June to August 1972, during a field project made possible by the Department of Epidemiology and International Health, University of Washington. The study was done in Ch'i-nan, a village in northern Taiwan, the same village I lived in from 1969 to 1970. Although I refer to "Chinese" for convenience, most of my data come from this Hokkien-speaking Taiwanese community. For background information on Ch'i-nan, see Emily M. Ahern, *The Cult of the Dead in a Chinese Village* (Stanford, Calif., 1973).

persons or substances are similarly counted as unclean? Principally, bodily effluvia associated exclusively with women are unclean: menstrual blood and postpartum discharge, which are believed to be the same substance. When a woman becomes pregnant, menstrual fluids accumulate in her body. These fluids emerge during childbirth and continue to flow, less and less heavily, for about a month afterward. Both menstrual and postpartum discharges are unclean, though the quantities of effluvia associated with birth make that event much dirtier. As one of my informants put it, "Menstruation is like one-hundredth of a birth."

In describing these substances, people used the word *la-sam*, a word also used to describe ordinary sorts of dirty things—a child's dirty face, for instance, or a dirty shirt. Alternatively, they described unclean substances as not clean, *bou chieng-khi*. Menstrual fluids are considered unclean in part because they are bad for the body. A woman is well rid of them. Numerous informants said something like this: "You want to get all the dirty stuff out. It's good to get rid of it; that blood is dirty. It is blood the body doesn't need." Such remarks make an implicit distinction between beneficent blood, i.e. the blood that flows through the veins, which is essential to health, and the blood that flows out during menstruation, which is harmful. Both kinds of blood escape during childbirth. A woman hopes to replace the good, ordinary blood by eating tonic foods after childbirth; the dirty blood, she feels, is a kind "no one would want."

Anyone who comes into contact with menstrual blood—male or female—is barred from worshiping the gods. Given the serious consequence of contact with menstrual blood, one would expect great care to be taken in its disposition. In fact, however, women treat the problem quite casually. They put the soiled papers or pads in the latrine, where they disintegrate. The fact that a latrine's contents ordinarily end up on rice fields in the form of nightsoil might be taken as indicating scant concern with unclean substances. Actually, however, concern with dirt reappears in another form: anything that has come into contact with the dirt on the ground is potentially offensive to the gods because unclean menstrual substances may be mixed in with ordinary dirt. A god's image, I was told, cannot be carried under a clothes-drying pole because pants (men's and women's) have probably been hung on it. "Pants are dirty because people's feet have passed through them when they put them on. People's feet are dirty because they often touch the ground and can come into contact with dirt even though we ourselves may not know it. The ground is full of dirty stuff—both real dirt [earth] and women's dirt. Our feet can't help coming into contact with this dirt." Even though in theory everyone comes into contact with menstrual blood in walking on the ground, in practice not everyone is prevented from worshiping the gods on that account. Only things touched by the feet must be kept away from the gods.

As the statement about dirt on the ground indicates, there are other kinds of dirt besides menstrual fluids. At this point, I will briefly introduce the other unclean substances as they were explained to me. Later in the paper, I will relate the unclean substances women produce to the entire class of unclean things. People talked about dirty substances in two basic ways. One approach was to consider any discharge from the body dirty; menstrual blood, semen, urine, feces, pus, and mucus are all dirty. One woman told me, "Menstrual blood, semen, urine, feces—all that stuff—is dirty." When I asked why, she replied, "How could something coming out from inside the skin be clean?" (*Baq-lai chut-lai na u chieng-khi?*)* The other approach to unclean substances was to divide them into two major types, the dirt associated with happy events (births) and the dirt associated with unhappy events (deaths). As one informant explained it, "The dirt from birth—menstrual fluids—is the dirtiest of all. Then there is the dirt from death—the corpse. Both of them are dirty in the same way, but the dirt of birth is the dirt of happy events (*hi-su*), and the dirt of a corpse is the dirt of unhappy events (*song-su*)." Ghosts, too, are said to be unclean by virtue of their association with death. Ghosts are spirits of dead persons, who for one reason or another cannot follow the normal route to the underworld. Rites to propitiate these ghosts are said to make the places they frequent cleaner. Most things people referred to as dirty were covered by the happy-unhappy typology. The major omission is sexual intercourse, which is not explicitly classified with the dirt of happy events despite its recognized connection with pregnancy and birth. I will discuss the dirt of sexual intercourse in more detail later.

The effect of contact with most dirty substances is the same as the effect of contact with menstrual blood: women who are menstruating or within a month of childbirth, anyone who enters a room in which a woman has given birth within the previous month, anyone who is in mourning, and anyone who has recently had sexual intercourse cannot

---

* Recent anthropological analyses of ritual pollution have shown the frequency with which bodily excretions are invested with special properties. Often they are considered both polluting and dangerously powerful. See, for example, Mary Douglas, *Purity and Danger: An Analysis of Concepts of Pollution and Taboo* (New York, 1966), pp. 114–28.

worship the gods. Here the term polluting will be applied only to dirty
substances that break communication between man and gods upon contact. Unclean things that do not affect the relationship between man
and gods are peripheral to my analysis. Some people made this distinction themselves, saying that bodily substances like urine, feces, and pus
(which do not affect worship of the gods) are "really" dirty, whereas
menstrual blood and corpses are dirty in a different sense. Someone who
has been in contact with a "really" dirty substance can be cleaned with
soap and water, whereas the dirtiness of someone who has been in contact with menstrual blood or with a corpse cannot be alleviated by soap
and water.

The polluting substances associated exclusively with women—menstrual and birth fluids—are closely associated with dangerous power.
Menstrual blood is most directly powerful in that, in the villagers' understanding, it creates babies. Some of the menstrual blood a woman
produces during pregnancy flows out during childbirth. The remaining
accumulated menstrual blood *becomes* the body of the child; "it creates
flesh and bones" (*si:-kut si:-baq*), informants said. The blood discharged
when a baby is born is residue of the creation process. To be sure, menstrual blood alone cannot produce a child. For that, "you need both the
mother's blood and the father's semen. The semen has '*thang*' in it,
which make the child start to grow. The thang are like seeds in the
ground from which a plant grows." The role of semen and the role of
plant seed are not identical. Whereas a seed itself turns into a grown
plant, semen merely starts the growth of a child; what turns into the
body of a child, into its flesh and bones, is menstrual blood. The woman's
role in procreation is thus seen as very substantial.*

The blood that surrounds the fetus and emerges during childbirth also
has great power. Beliefs about the potentially dangerous power of this
superfluous blood are related to beliefs about the behavior of a spiritual
entity called the Thai Sin. Although the name means Placenta God, Thai
Sin is also, and more importantly, regarded as the child's soul. One informant said, "You could say that just as adults have a *lieng-hun* [a soul],
so infants have a Thai Sin." The Thai Sin comes into existence the moment the child is conceived and stays until four months after birth. During its first nine months the spirit is not confined to the fetus, but moves
about inside the pregnant woman's bedroom. This movement causes

---

* Ancient ideas about women also depict them as the fount of life-giving forces.
Whereas men must copulate with women to absorb women's yin essence, women
themselves have an endless supply, which is not depleted by intercourse. R. H. Van
Gulick, *Sexual Life in Ancient China* (Leiden, 1961), pp. 46, 48.

difficulties: if one should happen to strike, break, or cut something in the woman's room when the Thai Sin is in the way, the child's body may be injured. If one cuts cloth at the wrong time, the child may be born with a cleft palate; if one breaks a stick, one of the child's limbs may be damaged; if one drives a nail in the wall or digs a hole in the floor, the child may be aborted or born prematurely. After birth the Thai Sin becomes attached to the child's body with increasing firmness, until, at about four months, there is no need to fear striking it inadvertently.[2]

Because the newborn child's soul is not firmly settled within his body, anything close to the child can affect his body through the medium of the Thai Sin. Because the Thai Sin may be present in the birth fluids, their disposal is most problematic. If they are disturbed while being removed, the infant may fall seriously ill. One informant said,

The birth fluids are caught on paper so they won't spill on the floor or bed. Afterward, the midwife takes the paper away and drops it gently into a large, free-running stream. She must be sure to drop it softly, because if she drops it with a jolt, the child will vomit continuously. The blood is very strong and powerful [*li-hai*]. If there is no stream, it can be buried but not burned. If fire were to touch the blood, the child itself would burn up, or else be marked with red spots. All the blood must be disposed of; if some soaks into an earthen floor you should dig up the earth in that place and dispose of it, too.

The power of this blood derives from its relation to the child; because the baby's soul is likely to be present in the blood, the treatment it receives can directly affect the baby's well-being.

In the case of birth fluids, every effort is made to avoid harming the child. In other cases, the potentially harmful power of menstrual blood may be deliberately exploited. About twenty years ago, I was told, two Ch'i-nan men named Li and Peq quarreled because chickens that belonged to one man ate some grain that belonged to the other. The quarrel finally escalated into a fight with long knives, in which Peq killed Li. Afterward, fearing the revenge the Li man's soul might exact, the Peqs hired a Taoist priest. The Taoist performed esoteric rituals using two key substances to ward off the vengeful soul: the blood of a black dog (a euphemism for menstrual blood) and a brass needle. The Taoist not only kept the soul away but also destroyed its power; as a result, it was said, the Li family has been declining ever since.

Other substances, similar to menstrual blood, are invested with similar powers. To be specific, blood flowing from bodies is in many cases regarded as powerful. In Ch'i-nan when a pig or chicken is slaughtered for the gods, the butcher captures a cupful of the blood that spurts from the jugular vein. A wad of ritual paper money may also be thrust into the stream of blood. These two items are presented to the gods as embodiments of the strength and life force of the slaughtered animal.

The power released at the moment when blood is spilled in slaughter, like menstrual blood, has potential for both good and evil. The man hired to slaughter a pig pastes a charm written on red paper (a prophylactic color) on the handle of the slaughtering knife. One such charm was used in Ch'i-nan when a man fell sick at the exact moment of the kill. The butcher soaked the charm in water and administered the resulting drink to the sick man. He soon recovered.

The double-edged power of blood is evident also from its use in exorcising evil spirits. The blood protects those who use it on the one hand and destroys those against whom it is used on the other. David Graham tells us that the blood of humans, chickens, or ducks can be used to exorcise demons.[3] According to J. J. M. de Groot, the blood of dogs is used for the same purpose.[4] Finally, *tang-ki*, spirit mediums who become possessed with the spirit of a god, commonly mutilate themselves and daub the resulting blood on charms that are then used to ward off evil spirits.[5]

Slaughter and exorcism seem a long way from menstruation and childbirth. Yet one element links them all, the escape and flow of blood. Moreover, in at least one instance menstrual blood is explicitly linked to the blood shed by tang-ki. A. J. A. Elliott notes that menstruating women are expected to stay away when a tang-ki is possessed: "If a menstruating woman is present while the *dang-ki* [sic] is possessed by the *shen* [god], she places both herself and him in great danger. If the *dang-ki* has cut himself as part of the performance, he may have great difficulty in stopping the flow of blood if such a woman is near him."[6] The escape of blood, any blood, from a living body seems to be associated with power. The life force in this power can be harnessed to produce a child, to please the gods with a potent offering, or to protect a person threatened by an evil spirit. At the same time, the destructive force in the power of blood portends death and danger—to the newborn child, the bystander at a slaughter, vulnerable spirits, and bleeding tang-ki.

The association of blood with both beneficial and destructive power may derive in part from the involvement of blood in both life and death. Blood is necessary for the development of a new life, but the menstrual blood that flows when a woman is not pregnant is, in a sense, a dead fetus. In earlier times, too, childbirth itself and the accompanying blood flow were all too often associated with the death of the mother, the child, or both. Moreover, the powerful blood that flows at a slaughter is necessarily accompanied by the death of an animal. The close association of both life and death with flowing blood is epitomized by a custom De Groot reported for Amoy: the blood that spurted from decapitated criminals was collected and used for life-strengthening medicines.[7] It may be partly the fundamental emotional response of people confronted with the momentous events of birth and death that invests flowing blood—which partakes of both—with its ambivalent power.

II. *Power and Danger in Women's Social Roles*

The comparison with other kinds of flowing blood gives us some understanding of the dangerous power of menstrual blood. For another kind of explanation we ask the question, what kinds of social powers do women have that might parallel the powers and dangers of menstrual blood?[8] If there are parallels between the characteristics of menstrual blood and the characteristics of women's social activities, one might hypothesize that the power of menstrual blood is an expression or a reflection of women's social role.

In searching for social parallels to the dangerous powers of menstrual blood, let us begin with the woman who has married but has not yet reached menopause. From the viewpoint of her husband's family, the woman's most important desirable power is her ability to produce offspring (chiefly sons) who will form the next generation in her husband's line of descent and ensure that offerings will be made to her husband's parents when they die. Although this capacity means great potential advantages for her husband's family, it is also potentially threatening. Like the menstrual blood that produces children, a woman's reproductive power is double-edged. A woman not only bears children, she also strives to form close, affectionate bonds with them so that she will be assured of a secure place for herself in the alien environment of her husband's family and security in her old age. Her ultimate goal is the separation of her uterine family (the term is Margery Wolf's) from the families of her sisters-in-law. This enables her to escape much of her mother-in-law's domination and to strengthen her influence within her own uterine family.[9]

A married woman's loyalties, at least initially, do not lie firmly with her new husband's family. As an outsider, an intruder, she is expected to make her own way, if need be by undermining her husband's authority. The few people I could persuade to talk about sorcery mentioned one form of sorcery almost to the exclusion of any other: attempts by a new bride to dominate her husband. In one incident recounted to me, a man and his wife quarreled. The wife packed up her things and set out for her natal family as if for good. To everyone's surprise she returned a few days later with her own mother. Not long afterward, the husband's behavior changed: he stopped cooperating with his brothers and sisters-in-law in paying their joint land tax, and he became very subservient to his wife. In my informant's opinion, the mother and daughter had procured a charm that would produce this effect and had devised a way to have the husband ingest it. The woman was assumed to be bent on manipulating her husband so that he would defer to her and weaken his own family ties.

The power young women wield as they build their uterine families and attempt to manipulate their husbands is of a peculiar kind. It consists in subverting and disrupting the family form that most Chinese men hold dear—the family that grows from generation to generation without interruption and without division. Sons, their wives, and their children should live in harmony under the guidance of the eldest male. The goals and desires of young married women conflict with this ideal, and it is largely their machinations that prevent its attainment. The *power* women have is their capacity to alter a family's form by adding members to it, dividing it, and disturbing male authority; the *danger* they pose is their capacity to break up what men consider the ideal family.

The kind of power married women exercise before menopause is, then, analogous to the kind of power inherent in menstrual blood in its two-sided potential for both great harm and great good. Does the parallel between women's social roles and the qualities of menstrual blood apply as well to other stages in the woman's life cycle? The pattern holds to some extent for a nubile but unmarried girl. At this stage, the girl's menstrual fluids are not likely to create a fetus; nor is she able to contribute in any crucial way to her natal family, as a young wife does to her conjugal family by bearing sons. The potential benefits both of the young woman's menstrual flow and of her social role are absent. What about the potential for harm? It is hard to see any parallel here. For the most part unmarried girls identify closely with the wishes of their elders and have little capacity or inclination for disruption. The most that can be said is that when they marry out they disrupt the family's finances and the emotional ties between themselves and others, but these are temporary problems that seem not to have a lasting, deep-felt effect.

Is there a clearer parallel in the stage of a woman's life that follows the menopause? We would expect women's potential for either good or evil to diminish along with the flow of menstrual blood. Their power to add to the family directly does indeed fall away. But activities that threaten male ideals continue, even though many of a woman's interests at this stage of her life seem to coincide with her husband's. Like him, she desires filial and obedient sons and daughters-in-law who will work to sustain the family and extend it to the next generation. In other ways, however, a woman's interests diverge from her husband's. Through what Margery Wolf has called the women's community, women—especially older women, established in the community—indirectly influence men's behavior in ways that men find threatening. The women's community, composed of loose, overlapping groups of women in a village, is most visible when women gather to wash clothes or do chores together. Much information is exchanged in this setting, some of it about the affairs of men.[10] Because, according to tenets accepted by everyone, to be talked about is to lose face, women affect men's behavior merely by talking about them:

We once asked a male friend in Peihotien just what "having face" amounted to. He replied, "When no one is talking about a family, you can say it has face." This is precisely where women wield their power. When a man behaves in a way that they consider wrong, they talk about him—not only among themselves, but to their sons and husbands. No one "tells him how to mind his own business," but it becomes abundantly clear that he is losing face and by continuing in this manner may bring shame to the family of his ancestors and descendants. Few men will risk that.[11]

According to the male ideal, power should be exercised by male heads of households, managers of lineages, and community leaders. No wonder the ability of women to exercise power of a very different kind, power wielded behind the scenes, unsupported by recognized social position, is seen as a threat to the male order. No matter how well-ensconced men are in the established positions of power, the surreptitious influence of women remains beyond their capacity to control.

Of course, this mode of influencing men is to some extent open to younger women as well. But it is the older women, themselves mothers-in-law, who set the tone of the women's community.[12] Outside the women's community, older women have ways of wielding power and influence that are not open to younger women. If they have gained the loyalty of their sons, they can exert considerable control over them, even after they are grown men with wives and children of their own. In many cases, too, older women take a strong hand in decisions about household management, investment, or social affairs. The gradual accretion of influence and power by older women by no means coincides with the end of menstruation. But the two processes work in opposite directions: as a woman's menstrual flow ends in her 40's or 50's, she gains increasing power over the people around her.

In sum, although the parallels between a woman's social power and the power of menstrual blood are at best tenuous before marriage or after menopause, they are quite convincing for the stage of life just after marriage. During this stage of women's lives their capacities are complex: the production of children for male lines of descent is regarded as essential and desirable, but in other respects their power is from a male point of view threatening and even dangerous. There is a clear parallel between these attributes and those of menstrual blood: both are able to cause substantial, desirable change, and both are potentially dangerous. Young women produce sons who form the next links in their husbands' lines of descent; menstrual blood creates the body and bones of the fetus. Young women can threaten male ideals of the family; menstrual blood can threaten the life of the fetus (at birth) and the wellbeing of anyone against whom it is directed by a sorcerer. The power of menstrual blood, then, can be seen as a symbolic representation of the actual social power of young married women. The power attributed to menstrual blood may also be the culture's way of recognizing that social power, which otherwise goes virtually unacknowledged in Chinese society.

The parallel between menstrual blood and young women's social role has one other noteworthy aspect. Young married women clearly use their powers intentionally, in order to achieve certain goals. The disruption caused by the men's perception of their activities as threatening is more than compensated by the increased security they gain. Is there a parallel with respect to pollution? Do women wield their supposed capacity to pollute as a weapon, intentionally directing it at others to gain their own ends? For an answer we must try to place beliefs about women's polluting capacities within the wider system of beliefs about pollution, including pollution from death. There we will uncover yet another way of interpreting the relation between women and pollution.

III. *The System of Ritual Pollution*

The defining characteristic of a polluting substance in Chinese society is that it prevents those who come in contact with it from associating with the gods. The prohibition is most rigorous for those who come into closest contact with birth fluids—the new mother and her baby. Both are confined to the house for one month to spare T'ien Kung, the highest god, the sight of them. While the mother is "within the month," she must not bathe or wash her hair; she must ingest only certain strengthening tonics. Only when the month is up may she resume normal activities.[13] As for the baby, during the first two or three days of life, efforts are made to cleanse him of the birth fluids he has been in contact with. The herbal tea he is given to drink is sweetened with brown sugar, a "clean" substance that will rid his stomach of any "dirty" blood swallowed during birth.* In Ch'i-nan this appears to be the sole act needed to cleanse the child of the mother's blood. An additional cleansing takes place one month after birth—the child's hair is shaved and he is given a bath in water mixed with several kinds of "clean" herbs—but this cleansing is said to rid the child of the dirt associated with death. "It is in case someone in mourning came into the child's room or touched him."

In some Chinese communities the dirt associated with birth requires more extensive cleaning. In Peihotien (also in northern Taiwan) Margery Wolf reports that one month after birth, a child is "ritually cleansed of the dirt she got from passing through 'the dirty part of a woman' by having her head and eyebrows shaved."[14] Marjorie Topley's Hong Kong informants believed the contamination from the womb to last well past infancy. The pustules that erupt during measles are caused by poison in the body that "came from the womb and was passed to the child. It was 'unclean' because of its origin."† In Ch'i-nan the sores accompanying measles are also considered a release of poison from the body, but my informants made no link between that poison and contact with the womb or birth fluids.‡

Even outside the immediate context of childbirth, women must take care to avoid offending the gods. The gods take offense if they are ex-

---

* In accord with a four-part classification of foodstuffs and herbs as cool, clean, hot, or poison, certain substances are considered clean and able to rid the body of unwanted poisons or dirt.

† Marjorie Topley, "Chinese Traditional Ideas and the Treatment of Disease: Two Examples from Hong Kong," *Man*, 5 (1970): 426. Topley also reports a serious disease called *so-lo*, contracted by men who have intercourse with a woman within 100 days of childbirth (*ibid.*, p. 424). I found no notion of any such disease in Ch'i-nan.

‡ This difference may reflect a more general difference in ideas about pollution prevalent in Hong Kong and in Ch'i-nan. In Ch'i-nan substances that exude from the body, e.g. pus, are often referred to as both poisonous and "really unclean." Ritually polluting substances or persons, however, such as menstrual blood and mourners, are called unclean (as opposed to "really unclean") but never poisonous. Hence it would make little sense for unclean substances associated with birth to appear later as bodily poisons. In Hong Kong, by contrast, the term poisonous can be applied both to things outside the body, like sex or pregnant women, and to ritually polluting things emanating from the body, like menstrual blood. (Marjorie Topley, "Cosmic Antagonisms: A Mother-Child Syndrome," in Arthur P. Wolf, ed., *Religion and Ritual in Chinese Society* [Stanford, Calif., 1974], p. 234.) Thus, the term poisonous provides a clear link between what my Ch'i-nan informants carefully distinguished as "unclean" and "really unclean." Such differences between Chinese communities make it premature to even attempt a description of beliefs about pollution for Chinese society as a whole.

posed to menstrual blood in any way; they may become angry and cause
harm to the offender. The Stove God, whose abode is closest to women's
work areas, will be angered if any article of women's clothing, any cloth
used by a woman to wash, or any basket that has contained women's
clothes should touch the stove. Outside the house, gods may take offense if a menstruating woman enters a temple, especially if she approaches the god's image too closely. Nor can she offer incense to the
gods, a necessary part of the act of worship. This latter prohibition reportedly is not based on fear of the god's anger; people said that when
you know you are dirty, you would not want to draw the gods' attention
to your dirty state by worshiping them because it would be embar-
rassing. Besides, a communication from a menstruating worshiper would
not "get through" to the gods anyway.

The presence of a polluted woman can prevent the gods from making
close contact with other people as well. Sometimes gods are beseeched
to diagnose an illness. To communicate his opinion, the god's spirit will
possess the body of a spirit medium (a tang-ki), using the medium's
voice to speak or hand to write. If a polluted woman is present at these
proceedings, the god's spirit will not possess anyone. Periodically it is
necessary to cleanse a god's image of polluting substances that have accidentally sullied it by carrying the image over a bed of hot coals. The
men who carry the image cross the coals in bare feet. They are not
burned because the god's spirit possesses them. The presence of a polluted woman prevents the god's spirit from entering the men; if the men
are unaware of this interference and proceed with the firewalk, their
feet may be severely burned.

To this point I have simplified the discussion in two ways. First, polluted women are not the only ones who are offensive to the gods and
can prevent communication with them. Any person, male or female,
child or adult, who sets foot inside the room in which a woman has given
birth within the previous month is equally offensive to the gods. No such
person can offer incense to the gods or attend a firewalk. The contamination lasts as long as the mother is within a month of childbirth. A man
whose wife is within the month is automatically considered polluted; it
is assumed that he cannot avoid polluting contact with his wife and child.

Second, other forms of pollution can produce the same effect. Gods
are offended by exposure to the pollution of death as well as to the
pollution of birth. Therefore the doors of any temple along the route
of a funeral procession are closed until it passes; in the room where a
corpse is laid out and encoffining takes place, ancestral tablets and gods'
images are covered by baskets or mats; anyone who is within the pre-

scribed 49-day mourning period refrains from offering incense to the gods. Further, although it is not absolutely essential because the gods will not necessarily be offended, people try to avoid sexual intercourse before worshiping, especially before a major festival. This is not just an extension of the pollution from women's bodies. Informants were quite clear that it is the act of sexual intercourse which is polluting, not just the male's contact with the female's genitals. At a firewalk, when a god is cleansed of all forms of pollution, those who are to carry the god's image must themselves be free of any form of pollution: they abstain from sex for six to twelve days prior to the event; they take care not to wear any clothes made of the cotton used in funeral dress (it goes without saying that they cannot be in mourning), and as a final ablution they pass each foot over an incense pot burning on the ground before beginning the walk.

Given the gods' extreme sensitivity to pollution, we are prompted to ask whether women are allowed less contact with the gods than men because they are more likely to generate pollution. When the higher gods are worshiped on special festival occasions, it is usually men who perform the act of worship. Unless they are menstruating, women are not barred from worshiping on such occasions, and they sometimes participate if the men of the household are absent. But men almost always make it their business to be home at those times. Special festivals are occasions on which a social group—a lineage or a village—is responsible for the celebration of a god's birthday. The group in charge provides sumptuous offerings and opera performances to please and honor the god. Two kinds of benefits may result. First, local leaders and the festival's organizers gain visibility in the community, and, if the festival goes well, political support. Second, it is hoped that the honored god will bestow on the festival's participants the universally sought-after blessings of wealth, many descendants, and family harmony. The same analysis applies when a lineage's early ancestors are worshiped: men worship when political and economic benefits are likely to ensue.

As far as I could determine, there are no festivals for high, powerful gods in Ch'i-nan in which women play a major role. Even cults that relate directly to women's interests and are given considerable prominence elsewhere are of minor importance there. The Weaving Maiden, for example, is worshiped in some areas by groups of women who ask for happy marriages.[15] The goddess is worshiped by some families in Ch'i-nan, but men perform the worship whenever they are home for the occasion.

Where low-ranking supernatural spirits are concerned, by contrast, women are quite free to play a predominant role. "Little low goddesses" like the Bed Mother or Cu-si: Niu-niu are often beseeched to bring sons or to cure a sickly child; their close association with childbirth makes them less clean than the other gods. These goddesses are worshiped regularly by most women in their own homes or at special altars in the back corners of temples, but there are no public festivals in their honor.*

Besides low-ranking supernaturals who reside in the world of the living, women are also permitted to traffic with residents of the world of the dead. When sessions are held in which villagers enter a trance, travel to the underworld, and visit deceased friends and kinsmen, women can participate fully either as observers or as mediums. Spirits of the dead and their world are unclean; hence women, also periodically unclean, may appropriately enter into contact with them. Indeed, in some parts of China practitioners who specialize in raising the souls of the dead are invariably women.[16]

Potentially malevolent spirits of the dead who are abroad among the living are often worshiped by women, not in hopes of their assistance, but in hopes of averting harm. For example, a *kho-kun* ceremony is held by every household on the first and fifteenth of each month. The spirits worshiped are *kui*, ghosts, who prey on the living, causing sickness and other misfortunes unless they are propitiated. Either men or women can worship these beings, but the responsibility seems to fall by default to women. Of the twenty households I observed performing kho-kun in one section of Ch'i-nan, in eighteen the worship was performed by women. In ten cases the woman's husband was not home, but in eight he was home yet made no move to take over the worship.†

It seems clear that there is a hierarchy of spiritual beings depicted here: at the top are clean, high gods worshiped at important times by men; at the bottom, dirty, low spirits and ghosts worshiped and tended by women. The common relegation of women to the worship of the low, unclean end of the hierarchy is appropriate because women are so frequently unclean themselves. Conversely, the near-monopoly by

* For lack of space I will not discuss here the other ritual roles in which women guard the welfare of children. There are principally two: in one the mother performs a certain ritual to call back the lost soul of her ailing child; in the other a child can be taken to a female ritual expert called a Sian-si:-ma, who can also call back the soul.

† These offerings are made privately by each household. Once a year, on the fifteenth day of the seventh month, a community propitiation for the ghosts is held. My notes from 1970 are unclear on whether men or women predominate in this rite, but my impression is that women do. If so, this may be the only public festival on which women more often worship than men. Still, its character is utterly different from that of festivals for the gods. One's only hope in worshiping is to be left alone.

men of the clean, high end of the hierarchy is appropriate because they are much less often unclean.

For a more accurate, albeit more complex, analysis of pollution, I turn now to consider the system of pollution, thus far presented piecemeal, as a whole. The idea of dirty or polluting substances as "matter out of place" is a familiar one.[17] The Chinese material lends itself to a similar notion: things the Chinese consider unclean threaten the order of or are a result of disorder in the family or in the human body. Disorder here has two specific meanings: anything that pierces the boundaries of these two entities is unclean, whether it is something that enters or something that leaves; anything that tends to undermine the tenets of order, any external threat to orderly entities, is unclean. This abstract formulation can be illustrated by drawing together the material already presented, supplemented occasionally by additional information.

In the family, for example, the entrance or exit of members is problematic and requires ritual action. The act of entering or exiting seems to make people dirty (productive of disorder) and in need of cleansing. For this purpose a special plant called *bua-a-chau* is cultivated and protected so its purity is ensured. It is grown in a fenced enclosure so that animals cannot defecate nearby. It is sheltered from birth and death: a woman who is menstruating or within the month cannot touch it; anyone in mourning cannot approach it. If the family cultivating it is in mourning, the plant, too, wears a mourning bracelet, which protects it from the pollution of death. This plant is then used to cleanse those who enter or leave the family. An infant is washed in water infused with it one month after birth, both to rid it of the dirt associated with leaving its mother's body and to mark its entrance into the mother's family.* A woman is washed with it on the day she marries out of her natal family.

When a person leaves a family through death, he or she becomes one of the most polluting objects—a corpse. Everyone who comes into association with the corpse takes measures to protect his family. When a mourner returns home from a funeral, he sets off firecrackers, burns incense, and prepares a tea infused with a charm to ward off the dead person's influence. This is drunk by the most vulnerable family members, the children. Even the deceased's immediate family takes mea-

---

* Adopted children seem to be an exception to this rule. If a child is adopted after the one-month washing, he need not be washed again. It may be that one cleansing of the dirt associated with entering a family is sufficient to cover a subsequent entrance into another family. Or the primary object of this cleansing may be to rid the baby of the pollution associated with birth, a cleansing that would not have to be repeated upon adoption.

sures to protect itself. Some of the ceremonies that follow a death are designed to separate the dead person from all his living relatives.[18]

After death, a spirit is normally reintegrated into his family as an ancestor, whereupon he ceases to be unclean. Those with no descendants to care for them, however, may become wandering, hungry ghosts and be termed unclean on that account. "Hungry ghosts without descendants are the dirtiest of all spirits. They come wandering around with missing heads or limbs, covered with filth and dressed in rags." These ghosts are the epitome of social disorder, contravening the most valued elements of orderly existence. They have no one to carry on their lines of descent, they are without resources, and they are excluded from any social group. Even worse, they destroy order where they can, causing illness and family quarrels.

If ghosts are the dirtiest supernatural beings, gods are the cleanest. They are so clean that besides taking the precautions discussed in the last section, people often wash in a bua-a-chau bath before worshiping them. In contrast to ghosts, gods are the epitome of social order. They are the source of all the things a ghost lacks: descendants, wealth, and peace. Moreover, in their capacity as supernatural magistrates, they can control and subdue disorderly ghosts.* In this same capacity, gods of various ranks literally define the boundaries of social groups, both large and small. In Ch'i-nan, each family worships the Kitchen God; each of the four lineage communities within the village worships the particular Earth God that governs its precincts; the village as a whole worships another Earth God in a central location; and the three villages that share the local market share responsibility for the worship of two more powerful gods called the Ang Kong. In short, most important social groups, from the family on up, are delineated by the worship of gods. The gods' cleanliness seems to derive from their association with right order and neatly bounded social groups.

Just as uncleanness in families is associated with the crossing of boundaries, so it is with the human body. We have already seen how substances that escape across body boundaries are considered unclean. Some of these, such as pus from sores, are indicative of disorder within the body, usually an imbalance of hot elements or an excess of poisonous ones.

Is the pollution attributed to sexual intercourse related to ideas of order and disorder in the body? It is hard to say, in part because vil-

---

* Villagers in Ch'i-nan said that some gods are unclean, i.e. corrupt gods who perform evil acts. Like corrupt government officials, corrupt gods encourage social disorder. Their association with disorder makes them unclean.

lagers are so reluctant to talk about sex that I am uncertain how it relates in their minds to pollution. Perhaps ideas about sexual intercourse widespread in China since ancient times influence the attitudes of country people today. According to these ideas, during intercourse a man absorbs the female yin essence, which strengthens his vital powers. Ejaculation, however, results in the debilitating loss of vital yang essence. Too frequent intercourse so drains a man's vital essence that he is vulnerable to several serious diseases. For this reason numerous techniques are recommended that enable men to avoid ejaculation; women are in no danger, for their supply of yin essence is inexhaustible.[19]

If some such ideas as these are believed by the villagers of Ch'i-nan (a possibility I can neither confirm nor reject), sexual intercourse may be considered polluting in part because it threatens to disrupt the balance of yang and yin in a man's body. If he cannot avoid emitting semen, his health may be impaired by the resulting imbalance. This would not differ greatly from an imbalance of hot and cold elements or an excess of poison in the body, which are sometimes associated with the emission of pus and other unclean fluids across corporeal boundaries.

Even if these ideas have influenced the villagers of Ch'i-nan, they take us only part way toward understanding why sexual intercourse should be considered polluting, for imbalance in the man's body would not pollute the woman. Future investigations may tell us whether the pollution of sex is related to order and disorder in the body, or to the crossing of body boundaries when the male enters the female or the fetal soul (the Thai Sin) enters the woman's body at the moment of conception.

The problematic case of sexual intercourse aside, if it is true that the system of pollution is based on the crossing of bodily or social boundaries, we should now be able to account for facts that initially seem puzzling. Why, for example, should birth be so extremely polluting that anyone who enters the room where it occurs becomes polluted, i.e. is barred from worshiping the gods? Even death pollutes only those in mourning, not all those who venture near a corpse or place of death. Our analysis shows us that unlike death, birth entails crossing both bodily and familial boundaries. Blood flows from the mother's body, and the family must be redefined to include the new member.

Again, why should the birth of a boy be considered less polluting by some Chinese than the birth of a girl? Doolittle writes that a woman is unclean for one month after bearing a son, but for four months after bearing a daughter.[20] And some of Margery Wolf's informants told her that if a newborn baby is a boy, only the mother is unclean, "and the visitors to her room would not suffer the same restrictions as they would had the child been a girl."[21] More graphically, Johannes Frick says that according to folk belief in Tsinghai:

At the time a boy is born, the pure sun sees the birth room submerged in blood and the mother sunk up to her neck in blood. At the birth of a girl the woman in childbed is so immersed in blood that her hair drips with it. The blood over-flows out of the birth room onto the whole courtyard. After the birth of a boy the lying-in period lasts by custom thirty days, but the birth of a girl requires forty days because she is more unclean than a boy.[22]

If integration into a family is part of what makes birth polluting, then it is reasonable that a boy should be less polluting than a girl. A male occupies a firm, permanent position in his family as a future heir to the family estate and as one of those who will perpetuate descent lines. His integration is therefore in a sense less problematic than a girl's, for she belongs to her natal family only temporarily, until she marries out and becomes part of her husband's family.

Beliefs in polluting and unclean things—because of their close asso-ciation with birth and death, and with the entrance and departure of people from social groups—involve problems or dilemmas of serious concern to both men and women.* The central dilemma might be ex-pressed this way: how can we keep families pure and homogeneous and their members united and loyal when, in order to grow, they need out-siders (women with competing loyalties and children whose loyalties are unformed) and when, in addition, all family members must even-tually die? The answer is that by ritual means, outsiders can be cleansed before entering the family, and mourners cleansed of the defiling con-tact with death. Temporary pollution remains a problem, and it is the cause of temporary ruptures between men and the gods. As long as a person's body or family harbors polluting disorder, he or she cannot establish communication with the gods, the most certain representatives of order.

In the foregoing section I have shown that women are not the sole source of pollution. The impression may still remain, however, that when a woman is involved in pollution, the invariable source is the woman's body. It is more accurate to say that problematic events—birth and death—are the sources of pollution, and both men and women are implicated in them. My informants pointed to this interpretation when

---

* See Sherry B. Ortner, "Sherpa Purity," *American Anthropologist* 75 (1973): 49–63, for an analysis that stresses the importance of concepts of pollution as a guide to action for people faced with fundamental problems of the human condition.

they referred to the dirt of happy and of sad events. Sometimes women are more closely associated with these events than men, as in childbirth. At other times men come to be polluted independently of women, as when a relative dies. Even for an event closely associated with women, men seem to be polluted not by the woman in question, but by the event itself. Pollution emanates from the place where childbirth occurs, not from the new mother. Now that more women have their children outside the home, in hospitals and clinics, within-the-month pollution is disappearing. When a baby is born in a hospital, only the delivery room is polluting; when the mother returns home, she leaves the contagion behind. Beyond this, some would say that a husband is automatically polluted when his wife gives birth and that he must wait as long as she to be clean again; it is as if he were affected by the birth in the same way as she.

Moreover, when women are in certain states they are considered dangerous and vulnerable, but not, in the sense used here, polluting. Pregnant women, for example, are often considered a menace to others: they can make children fall sick and cause difficulties for brides.[23] Because of the danger pregnant women pose for brides, in Ch'i-nan a ceremony called Sifting Four Eyes is performed before the bride's dowry is sent to the groom's house. All items in the dowry are passed over a large sieve so that pernicious influences, including those of pregnant women, can be sifted out. "Four Eyes" refers to the two beings in one that a pregnant woman represents—two eyes for her and two for the fetus. As Doolittle explains:

After the articles have been sifted, contact with them is carefully avoided by the female members of [the bride's] family. It is supposed that it would be especially unlucky for her and her affianced husband should any pregnant woman, or any person wearing mourning, handle, or in any manner come in contact with, any of the articles already sifted before they are carried over to the future home of the girl. Such a contact would be expected to produce death in her husband's family, or a future miscarriage on her part, or quarrels and misunderstandings between him and her, or some undesirable result.[24]

In I-ch'ang, Hupeh, during an initiation ceremony for young men on the eve of marriage, comparable protective measures are taken against pregnant women and widows. On the groom's breast "hangs a small bronze mirror about three inches in diameter. This custom rests on the belief that the mirror can counteract the evil influence of widows and 'four-eyed persons,' (i.e., pregnant women). In spite of the power of the mirror, widows and pregnant women are usually excluded from the marriage ceremonies."[25]

At the same time, pregnant women are vulnerable: according to Topley, if a pregnant woman encounters a child with measles, the woman will fail to give birth.[26] Similarly, at a funeral attended by Margery and Arthur Wolf in northern Taiwan, a cry went out to warn pregnant women to stay away when nails were about to be hammered into the coffin "or else something will happen." The Wolfs were told that if "one of the dead person's daughters or granddaughters is pregnant, she must stand astride the threshold of the house, holding a piece of white cloth over her stomach. Other pregnant women should be far enough away so as not to be able to hear the noise of the nails being pounded into the coffin."

We plainly have here a class of anomalous, marginal, or transitional people—pregnant women, widows, brides, grooms, mourners, children —who are both vulnerable and dangerous to others.* A full analysis of the beliefs underlying this classification would go beyond the limits of this essay precisely because pollution is not at issue; people in this category are not called "dirty" for that reason, and, though danger lurks, it does not threaten the relationship between human beings and the gods. I have brought up these beliefs simply to illustrate the difference between women who are dangerous and vulnerable because of their condition (pregnancy or widowhood), and women as potential polluters. Pollution, with its consequent rupturing between people and gods, derives from association with the events of birth and death, which can affect both men and women; pregnancy and widowhood are states known only by women. In this sense the danger associated with pregnancy, pregnant women, and widows is sex-linked in a way that pollution itself is not. Only women can be pregnant or widows, but men as well as women can come into contact with polluting events, though men are less likely to do so.

Conclusion

We are left, then, with three different interpretations of the dangerous power of women. The first looks to the emotional significance of death and birth, the second to women's social role, and the third to the system of ideas about pollution. Are these mutually exclusive or mutually compatible interpretations? Must we choose one or can we keep them all? I would argue that we can reject the second in favor of the third on the grounds that the second leads to an inconsistency, which can be seen by reopening a question raised earlier: does it make sense

* Topley discusses the beliefs of her Hong Kong informants about this class of people in "Cosmic Antagonisms: A Mother-Child Syndrome."

to say that women intentionally hurt men by polluting them in the same way they may hurt men by interfering with their ideal of the family? Women stand to gain security and control over their lives from deliberate interference with male ideals of the family; no such gain accrues to women from deliberate exploitation of their capacity to pollute. Preventing communication between men and the gods is no more in the interest of women than it is of men. If a polluted woman intentionally entered an area where a god was being implored to possess men, her presence might cause either an abortive firewalk and injury to the participants, or the failure of the gods to diagnose an illness. In either event the benefits the gods can bring—health, plenty, and peace—would be denied to kinsmen and neighbors as dear to women as to men, an outcome unlikely to further any woman's interests. Aside from the possibility of interfering with worship, women seem to have no special ability to unleash the destructive power of their menstrual discharge. Menstrual blood is a powerful component of sorcerers' potions, but the knowledge to use it belongs to ritual experts, available for hire by men and women alike.

If the dangerous power of menstrual blood reflects the social role of young women, the two should be parallel in all important respects. But in one important respect they are not parallel: the element of intention in young women's manipulation of the family is not present in their capacity to pollute. This discrepancy leads me to reject the second interpretation in favor of the third, which sees certain events as sources of pollution because of their impact on the stability and integrity of the body and the family. The first interpretation need not be rejected, however. The hypothesis that the emotional significance of blood derives from its association with birth and death is not incompatible with the third interpretation, but rather helps us understand why certain events and not others are seen as disturbing.

But lest we too quickly rule out the relevance of women's social role, let me note that the system of ideas about polluting events does not exist in isolation from the Chinese kinship system. It is no accident that women rather than men are considered outsiders, and that the children women bear must be anchored to their families by elaborate ritual means. It is because the kinship system is focused on male lines of descent that women are depicted on the boundaries, breaking in as strangers. It may be events that are polluting rather than women *per se*, but polluting events are events that intrude new people or remove old ones in a male-oriented kinship system.

This brings us to a final question. If, as I believe to be the case, women do not deliberately use their capacity to pollute against men, what happens when the shoe is on the other foot? Do men deliberately use beliefs in pollution as a weapon against women? Many of the most polluting substances emanate from a woman's reproductive organs, the source of her greatest power over her husband's family—her ability to produce descendants. Once the polluting nature of the sex act (which begins the child's development), menstrual blood (which becomes the child's flesh and bones), and childbirth (which brings the child into the husband's family) is established, the source of a woman's power is obscured, if not rendered invisible by a layer of negative sentiment. While this line of thought is suggestive, I know of no evidence that men intentionally and self-servingly perpetuate these beliefs.

Nonetheless, one cannot ignore the numerous messages that deal with women's reproductive capacity in a negative way. Perhaps the most striking of these is the belief that women who have borne children (or, some say, who die in childbirth) are punished in the underworld for having produced polluting substances. According to Frick, people in Tsinghai say that women who die in childbed are sent to a special section of the underworld called *hsieh-k'eng*, blood pit. There the woman's soul is pinned down by a heavy stone:

The soul groans, yes, cries out in agony. As its eyes anxiously dart all around it sees only blood. It eats only blood clots; it drinks only bloody fluid. It is not the fresh blood of animals—which in its raw state is already an abomination for the people of Tsinghai—but inevitably foul vaginal blood and fluid. The soul cannot rest in the dreadful torment that it endures. Incessantly it groans and cries, but no friendly spirit approaches to help it. All good spirits shun the soul of a woman who has died in childbed.[27]

Sometimes, however, a woman's sons will show their love and pity for her and attempt to lessen or eliminate this punishment by ritual means. As Doolittle explains it:

The object of the *Bloody-Pond ceremony* is to save the spirit of a deceased mother from the punishment of the *Bloody Pond*. Sometimes it is performed several times on the death of the mother of a family of children. This is one way by which they manifest their *filial love* for the deceased.[28]

It is remarkable that in the same ceremony, the fate that women suffer for engendering pollution in the exercise of their procreative powers and the gratitude and pity that at least some men feel for them should be so dramatically juxtaposed.

Doing Business in Lukang

DONALD R. DE GLOPPER

Today the old port of Lukang lies like a beached whale three kilometers inland from the west coast of Taiwan. During the Ch'ing dynasty it was the second largest city of the island, the economic center for a large region of central Taiwan. In the latter part of the nineteenth century the harbor silted up and the city began a slow decline. In the fifteen years after the Japanese occupation of Taiwan in 1895, the economy of Lukang declined precipitously. This decline was due primarily to the construction of the railroad and the reorientation of central Taiwan's trade away from Fukien, via Lukang, and toward Japan, via Keelung. As Lukang slipped down the central-place hierarchy, thousands of its people left to seek their fortunes in Taipei and the growing cities along the railroad. Throughout the Japanese Period (1895–1945), Lukang remained a backwater while other cities boomed.

Lukang is now a placid town of about twenty-eight thousand people. It is regarded by its inhabitants and by outsiders as quaint, old-fashioned, dull and bereft of opportunity, a place where the best way to get on is to get out. Seen from the outside, in an ahistorical perspective, it differs but little from the scores of other country towns that dot the Taiwanese landscape. There is no trace of the old harbor, and the town serves as a market center for the surrounding farmers. It is also a minor center of handicraft and small-scale light industry.

Many of the town's businessmen subsist by providing goods and services to the people of the villages that surround the town. The land around Lukang is intensively cultivated and densely populated, with a rural population density of about twenty-one hundred people per square mile. Most of the surplus agricultural produce of the area is not marketed through Lukang, but goes directly to the cities or to processing factories. This obviates any substantial brokerage role for the businessmen of the town. Farmers sell their crops for cash, some of which is spent in Lukang; they do not rely to any great extent on credit from Lukang shops.

Farmers can bypass Lukang and send their crops directly to the cities or to large wholesale markets some distance from their homes because of the highly efficient transport available in Taiwan today. Most villages have access to an all-weather road, and major cities are linked by paved roads and railroads. It is only twelve kilometers by paved road from Lukang to the city of Changhua, the regional economic center, and from there it is easy to reach the rest of Taiwan. Today it is possible for inhabitants of Lukang or of the surrounding villages to take a bus, a taxi, a motorcycle, or a motorized cart to Changhua, or to go another thirty kilometers to the metropolis of Taichung. Both Changhua and Taichung offer a wider selection of shops, cinemas, restaurants, and medical facilities than does Lukang. The retail shops and service enterprises of Lukang must compete with those of the larger cities. They must also compete with smaller establishments in the countryside. Population growth and the rural prosperity following land reform and technical improvements in agriculture have led to a great increase in the number of rural shops and to the growth of small new commercial centers in the countryside. The settlement of Ts'ao Kang, some seven kilometers north of Lukang, was as late as 1958 simply a large village with a police station, a primary school, and a bus stop for Lukang and Changhua. Two rows of concrete shop houses that have risen from the rice fields now supply the local farmers with their daily necessities.

Lukang's central-place functions and role as market town have been undercut, then, both by improved transportation facilities and by commercial growth in the countryside itself. On the other hand, population growth and a vastly improved standard of living have generated a much greater total volume of business, as well as a mass demand for many products and services that simply did not exist twenty years ago. There are now far more businesses in Lukang than twenty years before, and the town remains one of the major commercial centers of Changhua Hsien. Furthermore, the improvement of transport and the growing use of trucks rather than the railroad, along with the rapid growth of Taiwan's total economy, has made it possible for Lukang to become a center of light industry.

The city is now the site of some five hundred small factories and handicraft enterprises. Some of them produce things like plows, bricks, or coffins, which are consumed within the town or its marketing area. Others produce articles for the island-wide or the international market.

Small factories turn out hinges, twine, motorcycle reflectors, and phonograph cabinets for sale in Taipei or anywhere else in Taiwan. Others manufacture such things as scissors, toy parasols, and screwdrivers, which are shipped off to Thailand, Zambia, and the United States. This sector of the town's economy is firmly integrated with national and international markets. It is also the sector that has grown most rapidly in the past twenty years, and the one in which the largest profits can be made.

Today the population of Lukang is only slightly larger than it was in 1900, and many of its natives have emigrated to the booming cities of Taipei, Taichung, and Kaohsiung. Lukang has not experienced the sort of explosive growth that many of the towns in the area have, and it is no longer the regional commercial center that it was a hundred or fifty years ago. Natives of the town complain that there are no opportunities there, that business is not especially good. But many new enterprises have been founded, and some local businessmen have done quite well for themselves. It is true that if one wants to become really rich, to succeed in a big way, one must leave Lukang and try one's luck in the speculative, highly competitive business world of Taipei or Kaohsiung. But it is still possible to make a fair living in Lukang, to become moderately wealthy, and many people have chosen to stay at home rather than join the migrants. They are the subjects of this account, businessmen of small or medium scale in a quiet provincial town.*

In September 1968 the administrative units that make up urban Lukang had a registered population of 28,464 people. The none-too-accurate business registration statistics of the Changhua Hsien government listed 1,083 businesses in the city. A count of shops and street sellers in November 1967 showed 711 shops, 234 market and street stalls, and 129 street peddlers. Roughly, then, Lukang has one retailer of goods or services for every fourteen adults, a shop or stall for every five households, and one registered business for every seven males above the age of fifteen. Almost all the retail shops are family businesses, employing only the owner and his household, or are run by the wife to supplement family income. Few manufacturing or craft firms have more than ten employees. Such small-scale factories or workshops are of course not peculiar to Lukang; they are typical of Taiwan (Chen Cheng-hsiang 1963: 537–39).

One's first impression of business in Lukang is that there is so much of it on so small a scale. The town has no large factories, nor is its econ-

* My fieldwork in Lukang from 1967 to 1968 was supported by the Foreign Area Fellowship Program, whose support I gratefully acknowledge.

omy dominated by a single product. Woodworking is one of the most common local crafts, but it is carried out by scores of small enterprises, each producing one particular item, from night-soil buckets to carved altar tables. The economic structure of the town is best summed up as one of a large number of very small-scale enterprises with extreme functional differentiation and diversity. One small shop makes and sells bicycle seat covers, nothing else. On the streets of Lukang one can buy dried fish, teapots, a single needle, shirts of the latest gaudy fashion, electric pumps, hormone-enriched chicken feed, cabinets for ancestral tablets, and deep-fried oyster cakes. It is possible to have one's watch, motorcycle, thermos bottle, or insecticide-sprayer repaired, to have one's teeth capped with gold, or to hire a specialist to extricate one's grandmother's soul from the Buddhist hell. The natives of the town manufacture everything from bean curd, to the huge vats used by pickle makers, to the fake aborigine artifacts that will eventually be sold to Japanese tourists in Taipei.

There are no large factories or wholesalers. The streets are lined with many small and totally independent businesses, often selling or manufacturing the same thing. There are, for example, twenty-nine grocery stores, each selling canned goods, seasonings, flour, sugar, and the like. There are twenty-one Chinese drug stores, nineteen furniture shops, and nine photographers. One finds the same multiplicity of apparently identical small shops that Barbara E. Ward discussed in her article on cash and credit crops (Ward 1960: 148). It follows from this that there is no hierarchy of business in Lukang; that is, no pattern of relations between large and small firms, or between wholesaler and retailer.

Nor are the businesses of Lukang joined in any common formal association. There is no chamber of commerce. All trades in Taiwan are organized by the government into quasi-official trade associations (*t'ung-yeh kung-hui*). The territorial base of such associations is the county (*hsien*) rather than the town or city. There is no Lukang branch of the druggists' association; the local druggists are simply members of the Changhua Hsien druggists' association. In Lukang such trade associations are almost universally regarded as otiose, as something imposed from the outside by the government for its own ends. The usual response to questions about the functions of trade associations is a laugh, and the comment that they don't do anything. With the exceptions of the barbers' and butchers' associations, trade associations in Lukang do not regulate prices, control entry to the trade, or settle disputes between members. To a large degree, then, the small businesses of the town function as autonomous units, with few formal constraints on their operation or on the relations they establish with customers or suppliers.

At this point it is useful to raise the general question of business relations, and of the forces that shape or constrain such relations. Economic relations in Chinese society have been described as highly particularistic and functionally diffuse (Levy 1949: 352–58). Studies of Chinese business have demonstrated the importance of such things as kinship, common place of origin or schooling, and particularistic personal relations (see Fried 1953; Ryan 1961; Silin 1964; T'ien 1953; Ward 1960). To understand why economic relations take the form they do, it is necessary to understand the categories of personal relations and the solidarities that are thought to exist between persons whose relations are described in certain terms (Fried 1953; Silin 1964). It is also necessary to consider the conditions under which relations of trust can be established (Silin 1964) and the way credit is established and granted (T'ien 1953; Ward 1960), as well as hiring practices and the reasons given for trading with one firm rather than another (Levy 1949; Fried 1953).

Here I want to discuss the pattern of business relations in Lukang in 1967–68. I am interested in the sorts of things that shape, influence, and constrain such relations. I am also interested in the way the businessmen of Lukang describe their economic relations, in what they see as important or necessary for the establishment of some degree of mutual confidence. To discuss these matters it is necessary to say a bit about the social structure of Lukang, the matrix within which business relations are established, as well as about the sorts of businesses the description is based on.

It is important to point out that the population of Lukang is homogeneous, in the sense that nearly everyone who lives there was born there, as were their fathers and grandfathers. Many people have left Lukang, but hardly any have moved in. The few resident outsiders work as schoolteachers, police, or functionaries in public administration. They do not engage in business. All of the businessmen in town are natives, and, as far as I know, all the businesses are owned by local men. Everyone therefore shares a common place of origin; everyone is *t'ung-hsiang*. Furthermore, the people of Lukang share a strong sense of local identity and pride. The social boundaries between Lukang and the outside world are well defined. It is a very parochial place. Its inhabitants are given to frequent assertions of their solidarity and community, and claim that "in Lukang everyone knows everyone else, and people get along well." Since there are some twenty-eight thousand people, everyone does not in fact know everyone else, but people talk as if they did or could if they wanted to. The stress on parochial identity and solidarity goes along with a certain coolness toward those outsiders resident in the town. The manager of one of the two banks, a man from Taichung, described society in Lukang as extraordinarily self-contained, turned in on itself. This strong sense of local solidarity has consequences for business relations, for everyone I talked with agreed that it would be impossible, or at best very difficult, for an outsider, even a Taiwanese from Changhua city, to open a business in Lukang and make a success of it. "Maybe if he had lived here for ten years or so and knew a lot of people fairly well, or if he had a monopoly in something people had to have, then he could do it. But otherwise he'd fail."

If the people of Lukang stress the distinctions between themselves and everyone else, they minimize distinctions among themselves. They recognize certain obvious differences—some are rich, some poor; some live in one neighborhood, others in another; some have one surname, others another; some earn their living in one way, some in another. But each distinction cuts a different way. There are no highly visible or corporate subgroups within the population of the city. Lukang consists of a number of named neighborhoods, each with its own temple. But every neighborhood contains rich and poor, people of various surnames, and men who earn their living in many different ways. One can speak of the people of a neighborhood as a unit, a group, only when they are contrasted with the people of another neighborhood, as they may be on certain ritual occasions. Lukang's population bears three major surnames and a host of less common ones. But those of one surname have little in common besides that name. A man's surname is important if he is worshipping his ancestors or considering a marriage, but in other situations its significance is less certain. In short, within the general category of "Lukang men," every individual is a potential member of many subgroups, each defined by different criteria and important in certain specific contexts. There are no bounded and corporate groups between the town itself and individual households.

Businessmen I talked with were unanimous in asserting that such categories as surname or neighborhood, in and of themselves, were of no importance in doing business. Membership in such categories was acknowledged as important for some purposes, but not for business. The field of potential partners to a business relation extended to all natives of Lukang, and was not limited to fellow members of a defined segment of the town's populace. The autonomy and the freedom of the individual businessman were stressed, and I was assured that one was free to establish business relations with anyone one wanted to.

This does not mean, however, that business relations within Lukang are established at random, or that they consist only of relations of exchange, based on pure economic rationality in a free market. There are certain constraints on business relations, and pure economic rationality is not the sole determinant of the structure of economic relations. It is simply that some of the factors that influence business relations in overseas Chinese communities or in large urban centers do not operate in Lukang. After all, if all of one's potential partners in a business relation are one's *t'ung-hsiang*, and every third one bears the same surname, one cannot use such criteria to narrow down the field of possible partners, as one could perhaps in a large city or an overseas community. Other criteria will be used.

The very first thing to say about the structure of business relations in Lukang is that one does not do business with people one does not know. No one deals with strangers. Business relations are always, to some degree, personal relations. They need not be very close, but both participants in a business relation should be acquainted, familiar, "siek-sai" as the Taiwanese say (cf. Mandarin *shu-ssu*).

At this point it is appropriate to make clear just what sorts of business I am talking about, for the pattern of business and credit relations will vary from one trade to another. A vegetable retailer does not have the same sorts of relations as the owner of a factory that produces for the international market, and the owner of a rice mill deals with different sorts of people than a man who makes furniture. In some sorts of business, access to supplies or markets is restricted. In Lukang this is true of the trade in rice and fertilizer, for these commodities are controlled by local governmental and administrative bodies. It is also true of some building suppliers and contractors, most of whose business is devoted to public works. The owners of such businesses must establish and cultivate very close relations with those local officials who control their supplies and constitute their market. Since such relations depend to a large extent on favors and favoritism, they contravene the official regulations that, in theory, govern the allocation of scarce supplies and of contracts. They are technically illegal and are therefore shrouded in secrecy, and I do not intend my remarks to apply to them.

The businesses with which I am most familiar—like most of the businesses in Lukang—are those in which access to supplies, labor, and markets is relatively unrestricted. The owners of such businesses have a choice of many people with whom they can establish business relations, and potential customers have a choice of many establishments to buy from. The businesses are small and are managed directly by the owner or owners. Most businesses in Lukang fall into this category rather than the previous one. The ones I know best are the cloth retailers, the furniture manufacturers, the wood-carvers, the sawmills, the hardware stores and the vegetable retailers. A common vocabulary is used among them to discuss business relations, although the precise meaning of the terms varies somewhat from one trade to another.

In every case the most important concept, the term most often used in discussing business and its problems, is *hsin-yung*. This is a fairly complex concept, and can be translated in several ways, depending on its context. The dictionary definition is "credit," and it is used in this way in the term for a credit cooperative. Colloquially it means "to credit, to have confidence in; to be worthy of confidence and credit." One speaks of a man's *hsin-yung*, meaning his trustworthiness, his willingness and ability to meet his business and financial obligations. A man who can't pay his debts, who for whatever reason fails to meet his obligations, immediately loses his *hsin-yung*. Business relations of mutual confidence are described as having *hsin-yung*. The word also refers to the quality and reliability of goods. One may ask of a piece of cloth or a radio, "How's its *hsin-yung*?" Is it sturdy, does it work well, will it fall apart in a month?

Hsin-yung refers to an individual's or a firm's reputation, reliability, credit rating. It is the most important thing in business, a firm's most valuable asset. People say that to start a business one needs capital, but capital isn't enough. One must have *hsin-yung*, and to have *hsin-yung* one must know people, have a good reputation with some set of people, such as the other members of one's trade. Similarly, when a business fails, as often happens, the failure is described as the result of a loss of *hsin-yung*: "If someone, for whatever reason, can't pay his bills when they are due, he immediately loses his *hsin-yung*. No one will advance him any more money or goods, and his creditors start demanding immediate repayment. That's the end—he goes bust."

Hsin-yung is predicated on performance in business. It is not given or ascribed. Nobody has good *hsin-yung* just because his surname is Lin or Chen. It has no direct relation to an individual's moral character or general popularity. An unpleasant man who pays all his bills on time will have better *hsin-yung* than a good fellow who can't meet his obligations. In at least one sense *hsin-yung*, like a credit rating, is a scalar quantity, of which one can have more or less. And one can gain or lose it by increments, or, in the case of losing it at least, all at once.

Hsin-yung in the restricted sense of credit and *hsin-yung* in the more general sense of reputation and trustworthiness meet in the nearly universal practice of doing business with postdated checks. Retail transactions are usually in cash, but those between businesses almost always involve payment with a check dated anywhere from ten days to a year later. Thirty days seems to be the most common period, followed by ten and then by ninety days. The use of postdated checks is explained as being the "custom" of businessmen, "the way you do business. If you are a serious businessman, then you use checks." It is claimed that even marginal retailers and petty traders will open an account with the credit bureau of the farmers' association or the credit cooperative, simply so that they can write checks and thus be proper businessmen.

At one point the Ministry of Finance ruled that postdated checks are illegal and may be cashed immediately. Since anyone who refuses to accept postdated checks will have great difficulty doing business at all, the ruling has had little effect (Tenenbaum 1963: 73). Certainly no one I talked with in Lukang seemed aware that postdated checks were illegal, for everyone said that one great advantage of checks was that they were legal documents, admissible in court. If someone failed to pay his check when it was due, he could be taken to court. Even if he formally declared bankruptcy, one could at least get a settlement of 30 percent of what he owed. In fact very few people actually resort to the courts, but it is claimed that since everyone knows what would happen if they did, they simply settle for 30 percent of the debt.

People say that in the past, before 1945, there were no checks, or that they were used only by big businessmen. Business then was said to be based solely on verbal agreements, which made *hsin-yung* and mutual confidence far more important than they are now. The stress on *hsin-yung* and verbal agreements is said to have restricted the number of people one could deal with, since they had to be very well known to be trusted. The present system of checks is said to be better because it permits greater flexibility, and allows dealing between businessmen in the absence of very close personal ties.

The acceptance of postdated checks is of course a form of credit extended by the payee, and in this sense almost all business except retail sales operates on credit. The credit is not free. Businessmen claim that there is no interest on a postdated check—and indeed they charge no interest as such. But if they expect that most payments for what they are selling will be by postdated check, they simply allow for that factor in the quoted price and give a discount for immediate cash payment. Timber, for example, is sold by a cubic measure called a *ts'ai*. The price of timber fluctuates, but it is always cheaper by five *mao* (half a New Taiwan dollar, U.S. 1.25 cents) per *ts'ai* if the customer pays with cash instead of a thirty-day check. This amounts to an interest charge for credit.

It is impossible to determine the exact interest rate for postdated checks in general, for the cash discount varies both with the amount of the purchase and with the relation between buyer and seller. The precise wholesale price of commodities varies for different customers according to their informal credit rating, their *hsin-yung*. A large, well-established firm whose continued custom is desirable will usually get things at a lower unit price than a small, more marginal shop, even when both pay with a thirty-day check. Such variation can be regarded either as a price concession to the larger firm in the interest of higher volume and long-term sales, or as a higher interest rate on the credit extended to the poorer risk.

In general, however, interest charges on postdated checks appear to be equivalent to or slightly higher than those for unsecured personal loans. The following table represents the informed opinion of a bank official in Lukang, with interest calculated, as it so often is in Taiwan, as simple interest on a per diem basis.

INTEREST RATES IN LUKANG, MARCH 1968

Category	Interest Rate (New Taiwan dollars)
Secured mortgage loan	$3.9/10,000/day = 1.17%/month = 14.24%/year
Bank credit loan	5/10,000/day = 1.5%/month = 18.25%/year
Private loan (est.)	6/10,000/day = 1.8%/month = 21.9%/year
Postdated check (est.)	7/10,000/day = 2.1%/month = 25.6%/year

The figures for private loans and postdated checks are, of course, estimates, and instances of both higher and lower rates could be found. Woodworkers said that it was about 2 percent cheaper to buy timber for cash than to pay with a thirty-day check. An old, well-established draper's shop received a discount of 1.8 percent per month if it paid cash rather than using the customary sixty-day check.

A postdated check, then, represents a fairly expensive form of credit. One wonders why the practice is as common as it is. People in Lukang claimed that it was partly a matter of status and emulation, men using checks to demonstrate their standing as proper merchants, and tending to extend the period of their checks in a spirit of keeping up with the Chens: "If you give me a thirty-day check, then I'll give you one for thirty days. Then you'll give me one for sixty days, and so on. Why, right now in the Western drug business they're using checks that run for as long as a year. There's no real reason for that; it's just this sort of competition." Nevertheless, one tends to feel that there is something more involved than simple status emulation. Many small businessmen clearly use checks because they do not have the ready cash, and other, cheaper, forms of credit are not available to them. It is almost impossible for a small businessman to get a loan from a bank or from the credit cooperative without collateral, "a house and fields" as people say. A formal loan involves a great deal of fuss and red tape. It often necessitates asking rich men to serve as guarantors, which obligates one to them, and it is sometimes necessary to provide gifts or entertainment for the bank or credit cooperative officials as well. It is too much bother (*ma-fan*), say small businessmen, and not a practical alternative.

In spite of high interest rates, postdated checks do have some advantages. Like any other form of credit, they permit the retailer to stock his shop with a wider selection of goods, which he need not pay for unless he sells. Such increased inventories in retail outlets are also to the advantage of the manufacturer or wholesaler, for they promote better distribution and more sales. They also permit a certain degree of flexibility in business arrangements, more than would be the case if all transactions were in cash. Cloth sellers, for example, can return a bolt of cloth if they have not sold any of it during the sixty-day period of their checks, or they can keep it for another sixty days at no increased cost. If they cut the bolt, it is theirs and they must pay for it. This practice, incidentally, gives rise to occasional dramas at the draper's, when a customer has her heart set on a certain kind of cloth, which is one of the unpopular, uncut bolts. The shopkeeper does not want to sell her a few feet, lest he have to pay for the whole bolt and be stuck with it. He therefore quotes a ridiculously high price and refuses to be bargained down, tries to catch her fancy with other sorts of cloth, and offers another, more expensive, pattern at an actual loss, all the while trying to weigh up the relative disadvantages of refusing to sell her what she wants—perhaps losing her custom and that of her friends and relatives—and of letting her have it and losing on the sale.

One furniture-manufacturing firm decided to install power tools and thus raise its production. The tools arrived, but the workmen, skilled craftsmen used to making everything by hand, refused to use them. They justified their Luddite position by saying they were not familiar with the machines, wouldn't be able to make such fine, high-quality furniture with them, and were afraid of losing their fingers and being unable to work at all. They may also have been aware that a machine which does the work of two men puts one of the men out of a job, as had happened that year when another furniture-maker in town installed a set of machines. After a series of meetings with the disgruntled workmen, the owner of the firm stopped payment on the postdated check he had used to pay for the machines and told the factory to come take the machines back.

Postdated checks also permit businessmen to get credit from many different sources and thus avoid becoming too dependent on any single supplier. People in Lukang often cited this as one of the primary reasons for the popularity of postdated checks. Most businessmen in Lukang pursue a conscious policy of spreading their patronage, of purchasing goods from several suppliers. Grocery stores get soy sauce or soft drinks from two or three distributors; cloth retailers deal with fifteen or twenty wholesalers; and woodworkers purchase timber, often the same kind, from several sawmills. Such a practice also permits the retailer or small manufacturer to play wholesalers off against each other, to shop for credit. Salesmen court shopkeepers with promises of special deals and token gifts. Soft-drink companies distribute T-shirts and baseball caps bearing the name of their product, and every grocer in Lukang seems to clothe his children in shirts proclaiming the virtue of some soft drink. Similarly, building suppliers' children glory in hats advertising paint, while druggists' children go about in shirts emblazoned with the names of aphrodisiac tonics. Such conditions obtain only when there are several competing suppliers. If something is in short supply or is monopolized by one distributor the situation is reversed, and the retailers do the courting.

When compared with the old system of business relations based on verbal agreements, under which close relations of mutual confidence were of the utmost importance, the use of postdated checks can be seen as a sign of a shift toward a more legal-rational, functionally specific foundation for business relations. But *hsin-yung*, if not as all-important as in the past, is still very much a part of the businessman's world. Accepting a postdated check, after all, involves the extension of credit and trust to the writer of the check, and indicates some degree of mutual confidence. One does not accept a check from just anyone. Some checks are inherently better than others. Businessmen prefer checks from the bank to those from the credit bureau of the farmers' association, for it takes less money to establish an account with the farmers' association than with the bank, and people with such accounts are considered more likely to default.

A check will not be accepted from a complete stranger. The first few transactions in any business relation require payment in cash. Only after a few mutually satisfactory exchanges, when the participants have become more "intimate" and better acquainted, will a check be accepted. One must first establish the reliability of the other. The trustworthiness of wholesalers and suppliers is as problematic as that of anyone else, and retailers test them carefully. A draper explained to me that when a new wholesaler is introduced to him, a lot depends on just who introduces him, and on how well he trusts that man. The introducer is in no narrow sense responsible for the wholesaler; he is definitely not a guarantor, but his recommendations do carry weight. Some wholesalers, salesmen in fact, come by without being introduced. In such cases the retailer never buys anything at the first visit. The salesman returns, showing samples of his wares and offering cigarettes and betel nut, the tokens of sociability; and after he has come at least three times, the retailer may buy a little and see whether he is honest and trustworthy. The retailer will also discuss the salesman or wholesaler with other retailers, and see what their experience with him has been, what they think of him. If he proves reliable, the retailer will eventually buy more and more from him.

The wholesaler is of course equally concerned with the *hsin-yung* of his customers. When he approaches a shop, with or without an introduction, he will ask all the other wholesalers he knows about its *hsin-yung*. He will also inquire of the other shopkeepers he knows how the potential customer's business is going. *Hsin-yung* is based on a series of mutually satisfactory transactions, and reports of the transactions of others are also taken into account when calculating the *hsin-yung* of a particular businessman. In this latter sense, *hsin-yung* is reputation, informal credit rating. Within the confines of Lukang, where it is claimed with some exaggeration that "everyone knows everyone else," the reputation of most businessmen is well if not too accurately known to others in the same line, the *nei-hang jen*. All transactions take place before a potential audience, or chorus, of *nei-hang jen*, who observe and comment on each other's doings. This is why it is so disastrous for an individual to fail to pay a check when it comes due. Everyone hears about it, and the unhappy defaulter loses the confidence, not only of the person holding the worthless check, but of everyone else who might accept a check from him. He loses his *hsin-yung* and is on the way to failure unless he can somehow come up with the money in a hurry and convince his skeptical creditors that such a lapse will not occur in the future.

This quasi-public sense of *hsin-yung* as credit-rating in the eyes of one's *nei-hang jen* is one reason that it would be hard for an outsider to do business in Lukang, for he would not be privy to the gossip and speculation about each other's financial affairs that occupies so much of the time and energy of the natives of the town. Such information is public in that it is a matter of public concern and interest, but not public in the sense of being freely available, for each businessman attempts to keep his own financial affairs a matter of the deepest secrecy, while eagerly speculating on those of his fellows. A missionary once noted that "all China is a whispering gallery," and the statement certainly applies to Lukang. The extension of credit and trust depends on information, and, given the habit of extreme secrecy about financial affairs, one's fellow townsmen and those in the same line have more information, imperfect though it may be, than do strangers. One is more likely to obtain credit from fellow townsmen or relatives than from strangers, not because of the prescriptive solidarities of co-residence or common kinship, for such credit is in most cases paid for at fairly high rates, but because one's intimates have more information and are in a better position to judge their chances of being paid back.

Thus, in the furniture trade there is a fairly common pattern of buying timber from sawmills in Lukang with a check but paying cash for that purchased in the big timber centers of Chiayi and Fengyuan, where the mills are in no position to judge the reliability of a small firm in Lukang. Besides deciding whether or not to accept a check, one must also agree on when it will be paid. Since time is money, and interest is calculated by the day, it seemed reasonable to me that the time a check ran before payment was due would be associated with the *hsin-yung* of the writer. I assumed that long-term credit would be extended only to well-established firms, which would be less likely to default and more able to pay the presumably higher interest on a long-term check. However, those businessmen with whom I discussed the question were unanimous in asserting that the length of time a check ran had nothing to do with *hsin-yung*, attributing the period of a check either to established custom in certain trades or to status emulation. One explained, "Look, if I'm afraid you won't be able to pay your check, it won't make me any happier if it's for ten days instead of two months. And if I know you can pay it, then it's not too important when it comes due, because I know I can count on it." I remain dubious that the matter is quite so simple, but since it was not possible to get precise information on just how much different firms were paying for checks of varying length, I cannot flatly contradict what everyone told me. However, my material on the furniture trade, which is both fairly complete and fairly reliable, suggests that long-term checks are, in fact, used only by those firms with good *hsin-yung*. Old, well-established furniture-making concerns tend either to pay cash for their timber or to buy it with exceptionally long-running checks, up to three months. Smaller firms almost always pay with a thirty-day or occasionally a ten-day check, while the most marginal usually pay cash, presumably because no one is willing to accept a check from them.

The businessmen of Lukang recognize a category of relations called "business relations." With the exception of retail sales, business relations can be described as those in which postdated checks are exchanged. In such relations *hsin-yung* and some degree of intimacy are important. But all the businesmen I talked with insisted quite firmly that business relations can be established with anyone at all, and that they are not influenced or constrained by such things as kinship, co-residence, sworn brotherhood, or relations that could be said to involve an element of sentiment, of *kan-ch'ing*. *Hsin-yung* is said to be determined entirely by a man's performance as a businessman, and to have nothing to do with the solidarities of common surname, schooling, or worship. Business relations are described as explicitly predicated on economic rationality and mutual self-interest. They are narrowly defined, functionally specific ties, based on the satisfactory performance of contractual obligations and sanctioned ultimately by the legal system. As one man said after I had been asking about the relation of such things as affinal kinship, co-residence, and common schooling to *hsin-yung*, "Look, *hsin-yung* is just a matter of whether or not someone pays his checks when they come due. That's all there is to it."

The owner of a furniture shop carefully explained that although he could be said to be "intimate" with the owners of the sawmills from which he bought his timber, and that he might occasionally go to a feast or wedding at their homes or invite them to his, such social relations were not necessary for the conduct of business and did not influence his decision to buy from one sawmill rather than another. "There are many kinds of wood, and the quality of each kind varies. I need several kinds of wood to make furniture, depending on just what I'm making. If this week I should need some cedar or *wu-t'ung* wood, I go out and see which sawmill has it and how good it is. I buy it from the place that best suits my particular needs. And the quality of the timber is very important. A lot of the quality is determined by the skill of the workers in the sawmill. I bought a lot of wood last week from Mr. Chen's mill, because his craftsmen are so skillful. The man who runs the planer is careful, so the planks are smooth and of uniform thickness. My workmen don't have to waste time planing them down by hand, and I don't have to pay for expensive wood like cedar that gets wasted as shavings and scrap. In this business it's the quality of the materials and the skill of the workmen that counts. That's the most important thing. It's not a matter of intimacy or sentiment (*kan-ch'ing*) at all."

The same man employs some twenty-five skilled cabinetmakers and apprentices. None of them are his kinsmen. When he wants more craftsmen he tells his workers, who recommend their "friends" or *nei-hang jen*, who are not their kinsmen either. He decides to hire or fire workers, and determines their wages, on the basis of their skill, on how well they perform their jobs as craftsmen. He sells his furniture to customers who walk in from the street. They come from all over central Taiwan, for Lukang furniture has a high reputation. He estimates that perhaps 30 percent of his customers come because other satisfied customers have recommended the shop to them. But, like all the owners of furniture firms with whom I talked, he insists that customers always visit a number of shops to compare quality and prices, and that recommendations do not determine where a customer will buy.

People in Lukang tend to deny that other sorts of social relationships or solidarities have any relation to business. One restaurant owner responded to my questions about the utility of sworn brotherhood in business by replying, "No, no, you don't understand. Business is an affair of money. Sworn brotherhood has nothing to do with money. It's just an affair of sentiment, of *kan-ch'ing*." People from the same neighborhood are described as "intimate" because they all know each other, and they form a group defined by their relation to their neighborhood temple and its annual festival. But this sort of relation or intimacy is said to be one of pure sociability, with no instrumental purpose.

In ideal terms, people in Lukang describe the sum of their social relations with a set of discrete categories. There are business relations; there are kinship relations; there are neighborly relations; and there are what are usually called "social" relations. Each of these has its own principles and purposes, its own satisfactions and problems. One expects different things from, and owes different things to, the people in each category. If one defines business relations narrowly as relations of buying and selling, then other sorts of relations can be seen to have little to do with business. Here, it is important to keep in mind the extensive structural differentiation and the degree of integration with the national economy that characterize Lukang's economy. It is unlikely that the owner of a factory that makes scissors, some of which are exported to Ghana, will have very many kinsmen or neighbors who are even potential participants in his business relations. Nor will a retailer who deals with a fairly large number of wholesalers, many of them residents of other communities, be able to call on presumed solidarities of common residence or schooling.

But business involves more than just buying and selling, and in prac-

tice the different categories of social relations tend to overlap somewhat. Simple economic rationality and functional specificity suffice to
explain much of the pattern of economic relations in Lukang, but they
are not the only forces at work. If one looks at other aspects of business
life, one finds that, in certain situations, what may be loosely described
as particularistic and functionally diffuse personal relations are of considerable significance. Their importance is most easily seen if one looks
at problems of credit, of access to restricted or limited supplies or markets, and of partnership.

Most businesses operate partially on credit extended by suppliers
through postdated checks, on the basis of some degree of "intimacy"
and mutual confidence. But since a few satisfactory cash transactions
must take place before a check will be accepted, it is impossible to start
a business on credit. Nor is it assumed that a business will regularly
yield such smooth profits that all checks can be paid when they come
due. Difficulties and slack periods are to be expected. Yet if checks are
not paid on time, *hsin-yung* is lost. Often it is necessary to borrow or
somehow raise funds to pay a check and preserve one's reputation, or
simply to meet operating expenses during slack periods. Neither the
bank nor the credit cooperative is a practicable source of credit for most
small businessmen. Given the norm of extreme reticence about financial
affairs, the common practice of keeping two or more sets of books, and
the absence of certified public accountants and of any reliable public
system of credit ratings, the banks are in no position to make rational
economic decisions about which businesses are good risks. They perforce
fall back on making loans only with substantial collateral, a practice not
very different from pawnbroking (see Tenenbaum 1963: 73). Small businessmen in Lukang often remark that the only people who can get loans
from banks are those who don't need them. To start a business and to
meet unexpected difficulties, businessmen must rely on credit obtained
through informal, private channels.

The term used to describe such informal relations of credit and mutual assistance is *min-ch'ing*. Rotating credit societies, sworn brotherhoods and unsecured personal loans provide examples of *min-ch'ing*.
People say that *min-ch'ing* depends on verbal agreements; nothing is
written down. Obligations predicated on *min-ch'ing* are thus not legally
enforceable, since there is no properly witnessed and sealed piece of
paper to introduce as evidence in court. Such arrangements are sanctioned by reciprocity and appeal to community opinion. There is some
risk in all such relations, and people are reluctant to participate unless
they know and trust the others involved. It is assumed that people one

has grown up with, who are committed to life in Lukang and bound up in its complex nexus of local social relations, are more worthy of trust than are strangers. People who have a family in Lukang, who have a general reputation for probity and have demonstrated a concern for community opinion are good candidates for an association or relation based on *min-ch'ing*.

Min-ch'ing is described as quite distinct from "business relations," and indeed it is. But *min-ch'ing* relations have an important, if somewhat indirect, effect on business. Relations with others in temple or festival committees, in rotating credit societies, in sworn brotherhoods, or in the informal groups that habitually sit in shops and exchange gossip are not described as "business relations." Rather, they are described as participation in "society," as "knowing people," or as affairs of general-ized sociability, sentiment, or *kan-ch'ing*. By participating in such activ-ities, by contributing time and money to temples, and by occasional acts of charity, a man defines himself as a responsible member of the com-munity, a moral person concerned with the affairs of others and with their opinion of him. Such a person is likely to receive aid, including financial aid, when he needs it. It is possible to abstain from such activ-ities and suffer no immediate injury to one's business. As long as checks are paid on time and the goods one purveys are of competitive price and quality, there is no loss of *hsin-yung*. But should troubles arise, the unsociable merchant is on his own; no one will go out of his way to help him.

In an emergency it is possible to borrow money from close kinsmen, or from such people as sworn brothers, if one has any. But such aid, even from brothers, may be given grudgingly, and it may be made clear that it represents a favor. The favor as well as the money will have to be returned. People dislike being under a special obligation to anyone else, even their own brothers. It is also possible to get a personal loan from one of several wealthy men in the city who act as moneylenders. This is to be avoided if at all possible. Not only is the interest high, but one is obligated to the wealthy man and perhaps to the person who act-ed as go-between in arranging the loan. The men who make such loans are in many cases local political figures who use moneylending as one way to extend their influence. Once indebted to such a man, in any way, a small businessman loses some of his autonomy, and his freedom to do business with whomever he pleases is curtailed. He may find himself under pressure to deal with associates of the moneylender, or to extend favors or support to them.

The best way to raise money and provide insurance against emergencies is through a rotating credit society. Such associations in Lukang resemble those described in other Chinese communities, and no extensive account is necessary (A. Smith 1900: 152–60; Gamble 1954: 260–70; Burton 1958). Credit associations in Lukang are fairly large, sometimes ranging up to twenty-five members, and they do not usually gather for monthly meetings or feasts. Members deal only with the organizer of the association, and may not even know who all the other participants are. It is claimed that almost every household in the town participates in at least one rotating credit association, and it is possible to take part in as many as one can afford. Many businessmen participate in several . at a time, and some people speak of belonging to as many as twenty. It is usually possible to arrange one's monthly bids so as to get the principal from each association at the same time. This is a common way of raising at least some of the capital necessary to start a business, and it is the preferred method of meeting emergencies and getting over temporary periods of slack business. By using rotating credit societies businessmen obtain short-term credit from many sources. Just as they prefer, if possible, to deal with many suppliers rather than one, so they prefer to borrow money in small amounts from many people rather than ask one person for a large loan. The participants in a rotating credit society are defined as equals, and their rights and obligations are clearly understood. Obtaining money from such a source permits one to avoid having to ask a kinsman, a semi-professional moneylender, or a bank official for a loan, and so obligating one's self to one of them.

Of course there are risks in rotating credit associations, for if one member fails to make a payment when it is due, the association is likely to collapse, and those members who have not yet had the principal lose their entire investment. It is best to be cautious both in joining and in asking others to join one. I cannot say just how often credit associations do fail or what the exact risk of losing one's money is, but they fail often enough for people to be very well aware of the dangers involved. The first response of an acquaintance of mine, a young engineer, to a question about rotating credit associations was to warn me, "Don't join any. You don't know people well enough." It is felt that the possibility of losing one's investment can be minimized by joining only with people one knows very well, or has known for a long time. The actual decision of whom to ask or whose invitation to accept is said to depend on a careful estimate of one's relations with the other person involved, of his credibility and of the likelihood of his meeting his obligations. One of the many factors considered is his past record in credit associations. A man who has participated in several associations, and thereby both rendered aid to the organizer and demonstrated his reliability, will find it easier to organize one when he wants to than would an equally wealthy man who has never taken part.

Unlike "business relations," which are understood to consist of limited, well-defined exchanges of money or checks for goods and services, those relations described as based on *min-ch'ing* depend on an assessment of a man's total personality and his place in the social structure. One establishes the good character necessary for acceptance in the sphere of *min-ch'ing* only by participating in "society," by knowing a lot of people and interacting with them in the role of community member rather than in a narrowly defined occupational role. The life of a small businessman in Lukang is uncertain enough as it is, and the insurance provided by relations based on *min-ch'ing*, which permit him to extend his relations of debt and credit to a circle of people quite distinct from those he has "business relations" with, may make the difference between success and failure in business. The ideal businessman, therefore, should not confine himself to his shop and deal only with the others in his line. He should supplement "business relations" with "social relations." And since, in Lukang, participation in "social relations" and community affairs is restricted to natives of the town, any outsider who attempted to establish a business would lack the insurance provided by *min-ch'ing*, and would be more vulnerable than a native.

A businessman's personal, particularistic relations are also important in partnership. Partnerships are quite rare in Lukang, and it is said that the relation between partners, unlike that between men who exchange checks, should be close, intimate, and "thick." Partnership in business is described as an inherently fragile arrangement, easily disrupted and best avoided. The problems were explained to me as follows: "Say three men who are very intimate and whose *kan-ch'ing* is good decide to form a partnership and do business together. One contributes $2,000 N.T., one $1,800 N.T., and one $1,700 N.T. When some difficulty in the business arises, the one who put in 2,000 will say, 'I put in 2,000, and all I get for it is an equal share with you.' The one who put in 1,700 will reply, 'My investment was less, but I'm here all the time working for the sake of the business. If you'd pay more attention to the business instead of running around wasting time, we wouldn't have the trouble we have now.' Dissension arises and their relations get worse. So they break up." It seems to be expected that partnership entails absolute equality between partners, but that balancing each partner's interests, rights, duties, contributions, and rewards to insure perfect equity is ultimately impossible.

Most partners in Lukang businesses are brothers, or fathers and sons. Such partnerships do not represent large, complex families that have postponed the usual division of the family. Large, undivided households are rare in Lukang, and those few that exist are regarded more as curiosities than as status-generating realizations of a cultural ideal. In almost all cases, brothers who are business partners have separate households, each with its own budget, often dwelling in different houses. The business is described as "just like a corporation; we each have a share and get so much money a month, no matter how many people there are in each household."

Partnerships between brothers do not endure indefinitely, and there are no large, complex businesses run jointly by several brothers and their sons. Such enterprises do exist in Taiwan's major cities, and their absence in Lukang may simply reflect the fact that Lukang is not a terribly good place to do business, or that economies of scale are not very important in its retail shops and small factories. The family business that goes on for generations, on the European or Japanese model, is not found in Lukang, although one should keep in mind that most of the town's businesses, especially in the industrial sector, have been founded only in the last twenty years. The histories of some of the older firms, such as rice mills and furniture factories, reveal a pattern of ameboid fission. The oldest existing furniture shop, still one of the largest and most successful, was founded in 1908 by six brothers. Today it is managed by the fifth and only surviving brother, a man of seventy-two, and one of his middle-aged sons. Next door is another furniture shop, run by the son of the oldest brother and his two young married sons. Across the street the widow of another of the original six brothers runs yet another shop with her two adult sons. The two others split off from the original shop sometime in the mid-1930's, following the deaths of some of the founding brothers. The elderly survivors are vague about the reasons for the split, and members of the younger generation say they have no idea why the family and the business were divided. There are said to have been at least four other furniture shops in Lukang in the past thirty years run by descendants of the original six brothers. There are also said to be at least five furniture establishments in Taipei, Taichung, and Chiayi run by descendants of the six brothers, some of whom moved their business from Lukang. In Lukang, then, it is rare to find family firms run as a joint estate by several adult brothers. More commonly the brothers act as partners, much as would unrelated men. Over time, these arrangements, too, break down, resulting in fission of the business into small independent firms.

People describe brothers cooperating in business not in terms of maintaining an undivided family estate, or in terms of prescriptive fraternal solidarity, but in terms of the personal relations between particular brothers. Brothers are said to be better as business partners than unrelated men, not so much because they occupy the status of "brother," but because they know each other so very well, and are so "intimate." They are said to be well aware of their common interest, and less likely to be disturbed by relatively minor upsets and difficulties. Hence, each is willing to work hard for the sake of the business without worrying about exactly how much time and effort the other is devoting to it.

Some brothers cooperate in business, others do not. If they do, it is said to be because their personal relations are good, their *kan-ch'ing* is good. *Kan-ch'ing*, as the term is used in Lukang, refers to the affective component of all human relations. It does not necessarily vary with the closeness or structural importance of the tie. It applies to relations between brothers and close kinsmen as well as to all other persons. Girls hope to marry into a family where the *kan-ch'ing* is good, where there isn't a lot of quarreling and fighting. Some brothers have good *kan-ch'ing* and a lot of interaction (*lai-wang*), and others do not (Pasternak 1968; Wolf 1970). The quality of the affective bond between brothers does not, or should not, affect the axiomatic base of the relation. Brothers owe certain things to each other, simply because they are brothers, and fraternal duties and obligations exist whether brothers like each other or not. Brothers are one's ultimate security, the people one can rely on automatically in times of crisis, and the man who has no brothers is to be pitied. Should a man be injured, or struck down with a severe illness, his brother will look after him and his family for as long as necessary. Should he be killed, his brother will look after his family. The attitude toward fraternal obligations can be summed up as "Home is where, when you have to go there, they have to take you in."

The relations between brothers and between all close kinsmen can be described as consisting of a core of axiomatic obligations, upon which is superimposed an affective personal bond. In the long run, and in crises, one can depend on one's brothers. But no one wants to be dependent on his brothers, and an able-bodied man should not expect his brothers or kinsmen to make many sacrifices for his sake. And in Lukang cooperation or special help in business affairs is not considered one of a brother's axiomatic obligations. Any use of one's brothers in business is a function of the personal relation, the *kan-ch'ing*, that exists.

The same could be said of all kinship relations. One is not obliged to do business with or to hire another person simply because he is a kinsman. Most of the retail businesses in Lukang are so small that there is no question of hiring anyone at all, all work being done by the owner and his household. Most jobs in industry or handicraft either demand technical skill of a fairly high order or are so hard and so poorly paid that giving one to a kinsman would constitute no great favor. Most of the assistance or support a man gets from his kinsmen takes the form either of services, such as help with the cooking for a feast or a wedding, or of money, the universal medium of exchange. If the owner of a metal-working factory were to help his brother's son who had failed his middle-school entrance examination, he would be more likely to use his influence to get the boy admitted to a private school, or to help pay his tuition, than to give the boy a sweatshop job.

Retailers are expected to give close kinsmen a lower price, but the kinsman is also expected to buy without a lot of quibbling. An unusually candid cloth retailer told me that he gave his close relatives a more "honest" price. But they did not constitute any appreciable proportion of his clientele, and he did not make very much profit from selling to them. "So I don't really care if they buy here or not; I don't get that much out of it anyway." One old lady carefully avoided shopping at the mixed-goods shop run by her sister's son because she would feel obliged to buy once she went in. If she wanted a blue thing and all they had were red ones, she would have to take a red one. So she went to the shop of a non-kinsman where she could carefully look for something that exactly suited her taste, walk out if she didn't find it, and bargain fiercely if she did.

Had the old lady been sure she could get exactly what she wanted at her nephew's shop, she would have gone there and saved money. If there is a choice, and everything else is equal, one will indeed prefer to deal with a kinsman or a person with whom one has something in common, or with whom one is at least acquainted. It is better than dealing with strangers. Kinsmen or *t'ung-hsiang* are people with whom one has the potential of establishing closer relations, relations involving some degree of mutual confidence. But, such relations are potential, and mutual confidence cannot be taken for granted. To do someone a favor or to extend trust to him simply because he is of the same surname or attended the same school would be regarded as a bit simple-minded. Other things being equal, in the absence of any other criteria, business relations would be influenced by membership in such common categories as surname, schooling, or residence. But in Lukang, in business, other things are very seldom equal. As the owner of a furniture shop pointed out above, a great many things are taken into account when deciding just whom to do business with. Kinship, membership in some recognized social category, or the affective content of the relation is considered, but so are many other things. A friend of mine noticed that his wife patronized a shop in the market rather than the one across the street. He asked her why she went all the way to the market when the owner of the local shop was a neighbor (*t'ung-hsiang*) and of the same surname (*t'ung-hsing*) as well. She replied, "At the shop in the market the prices are lower and the selection is better."

In the absence of any other criteria, people will prefer to deal with kinsmen, fellow townsmen, or schoolmates because they "know them better." One has the impression that if a native of Lukang were suddenly dropped into the anonymous urban bustle of Taipei or Singapore, such categories as *t'ung-hsiang* and *t'ung-hsing* would become very important indeed, and that he would carefully cultivate close personal relations, described in terms of *kan-ch'ing*, with those who were in a position to affect his livelihood. But at home, in Lukang, such gross categories are rejected in favor of more complex and subtle criteria that operate beneath the bland surface of "friends and neighbors." People are quite reluctant to discriminate within the category of "friends and neighbors," to say who is more intimate, more trustworthy, more likely to be asked to join a rotating credit society. Unique personal relations, acquaintance, and mutual interaction are stressed, and people insist that one cannot talk about such general categories as "affinal kinsmen," for "it all depends on the person himself." Sentiment rather than structure is emphasized, and the vocabulary used to describe social relations beyond the narrow confines of immediate kinship consists largely of such imprecise expressions as "people you know," "people you've known a long time," "people with whom you have a lot of interaction (*lai-wang*)," or "those with whom your *kan-ch'ing* is good." Relations are described in what seems a deliberately vague terminology, one that blurs distinctions and avoids making any categorical statement of mutual obligations. Such social relations are thought of, or at least spoken of, in terms of natural human sociability rather than as positions in a social structure or as calculating, instrumental relations.

Relations with others in one's personal network, one's friends and neighbors, the people one invites to feasts or joins in a rotating credit society, are seen as rooted in affect. Associations of such people are referred to as based on *min-ch'ing*, which might be translated as "sentiments of sociability or community." But such relations are not necessarily or even ideally very close or intimate. The aim seems to be a lot of amiable, matey, but not too intimate ties with as many people as possible. People give the impression of being hesitant about getting too close, too deeply involved with or committed to anyone else. Amiable relations may break down if too much is expected of them. In business one should not expect others to do business or give concessions only because of affective, amiable feelings, which would be described in terms of "intimacy" or *kan-ch'ing*. Indeed one of the most common uses of the term *kan-ch'ing* is in a negative retroactive sense, to explain why two people don't get on so well any more. "Their *kan-ch'ing* used to be very good, but then something happened, and it broke up." Such usage is common in discussing business partnerships.

The rather diffuse, particularistic relations referred to as those of acquaintance or affective attachment are seen, then, as rather fragile, and not to be relied on in business. And in spite of the rhetoric of mutual support and affect, it is recognized that particularistic relations based on *min-ch'ing* can be exploited, one man profiting from the misplaced trust of another. Apparent concessions and special favors, allegedly based on particularistic bonds, may turn out to be no favors at all, or may be extended only to obligate the recipients. Cloth retailing is described as being largely a matter of salesmanship, since the cloth sold in all the shops comes from the same factories and wholesalers. One of the principles of successful cloth retailing is said to be the establishment of a personal relation with the customer, thus making the transaction something more than a pure encounter between strangers. A skillful retailer will chat with the customer, seeking something they have in common, and trying to persuade him that he is being granted a special concession because of the supposed relation. The retailer may point out that they are both graduates of the same primary school, or have a friend in common, or claim that because the customer has the same surname as the retailer's wife they are in some sense affinal kinsmen. The recognition of the relation will, ideally, make the customer feel more obliged to buy. One retailer explained as follows. "I take a common sort of cloth that most people know the price of and say, 'Usually this is ten dollars a foot, but since you are my affinal kinsman and are bringing me so much business, I'll let you have it for only nine a foot.'" The customer, pleased at such a bargain, does not realize that the wily draper is raising the price of another, less well-known sort of cloth by an equivalent amount. It is claimed that this sort of approach works best with rustics, who are reputed to take such things as kinship solidarity more seriously, and to be more socially naïve than the cynical townsmen. The same retailer told me that if he were to try the same sort of approach on a middle-class native of Lukang, the man would feel that he was being tricked and become even more suspicious than customers usually are.

In a similar vein, the woman who ran the very small and poorly stocked general store across the street from our house used to tell my wife that we should buy all our soap and toothpaste from her rather than the larger shops in the market "because we're neighbors."

Most people, and most businessmen, are perfectly aware that *min-ch'ing* relations can be exploited, and are therefore reluctant to appeal to them and rather suspicious of those who do. One man I knew ran a hardware shop, specializing in the sale and installation of pumps and pipes for irrigation. He spent a lot of time out in the countryside, and was often invited to rural weddings and village festivals, where he met a lot of people. Often someone he had met at such an affair would show up at the shop to buy something, which was all to the good. But the customer would demand credit or promise to pay after the harvest because, having eaten and drunk together, he and the shopkeeper were "friends." The shopkeeper claimed that such demands for credit or failures to pay bills on schedule were his greatest problem. He was confident that he would get his money eventually, but he himself had checks to pay and wanted his money as quickly as possible. He doubtless used the rather superficial relations of "friendship" existing between himself and the farmers to try to persuade them to buy from his shop rather than another, but suffered when they used the same superficial relation as an excuse for delaying payment. He claimed that he tried, as far as possible, to do all business on a cash basis, but that this was simply not possible when dealing with farmers who did not have a regular cash income.

When sources of supply or custom are limited, businessmen will try to cultivate close personal relations of a particularistic nature, but this is usually considered a second choice, something one does only when there is no alternative. During my stay in Lukang, cement was hard to get, since Taiwan was exporting vast quantities of it to Vietnam. The price of cement rose, and still there was none to be had. Building projects came to a halt or were delayed for months, and building suppliers in Lukang, at the end of the distribution network, were frantic. They sought out cement wholesalers and took them out to winehouses, entertaining them lavishly and pointing out what good customers they were. They stressed their *kan-ch'ing* with the suppliers, and tried to use any potential common category they could, begging for a few bags of cement, regardless of price, to satisfy their own customers and maintain their own *hsin-yung*. They did not enjoy doing this, and described the wholesalers as taking advantage of the situation in spite of protestations of fellowship and good feeling, but said that they had no choice.

Businessmen are wary of attempts to make use of particularistic relations, not only because such relations may be exploited, but because any special favor received puts one under obligation and thus reduces one's autonomy. The old man who ran the town's largest furniture enterprise asserted that he never accepted invitations to feasts or trips to wine-houses, because if he ate someone else's food he was indebted to the host, which was a bad thing. He would, he said, go to weddings because there the guests contribute a red envelope with money and, in a sense, pay for their food. Factory workers and such skilled craftsmen as wood-carvers made a point of not asking their employers for loans or advances in pay, since that would obligate them too deeply to the boss. If they had troubles they turned to their "friends and neighbors," and to associations based on *min-ch'ing*. The organization of the numerous small factories and workshops was anything but paternalistic, and both owners and workers seemed content with a "business-is-business" approach to their relations.

To do business in Lukang one must know people and establish relations of mutual confidence, but one need not know people terribly well, and it is better to have limited relations with a lot of people than very close ties with only a few. Close, particularistic relations are important only in special circumstances. The small businessmen of Lukang desire to maximize their autonomy and freedom of choice, and prefer limited, functionally specific relations to diffuse ties, fused with personal relations. Such close personal relations are of less importance in Lukang's business relations than in those of Chinese communities described by other anthropologists (T'ien 1953; Ward 1960; Fried 1953; Ryan 1961; Silin 1964). The businessmen of Lukang, it must be recalled, operate on a small scale in their home community, one that is unusually homogeneous and that thinks of itself as perhaps even more homogeneous than it is. They do business in a booming national economy with a stable currency, and have access to fairly adequate if not ideal sources of capital, credit, and goods. Their customers have money to pay them, and they need not extend credit or ask any special favors to survive in business. T'ien explains the particular pattern of business relations in Sarawak by pointing out that "the characteristic features of business in Sarawak are lack of capital and emphasis on speculation; both of which provide ideal conditions for those who lend money to extend their influence" (T'ien 1953: 70). Such conditions simply do not apply in Lukang. The small businessmen of Lukang operate under a different set of economic and social conditions than the Chinese businessmen of Sarawak, Chu Hsien, or Modjokuto, and the particular pattern of business relations in Lukang is to be understood as a response to a particular situation.

The businessmen of Lukang are doubtless as devoted to success and the pursuit of wealth as their colleagues in Hong Kong or the Nanyang, but, when asked what they think is necessary for success, do not reply in terms of cultivating *kan-ch'ing* or of striving to "fuse business relations with personal relations" (Ryan 1961: 22). Nor do they put much emphasis on industry and frugality. These qualities are not denigrated, but are taken for granted. Everyone is industrious and frugal. Industry and perseverance do not bring a sure reward; they permit one to get by, to be a respected member of the community. A hard-working man will be able to support his family at a reasonable level, but no one expects him to become wealthy. Farmers and laborers are regarded as industrious and frugal, but they are not thought of as incipient tycoons.

To become rich one should of course be willing to work hard, but that is not the essential quality. What one needs is brains, cleverness. It is recognized that some people have a talent for doing business and making money, and others do not. Anyone can work hard and get by, or run a small shop, but only a few are clever enough to become wealthy. A Lukang proverb says: "It's difficult to raise a child who can do business." Another points out: "Without cleverness one will never become a merchant."

Cleverness is important, but success in business is not usually ascribed to sharp practice or low cunning alone. Success takes more than that. The essential quality of a good businessman could be summarized as the ability to look at a situation, interpret it in terms of business success, and adapt one's own behavior to the situation. The world is complex, and it is difficult to perceive just what a given situation holds in the way of business advantage, or how it is likely to change. The man who can best do this, and thinks of a way to turn a situation to his advantage, is the one who succeeds, who becomes rich.

A cloth retailer explained that in the cloth business one has to be smart and use one's head. "When a customer comes in you should be able to size him up, to know just what he wants and how much he's willing to pay for it. Cloth is very complex now; there are all sorts, colors, patterns, and degrees of quality." The retailer has to match up the customer's specific wants, which the customer himself may not be very well aware of or able to articulate, with one of the several hundred possible sorts or combinations of cloth. To sell cloth successfully one has to be able to think fast, to empathize with each unique customer and respond to him in the appropriate way. "You have to 'research,' to know all kinds of people and what is in people's hearts."

Rather than discussing competition with other businessmen in the same line, the merchants and craftsmen of Lukang prefer to speak more vaguely of an impersonal market or "conditions." To succeed, one must be able to meet the demands of the market. Business failures are usually described as the result of insufficient capitalization, getting too far in debt, and inability to satisfy the market, rather than as the result of the competition of other businessmen. Rather than recognizing an antagonistic relation between those in the same line, the *nei-hang jen*, people speak of an abstract "market" or "conditions," which everyone in a given sort of business must try to satisfy. Retailers stress the contest with the customer rather than that with the *nei-hang jen*. Cloth sellers ascribe success to their ability to size up customers and manipulate them, and celebrate the virtues of the salesman. "People say that a really skillful Lukang cloth seller can go up to a dead person and start talking with him, cajoling him, and gradually the dead person will rise up, bit by bit. In this business a clever tongue is what really counts." Craftsmen such as furniture makers or wood-carvers stress their skill and the quality of their products, the *hsin-yung* of these products as well-made objects. They say that one has to satisfy customers, give them what they want, but that customers can recognize quality, and will choose to buy from one firm rather than another because of the quality of the goods offered.

The emphasis is on fitting, matching up with what seem to be impersonal, given conditions. One merchant said that each person has his own way of looking at things, his own orientation to conditions and the market. Some ways of approaching things are better than others, for they accord with the demands of the market, and the man who is able to fit in with the conditions of the trade will prosper. A good cabinetmaker has to select the right kind of wood and decide the best use for each unique piece. A retailer must treat each customer differently, cater to him. He must know which customers like to look at a lot of things and bargain hard before they buy, and which prefer a simple transaction and will walk out if the merchant quotes his initial bargaining price instead of the one he is willing to sell for. Circumstances are constantly changing and one must keep up with them. Behavior that is appropriate in some circumstances will be inappropriate in others.

The qualities of a good businessman are summed up in the success story of Mr. Lin, a Lukang man who made a fortune in Taipei. As a young man Mr. Lin was very poor and could find no work in Lukang, so he went to Taipei to seek his fortune. There he worked at seal carving, a genteel but low-paying street trade. Somehow he managed to save or get his hands on a little money. With it he bought a small piece of land. The land was the least desirable in the city, the waste land where trash was dumped and burned. It was therefore quite cheap, and Mr. Lin gradually bought more and more until he owned two whole trash dumps. Taipei grew and the price of the land rose tremendously. Mr. Lin's two trash dumps, close to the center of the city, became very valuable and he sold them at an immense profit. He invested the money in an import-export business and so became very wealthy.

Like the protagonist of a Taoist parable, Mr. Lin succeeded because he was able to see the value of the useless and the unwanted. He saw an advantage that others did not, and was able to adapt his behavior to the demands of the situation, the market. And he succeeded because he was free to invest in trash dumps; he did not have to explain what he was up to, or get the approval of anyone else. He was clever and he maintained his autonomy. Many of the small businessmen in Lukang could be said to be trying, each in his own way, to emulate the legendary Mr. Lin. By insisting on their freedom to do business with whomever they choose, by maintaining strict secrecy about the details of their financial affairs and their intentions, and by spreading their debts and obligations as widely as they safely can, they are maximizing their autonomy and their ability to take advantage of any opportunity that comes their way.

Cantonese Shamanism

JACK M. POTTER

Although they are an important aspect of life in Cantonese villages, the *mann seag phox*, "old ladies who speak to spirits," have been neglected by most students of Chinese society. The only references I have found to them are J. J. M. de Groot's description of similar female shamans in Amoy at the turn of the century (De Groot 1969: VI, 1323–33), and a brief account of Cantonese female mediums in Alan J. A. Elliott's *Chinese Spirit Medium Cults in Singapore* (1955: 71, 135–38). In this paper I shall describe the three female shamans I observed in 1961–63 in Ping Shan, a Cantonese lineage comprising eight villages in Hong Kong's New Territories. Whether the practices I observed there are characteristic of other regions of China, I cannot say.[1]

The mann seag phox (alternatively, *mann mae phox*; see below, p. 219) act as intermediaries between the villagers and the supernatural worlds of heaven and hell.[2] Assisted by their familiar spirits, the seag phox send their souls to the supernatural world, where they communicate with deceased members of village families. They also know how to recapture the kidnapped souls of sick village children, and they can predict the future. They care for the souls of girls who die before marriage, and protect the life and health of village children by serving as *khay mha*, fictive mothers.

[1] I wish to thank the Ford Foundation's Foreign Area Training Fellowship Program for financing my research in Hong Kong, and my wife, Sulamith Heins Potter, for many useful suggestions. See Potter 1968 for a general account of Ping Shan.

[2] The other important religious practitioners in Ping Shan were the Buddhist nuns and priests, and the Taoist priest or Naam Mo Sin Shaang, also called the Naam Mo Lhoo, who served as master of ceremonies for many village rites. See Potter 1970 for a general discussion of Cantonese village religious beliefs and practices and the relation between them.

The Group Seance

In 1962, at the time of the Moon Cake Festival on the fifteenth day of the eighth month, the three spirit mediums of Ping Shan held their annual free group seance open to all the villagers. At dusk the villagers, young and old, men and women, gathered on the cement rice-threshing floor in the open area west of Ping Shan's central ancestral halls. As darkness fell and the full moon filled the sky with light almost as bright as day, the most accomplished shaman of the three, known as the Fat One, took her place on a low stool before a small, improvised altar table. As the incense sticks on the altar burned down, the Fat One, her head covered with a cloth, went into a trance. She jerked spasmodically and mumbled incoherent phrases. Then she started to sing a stylized, rhythmic chant, as her familiar spirits possessed her and led her soul upward, away from the phenomenal world into the heavens. Their destination was the Heavenly Flower Gardens.

Many of the villagers were less interested in the Fat One's destination than in the ghosts (*kuei*) she met along the way. These were the souls of their deceased relatives and neighbors, who took advantage of this opportunity to communicate with the living. They asked for news, gave advice, and sometimes voiced complaints.

The first ghost the medium encountered spoke as follows: "It was not time for me to die. My head was severed by a Japanese sword. I am angry and lost because my bones are mixed with those of other people." The assembled villagers immediately recognized this as the voice of Tang Tsuen's younger brother, who was one of ten villagers executed by the Japanese for smuggling during World War II. The villagers believe that anyone who meets such an unnatural death has an understandable grievance against the living, and his ghost is greatly feared. Tang Tsuen's wife, who was attending the seance, beseeched the ghost in a frightened voice to "protect the luck and safety of my husband." Tang Tsuen and his wife had worried for years about this ghost. To pacify him, they had planned to buy a silver plaque with the brother's name engraved on it, place it in a *kam taap*, a ceramic funerary vessel, and bury it in a permanent tomb where, they hoped, the brother's spirit would rest in peace.[3]

The ghost of the dead brother, speaking through the medium, told Tang Tsuen that a costly permanent tomb was unnecessary because he had died unmarried and an elaborate burial was therefore inappropriate. All Tang Tsuen and his wife had to do, the ghost said, was to write

[3] *Ibid.*, pp. 145–47.

his name on a piece of silver paper and hang it beside their ancestral altar. "If you do this," the ghost said, "I will try to help you, my brother, and your wife to have good luck and many children." As an afterthought, the spirit mentioned how pleased he was that his elder brother's wife had burned so much gold paper for him to spend and had offered him such excellent fruit during festival worship.

Later, while discussing the seance with a villager, I learned that the matter went much deeper than I had realized. Shortly after the war ended, Tang Tsuen's mother had, in fact, been bothered by the restless ghost of her younger son. As the villagers explain it, people accept death without resentment if they have lived a full, normal life and their death mandate is entered in the King of Hell's book in the usual fashion; this is fate, and nothing can be done about it. Executed in his youth by the Japanese, Tang Tsuen's brother had been deprived of the normal balance of his lifespan. The result was a troubled ghost, who could neither find peace himself nor leave his family any. Plagued by her son's ghost, Tang Tsuen's mother became physically and mentally ill, and died less than a year after her son's execution. Convinced that the ghost had driven the old lady to her grave and fearing for their own lives, Tang Tsuen and his wife tried to placate this restless family spirit. On the first and fifteenth days of every month, they made elaborate offerings in the doorway of their house, calling out to the bothersome ghost, "We are giving you money and offerings; take them and be satisfied! Don't come back to bother our family." Tang Tsuen also had gone to the expense of having his brother's spirit exorcised by a famous Taoist priest in the nearby market town during the Hungry Ghost Festival, when great quantities of food and paper money were offered the wandering ghosts of the countryside in hopes of appeasing restless spirits and driving them away.

Nothing seemed to work, however. The ghost continued to haunt the couple's household, causing Tang Tsuen and his wife to fall ill repeatedly, and, they believed, to remain childless. Trips to spirit mediums confirmed that the couple's tragic barrenness was the work of the dead brother's jealous ghost. Tang Tsuen's wife was terrified when she heard the family ghost begin to speak through the medium that night.

Then, suddenly, the voices of children were heard through the medium, quarreling and fighting over the orange and peanuts that were part of the offering. One child's voice said, "These are mine"; another, a little girl's, screamed angrily, "No! These things are not for you; they were purchased as an offering!" Shrilly she continued, "These things belong to my parents and you stole them." The village women shouted in reply, "No, money was spent for this food; go away and don't bother us." By this time all the villagers had recognized the stubborn little girl as the deceased daughter of Tang Kau, the shopkeeper from whom Tang Tsuen's wife had purchased the offerings.

Suddenly the ghost of the girl spoke again: "When I took sick you did not call a doctor; after I became seriously ill you finally called one, but by then it was too late and I died." Speaking through the medium, the voice repeated this accusation again and again. Finally the women of the village grew angry and scolded the ghost, saying, "We don't want to hear any more of this; you are too young to know about things like this." The little girl had, in fact, died four years earlier, when she was two years old.

Tang Kau and his wife, the dead girl's parents, stood among the villagers without saying a word. They were ashamed to have the circumstances of their daughter's death rehearsed before the entire village, and they now feared that the girl's unhappy ghost would return to make her brothers and sisters ill. From the night of the seance on, Tang Kau and his wife dutifully burned silver paper for her on the first and fifteenth of every month. If the family's luck turns bad, they will blame their misfortune on their daughter's angry ghost. Resentment at their failure to call a doctor in time and jealousy of her surviving brothers and sisters are considered sufficient grounds for her returning to haunt the family.

The interview with the child's ghost ended as her final plaintive words drifted across the darkened village: "My parents were careless. When I died, they hired someone who buried me so shallowly that my body was not completely covered and the dogs got at me. I cannot rest."[4]

The other villagers believed that the Fat One had deliberately brought up the case to frighten the guilt-ridden Tang Kau into placing the soul of his dead daughter under the medium's care. The villagers predicted that Tang Kau would wait and see if ordinary ritual procedures pacified his revengeful child's spirit. At the first sign of illness in the family or financial reverses, he probably will ask the Fat One to take charge of his daughter's spirit, a service for which she would of course charge a sizable fee.

The next village spirit the Fat One encountered on her heavenly voyage was Tang Mok-leung's father. The old man had died years earlier, when he was over sixty years old. He was, in the terminology sometimes used by the villagers, an old ghost. Young ghosts, i.e. ghosts of the newly dead, are very powerful beings; if dissatisfied, they usually return to harry people. Like an aging person, the ghost grows progressively weaker as he ages, and he also becomes increasingly disposed to

---

[4] Young children are not given an elaborate funeral like older people. Usually they are perfunctorily buried in a makeshift coffin.

help rather than harm the living. Once a person has been dead more than sixty years, his ghost no longer inspires much fear; he may even be born again as a different person. Occasionally spirit mediums are unable to locate an aged ghost because it has been reborn into another life. Thus supernatural potency diminishes as the personality of the ghost dims in the minds of the living.

Tang Mok-leung and his aged mother were present at the seance. They heard the old man speak through the medium: "Everyone is well; my eldest son, I see, has sent $1,000 from abroad to help the family." Tang Mok-leung remained silent at this, so everyone present assumed that he had in fact received such a sum from his elder brother, who had emigrated to Europe. The old ghost continued speaking in a good-humored vein, now addressing his wife: "You, old 'ghost' [kuei], are very lucky, aren't you? Now that our son has sent you all this money, you have money to gamble with every day." The conversation represented an affectionate exchange between an old married couple; the old man was clearly pleased that his wife and family were doing so well. The good fortune of the family, until now just unsubstantiated gossip, was publicly confirmed, and the fortune and status of the aged woman recognized. In such cases the annual seance served to take stock of the gossip about villagers that has accumulated during the year and deal with it in a public manner.

The interview ended with the old ghost counseling his son and daughter-in-law: "Daughter-in-law, obey your mother-in-law; son, obey your mother. Be careful in doing things; do not quarrel," he said as his voice faded away. Benevolent old family ghosts typically give their families such advice during these seances. Their message affirms the society's normative structure.

The next spirit the medium encountered was the younger brother of Tang Soo's father. Through the medium he admonished his widow: "No matter how much money you make working for your nephew, you always give it to your daughter. You must keep some back for yourself." The old woman would have none of this, and scolded her husband's ghost: "Don't tell me what to do! If I'd known you were going to die so young, I wouldn't have married you because now I am left alone and have to work as a servant to support myself." Good-naturedly the old ghost replied, "But you are very happy now. Your nephew lets you stay with his family and so you have a new house to live in." The old woman scolded her husband again and he riposted. The dialogue continued for some time, until the entire audience was laughing at this incongruous quarrel between the old woman and her husband's ghost.

The shaman continued on her trip to the Heavenly Flower Gardens, describing the beautiful scenery she saw along the way. As she traveled on, she suddenly met a woman's ghost holding three children's souls in her hands. The medium asked the ghost who the three souls belonged to and why she had stolen them. The ghost replied that she was starving and had kidnapped the three children's souls in hopes of receiving ransom money for them. The medium summoned her tutelary spirits—the souls of her own dead children—to question the children's souls in hopes of eliciting their identity. When the spirits asked the children who their fathers and mothers were and how many brothers and sisters they had, the answers made it plain to all that they were the souls of village children whose mothers were in the audience. The mothers berated the woman ghost. "You must be crazy! Why have you stolen our children's souls?" The women asked the medium to send spirit soldiers to recover their children's souls. The ghost, unintimidated by this prospect, defiantly insisted on ransom money before she would release the souls.

The three mothers ran back to their homes to fetch gold paper to burn as ransom, and an article of their child's clothing to be used in retrieving its soul. Once home they examined the children and found they were not well. Their complexions were yellowed, their appetites gone—symptoms of soul loss. If the souls were not recovered, the children would sicken and eventually die.

The three mothers rushed back into the arena and burned the gold paper as an offering to the ghost. After the ransom was paid, the ghost released the children's souls, and the medium's tutelary spirits brought them back down to earth with a loud, whistling sound. The medium then placed the soul of each child in its garment, which the women clutched tightly as they ran right home. As they ran they called their child's name, urging the rescued souls not to worry, they would soon be home and be given sweets to eat. The mothers rushed into their houses still repeating these assurances. Then, after hurriedly bowing before the ancestors, they each laid the garment beside the child it belonged to, so that the soul would easily recognize and reenter the body.

It turned out later that most of the villagers knew from the ghost's description that it was the notorious wife of Bean Curd Jong. Many years earlier, Bean Curd Jong married an evil young woman. From the beginning, the household was unhappy because the wicked daughter-in-law worried and scolded her mother-in-law night and day. Finally, the old lady could bear no more, and hanged herself dressed in a bridal costume. The villagers believe that a woman who dies dressed this way will become a fierce and powerful ghost; perhaps Bean Curd Jong's mother had this in mind. After her death—as the daughter-in-law learned when she consulted a spirit medium about an illness—the old lady complained to the King of Hell about her daughter-in-law's wickedness, and she and the King of Hell together plotted the untimely death of the whole family.

First the ghost of the old lady stole the soul of her son, who had violated his filial obligations by supporting his wife against her. Bean Curd Jong died shortly after his mother. His daughter was the next to die, then the evil daughter-in-law, and finally the son. Although the old lady had killed off the entire family, the villagers said the root cause of the family's troubles was the wickedness not of the mother, but of the daughter-in-law. As a ghost she has been even more ferocious than her mother-in-law, repeatedly bringing harm to the villagers, who are still terrified of her. Her favorite haunt is her family's old house. After the family died out, it was rented to outsiders because no village family would live there for fear of the ghost.

After the children's souls had been ransomed and returned to their owners, the medium and the village women scolded the ghost. "Don't do this again. If you do, spirit soldiers will be sent to catch and beat you. All those children have their own parents, why do you bother them? You must stop doing these evil things."

The evening wore on, with the spirit medium continuing her travels until well past midnight. She continued to run across the villagers' family spirits. Rather than identifying them directly by name, she questioned the spirits, asking such questions as how many daughters-in-law they had, how many siblings, how many children. Given a few general clues, the villagers were able to guess the spirit's identity. Among the spirits there was much quarrelsome jockeying for the opportunity to talk with their families. The questions typically asked of the spirits were the same as those that would be asked in a private consultation with the medium. The most common questions were about the dead person's well-being. This is a matter of great concern because if family spirits are not content and comfortable, their descendants will not prosper.[5]

Finally, after an eventful journey through the heavens, the spirit medium passed through the portals leading to the four Heavenly Flower Gardens, where every living person is represented by a potted flowering plant. The East and South Gardens are large, the North and West Gardens small. When a woman conceives a child, a heavenly flower is planted in one of the small gardens, and a seed is sent down from heaven into the uterus of the woman. The villagers liken the uterus to a flower that begins to enlarge and open after conception. The growing life

[5] See Potter 1970: 147.

flowers remain in the small gardens until the people they represent are between twelve and sixteen years old, when they are transplanted into one of the large gardens. When a person's plant is moved to a large garden, it is placed alongside that of his or her future spouse. The villagers believe that the old, arranged marriages were fixed in heaven in this manner.

Two female deities, Lee Paak and Zap Yih Nae Neung, tend the flowers while they are in the small gardens. The two deities watch over all the world's children, deciding which shall flourish and which shall die. They also decide which women shall have children and which shall remain barren. Understandably, they are very important deities to Cantonese women. There is an image of Zap Yih Nae Neung in the Hang Mei Village temple of Ping Shan. Women pray to it that they may have children and that their children may be protected from harm.

The medium journeys to the Heavenly Flower Gardens in order to inspect the villagers' flowers. This "inspection of the flowers," or *chan fa*, is a form of fortune-telling. The medium examines the condition of a person's flower: are there yellowed leaves or spider webs on the plant, does the flower seem in poor condition? The medium examines the flower to see how many red flowers (representing daughters) or white flowers (representing sons) are in bloom; unopened buds on the plant represent future offspring. If the pot contains bamboo, a woman will be barren; if it holds tangerines, she will have many children. The condition of a villager's flower tells the medium important things about that person's future.

When she had reached the Heavenly Gardens, the Fat One began to tell the villagers' fortunes by chan fa. One of the many villagers whose flowers she inspected was Tang Soo-kwai, a 48-year-old man. Soo-kwai did not attend the seance, but his mother and his wife were there. Soo-kwai's mother gave the Fat One the eight characters denoting the year, month, and day of her son's birth. This was necessary so the medium could locate Soo-kwai's pot, which has the same eight characters written on it. Soo-kwai's plant, the Fat One reported, had one white and three red flowers, representing his three daughters and one son, plus an unopened white bud, indicating that eventually he would have another son.

Suddenly, the Fat One called out that she saw a woman's ghost hovering around Soo-kwai's plant, an announcement that riveted the villagers' attention. Speaking through the medium, the ghost informed the spectators that this flowerpot belonged to her husband. Everyone then knew that the ghost was Tang Soo-kwai's deceased first wife. From the look on the face of Soo-kwai's second wife, this was a bad omen.

The ghost assured her, however, that she would not bother her husband or his family and was merely visiting his plant because she was lonely. Soo-kwai's second wife relaxed a bit. The ghost conversed with several women in the audience. She expressed anxiety about her son and daughter, and admonished the second wife to take good care of them and see that they were well brought up and properly educated. Soo-kwai's younger brother's wife was also at the seance, and the ghost told her that since they had known and liked each other in life, she had nothing to fear. "Now I am a ghost [kuei]," she said, "but I have a good heart and will not bother you. When I was alive we were good friends, and now we are still like sisters." This was a relief to the brother's wife, and Soo-kwai's second wife was also pleased to hear the ghost expressing good will rather than malevolence.

The final event of the seance was a remarkable attempt by the spirit medium to preserve traditional religious beliefs and practices among the younger generation, which is increasingly affected by modern secular ideas. A young couple had just built a modern-style house in the village without installing the paper images that represent the traditional guardian deities of village houses. The spirits of the new household spoke through the medium. They said they had nothing to eat and no permanent place of their own, and so had to flit around restlessly. The spirit generals of the doors, the guardian spirit of the house, and the kitchen god all said that if a suitable resting place and proper worship were not arranged for them, the household would soon meet with disaster. So effective was this warning that the modern young couple installed the traditional deities and began to worship them the very next day.

The Regular Duties of the Spirit Medium

The dramatic group seance takes place only once a year, during the eighth month, which is an especially propitious time for communicating with spirits. Throughout the rest of the year the spirit mediums cure illness, converse with villagers' family spirits, tell fortunes, and care for their fictive children.

The professional headquarters of the spirit mediums are their altar houses or shrines, *pay dhaan*. Each pay dhaan contains an altar on which the medium's special tutelary deities are enshrined, sometimes along with the souls of girls who died unmarried, other spirits entrusted to her special care, and assorted religious paraphernalia. It is here that people come to consult the spirit medium, and it is here that she customarily goes into trances and communicates with the supernatural world. When the medium's altar house serves as a repository for the souls of unmarried village girls as well as the medium's tutelary spirits, it is called a *dsox zan dhaan*, or "shrine where spirits reside."

In 1963 there were two dsox zan dhaan in Hang Mei Village, belonging to Kao Paak-neung and the Fat One, the two spirit mediums of Hang Mei; and there was a pay dhaan in the adjacent village of Hang Tau, which belonged to the elderly spirit medium from China proper. The altar houses of the Fat One and the Old Woman from China were dingy lean-tos, built against walls of their houses. Kao Paak-neung's altar house was a recently built little one-room shrine, situated between the fish pond and the Hang Mei Village temple. Kao Paak-neung had formerly practiced in a lean-to like those of the two other mediums, but in 1957 Tang Nai-men, in gratitude for her efforts on behalf of his many children, had built her a new one.

Kao Paak-neung's altar house was sparkling white inside and out, with colorful testimonial banners given her by Tang Nai-men hanging on the wall. The most striking feature of the shrine was the altar itself, a large piece of orange-red paper, which was affixed to the wall and had written on it in bold black characters the names of the spirits and deities who aided Kao Paak-neung in her profession. Before the altar was a large table, which held a variety of ritual objects: vases of plastic flowers intended to brighten the shrine and please the spirits of the altar; mirrors to gratify the souls of the young girls who dwelled in the altar; tea and fresh fruit for the spirits to eat along with the incense that the villagers considered the spiritual equivalent of rice; a bowl of fresh water so the spirits could wash their hands before eating; and a copper incense burner and candlesticks used in the medium's ritual performance.

Alongside the altar hung five dresses, belonging to five young girls whose spirits dwelled in the altar. These were placed there because the villagers are uncertain how to treat the spirits of women who die before marriage. The spirit tablets of adult men and married women are kept on their family's ancestral altar, and those of unmarried men are placed either on the altar or on a wall beside the altar (cf. the case of Tang Tsuen's unmarried brother, p. 322). Women who die before marriage present a problem because they have no husband and are not members of their father's lineage. People are afraid to put their tablets in the home because they might haunt the family. The solution is to put the spirits of unmarried daughters under the shaman's charge. The medium has the names of her spiritual charges written on her altar, where she worships them twice daily and on festival days. When village parents place a daughter's spirit under the medium's care, they usually bring one of the deceased child's garments to hang near the altar so the child's spirit knows the shrine is her home. Parents visit their dead daughters' spirits during the Spring and Autumn Festivals, when the villagers worship the spirits of their dead kin.

On Kao Paak-neung's altar are written the names of seven deities, the names of her dead son and two dead daughters, who serve her as spirit helpers, the names of six young female spirits entrusted to her care, and the name of Tang Fang-cheung, her husband's younger brother, who died before marriage. Fang-cheung's name appears on the altar because he ended an unhappy life as an opium addict by committing suicide in his lineage's ancestral hall. His spirit was presumed to have been made so unhappy by his unfortunate way of life and manner of death that it was greatly feared. Kao Paak-neung propitiated it daily.

The six powerful *poo-sat*, deities whose names are on the altar, are Yok Waang Daay Tay, Laan Sio Tzex, Cau Kong, Dsann Kux Loo Ye, Kun Iam Mha, and Wa Dho.

Yok Waang Daay Tay is the Jade Emperor, who according to the medium rules over all the spirits and deities of heaven. He is the most powerful deity, commanding the obedience of all the heavenly officials. Because she considers the Jade Emperor a good deity who helps people, Kao Paak-neung always invites him to come down and help her.

Laan Sio Tzex, Miss Laan, is a deity unknown to anyone else in Ping Shan. She is Kao Paak-neung's familiar spirit. Before Kao Paak-neung became a spirit medium, this spirit entered her body and made her ill. Kao Paak-neung had no idea who was making her ill until her children's spirits told her she was being possessed by Miss Laan of heaven. They instructed her to write Miss Laan's name on her altar, and promised that this new spirit would always respond to their mother's request for help. Kao Paak-neung followed her children's instructions, and now Miss Laan is her familiar spirit. The medium knows that Miss Laan is a good friend of her two dead sons because when she calls her sons' spirits down, Miss Laan always accompanies them. She suspects that Miss Laan is a maidservant of Kun Iam, the Goddess of Mercy, but is not certain.

Cau Kong is a well-known Chinese deity who is famous for his invention of the Chinese divination blocks, the *pok kwah*. A pair of wooden blocks shaped like tortoise shells, convex on top and flat on the bottom, the pok kwah are used for divination by spirit mediums and other religious practitioners. The diviner, whether a spirit medium, a Taoist priest, or a fortune-teller, first has to invoke Cau Kong. Then the blocks are thrown, and their position gives a positive or negative answer to a query. Cau Kong assists the spirit medium in her divinations and fortune-telling.

His Excellency Dsann is, according to Kao Paak-neung, a mountain spirit, *saan zan*, who helps and protects people. When a child or adult becomes ill, the medium can call on Dsann to cure the illness.

Kun Iam Mha, Mother Kun Iam, is the famous Buddhist Goddess of Mercy, one of the most popular deities in all China, a deity who embodies all the warm, tender, and merciful female virtues. Strangely enough, Kao Paak-neung claims to know little about Kun Iam except that she protects and helps people. When ghosts see Kun Iam, who is very powerful, they run away in fright.

Wa Dho is the major deity on Kao Paak-neung's altar; he is her teacher and helper, and she is his disciple. Before Kao Paak-neung became a spirit medium there was a struggle between her daughter's spirit, who wanted her to become a spirit medium, and her son's spirit, who wanted her to become a Wa Dho curing specialist. A compromise was finally reached; she became both a spirit medium and a Wa Dho curer.

According to Kao Paak-neung, Wa Dho was the first famous doctor of China. He lived in the third century A.D., in the age of the Three Kingdoms. When Kwan Kong, China's renowned general of the period, fell ill, Wa Dho cured him. Then Tsao Tsao, the famous rival and enemy of Kwan Kong, became ill with a terrible headache, and he consulted the famous doctor. Wa Dho reportedly told him that something was wrong with his brain, and that to cure him it would be necessary to cut it out and wash it before replacing it. Tsao Tsao quite naturally suspected Wa Dho of being in league with Kwan Kong, and had him killed. Kao Paak-neung says this was a disaster, because all of Wa Dho's knowledge died with him. Had he lived longer, the Chinese could have learned a great deal from this famous physician. It is said he was so able that he could cure people simply by blowing on them. After his death, he became the patron saint of Chinese doctors and religious curers.

Alongside Kao Paak-neung's altar hangs a magic horsetail brush like the one Wa Dho supposedly used. When someone is ill because an evil ghost has possessed him, Kao Paak-neung drives the malicious spirit away by waving the brush over and around the sick person. She then brushes the patient all over from head to foot, to rid his body of the intrusive spirit.

The final entry on Kao Paak-neung's altar reads "all Tang ancestors." All altars in the village, the spirit medium said, have this entry because the Tang lineage ancestors always protect their descendants. Not written on her altar but still important in her practice are two other local spirits. One specializes in caring for sick children and the other helps the medium mobilize spirit soldiers to fight recalcitrant ghosts.

Kao Paak-neung's rival, the Fat One, is a more successful medium with a more elaborately equipped altar house. The Fat One's altar has face powder and feather fans for the spirits of little girls, as well as mirrors for them to use. It also has a bowl of pomelo leaf water—the standard purifying agent for the Cantonese—which the Fat One uses to cleanse herself of pollution before dealing with the spirits.

The Fat One also has two wooden buckets, one of which holds lighted candles stuck in rice, the other rice and an egg. The rice is essential for a medium's contact with the supernatural. After the medium has gone into a trance with her head covered by a cloth, the spirit that possesses her tosses handfuls of rice around the room at any of its relatives that are present, thus helping to identify itself. Because of this practice, one of the common names for a spirit medium is *mann mae phox*, "ask-rice woman."

The altars of the three spirit mediums—Kao Paak-neung, the Fat One, and the Old Woman from China—all have different deities inscribed on them, having in common only Kun Iam and Wa Dho. Each shaman has her own ancestors and dead relatives and children to serve as her familiar spirits. Since the names of the altar deities are dictated by the spirits who make a person become a medium (more on this below), and since the Chinese have many deities of rough functional equivalence, the variation in altar deities is not surprising.

When a sick person or a concerned relative comes to the altar house to seek the spirit medium's help, she begins by ascertaining the patient's home village and eight characters. Because the supernatural world is organized bureaucratically, the spirits need the name of the person's village so they know where to start their investigations. The eight characters help them identify the specific soul that is lost. If the patient is seriously ill, the medium then throws the divination blocks to determine whether a cure is possible; if the blocks say the illness is mortal, there is no use proceeding further.

A village woman who was an apprentice shaman told me about one of Kao Paak-neung's untreatable cases. A man from Mai Po Village fell ill, and his wife asked Kao Paak-neung to come to their house and treat him. When Kao Paak-neung called down her tutelary spirits, they told her that the man was dying and there was nothing she could do for him. The ailing man refused to accept this verdict. Speaking through Kao

Paak-neung, he promised her tutelary deities that he would establish a fictive kinship relation with them if they restored his health. But the spirits reiterated that his case was hopeless: his sister in hell had prepared his coffin and he was doomed. The sick man and his family still doubted Kao Paak-neung, but soon afterward she learned that he had died as predicted. (Kao Paak-neung attributes the man's death to his evil sister. Married off to a very poor farmer, she had had a hard life. When she fell sick her husband had no money for a doctor, and she died. After her death her husband did not worship her. Her lonely, dissatisfied soul returned to her father's house, where her brother lived. She caused her brother to die so that his soul would keep her company.) An able spirit medium like Kao Paak-neung should always know whether or not a person can be treated. Kao Paak-neung claimed that of the many cases she had treated over the previous decade, only about ten of her patients had died, and that in each case she had predicted the outcome beforehand with the aid of her tutelary spirits.

If the divination blocks indicate that treatment is possible, the spirit medium proceeds to go into a trance, call down her familiar spirits, and begin a search for the ghost who has stolen the sick person's soul. First she lights two ritual candles and burns three sticks of incense. Then she settles herself in front of her altar. She covers her head and face with a scarf because when she sings she opens her mouth very wide. The scarf spares onlookers the painfully ugly sight of her distorted face.

Usually by the time the three incense sticks have burned down, the medium is already entranced and has called down her familiar spirits to enter her body. She always calls the spirits of her dead children first because she is powerless without their help. They are the intermediaries through whom she contacts the more powerful deities on her altar. Sometimes the children's spirits refuse to enter their mother's body, in which case she can do nothing. The children's spirits are very young and sometimes would rather go off and play. They also may be uncooperative or even vindictive when they feel slighted. For example, about five or six years earlier two women came to play cards with Kao Paak-neung. Her guests arrived early, and Kao Paak-neung, who had not had time to buy party food, took some cakes from the altar to offer them. A few minutes later her eyes suddenly turned glassy and she went into a trance. The souls of her children had retaliated for the misappropriation of their cakes by possessing the medium. For several days she either stared fixedly without speaking or talked gibberish, giving nonsensical answers to questions put to her. She had no appetite, her head ached, and she was always exhausted. She recovered only after she had propitiated the spirits with special offerings.

Usually, however, the medium is on good terms with her tutelary spirits and is able to go into a trance whenever she holds a curing seance. She begins to shake and her body grows cold—signs that the spirits are entering her. As she trembles, she cries out the names of the spirits on her altar, asking them to find the soul of her patient. In searching for the patient's soul they follow a route much like the route to the Heavenly Flower Gardens followed in the annual group seance. Almost always the lost soul is discovered in the hands of a ghost that has kidnapped it. The spirit medium tries to learn the identity of the malevolent ghost and its relation to her client. She asks leading questions, drawing upon her intimate knowledge of village families. The client searches his memory for family ghosts with reason to bother their living relatives. Usually he has a good idea who the ghost might be and helps the medium in her search. At other times, the medium puts leading questions to the client until he cries out, "It must be —." The medium outlines the steps necessary to achieve a cure. If the illness is not serious and the ghostly kidnapper not very powerful, the medium tells the child's mother or some other female relative the kinds of food and amount of paper money required to ransom the ailing person's soul. She uses her divination blocks to find out how long the patient will take to recover. The medium ends the session by scattering rice around to feed her tutelary spirits, and giving her callers rice to take home to the patient.

If the illness is serious or the offending ghost exceptionally powerful, the medium arranges for a ceremony at the patient's home. Lasting from nine in the evening until four in the morning, such a ceremony is very expensive and is usually a last resort. For a ceremony at a patient's home, the medium arrives in the evening. Incense, candles, offerings, and so on have been prepared for her use. She goes into a trance and calls on her spirit helpers to wrest the soul away from the ghost and return it safely home. The battle is often prolonged and difficult. The medium calls on powerful deities, spirit soldiers, and spirit policemen to help her rescue the soul. If she has not located the lost soul in earlier sessions, much of the evening is devoted to the quest. If she already knows where the lost soul is and who has taken it, she concentrates on wresting it away from the kidnapper. By midnight the medium has found the patient's soul and secured its release with offerings of paper money; from then until about 4 A.M. the medium escorts the soul home through the heavens.

In many of these elaborate home seances, the medium places a wooden container holding burning incense, red flags, and lighted candles on her head, invites spirits to possess her, and while possessed marches around in this makeshift headdress. Her purpose is to attract the souls of frightened children, or, less often, of adults. Mediums sometimes perform spectacular feats at these special seances. People say they climb ladders that are unsupported by anything more material than the medium's tutelary spirits, and make eggs stand upright on the floor and then split them exactly in half.

Kao Paak-neung can cure with the help of Wa Dho as well as in her own capacity as a spirit medium. Wa Dho is an ugly, angry-looking spirit, with a long beard. When Kao Paak-neung calls on Wa Dho's spirit to possess her, she shakes almost uncontrollably as he enters her body. She waves Wa Dho's horsetail brush wildly to frighten off evil spirits. She then turns to her patient, brushing intrusive spirits out of his body. Wa Dho also enables Kao Paak-neung to write out magical protective and curative charms. With Wa Dho moving her arms (she is illiterate without his aid), she writes out strange-looking characters in red ink on yellow paper with a Chinese writing brush. The written charms, called *vu*, are burned; the patient then drinks the ashes in tea, so that he will absorb the characters' curative power and suffer no more from intrusive spirits. After Kao Paak-neung has retrieved a soul and returned it safely to the patient's body, she has Wa Dho write a vu, which is placed on the patient's body or given him to drink in water as protection against further attacks by ghosts. This is important in cases of soul loss because the mere fact that a person's soul has been kidnapped shows him to be suffering very bad luck; a ghost cannot steal the soul of a lucky person.[6]

Cantonese villagers attribute most children's illnesses to soul loss. The souls of small children are loosely attached, and are easily frightened out of the child's body, making the child ill. Or a hungry or malicious ghost may enter a person's body and steal his soul. Usually the ghost holds the soul for ransom, releasing it in return for offerings of food and money. Sometimes the assistance of deities and spirit soldiers is needed to force a powerful and determined ghost to release a kidnapped soul. Intrusion of a ghost into a person's body is a third possible cause of illness. Because children are such easy prey for malicious spirits, sick children constitute most of the spirit medium's caseload.

One means of making a child less vulnerable to soul loss is to establish a fictive kinship relationship, known to the Cantonese as *khay*, between the child and a lucky person or beneficent deity. Parents are most likely to establish such a relationship if the child's future health and safety seem particularly doubtful. For example, a few weeks after a

[6] *Ibid.*, p. 150.

child is born, the mother usually goes to the market town to consult a fortune-teller, who may also be a Taoist priest. On the basis of the exact time of birth, the fortune-teller tells the mother such things as the names of the child's "flower mother" and "flower father," i.e. its mother and father in its previous existence, and which of the Heavenly Flower Gardens it has come from. Then the baby's fortune is told. If it is inauspicious, if there is some fear for the child's life, the fortune-teller will recommend the establishment of a protective fictive kinship relation with a person or deity. A couple that has had demonstrably poor luck in raising children to maturity is also likely to establish a fictive relationship for subsequent children—usually with a woman who has raised many children to maturity and whose husband, too, is lucky and prosperous—in the hope that the luck of the new parents will be extended to their fictive children. The same rationale applies when the fictive parent is a deity. The deity protects his human godchild as it grows up.

Fictive kin relationships may also be established out of gratitude to a deity who helped a child recover from illness. Kao Paak-neung once participated in the establishment of such a relationship. A two-year-old boy in Hang Tau Village was seriously ill. He had no appetite and vomited what little he ate; then he started refusing all food. At night he lay awake, crying. The boy's mother blamed his suffering on the jealous ghost of his deceased elder brother, who could not bear to see the living boy loved and cared for. The old spirit medium of Hang Tau Village confirmed the mother's suspicion; she had seen the ghost of the elder brother entering the family's house. Then the sick child began refusing even his mother's breast. It was as if the dead son was so jealous that he was preventing his brother from nursing. The mother tried expressing milk from her breast and putting it in a cup outside her door, as a propitiatory offering to the jealous ghost. But the ghost was not appeased, and the child seemed near death. Kao Paak-neung was called in. Once entranced, she confirmed that the deceased elder brother was the guilty party. Before the sick child's soul was finally retrieved and returned to his body, Kao Paak-neung and her tutelary spirits had to dispatch spirit soldiers and policemen. She then threw the divination blocks to learn how long the child's convalescence would take, and predicted that he would recover in three or four days. The grateful parents promised to make the boy a fictive son of Wa Dho, Kao Paak-neung's master, if the child recovered as predicted.

The child did recover, and his parents kept their promise. After the divination blocks assured Kao Paak-neung that Wa Dho would accept the child as his fictive son, a lucky day was selected from the almanac for the ceremony. When the day came the boy's parents brought him to Kao Paak-neung's shrine. They brought with them as an offering fresh fruit, pork, chicken, rice wine, rice, a ceremonial wooden box full of sweets, and some candles. Then the boy knelt before the altar and bowed three times to show respect. Kao Paak-neung addressed the deity: "Help the child to grow up quickly and in good health; and let him bring fortune to his parents and his brothers and sisters." Then the medium gave the boy a new pair of trousers, a pair of wooden shoes with a plastic strap, a bowl of rice, a pair of lucky red chopsticks, and a packet of lucky red money. She also gave him a red string to wear for luck.

From this day on, Wa Dho was the boy's *khay kong*, or fictive father, and he was Wa Dho's *khay jair*, fictive son. On all major holidays the boy's family had Kao Paak-neung worship Wa Dho on their son's behalf. If the child fell ill his family had her worship the deity again, with a special request for protection against the illness. The fictive kinship relationship does not end until just before the child's wedding. At this point the child comes to the altar and worships (*dsaau zan*) to repay the deity for his protection during childhood and youth. After the young man or woman worships and bows before the deity for the last time, the relationship between them is formally at an end. It is believed that anyone who failed to thank his spiritual godfather at this time would be most unlucky for the rest of his life.

One of the shaman's major duties, then, is to protect her clients' children by establishing and maintaining fictive kinship relations between them, herself, and appropriate deities. Both boys and girls can establish fictive kinship ties, although the practice is more common with boys because they are valued more highly by their families. A spirit medium who gains a reputation for successfully raising children to adulthood may acquire dozens of fictive children from families in her village and the surrounding countryside. Such relationships bring the medium both prestige and profit. It was, for example, the parents of Kao Paak-neung's fictive children, guided by the local political leader, who helped pay for her new altar house.

Another duty of spirit mediums is the questioning of family spirits. Cantonese burial practices and beliefs about the afterlife make it important to ensure the comfort of family spirits and to seek their advice when problems arise. A person's remains are buried three times, and on each occasion a ghost, if made unhappy, may bring his family grief. When a person dies, he is first placed in a wooden coffin and interred in a burial hill near the village. Five to ten years later, the bones are dug up, ritually washed with wine, and placed in a *kam taap*, a ceramic funeral pot. The pot is buried in a hill, where it remains for several years, pending reburial in an elaborate permanent tomb. The villagers believe that the location of an ancestral spirit's tomb profoundly affects the lives and fortunes of his descendants for generations, and the whole process of burial, disinterment, and reburial is fraught with danger and uncertainty.[7]

To assure themselves that they are handling matters properly, the villagers have the spirit medium contact their deceased relatives to discuss the ghost's wishes with respect to burial. The consultation takes place in a private ceremony attended only by the family members concerned and the shaman herself. The family asks if the dead person is comfortable and content in his grave, and if it is time for them to disinter his bones and place them in a permanent tomb. They do as the spirit directs (see the consultation with the spirit of the man executed by the Japanese, p. 322 above).

When the bones have been placed in a permanent tomb (its site chosen in careful accordance with geomantic principles), the ancestral spirits are asked if the tomb is satisfactory and comfortable. An ancestral spirit who is not comfortable in his tomb will become troubled and restless, and his living descendants will suffer for it. If the ancestral spirit says he is unhappy and dissatisfied, a family may even destroy the tomb and move the ancestral remains to another location to ward off misfortune.

Becoming a Shaman

The Ping Shan mediums share the ability to be possessed by spirits and go into trances. The villagers explain this gift by saying the mediums have *sin kwat*, "fairy bones," and *sin low*, a "fairy road."

An unborn child is connected to the Heavenly Flower Gardens by thirty-six ethereal bones. The bones are usually severed when the child is born, but sometimes one bone is not severed, which alters the child's spiritual outlook gravely. During the Ching Ming Festival in the spring, the Dragon Boat Festival, and other major holidays, the child with fairy bones loses his appetite and becomes ill. During these festivals the spirits of adults with fairy bones roam around heaven, to their mortal danger. Since the souls of people with fairy bones move freely and easily from their bodies to heaven, they are particularly vulnerable to attack by malicious ghosts. And if the fairy bones are not severed before marriage,

[7] *Ibid.*, p. 145.

marriage itself may cause death. People with fairy bones live in special danger.

The shamans of Ping Shan are not in agreement on fairy bones and the fairy road. The Fat One and Kao Paak-neung refer only to fairy bones. The Old Woman from China, a woman of some eighty years who has been a shaman for over fifty of them, distinguishes between the two concepts. A thread that connects a person to heaven, she calls a fairy road. Fairy bones also link a person's soul to the spirit world, but in less easily definable ways. Whereas a person with fairy bones can go into trances, a person with both fairy bones and a fairy road is easily possessed by spirits and is better able to travel to heaven with the aid of supernatural beings. The Old Woman from China says that only women with both fairy bones *and* a fairy road can become shamans.

Women having this capacity only become shamans if events in their personal lives drive them to it. The lives of the three spirit mediums of Ping Shan follow a remarkably consistent pattern. In each case the woman became a shaman only after a severe crisis—the death of several children, of her husband, or both. After her traumatic loss, each of the women was visited in her dreams by her children's spirits, who urged her to become a shaman. (Deceased children, who mediate between their mother and the supernatural world, are essential to a career as a spirit medium.) In each case the woman resisted, and in the case in which the husband was alive, he opposed his wife's becoming a spirit medium, not out of jealousy of the spirits who would possess his wife, but because shamans are low in status and viewed with distrust. Usually the struggle between the unwilling woman and her insistent children goes on for some time. As the pressure on the woman increases, she suffers attacks of seeming madness, during which she jumps around the house, leaps on top of tables, answers questions nonsensically, and so on. Finally, the reluctant candidate appears to die, and she must choose between becoming a spirit medium and dying permanently. The experiences of the three shamans of Ping Shan all follow this pattern.

The Fat One, considered the best spirit medium in the lineage, had five daughters and two sons, all of whom died very young. Soon after the death of her last child, her husband also died. Her losses left her grief-stricken, depressed, and continually ill. Every night she dreamed of visits from her dead children's souls. They taught her to "sing" in the rhythmic fashion characteristic of all professional shamans during conversations with the spirits, and then they asked her to become a spirit medium so she could help others and also earn extra money for herself. They knew that she had fairy bones because they had seen her call up spirits during the eighth month. They told her they had connections with other spirits and deities and would use their influence to help her deal with the supernatural world.

The Fat One resisted her children's advice, but they persisted in possessing her and forcing her to sing. She became ill, and they made her appear to die many times. Finally she agreed to become a spirit medium.

After making this decision, she sought the aid of an older spirit medium, and together they erected an altar in a shed alongside her house. She had written on her altar the names of her dead children and the names of powerful deities dictated by the children's spirits. After she had worshipped before her altar for many days, her health was restored and she was convinced of her supernatural powers. Parents began to bring sick children to her to be cured, and gradually she won a sizable following as a shaman and curess.

The experience of Kao Paak-neung, the second shaman of Ping Shan, was similar. As a young woman she had three daughters and one son, but they all died while very young. A year after her third daughter died, the daughter's soul entered Kao Paak-neung's body and asked her to become a spirit medium. But her dead son possessed her simultaneously, insisting that she become a curing specialist under the guidance of Wa Dho. The struggle between the two spirits made her continually ill and almost drove her mad. She wandered around the countryside worshipping at all kinds of temples and altars in an attempt to free herself from their demands. Neither she nor her husband wanted her to become a spirit medium and curer.

After a time the spirits of her daughter and son compromised, deciding that she should become both a spirit medium and a curing specialist following Wa Dho. Her husband continued his opposition to the spirits' demands until one day her daughter's spirit entered Kao Paak-neung's body and took her soul up to the heavens, making her appear to die several times during one long evening. Finally, at two in the morning, the husband relented and said she could become a shaman. Kao Paak-neung went wild with joy, jumping on tables and chairs, eating silver paper, incense, and candles, and singing loudly.

Shortly thereafter, she established an altar in her house. On the altar a Taoist priest wrote the names of her children, of Wa Dho, and of deities whose names were given her by her children's spirits. The priest reportedly addressed the deities as follows: "Here is a woman who, with the aid of her children's spirits, wishes to become a spirit medium. Please help her." After worshipping at the new altar, she was cured of her illnesses. The villagers heard about this, and began coming to her for help when their children were ill.

The history of Ping Shan's third shaman, the Old Woman from China, follows the same pattern. Her most important tutelary spirit is that of a son who died at age nine. After his death, she was ill for three years. During this period her son's spirit visited her many times, repeatedly kidnapping her soul and making her appear to die. This ended when she finally agreed to become a shaman. She learned the profession from her father's mother's sister, a woman who lived to be 120 years old and practiced as a spirit medium for almost a century.

The Old Woman from China claims that when she was younger, before World War II, she was famous throughout the countryside and had been consulted by people from many villages, including some quite distant ones. "I was popular," she says, "not only because of my ability, but because I charged less than the going rate for my services." When she was in her prime, many New Territories people established fictive kinship relations with her and her tutelary deities, and she now has over one hundred fictive sons in Ping Shan alone.

The personal tragedies each medium suffered were psychic shocks of the first magnitude. Their profession gives these women a useful and important social role that replaces their aborted family relationships. Perhaps the spirit mediums find sustenance in their contact with the spirits of the children who would have been of such emotional and social importance to them had they lived to adulthood.

The Shaman and Village Society

The supernatural world of Cantonese villagers is divided into two parts, which reflect the two aspects of their social world. One part belongs to the benevolent ancestral spirits who represent and celebrate the valued goals of lineage existence and the powerful and lucky deities who fill the imposing temples. These spirits and deities bring success and fortune to some of the villagers. The second part is the realm of the malevolent ghosts who bring the villagers sorrow and misfortune. These ghosts represent the unsuccessful, the unfulfilled, the jealous, the angry. The Cantonese shaman contributes to village society by controlling the dark side of the supernatural world.

The lineage of Ping Shan consists of most of the inhabitants of eight villages, all situated around a central ancestral hall. The men of the lineage, surnamed Tang, are descended in a direct line from a common ancestor, who founded the lineage over eight hundred years ago. Seen from outside, the lineage appears to be a highly solidary, unified social group, which struggles for power, status, and wealth with other such social groups. In the ideal view of the villagers, too, the lineage is a unitary group of brothers and kinsmen who enjoy equal status and a common social identity. Seen from within, however, the lineage is a hatchwork of competing families and sublineages. The ideal of fraternal equality is undermined by a drive for achievement that pits brother against brother. After death men who fail to rise in village society join the ranks of malevolent ghosts who populate the dark supernatural world of the spirit medium. Cantonese villagers believe that a person should be born into a nurturing family, grow to maturity in good health, prosper, have sons, and live to an advanced age. Anything that upsets this normal sequence is considered unlucky, and the person who dies young, who suffers particularly dire poverty, or who in some other way fails to taste the fruits of what the villagers consider a successful life has received less than his due. When such a person dies, the dissatisfied spirit becomes a malevolent ghost.

That most malevolent ghosts are female is surely no accident. Ground down by the lineage and family system, women may not join the competition for power, wealth, and prestige except vicariously, through their husbands and sons. They are the most downtrodden group in village society. When they marry they leave their parents' home and all their friends in the village of their birth. In their husband's village they must defer to their mother-in-law, to their husband, and to their husband's family. In many cases they are mistreated. Often they must endure the humiliation of seeing their husband take a mistress or a second wife. The frustrations of Cantonese women from one village could supply enough discontented, angry, revengeful ghosts to populate ten village hells.

A third group of malevolent ghosts are products of the conflicts, rivalries, and jealousies inherent in Cantonese family structure. Most malevolent ghosts are those of close kinsmen, usually members of the immediate family. Although the solidarity of brothers is a keystone of family and lineage structure, brothers compete for their parents' love and favor while they are growing up and for their property after their father's death. In Ping Shan numerous ghosts of brothers came back to haunt their living brothers and their families, a reflection of the ambivalence of fraternal relationships in village families.

Another common theme in the cases treated by shamans is the return of a sister's ghost to bother her living brother. Sometimes the sister's ghost is jealous of her brother and is malevolent, but usually the sister's ghost longs for her brother, who stands for the lost world of her natal family. This reflects the reluctance of many women to leave their parental home when they marry. Women pay a heavy psychological price for the Chinese patrilineal system. They do not really belong to their father's and brothers' family while they are growing up, and when they marry they are wrenched away from their parents and siblings to spend the rest of their lives among strangers.

In the case of unmarried females returning to haunt their family, the theme of sibling jealousy is evident. These ghosts are particularly dangerous because they are social anomalies; they do not belong to their father's family, yet they have no husband to care for their soul after death. So dangerous are these abnormal ghosts, they must be placed under the special care of the spirit medium. Ghosts of deceased first wives are also considered dangerous by the villagers, because they are so jealous of their successor. As might be expected, the tensions inherent in the notoriously difficult relations between mother-in-law and daughter-in-law find frequent expression in cases handled by spirit mediums. Daughters-in-law come back to seek revenge on a cruel mother-in-law; and mothers-in-law return to punish rebellious daughters-in-law for unfilial disrespect.

Village society is dominated by rich and successful males, the heads of successful families and sublineages. It is they who reap the rewards of Chinese society. It is the ancestors of these successful men who fill the ancestral halls of the lineage and are buried in impressive tombs. Only the rich and successful are immortal in China because it is only their descendants who can afford to build tombs and ancestral halls to house tablets and remains and to carry out the yearly ancestral rites. Even after death, the rich in rural China flaunt their wealth and status within the village, making the failure of the less fortunate members of village society even more galling than it would otherwise be.

Like villagers in many parts of the world, the inhabitants of Ping Shan share the image of limited good (Foster 1965). Because all good things in life are in short supply, if some members of the community attain wealth and success, it must be at the expense of others who are deprived of their rightful share. The poor people of Ping Shan hate their successful kinsmen with passion. Deprived of their share of life's fruits when alive, they form a mirror image of village society when they die. The most unsuccessful villager in life becomes the most powerful malevolent ghost after death. By kidnapping the souls of the living, by possessing their bodies and making them ill, the aggrieved ghosts blackmail the living into giving them gold and silver money and succulent food—all beyond their reach when they were alive. They so often attack children because they are not only the most vulnerable, but the most valued possessions of the living.

The spirit medium is the high priestess of this black half of the villagers' supernatural world. She rules over the dark world inhabited by the malevolent ghosts of the unsuccessful, the discontented, the abnormal, and the exploited. Her major function in village society is to deter these discontented and dangerous beings from wreaking their vengeance on the living villagers.

Notes and References

Cities and the Hierarchy of Local Systems

1. I am grateful to Sophie Laden La and John R. Ziemer for their able research assistance and to J. G. Bell for a critical reading of an earlier draft.

2. See Table 2 in my "Regional Urbanization in Nineteenth-Century China," in G. William Skinner, ed., *The City in Late Imperial China* (Stanford, Calif.: Stanford University Press, 1977), p. 224, for a summary of my numerical model of central places in agrarian China as of 1893.

3. It does appear to be the case that however Chinese settlements originated—whether as administrative capitals, garrison towns, religious centers, mining towns, or manufacturing centers—in the course of time they almost invariably acquired commercial central functions for a surrounding hinterland.

4. For market towns, see my "Marketing and Social Structure in Rural China, Part I," *Journal of Asian Studies*, 24, no. 1 (1964): 32–43.

5. *Ibid.*: 37–38.

6. Cf. John R. Watt's discussion of Ch'ing urban strategy in "The Yamen and Urban Administration," in G. William Skinner, ed., *The City in Late Imperial China* (Stanford, Calif.: Stanford University Press, 1977), p. 359.

7. The classic studies are Walter Christaller, *Die zentralen Orte in Süddeutschland* (Jena: Gustav Fischer, 1933), trans. by C. W. Baskin as *Central Places in Southern Germany* (Englewood Cliffs, N.J.: Prentice-Hall, 1966); and August Lösch, *Die räumliche Ordnung der Wirtschaft* (Jena: Gustav Fischer, 1940), trans. by W. H. Woglom and W. F. Stolper as *The Economics of Location* (New Haven, Conn.: Yale University Press, 1954). Among the most accessible general treatments of central-place theory are Brian J. L. Berry, *Geography of Market Centers and Retail Distribution* (Englewood Cliffs, N.J.: Prentice-Hall, 1967); John U. Marshall, *The Location of Service Towns: An Approach to the Analysis of Central Place Systems* (Toronto: University of Toronto, Department of Geography, 1969), chaps. 2 and 3; and

Carol A. Smith, "Economics of Marketing Systems: Models from Economic Geography," in Bernard J. Siegel, ed., *Annual Review of Anthropology, Vol. 3* (Palo Alto, Calif.: Annual Reviews, 1974), pp. 167–201. As Smith points out (p. 169), the basic assumptions and simple models of central-place theory require "less modification for the analysis of agrarian marketing systems than they do for industrial economies complicated by modern transport and localized production."

8. See in particular R. D. McKenzie, *The Metropolitan Community* (New York: McGraw-Hill, 1933); and R. E. Dickinson, *City Region and Regionalism* (London: Kegan, Paul, 1947).

9. This approach as well as the first are variants of what has been called the human-ecological theory of regionalization. See Harry W. Richardson, *Regional Economics: Location Theory, Urban Structure, and Regional Change* (New York: Praeger, 1969), pp. 170–76, 227–29. The functional interconnections of cities are most often studied as the movements of commodities (trade), persons (migration and labor recruitment), or messages (news, postal service, and in modern times telegraph and telephone service). A relevant and theoretically interesting study of interurban communications in a preindustrial society is Allan R. Pred, *Urban Growth and the Circulation of Information: The United States System of Cities, 1790–1840* (Cambridge: Harvard University Press, 1973).

10. As Minshull points out, it is quite possible to "start a regional description with the facts of population," and this approach in fact follows the lead of Vidal de la Blache, the founder of modern regional geography. Roger Minshull, *Regional Geography: Theory and Practice* (Chicago: Aldine, 1967), p. 24.

11. Philippe Buache, *Essai de géographie physique* (1752). See the discussion in Minshull 1967, pp. 21–22.

12. See E. L. Ullman, "Rivers as Regional Bonds," *Geographical Review*, 41 (1951).

13. Yun-Kwei was a notable exception. The Kunming-Kweiyang trade was most likely exceeded both by Kunming's trade with Hsü-chou-fu and by Kweiyang's trade with Chungking.

14. The upward shift of functions to centers at the next higher level of the hierarchy appears to be a general concomitant of declining population densities. For examples and rationale, see Berry 1967, pp. 32–35, and Marshall 1969, pp. 152–61.

15. Skinner 1964: 17–31.

16. For a lively discussion of the causes of deforestation in China, see Yi-fu Tuan, *China* (Chicago: Aldine, 1969), pp. 37–41.

17. In his account of the soils of China, Kovda estimates that the river system that dominates the Lingnan region transports some 28 million tons of silt annually. V. A. Kovda, *Soils and Natural Environments of China* (Washington, U.S. Joint Publications Research Service, 1960), p. 63.

18. See Franklin H. King, *Farmers of Forty Centuries*, 2d ed. (New York: Harcourt Brace, 1927), p. 75.

19. Keith Buchanan, *The Transformation of the Chinese Earth* (New York: Praeger, 1970), p. 90.

20. This analysis of the Upper Yangtze region rests primarily on data

culled from 60-odd county and prefectural-level gazetteers spanning the century from the 1830's to the 1930's. The more important of the Western sources used include *Baron Richthofen's Letters, 1870–1872* (Shanghai: North-China Herald, 1872); Ferdinand Paul Wilhelm von Richthofen, "Das Südwestliche China (Provinzen Sz'tshwan und Kwéitshou)," in *China: Ergebnisse eigener Reisen und darauf gegründeter Studien* (China: Results of my travels and studies based on them; Berlin: Reimer, 1912), vol. 3, 1–286; Chambre de commerce de Lyons, comp., *La Mission lyonnaise d'exploration commerciale en Chine, 1895–1897* (Lyons: Rey, 1898); G. J. L. Litton, *China: Report of a Journey to North Ssu-Ch'uan* (London: Her Majesty's Stationery Office, 1898; Gt. Brit., Foreign Office, Diplomatic and consular reports, misc. series, 457); Alexander Hosie, *Three Years in Western China: A Narrative of Three Journeys in Ssu-ch'uan, Kuei-chou, and Yün-nan*, 2d ed. (London: George Philip, 1897); Alexander Hosie, *Szechwan: Its Products, Industries, and Resources* (Shanghai: Kelly and Walsh, 1922); S. C. Haines Watson, "Journey to Sungp'an," *Journal of the China Branch of the Royal Asiatic Society*, 36 (1905): 51–102; and Edwin J. Dingle, *Across China on Foot: Life in the Interior and the Reform Movement* (New York: Holt, 1911).

21. The following passage from *Baron Richthofen's Letters* (1872, p. 162) catches the flavor of water transport in the Upper Yangtze region: "All the affluents [of the Yangtze] below Ping-shan can be navigated by small boats as far as the limits of the Red Basin extend. . . . All rivers of Sz'chwan have a strong current, even at low water, and are beset with rapids. Downstream, vessels travel at a quick rate; upstream they are dragged slowly and at great expense. Either way more hands are required than is usually the case in Chinese waters. . . . The expense of freight increases with the distance from the great rivers. Not one artificial canal for navigation exists in the province, the country being totally unfit for their construction."

22. "Communication by land," Baron Richthofen tells us (*ibid.*, p. 163), "is difficult everywhere, with the exception of the plain of Ch'eng-tu-fu [Chengtu]. The Peking road . . . is the greatest highroad in the country. Another much travelled road connects Ch'eng-tu-fu with Ch'ung-ch'ing-fu [Chungking] by way of Tzu-chou; a third goes from Ch'eng-tu-fu to Tung-ch'uan-fu and Pao-ning-fu; another to Ya-chou-fu, where the roads to Tibet and Ning-yüan-fu commence. . . . All these highroads . . . are well paved with flagstones, wide enough for the packtrains to pass each other, and kept in excellent repair. But little care is bestowed upon the grading. At steep places, flights of stairs are made, sometimes of a few hundred steps at a time, with little interruption. . . . In general, animals are not much employed in Sz'-chwan. Usually, travellers go in chairs, and the transportation of goods is done by coolies. Away from the highroads, these are the only modes of traffic." [In this quotation city names have been converted to Wade-Giles transcriptions.]

23. The standard guide to the formal structure of administration in the late Ch'ing is H. S. Brunnert and V. V. Hagelstrom, *Present-Day Political Organization of China*, translated from the Russian by A. Beltchenko and E. E. Moren (Shanghai: Kelly and Walsh, 1912). The two most important monographic studies are T'ung-tsu Ch'ü, *Local Government in China under the Ch'ing* (Cambridge: Harvard University Press, 1962; reissued Stanford, Calif.: Stanford University Press, 1969); and John R. Watt, *The District*

Magistrate in Late Imperial China (New York: Columbia University Press, 1972). Most of the data used here were culled directly from the Kuang-hsü edition (1899) of *Ta-Ch'ing hui-tien* and from the Autumn 1893 issue of *Chin-shen ch'üan-shu.* Data are standardized throughout to 1893.

24. The exceptional nature of governmental arrangements at Nanking derived in part from its one-time role as secondary imperial capital. See F. W. Mote, "The Transformation of Nanking, 1350–1400," in G. William Skinner, ed., *The City in Late Imperial China* (Stanford, Calif.: Stanford University Press, 1977), pp. 101–53.

25. The tabulations (of 1893 data) on which this assertion rests cannot be reproduced here for want of space. The differences noted are statistically significant at the .05 level or better.

26. Brunnert and Hagelstrom 1912, p. 426.

27. The exception was Li-fan *t'ing* in Mao autonomous *chou,* Szechwan. Ch'ü 1962 (Chart 1, p. 5) errs in indicating that ordinary *chou* could be subordinate to autonomous *t'ing* as well as to prefectures.

28. The differences cited are statistically significant at the .05 level or better.

29. See Brunnert and Hagelstrom 1912, pp. 426–27; Ch'ü 1962, p. 15; and Rozman 1973, p. 155.

30. The differences reported in this paragraph are all statistically significant at the .05 level or better.

31. Rozman (1973, p. 154 and chap. 5) cites several instances of *chou* cities situated at the gateways to major capitals.

32. Watt 1972, p. 47.

33. *Ibid.,* p. 48.

34. It goes without saying that the geography of rebellion throughout Chinese history would be clarified by systematic attention to the structure of regional systems.

35. I am in no position to broach the enormous complexities of taxation and fiscal management in late imperial China. The most detailed monographic study is Ray Huang, *Taxation and Governmental Finance in Sixteenth-Century Ming China* (Cambridge: Cambridge University Press, 1974). For a guide to the relevant literature on Ch'ing fiscal management, see the first three temporal subheadings under the main headings "14.5 State Revenue and Expenditure" and "24.5 Local Revenue and Expenditure" in each of the three volumes of G. W. Skinner et al., eds., *Modern Chinese Society: An Analytical Bibliography* (Stanford, Calif.: Stanford University Press, 1973). An analysis of the political geography of revenue collection in China may be found in Joseph B. R. Whitney, *China: Area, Administration, and Nation Building* (Chicago: University of Chicago, Department of Geography, 1970), chap. 4.

36. All county-level units were expected to be self-sufficient in fiscal terms, but there was a wide range in the ratio of retained to transferred revenue. When all transfers, remittances, and grants-in-aid are taken into account, deficit county-level units are identifiable; it would appear that ordinary *t'ing* were prominent among them. See Hosea Ballou Morse, *The Trade and Administration of China,* 3d rev. ed. (Shanghai: Kelly and Walsh, 1921), pp. 92–135; E-tu Zen Sun, *Ch'ing Administrative Terms* (Cambridge: Harvard University Press, 1961), pp. 76–186; and Huang 1974, pp. 21–29.

37. Cf. Huang 1974, p. 21: "The primary consideration behind the organization of the provincial and local governments was that of fiscal management." In this regard, however, Huang makes nothing of the differences in the size of counties or prefectures; see pp. 21 and 27.

38. Rozman (1973, p. 155) considers F to be primarily an indicator of population size.

39. Cf. the categorization suggested by Rozman 1973, p. 155.

40. For further details, see John R. Watt, "The Yamen and Urban Administration," in G. William Skinner, ed., *The City in Late Imperial China* (Stanford, Calif.: Stanford University Press, 1977), pp. 353–90. Ch'ing appointment procedures are treated in full in Watt 1972, chap. 3.

41. Ch'ü 1962, pp. 32–35; quotation at p. 34.

42. *Hsia-men chih* (Gazetteer of Amoy), 1839, ch. 2, p. 2b.

43. Brunnert and Hagelstrom 1912, p. 424.

44. *Sung-chiang fu chih* (Gazetteer of Sung-chiang prefecture), 1817, ch. 37, pp. 1a–1b.

45. *Hu-pei t'ung chih* (Hupeh provincial gazetteer), 1921, ch. 115.

46. *Hsü Yün-nan t'ung chih kao* (Draft continuation of Yunnan provincial gazetteer), 1901, ch. 5, p. 3b.

47. Skinner 1964: 40–41.

48. Local organization above the level of the village is a vastly complex subject. It is clear from work published in the last decade that the internal structure of the standard marketing system was more variegated and interesting than my 1964 article began to suggest. Extravillage local systems below the level of the standard marketing community were variously structured by higher-order lineages, irrigation societies, crop-watching societies, politico-ritual "alliances" (under a variety of terms including *yüeh, she*, and *hsiang*), and the jurisdictions of particular deities and temples; many if not most were multipurpose sodalities manifesting more than one organizing principle. It would appear that, in some instances at least, these local systems—for which Maurice Freedman has suggested the generic term "vicinages"—were not wholly contained within marketing systems but rather continued the overlapping mode of hierarchical stacking that I have shown to be characteristic of the "natural" economic hierarchy. The general importance of standard marketing communities as informal political systems, however, is generally supported by new research. See in particular Maurice Freedman, *Chinese Lineage and Society: Fukien and Kwangtung* (London: Athlone Press, 1966), pp. 23–25, 79–96; Philip A. Kuhn, *Rebellion and Its Enemies in Late Imperial China: Militarization and Social Structure, 1796–1864* (Cambridge: Harvard University Press, 1970), pp. 76–104; Sidney D. Gamble, *North China Villages: Social, Political and Economic Activities Before 1933* (Berkeley: University of California Press, 1963), chaps. 3–5; Wang Shih-ch'ing, "Religious Organization in the History of a Taiwanese Town," in Arthur P. Wolf, ed., *Religion and Ritual in Chinese Society* (Stanford, Calif.: Stanford University Press, 1974), pp. 71–92; John A. Brim, "Village Alliance Temples in Hong Kong," in Wolf, ed., 1974, pp. 93–103; and Arthur P. Wolf, "Introduction," in Wolf, ed., 1974, pp. 5–6.

49. Most of the relevant scholarship has focused on paramilitary organization rather than on politico-administrative organization per se, and most pertains to the nineteenth century. For the relationship between militia and

the marketing hierarchy, see Robert G. Groves, "Militia, Market, and Lineage: Chinese Resistance to the Occupation of Hong Kong's New Territories in 1899," *Journal of the Hong Kong Branch of the Royal Asiatic Society* 9 (1969); Kuhn 1970, pp. 82–87; Winston Hsieh, "Peasant Insurrection and the Marketing Hierarchy in the Canton Delta, 1911," in Mark Elvin and G. William Skinner, eds., *The Chinese City Between Two Worlds* (Stanford, Calif.: Stanford University Press, 1974), pp. 119–41; and Maurice Freedman, "The Politics of an Old State: A View from the Chinese Lineage," in John H. R. Davis, ed., *Choice and Change: Essays in Honour of Lucy Mair* (London: Athlone Press, 1974), pp. 82–88.

50. "The prefect's fiscal responsibility was largely supervisory. [He] saw to it that all the scheduled tax deliveries were properly carried out [by county-level magistrates] and the reserves were kept in good order. He also operated a number of revenue and service agencies. . . ." Huang 1974, p. 26.

51. Chung-li Chang, *The Chinese Gentry: Studies on Their Role in Nineteenth Century Chinese Society* (Seattle: University of Washington Press, 1955), pp. 197–202. On the significance of the last mentioned sanction, see Maurice Freedman, "Shifts of Power in the Hong Kong New Territories," *Journal of Asian and African Studies*, 1, no. 1 (Jan. 1966): 6.

52. For details and evidence on this point, see my "Mobility Strategies in Late Imperial China: A Regional-Systems Analysis," in Carol A. Smith, ed., *Regional Analysis, Vol. 1, Economic Systems* (New York: Academic Press, 1976), pp. 327–64.

53. In late imperial times Ch'u-chou, Anhwei, was the capital of an autonomous *chou* and a local city in the economic hierarchy. When Morton H. Fried studied the town and its environs in the republican period, he found that "successful landlords, merchants, artisans, and officials tend to associate socially on a basis of approximate equality. Wealthy landlords associate with wealthy merchants rather than with poor landlords; successful artisans prefer the company of wealthy merchants to that of indigent co-specialists. . . . The leadership of the various guilds is often vested in a gentleman of the town, the leadership of the combined guilds is always so vested." Ping-ti Ho's discussion of the relations between merchants and gentry in the Ch'ing period suggests that the situation portrayed by Fried can hardly be dismissed as a modern aberration. Ping-ti Ho, *The Ladder of Success in Imperial China: Aspects of Social Mobility, 1368–1911* (New York: Columbia University Press, 1962), chap. 2.

54. "Inland Communications in China," *Journal of the China Branch of the Royal Asiatic Society*, 28 (1893–94): 1–213.

55. See n. 10 to my "Regional Urbanization in Nineteenth-Century China," in G. William Skinner, ed., *The City in Late Imperial China* (Stanford, Calif.: Stanford University Press, 1977), pp. 708–9.

56. For a sophisticated analysis of gazetteer data on markets, see Ishihara Hiroshi, "Kahoku shō ni okeru Min Shin minkoku jidai no teiki ichi" (Periodic markets in Hopei during the Ming, Ch'ing, and Republican periods), *Chirigaku hyōron*, 46, no. 4 (1973): 245–63.

57. *Ch'ing-p'ing hsien chih*, 1911, ch. 5, pp. 11–13.

58. Skinner 1964: 21–24.

Peasant Insurrection and the Marketing Hierarchy in the Canton Delta, 1911

1. Winston Hsieh, *Chinese Historiography on the Revolution of 1911: An Analytic Survey and a Selected Bibliography* (Stanford, Calif.: Hoover Institution Press, 1975).

2. Information on the Shih-ch'i uprising, unless otherwise noted, is based on Cheng Pi-an, "Hsiang-shan ch'i i hui i" (Recollections of the Hsiang-shan uprising), in Chung-kuo jen min cheng chih hsieh shang hui i, Ch'üan kuo wei yüan hui, Wen shih tzu liao yen chiu wei yüan hui, ed., *Hsin hai ko ming hui i lu* (Recollections of the Revolution of 1911; Peking: Chung-hua shu chü, 1962), 2: 338–42. In addition to participating as a T'ung-meng Hui activist in the 1911 uprising, Cheng served in the 1940's as Director of the Hsiang-shan County Historical Commission, which sponsored the compilation of accounts of the uprising. Cheng's material is supplemented by my interviews with Mo Chi-p'eng (1892–1972), another participant in the Revolution of 1911. Copies of the unpublished interview records and the manuscript copies of his memoirs are deposited at the Academia Sinica's Institute for Modern History in Taipei and at Columbia University's East Asian Institute in New York City.

3. The name of the Ch'ing army commander killed at Hsiang-shan is recorded in Shang Ping-ho, *Hsin jen ch'un ch'iu* (Spring and autumn annals for the years 1911–12; Peking [?], 1924), ch. 44, p. 10a.

4. Data on lineages in the Lung-tu area are supplied in the following sources: (a) *Hsiang-shan hsien chih hsü pien* (hereafter HSHCHP; County gazetteer of Hsiang-shan, a supplement), which covers data primarily through 1911, though published in 1924; (b) "Shih tsu chih ch'u kao" (Section on genealogies, a preliminary draft), part 2, in *Chung-shan wen hsien* (Documents on Chung-shan [county]), no. 2 (May 1948), 57–70; (c) *Hsi-chiao yüeh pao* (Monthly magazine of Hsi-chiao hsiang), vol. 2 (1948), nos. 4 (Apr.), 6–7 (June-July), 11 (Nov.); and vol. 3 (1949), no. 2 (Feb.); and (d) *Hsiang-kang Chung-shan Lung-chen t'ung hsiang hui fu hui ti ssu chieh chi nien t'e k'an* (Special issue in commemoration of the fourth anniversary of the restoration of the Hong Kong Association for Natives from Lung-tu of Chung-shan [county]), 1964. For an analytical treatment of lineages see Maurice Freedman, *Lineage Organizations in Southeastern China* (London: Athlone, 1958) and *Chinese Lineage and Society: Fukien and Kwangtung* (London: Athlone, 1966).

5. G. William Skinner, "Marketing and Social Structure in Rural China, Part II," *Journal of Asian Studies*, 24, no. 2 (Feb. 1965), p. 221.

6. For the Hsiang-shan people's version of the disputes, see HSHCHP, ch. 16, pp. 5a–6b; for the Shun-te version, see Chou Ch'ao-huai et al., eds., *Shun-te hsien hsü chih* (County gazetteer of Shun-te, a supplement), 1929, ch. 24, p. 14b. For scholarly investigation, see Sasaki Masaya, "Shun-te ken kyōshin to tōkai juroku-sa" (The local gentry of Shun-te county and the Sixteen Delta Sands of the Eastern Sea), *Kindai Chūgoku Kenkyū* (Studies on modern China), 3: 163–232. For a historical perspective on militia control in this area as well as in the Canton delta in general, see Frederic Wakeman, Jr., *Strangers*

at the Gate: Social Disorder in South China, 1839–1861 (Berkeley: University of California Press, 1966), esp. chap. 15.

7. For lists of annual import and export figures, presumably of years around 1911, see HSHCHP, ch. 2, pp. 15a–16a.

8. *Ibid.*, ch. 5, pp. 3b–4b.

9. See, for example, *Tung fang tsa chih* (hereafter TFTC), 1910, nos. 3, 4, 5, 7, 8, and 10, including incidents in Kwangtung, Kiangsi, Kiangsu, and Anhwei.

10. This specific incident is reported in TFTC, 1910, no. 6. For information on other "tax rebellions" in the late Ch'ing years, see the TFTC news reports and the documents from the Grand Council archives to be found in the section entitled "Jen min fan Ch'ing tou cheng tzu liao" (Materials on popular struggles against the Ch'ing), in Chung-kuo shih hsüeh hui, ed., *Hsin hai ko ming* (The Revolution of 1911; Shanghai: Sheng chou kuo kuang she, 1957).

11. Information on the Kuan-lan uprising in this section is based on Wang Hsing-chung, "Yüeh sheng ti ssu chün ko ming jih chi" (A day-to-day account of the revolutionary struggle of the Fourth Army in Kwangtung), annotated and edited by Chou Hui-chün, in Kuomintang Archives, comp., *Chung-hua min kuo k'ai kuo wu shih nien wen hsien* (Documents in commemoration of the fiftieth anniversary of the founding of the Republic of China), Part 2, vol. 4, pp. 433–39.

School-Temple and City God

1. For the two prefectures I investigated (Ning-po and T'ai-wan), I have data from all eleven counties formed before 1875. Only three types of shrines of the *ssu-tien* occurred in all eleven. They were City God temples, school-temples, and temples to Kuan-ti. In ten counties there were one or more open altars to the Land and Grain (*She-chi t'an*), to Wind-Rain-Thunder-Clouds (*Feng-yü-lei-yün t'an*), to Mountains and Rivers (*Shan-ch'uan t'an*), and to unworshiped dead (*Li t'an*). Regional variation comes into play with the God of Literature (*Wen-ch'ang*) and the God of the Eastern Peak (*Tung-yüeh*), who are more a feature of Ning-po than of T'ai-wan, and with the God of Agriculture (*Hsien-nung*) and T'ien-hou, whose shrines were more frequent in T'ai-wan than in Ning-po.

C. K. Yang used eight county gazetteers dating from the 1920's and 1930's for his *Religion in Chinese Society* (Berkeley: University of Calif. Press, 1961). The counties were scattered throughout China—two in Hopei, two in Kiangsu, two in Kwangtung, and one each in Hupeh and Szechwan. Extrapolating official shrines from his more general survey I find that, of the open altars, Land and Grain, Wind-etc., and Hsien-nung occurred in all eight counties, unworshiped dead in six. Of the temples, those to the City God, to Confucius, to Kuan-ti, and to Wen-ch'ang occurred in all eight. But so too did temples to the God of the Eastern Peak and to Dragon Kings (gods for the control of rain, but not constituting a single cult and only marginally part of the official religion), while T'ien-hou occurred only in the four *hsien* of Kiangsu and Kwangtung.

2. The two main difficulties in compiling this list were (1) that for many

temples there were no records of establishment or repair, and (2) that more than one Kuan-ti, T'ien-hou, and Wen-ch'ang temple in each county was sponsored by officials, making it difficult to know which was the one used in the annual official rites. The sources for Taiwan (all of them in the Bank of Taiwan edition) were Cheng P'ei-kuei, *Tan-shui t'ing chih*, 1872; Chou Chung-hsüan, *Chu-lo hsien chih*, 1718; *Fu-chien t'ung chih T'ai-wan fu*, 1830–69; Lien Heng, *T'ai-wan t'ung shih*, 1918; Lin Hsiung-hsiang, *T'ai-wan sheng t'ung chih kao*, ch. 2, ts'e 1, 1956; *T'ai-wan hsien chih*, 1721; *T'ai-wan t'ung chih*, 1897. For Ning-po prefecture I used *(Chia-ch'ing) Ning-po fu chih*, 1560; *(Ch'ien-lung) Ning-po fu chih*, 1733; *(Ch'ien-tao) Ssu-ming t'u ching*, 1169; *(Pao-ch'ing) Ssu-ming chih*, 1228; *(K'ai-ching) Ssu-ming hsü chih*, 1259; *(Yen-yu) Ssu-ming chih*, 1320; *(Chih-cheng) Ssu-ming hsü chih*, 1342; *(Ch'ien-lung) Yin hsien chih*, 1788; *(Kuang-hsü) Yin hsien chih*, 1876; *(Min-kuo) Yin hsien t'ung chih*, 1936, book 7, 19.

3. For examples of the *fen-hsiang* links of Taipei's major temples, and for a general description of the process of subdivision, see my paper "City Temples in Taipei Under Three Regimes" in Mark Elvin and G. William Skinner, eds., *The Chinese City Between Two Worlds* (Stanford, Calif.: Stanford University Press, 1974).

4. Yang 1961, pp. 98–99.

5. Meng-tzu, *T'eng Wen kung*, Part II, which is *Mencius*, Book III, Part II, chap. 9, paragraph 9 in Legge's translation.

6. *Chu-lo hsien chih*, ch. 5, Hsüeh hsiao chih.

7. *Hung kung ching shih lu* (Record of paying respects in the school-temple), "Shih-tien Hsü" (The order of the rites of *shih tien*), 1686, edition of 1835.

8. This is the phrase used in John K. Shyrock's translation in *The Origin and Development of the State Cult of Confucius* (New York: Appleton-Century, 1932), p. 225.

9. Lien Heng, *T'ai-wan t'ung shih*, ch. 4, "Shen-chiao." This history of Taiwan was published in 1918 after ten years of preparation. Lien was a patriot writing under Japanese occupation, and he had obviously had a traditional classical education. His story is much like an extended gazetteer, like traditional Chinese historiographic writing. I think I am justified in taking it as a product of late Ch'ing China.

10. See the *Tz'u hai* dictionary's entry on *t'ien* for quotations from the *Shih ching* and the *Hsiao ching*.

11. Yūji Muramatsu, "Some Themes in Chinese Rebel Ideologies," in Arthur F. Wright, ed., *The Confucian Persuasion* (Stanford, Calif.: Stanford University Press, 1960), p. 255, suggests the broad outlines of a middle class of priests, monks, jobless lower degree-holders, fortune-tellers, and sorcerers that fell between the emperor and officials above and peasant farmers, merchants, and artisans below.

12. The description of the worship at the Altar of Heaven is taken from my own reading of the K'ang-hsi edition of the *Hui tien* and from E. T. Williams's reading of various other editions and his personal observation of the ceremony during the closing days of the dynasty reported in "The State Religion of China during the Manchu Dynasty," *Journal of the North China Branch of the Royal Asiatic Society*, new (2d) series 44 (1913): 11–45.

13. The magistrate of Wei *hsien* in Shantung, a noted calligrapher, poet, scholar, and wit, in 1752 wrote a commemoration of his repair and extension of the City God temple. He drew attention to the substance and brilliance of the new images and the contents of the temple. "Moreover, outside the principal gate of the temple a stage for theatrical performances has been erected. . . . Can it be that there are *shen* who delight in theatrical performances? Of course not. . . . It is simply because people wish to give expression to their feelings of gratitude that they are led to pay court to the great *shen* in these multiplied acts of love and worship. Now, as to the city god, since it is sacrificed to as though it had a personal existence, why should not such things as songs and dances be employed to give it enjoyment. But let the plays be about ancient times so that they be instructive and prohibit the low, clandestine, vulgar, and grosser passions. Fu Hsi, Shen Nung, Huang-ti, Yao, Shun, Yü, T'ang, Wen-wang, Wu-wang, Chou-kung, and Confucius [the whole line of legendary sage-kings] having been men were later deified. It is proper to sacrifice to them as those who had a personal existence. But Heaven, Earth, Sun, Moon, Wind, Thunder, Hills and Streams, Rivers and Mountains, Soil and Grain, Walls and Moats [= Ch'eng-huang, the City God], the Impluvium, and the Stove [this is the full range of nonhuman deities in the official religion], although deified, have no personal existence and should not be sacrificed to as if they had. Yet from ancient times even the sages have all sacrificed to them as though they had a personal existence" (translation by the Reverend McCartee in *Journal of the North China Branch of the Royal Asiatic Society*, 1869–70, article XI). I take this to be typical of the agnostic Confucian official line, didactic and paternal in the rationalization of popular religion and perplexed by its similarity to the official rites.

14. This is the shortest of the oaths I have found and comes from the 1788 *Yin hsien chih*. The oath given from an inscription of 1810 in the *Chang-hua hsien chih, I wen chih*, as cited in *T'ai-wan sheng t'ung chih kao*, pp. 207–8, has the newly appointed magistrate declaring confidence in himself as the imperial delegate to look after the people. But his family might be unprincipled. He cannot control what is beyond his ears and eyes and knowledge. The god and his assistants can, however, so the magistrate asks the god to lend him power to fortify his virtue.

15. Kung-chuan Hsiao, *Rural China: Imperial Control in the Nineteenth Century* (Seattle: University of Washington Press, 1960), chap. 6, makes this quite clear—see particularly notes 193 and 197 to that chapter.

16. John H. Gray, *China: A History of the Laws, Manners and Customs of the People* (London: Macmillan, 1878), vol. 1, pp. 118–19.

17. J. J. M. de Groot, trans. by C. G. Chavannes, "Les fêtes annuellement célébrés à Emoui," *Annales du Museé Guimet*, 11 (1886): 68–72: 12 (1886): 586ff.

18. The prayer of Hu Ch'eng-kung, appointed subcircuit military intendant of Taiwan in 1824, is to be found in *T'ai-wan wen hsien*, 11, no. 2 (June 1960): 256.

19. The limits of the official religion as a matter of rank and dignity, and the official interpretation of the people's religion below it as an extension of it, are well demonstrated in an account by Magistrate Wang of Ning-yüan *hsien*, Hunan, in 1789, quoted by Hsiao 1960, chap. 6, note 204. Wang relates how it was the custom in the rain ceremony for images from all the local temples

to be carried in procession to the yamen where the officials were to bow to them—a ritual similar to that described for Amoy by De Groot. When the rain ceremony occurred in 1789, Magistrate Wang refused to bow, despite the urgings of the clerks of the Division of Ritual. He explained that the local temple gods were only the equivalents of local elders, and since his office was superior to that of local elders he should not be expected to bow to their images.

20. Hsiao 1960, pp. 226–29.

21. See especially J. J. M. de Groot, *Sectarianism and Religious Persecution in China* (Amsterdam: Johannes Müller, 1903, 1904; 2 vols.; reprinted Taipei: Ch'eng-wen, 1971), pp. 102–9, 113–18, 244–48. See also Yang 1961, pp. 187–91, 308.

22. For histories of Kuan-ti and Wen-ch'ang and their canonization, see A. S. Goodrich, *The Peking Temple of the Eastern Peak* (Monumenta Serica, Nagoya, 1964), pp. 120ff and 128ff. This temple seems to have been to the imperial capital what the Ling-ying miao was to Ningpo and the Lung-shan ssu was to Taipei—the most important popular temple, and bordering on the official religion. The gods enshrined in it ranged from those worshiped by scholar-officials for luck in the examination and related areas through almost every kind of god worshiped for luck in northern China. This admirable book documents them all.

23. The Ch'ing emperors also had an exclusively Manchu official religion that came under the Department of Ceremonial of the Imperial Household. I am indebted to Jonathan Spence for informing me of this.

Gods, Ghosts, and Ancestors

Addison, J. T. 1925. *Chinese Ancestor Worship: A Study of Its Meaning and Relations with Christianity.* Shanghai.

Ahern, Emily M. 1973. *The Cult of the Dead in a Chinese Village.* Stanford, Calif.

Ayscough, Florence. 1924. "Cult of the Ch'eng Huang Lao Yeh," *Journal of the Royal Asiatic Society, North China Branch*, 55: 131–55.

Bryson, Mary. 1900. *Child Life in China.* London.

Ch'ü, T'ung-tsu. 1962. *Local Government in China Under the Ch'ing.* Cambridge, Mass. Paperback ed.: Stanford, Calif., 1969.

Coltman, Robert. 1891. *The Chinese, Their Present and Future: Medical, Political, and Social.* Philadelphia.

Cormack, Mrs. J. G. 1935. *Everyday Customs in China.* Edinburgh.

Day, Clarence Burton. 1940. *Chinese Peasant Cults: Being a Study of Chinese Paper Gods.* Shanghai.

Diamond, Norma. 1969. *K'un Shen: A Taiwan Village.* New York.

Doolittle, Rev. Justus. 1865. *Social Life of the Chinese.* New York, 2 vols.

Fabre, P. Alfred. 1935. "Avril au pays des aieux," *Catholic Church in China: Commissionis Synodalis*, 8: 111–31.

Fei, Hsiao-tung. 1939. *Peasant Life in China.* New York.

Feuchtwang, Stephan. 1974. "Domestic and Communal Worship in Taiwan." In Arthur P. Wolf, ed., *Religion and Ritual in Chinese Society.* Stanford, Calif.

Freedman, Maurice. 1966. *Chinese Lineage and Society: Fukien and Kwangtung.* London.

———— 1967. "Ancestor Worship. Two Facets of the Chinese Case." In Maurice Freedman, ed., *Social Organization: Essays Presented to Raymond Firth*. Chicago.

Giles, Herbert A. 1915. *Confucianism and Its Rivals*. London.

Harrell, C. Stevan. 1974. "When a Ghost Becomes a God." In Arthur P. Wolf, ed., *Religion and Ritual in Chinese Society*. Stanford, Calif.

Hsu, Francis L. K. 1952. *Religion, Science and Human Crisis*. London.

———— 1963. *Clan, Caste and Club*. Princeton, N.J.

Johnston, R. F. 1910. *Lion and Dragon in Northern China*. New York.

Jordan, David K. 1972. *Gods, Ghosts, and Ancestors: Folk Religion in a Taiwanese Village*. Berkeley, Calif.

MacKay, George Leslie. 1895. *From Far Formosa: The Island, Its People and Missions*. New York.

Pruen, Mrs. William L. 1906. *The Provinces of Western China*. London.

Schipper, Kristofer M. 1977. "Neighborhood Cult Associations in Traditional Tainan." In G. William Skinner, ed., *The City in Late Imperial China*. Stanford, Calif.

Shen, Chien-shih. 1936–37. "An Essay on the Primitive Meaning of the Character *Kuei*," *Monumenta Serica*, 2: 1–20.

Shryock, John. 1931. *The Temples of Anking and Their Cults*. Paris.

Smith, Arthur H. 1899. *Village Life in China*. New York.

Wang Shih-ch'ing. 1974. "Religious Organization in the History of a Taiwanese Town." In Arthur P. Wolf, ed., *Religion and Ritual in Chinese Society*. Stanford, Calif.

Wang Sung-hsing. 1973. "Ancestors Proper and Peripheral." Paper presented at the Symposium on Ancestor Worship, IXth International Congress of Anthropological and Ethnological Sciences. Chicago.

Developmental Process in the Chinese Domestic Group

Ch'en Ta. 1938. Nan-yang Hua-ch'iao yü Min-Yüeh she-hui. Shanghai.

————. 1940. *Emigrant Communities in South China*. Institute of Pacific Relations, New York.

Chow Yung-teh. 1966. *Social Mobility in China*. New York.

Cohen, Myron L. 1967. "Variations in Complexity among Chinese Family Groups: The Impact of Modernization," *Transactions of the New York Academy of Sciences*, Ser. 2, vol. 29, no. 5.

———— 1968. "A Case Study of Chinese Family Economy and Development," *Journal of Asian and African Studies*, vol. 3, no. 3.

Fei Hsiao-tung. 1939. *Peasant Life in China*. London.

Fei Hsiao-tung and Chang Chih-i. 1949. *Earthbound China*. London.

Freedman, Maurice. 1958. *Lineage Organization in Southeastern China*. London School of Economics Monographs on Social Anthropology, 18.

———— 1961–62. "The Family in China, Past and Present," *Pacific Affairs*, vol. 34, no. 4.

Fried, Morton H. 1953. *Fabric of Chinese Society*. New York.

Ho Ping-ti. 1962. *The Ladder of Success in Imperial China*. New York.

Hu Hsien-chin. 1948. *The Common Descent Group in China and Its Functions*. Viking Fund Publications in Anthropology, 10, New York.

Kulp, Daniel H. 1925. Country Life in South China. New York.

Lang, Olga. 1946. Chinese Family and Society. New Haven.

Levy, Marion J. 1949. The Family Revolution in Modern China. Cambridge, Mass.

Lin Yueh-hwa. 1948. The Golden Wing: A Sociological Study of Chinese Familism. New York.

McAleavy, Henry. 1955. "Certain Aspects of Chinese Customary Law in the Light of Japanese Scholarship," *Bulletin of the School of Oriental and African Studies*, vol. 17.

Moench, Richard U. 1963. Economic Relations of the Chinese in the Society Islands. Unpublished doctoral dissertation, Harvard University.

Osgood, Cornelius. 1963. Village Life in Old China: A Community Study of Kao Yao, Yünnan. New York.

Simon, G. E. 1887. China: Its Social, Political, and Religious Life. London.

Smith, Arthur H. 1900. Village Life in China: A Study in Sociology. Edinburgh and London.

Tawney, R. H. 1932. Land and Labour in China. London.

Yang, C. K. 1959a. The Chinese Family in the Communist Revolution. Cambridge, Mass.

———— 1959b. A Chinese Village in Early Communist Transition. Cambridge, Mass.

Yang, Martin C. 1945. A Chinese Village: Taitou, Shantung Province, New York.

The Sociology of Irrigation: Two Taiwanese Villages

Brief Introduction of Chia-nan Irrigation Association. 1967. Tainan: Chia-nan Irrigation Association.

Chen Cheng-siang. 1963. *Taiwan: An Economic and Social Geography*, vol. I, Research Report no. 96. Taipei: Fu-min Geographical Institute of Economic Development.

Chia-nan ta-chün hsin-she shih-yeh kai-yao (Principles of recent canal construction in Chia-nan). 1930. Tai-wan Jih-jih Hsin-pao She [in Japanese].

Cohen, Myron L. 1967. "Variations in Complexity Among Chinese Family Groups: The Impact of Modernization," *Transactions of the New York Academy of Sciences*, ser. II, vol. 29, no. 5: 638–44.

Eisenstadt, S. N. 1958. "The Study of Oriental Despotisms as Systems of Total Power," *Journal of Asian Studies*, 17: 435–46.

Gallin, Bernard. 1966. Hsin Hsing, Taiwan: A Chinese Village in Change. Berkeley: University of California Press.

Geertz, Clifford. 1970. *Agricultural Involution*. Berkeley: University of California Press.

Hsieh Chiao-min. 1964. *Taiwan—Ilha Formosa*. Washington, D.C.: Butterworth.

Leach, E. R. 1959. "Hydraulic Society in Ceylon," *Past and Present*, 15: 2–25.

Lijphart, Arend. 1968. *The Politics of Accommodation*. Berkeley: University of California Press.

Orenstein, Henry. 1956. "Irrigation, Settlement Pattern, and Social Organization," in Anthony F. C. Wallace, ed., *Selected Papers of the Fifth Inter-*

national Congress of Anthropological and Ethnological Sciences. Philadelphia: University of Pennsylvania Press.

———. 1965. "Notes on the Ecology of Irrigation Agriculture in Contemporary Peasant Societies," *American Anthropologist,* 67: 15–31.

Pan-American Union. 1955. *Irrigation Civilization: A Comparative Study.* Washington, D.C.

Pasternak, Burton. 1968. "Social Consequences of Equalizing Irrigation Access," *Human Organization,* 27, 4: 332–43.

Report on the 1964 Irrigated Land Survey of Irrigation Associations in Taiwan, The Republic of China. 1965. Taiwan Provincial Water Conservancy Bureau.

Steward, Julian. 1955. *Theory of Culture Change.* Urbana: University of Illinois Press.

Tai-nan Hsien-chih kao tzu-jan chih (Gazetteer of Tainan Hsien, Natural History), vol. 1, no. 1. 1960. Tainan Hsien Wen-hsien Wei-yüan Hui.

Tai-wan Sheng t'ung-chih kao (Taiwan Province Encyclopedia of Geographical and Topical Matters), vol. 4, no. 1. 1955. Taipei: Tai-wan Sheng Wen-hsien Wei-yüan Hui.

Wittfogel, Karl A. 1935. "The Foundations and Stages of Chinese Economic History," *Zeitschrift für Sozialforschung,* 4: 26–60.

———. 1938. *New Light on Chinese Society: An Investigation of China's Socio-Economic Structure.* International Secretariat, Institute of Pacific Relations.

———. 1957. *Oriental Despotism.* New Haven: Yale University Press.

Child Training and the Chinese Family

Lang, Olga. 1946. Chinese Family and Society. New Haven.

Whiting, John W. M., Irvin L. Child, and William W. Lambert. 1966. Field Guide for a Study of Socialization. New York.

Wolf, Margery. 1968. The House of Lim. New York.

Marriage Resistance in Rural Kwangtung

1. Wu Shang-shih and Tseng Chao-hsüan, *"Chu chiang san chiao chou"* (The Pearl River delta), *Ling-nan hsüeh pao,* 8.1 (Dec. 1947): 105–22. Translated into English by Winston Hsieh and P. Buell in "Metaphysics Involved in Defining a Region: The Case of the Canton Delta Region" (background paper for the Canton Delta Conference, held at the University of Washington, Seattle, June 13–15, 1971).

2. Glenn T. Trewartha, "Field Observations on the Canton Delta of South China," *Economic Geography,* 15.1 (Jan. 1939): 9–10.

3. *Ibid.,* p. 8.

4. *Ibid.,* p. 6.

5. Benjamin Henry, *Ling-Nam: or, Interior Views of Southern China* (London, 1886), p. 66.

6. Trewartha, pp. 9–10.

7. Henry, p. 67.

8. John Kerr, *A Guide to the City and Suburbs of Canton* (rev. ed.; Hong Kong, 1904), p. 66.

9. Henry, p. 67.

10. Agnes Smedley, *Chinese Destinies* (New York, 1933), p. 178.

11. Robert F. Spencer and S. A. Barnett, "Notes on a Bachelor House in the South China Area," *American Anthropologist*, n.s., 50.3 (July–Sept. 1948): 463–78.

12. *Ibid.*, p. 474.

13. Henry, *Ling-Nam*, p. 68.

14. *Shun-te hsien-chih* (Shun-te county gazetteer), 1853, vol. 3: *Feng-ssu* (Customs), p. 39.

15. Marjorie Topley, "The Great Way of Former Heaven: A Group of Chinese Secret Religious Sects," *Bulletin of the School of Oriental and African Studies*, 26.2 (June 1963): 386–87.

16. Marjorie Topley, "Chinese Religion and Rural Cohesion in the Nineteenth Century," *Journal of the Royal Asiatic Society, Hong Kong Branch*, 8 (1968): 27.

17. *Ibid.*, p. 29.

18. Topley, "The Great Way," pp. 369–71.

19. Mrs. Edward Thomas Williams, "Some Popular Religious Literature of the Chinese," *Journal of the Royal Asiatic Society, China Branch*, n.s., 33 (1899–1900): 11–29.

20. Justus Doolittle, *Social Life of the Chinese* (2 vols.; New York, 1865), 1: 196–97.

21. I am grateful to Emily Ahern for this reference.

22. Ho It Chong, "The Cantonese Domestic Amah; a Study of a Small Occupahome Group of Chinese Women" (Research paper, University of Malaya [Singapore], 1958), p. 135.

23. James Dyer Ball, *The Shun-Tak Dialect* (Hong Kong, 1901), p. 6.

24. Cf. Ho It Chong, p. 47.

25. Marjorie Topley, "The Organisation and Social Function of Chinese Women's *Chai T'ang* in Singapore" (Ph.D. dissertation, University of London, 1958).

26. *Shun-te hsien-chih*, 1853, 3: 35.

27. W. P. Morgan, *Triad Societies in Hong Kong* (Hong Kong, 1960), p. 284.

28. James Dyer Ball, *Things Chinese* (5th ed.; Shanghai, 1925), p. 6.

29. Ch'en Tung-yuan, *Chung-kuo fu-nü sheng-huo shih* (History of women's life in China; Shanghai, 1928), chap. 8; *Chung-hua ch'üan-kuo feng-ssu chih* (Gazetteer of Chinese customs; n.p., n.d.), vol. 7: *Kuang-tung* (Kwangtung), Book 4, *hsia chieh*, pp. 30–33; S. H. Peplow and M. Barker, *Hong Kong Round and About* (Hong Kong, 1931), p. 118; Agnes Smedley, *Battle Hymn of China* (New York, 1943), p. 87.

30. Cf. *Chung-hua ch'üan-kuo feng-ssu chih*, loc. cit.

31. Ho It Chong, "Cantonese Domestic Amahs," p. 36.

32. Dyer Ball, *Things Chinese*, p. 372.

33. Arthur H. Smith, *Village Life in China* (New York, 1899), p. 287.

34. *Ibid.*, pp. 258–311; Margery Wolf, *Women and the Family in Rural Taiwan* (Stanford, Calif., 1972).

35. Cf. Olga Lang, *Chinese Family and Society* (reissue; New Haven, Conn., 1968), p. 43.

36. Smith, p. 262.

37. Ho It Chong, pp. 24, 135.

38. Smith, p. 287.

39. Ho It Chong, "Cantonese Domestic Amah," p. 28.

40. Lang, p. 42.

41. Cf. Doolittle, *Social Life of the Chinese,* 1: 61.

42. Smith, *Village Life,* p. 289.

43. Ho It Chong, p. 29.

44. *Chung-hua ch'üan-kuo feng-ssu chih,* loc. cit.

45. Ho It Chong, p. 25.

46. Smith, p. 287; Dyer Ball, *Things Chinese,* p. 375; and Peplow and Barker, *Hong Kong Round and About,* p. 117.

47. Dyer Ball, *Shun-Tak Dialect,* p. 7; cf. his *Things Chinese,* p. 375.

48. Cf. Ho It Chong, "Cantonese Domestic Amah," p. 30.

49. Cf. *Hsin-chiu hun-yin tui-pi t'u* (Chart comparing old and new marriage; Canton, 1952).

50. Ho It Chong, p. 36.

51. Maurice Freedman, "Ritual Aspects of Chinese Kinship and Marriage," in Freedman, ed., *Family and Kinship in Chinese Society* (Stanford, Calif., 1970), pp. 181, 183.

52. Cf. Ho It Chong, p. 115.

53. Lang, *Chinese Family,* p. 109.

54. Smedley, *Chinese Destinies,* p. 177.

55. W. L. Blythe, "Historical Sketch of Chinese Labour in Malaya," *Journal of the Royal Asiatic Society, Malaya Branch,* 20 (1947): 103.

56. *Hsin-chiu hun-yin tui-pi t'u.*

57. Cf. Ho It Chong, p. 120.

58. *Ibid.,* p. 21.

59. *Ibid.,* p. 27.

60. Topley, "Organisation and Social Function of Chinese Women's *Chai T'ang.*"

61. Janet Salaff, "Social and Demographic Determinants of Marital Age in Hong Kong," in Henry E. White, ed., *The Changing Family, East and West* (Hong Kong, 1973), pp. 72 *et seq.*

62. Fei Hsiao-t'ung, *Peasant Life in China* (London, 1943), p. 235.

63. Topley, "Organisation and Social Function of Chinese Women's *Chai T'ang.*"

64. Graham Johnson, "Rural Chinese Social Organization: Tradition and Change," *Pacific Affairs,* 46.4 (Winter 1973–74): 562.

65. *Ibid.,* pp. 563–64.

The Power and Pollution of Chinese Women

1. Ida Pruitt, *A Daughter of Han: The Autobiography of a Chinese Working Woman* (1945; reissue, Stanford, Calif., 1973), p. 179.

2. See Ho Lien-k'uei and Wei Hui-lin, *Tai-wan feng-t'u chih* (Customs of Taiwan; Taipei, 1970), pp. 65–66.

3. David C. Graham, *Folk Religion in Southwest China* (Washington, D.C., 1961), p. 140.

4. J. J. M. de Groot, *The Religious System of China*, 6 vols. (1892–1910; reissue, Taipei, 1967), 6: 1006–9.

5. A. J. A. Elliott, *Chinese Spirit Medium Cults in Singapore* (London, 1955), pp. 56–57, 88; Norma Diamond, *K'un Shen: A Taiwan Village* (New York, 1969), p. 103.

6. Elliott, p. 48.

7. De Groot, *Religious System of China*, 4: 377.

8. See Mary Douglas, *Purity and Danger: An Analysis of Concepts of Pollution and Taboo* (New York, 1966); Ian Hogbin, *The Island of Menstruating Men* (Scranton, Pa., 1970); and Marilyn Strathern, *Women in Between: Female Roles in a Male World: Mount Hagen, New Guinea* (New York, 1972) for other efforts to analyze the relationship between pollution and social roles.

9. Margery Wolf, *Women and the Family in Rural Taiwan* (Stanford, Calif., 1972), pp. 32–37, 164–67.

10. *Ibid.*, pp. 37–52.

11. *Ibid.*, p. 40.

12. *Ibid.*, pp. 39–40.

13. See Wu Ying-t'ao, *Tai-wan min-su* (Taiwanese customs; Taipei, 1970), p. 22.

14. Wolf, p. 57.

15. V. R. Burkhardt, *Chinese Creeds and Customs*, 1 (Hong Kong, 1955): 33.

16. Elliott, *Chinese Spirit Medium Cults*, p. 70; De Groot, *Religious System*, 6: 1323.

17. Douglas, *Purity and Danger*, pp. 1–4.

18. See Emily M. Ahern, *The Cult of the Dead in a Chinese Village* (Stanford, Calif., 1973), pp. 171–72.

19. R. H. Van Gulick, *Sexual Life in Ancient China* (Leiden, 1961), pp. 34, 46, 48, 144–47, 193–200, 279–84 *passim*.

20. The Rev. Justus Doolittle, *Social Life of the Chinese* (1865; reissue, Taipei, 1966), p. 196.

21. Wolf, *Women and the Family*, p. 57.

22. Johannes Frick, "Mutter und Kind bei den Chinesen in Tsinghai, I: Die Sozialreligiöse Unreinheit der Frau," *Anthropos* 50 (1955): 341–42.

23. Marjorie Topley, "Chinese Traditional Ideas and the Treatment of Disease: Two Examples from Hong Kong," *Man*, 5 (1970): 427.

24. Doolittle, p. 74.

25. Feng Han-yi and J. K. Shryock, "Marriage Customs in the Vicinity of I-Ch'ang," *Harvard Journal of Asiatic Studies*, 13 (1950): 393.

26. Topley, "Chinese Traditional Ideas," p. 427.

27. Frick, p. 358.

28. Doolittle, pp. 196–97.

Doing Business in Lukang

Burton, Robert A. 1958. "Self-Help, Chinese Style," *American Universities Field Service Reports*, East Asia Series 6, 9 (July).

Chen Cheng-hsiang. 1963. *Taiwan: An Economic and Social Geography*. Taipei: Fu-Min Institute of Economic Development.

Fried, Morton H. 1953. *The Fabric of Chinese Society: A Study of the Social Life of a Chinese County Seat.* New York: Praeger.

Gamble, Sidney D. 1954. *Ting Hsien: A North China Rural Community.* New York: Institute of Pacific Relations (reissued in 1968 by Stanford University Press).

Levy, Marion J., Jr. 1949. *The Family Revolution in Modern China.* Cambridge, Mass.: Harvard University Press.

Pasternak, Burton. 1968. "Atrophy of Patrilineal Bonds in a Chinese Village in Historical Perspective," *Ethnohistory* 15, 3 (Summer).

Ryan, Edward. 1961. The Value System of a Chinese Community in Java. Unpublished Ph.D. dissertation, Harvard University.

Silin, Robert. 1964. Trust and Confidence in a Hong Kong Wholesale Vegetable Market. Unpublished M.A. thesis, University of Hawaii.

Smith, Arthur H. 1900. *Village Life in China.* London: Oliphant, Anderson, and Ferrier.

Tenenbaum, Edward A. 1963. *Taiwan's Turning Point.* Washington, D.C.: Continental-Allied.

T'ien Ju-k'ang. 1953. *The Chinese of Sarawak: A Study of Social Structure.* London: London School of Economics Monographs on Social Anthropology, 12.

Ward, Barbara E. 1960. "Cash or Credit Crops? An Examination of Some Implications of Peasant Commercial Production with Special Reference to the Multiplicity of Traders and Middlemen," *Economic Development and Cultural Change* 8, 2 (Jan.).

Wolf, Margery. 1970. "Child Training and the Chinese Family," in Maurice Freedman, ed., *Family and Kinship in Chinese Society.* Stanford: Stanford University Press.

Cantonese Shamanism

De Groot, J. J. 1969. *The Religious System of China.* 6 vols. Taipei. (Originally published 1892–1919.)

——— 1912. *The Religion of the Chinese.* New York.

Doolittle, J. 1966. *Social Life of the Chinese.* Taipei. (Original publication: New York, 1865.)

Elliott, Alan J. A. 1955. *Chinese Spirit Medium Cults in Singapore.* London.

Foster, George M. 1965. "Peasant Society and the Image of Limited Good," *American Anthropologist,* 67: 293–315.

Potter, Jack M. 1968. *Capitalism and the Chinese Peasant: Social and Economic Change in a Hong Kong Village.* Berkeley, Calif.

——— 1970. "Wind, Water, Bones and Souls: The Religious Life of the Cantonese Peasant," *Journal of Oriental Studies* (Hong Kong), vol. III, no. 1, pp. 139–53. (Reprinted in Laurence G. Thompson, ed., *The Chinese Way in Religion,* Belmont, Calif., 1973.)

Index